Desire Street

Desire Street

A True Story of Death and Deliverance in New Orleans

JED HORNE

Farrar, Straus and Giroux

New York

Farrar, Straus and Giroux
19 Union Square West, New York 10003

Copyright © 2005 by Jed Horne
All rights reserved
Distributed in Canada by Douglas & McIntyre Ltd.
Printed in the United States of America
First edition, 2005

Uncredited photographs are provided by the State of Louisiana, from the case files of
State of Louisiana v. Curtis Kyles.

Library of Congress Cataloging-in-Publication Data
Horne, Jed, 1948–
    Desire Street: a true story of death and deliverance in New Orleans / Jed Horne.— 1st ed.
    p. cm.
    ISBN-13: 978-0-374-13825-7
    ISBN-10: 0-374-13825-7 (hardcover : alk. paper)
    1. Kyles, Curtis. 2. Dye, Delores, d. 1984. 3. Kyles, Curtis—Trials, litigation, etc.
4. Murder—Louisiana—New Orleans. 5. Trials (Murder)—Louisiana—
New Orleans. I. Title

HV6534.N45H45 2005
364.152'3'0976335—dc22

                                                                              2004009527
Designed by Patrice Sheridan

www.fsgbooks.com

1   3   5   7   9   10   8   6   4   2

For Jane and Jed and Eli

Desire Street

PROLOGUE

I found myself studying his hands, the way the weave of veins and sinew fitted over the bone like gloves, the nails pale against black skin. I absorbed myself in his hands partly because of their elegance and animation, partly as respite from Kyles's eyes. The eyes were going to take some getting used to.

More than once as we spoke, the pager on his belt beeped and Kyles glanced at it, making mental note of a call he could put off returning. The sonorousness of his voice and the almost biblical turn of his phrasing were reminders that his roots were in rural Mississippi, not in the cutthroat, heebie-jeebie world he had come to know in New Orleans. But in other respects, Kyles's style was urban. He had chucked the schoolboy costume his lawyers dressed him in for court—the gray flannel pants and loafers, the Oxford-cloth shirt. These had given way to a more credible look built up of fitted black denim and black acetate. Prison had taken fourteen years of his life, yet I could not help thinking the experience had been a kind of amber. At thirty-nine, Kyles was as scrawny as a teenager, though his coiled energy seemed to draw more on anxiety than on the juice of boyhood.

As we talked, his thumb prowled the undersides of adjacent fingers, now and then ratcheting one or another of his rings a few degrees this way or that, a fidget of some precision. If the prosecutors were right, the same precision fourteen years earlier had been applied suddenly and fatally to the trigger of a .32-caliber revolver pressed to the temple of a woman Kyles was trying to rob. And in broad daylight, in the parking lot of a New Orleans supermarket, a tough, good-looking sixty-year-old named Delores Dye had slumped to the pavement and expired in the puddle of fluids leaking from her skull like a dropped egg. Delores Dye, while exceptional in her way, served handily in the public imagination as a proxy for her class and gender. A housewife and grandmother who kept the books for her husband's drywall company, she was Everywoman. There being no reason for her murder—a mundane murder, at that, a garden-variety robbery gone wrong—it carried the eerie overtones of a fate that could befall anyone. And, in her assailant, New Orleans believed it had glimpsed the early incarnation of a social horror that would loom suddenly much larger in the mythology of the Reagan '80s: the predator—the young man who would as soon kill you as look at you, even after you handed over your wallet and car keys. Kyles was twenty-five in 1984, the father of four with a fifth on the way, when police snatched him from the driveway of his home in the city's ramshackle Ninth Ward and charged him with Dye's murder. It was a murder only more terrifying to New Orleans—in particular to the city's dwindling white population—for being so utterly unprovoked. There was almost certainly no connection between assailant and victim, no web of intrigue on which the public could meditate and, in that way, reinforce the sense of distance, the sense of otherness, that lies in the particulars of someone else's life.

The conversation was roundabout at first, as Southern etiquette requires. My years as a reporter working the wrong side of the tracks had taught me better than to be surprised when a canny and sophisticated mind expresses itself in the language of the unschooled. Illiterate when he entered prison, Kyles by now had read a lot—Claude Brown and Jack Abbott, the literature of race and the subset of it that is the literature of prison. He was quick with the politics of his case and the nuances of the legal maneuvering that had carried him thus far. And there had been a lot of it. What began as a textbook example of summary justice was, by the end of Kyles's fifth trial, perhaps the most adjudicated murder case on record—albeit still, in legal terms, unresolved. Now and then Kyles would fall silent, as though relapsing into the interior monologue that had been his only conversation for twenty-three hours a day during his years on death row, and it seemed best for a while to ponder the sunset through the window of his lawyer's twenty-seventh-floor aerie and the sweep of the Mississippi River coiling across the flatlands of southeast Louisiana toward the Gulf of Mexico. Damaged but intact, Kyles had survived a legal train wreck. I was interested to know what had caused that wreck and what it said about the railroad on which he—and not he alone—had been riding. Kyles said he was interested in giving it a try.

I told Kyles that I would need more than his protestations of innocence before I could believe he had been wrongly sentenced for the crime that had ruined his life. I told him that to tell his story, even the narrow stripe of it that had made him briefly a cause célèbre, I would need to know more about him than his lawyers had known or perhaps wanted to know, more than he might be comfortable telling a stranger, let alone a white. Except I said "honky" instead of "white," eliciting a snort from Kyles that I took to be a stifled laugh. I glanced up to see a spark light his eyes and then fade out as quickly. I put it to him point-blank. How could he expect to convince me of his innocence when his attorneys had failed to convince five juries?

Kyles's answer was unexpected. "I ain't no goody two-shoes," he said. I took it as a caveat but also as a strategic proposal. To understand the truth about the Dye murder, Kyles seemed to be saying, I would have to understand his life and the code of values that had shaped it.

Real life is ambiguous in ways that cost it the clarity of art, but as I settled down to talk with Kyles, I could not help thinking that ambiguousness itself had found an exact metaphor in the minor medical disorder that had put its stamp on his face. During his years in prison, Kyles had developed Bell's palsy, a neurological condition brought on by traumatic stress. One corner of his mouth, the left side, had been pulled down in something like a permanent sneer or scowl. The other corner kept the usual mobility, such that when he spoke, and especially when he smiled, his face was the carnival mask that both grins and glowers, a rictus at once sinister and jolly, defiant and defeated.

When he held out his hand to shake mine, I noticed the bullet hole—there was no mistaking it for anything else—scarred over near the butt of his palm. I thought better of asking him how he came by it. I was surprised I hadn't noticed it earlier.

PART ONE

ONE

This much is certain and always was. That on a Thursday afternoon in late September 1984, a housewife named Delores Dye—Dee to her husband and friends—ran afoul of a thief as she loaded a shopping cart of groceries into her car out front of a New Orleans supermarket.

The skies are hazy in the hot afternoon, and the parking lot of the Schwegmann Bros. Giant Supermarket is perhaps a third full. The general hubbub of passing traffic, the stream of cars and vans and delivery trucks and light pickups is deepened by the throb of heavy equipment: a pipe crew laying a gas line along the curb that divides Old Gentilly Road, an artery leading east to the suburbs, from the vast field of tar in which Delores Dye has parked her red Ford LTD.

At sixty, Mrs. Dye is spry and vigorous enough to leave at least one eyewitness to her death convinced she is much younger. Reared Mormon, a rodeo queen in her day, she has strayed from her Wyoming homeland, but not from her values. She is, by all accounts, a no-nonsense woman in a no-nonsense marriage. Her husband is a small-time contractor in the construction business. She bills the customers, pays the subs, banks the money, keeps him on an allowance, shops, cooks, cleans. She has raised two sons and intends to have a hand in raising the grandson one of them, at long last, has provided her.

Mrs. Dye is not unmindful of crime, even here in Gentilly, a modest, thoroughly middle-class neighborhood which—like every modest middle-class neighborhood and some very posh ones as well—is not far from a stretch of rotting slums and the enormous, half-empty public housing projects they surround, this being New Orleans, one of the poorest cities in America, especially if you are black.

Out of habit, or perhaps in response to some special premonition, Mrs. Dye has set her purse in alongside the groceries before slamming the lid of the trunk. She has her keys out and is moving toward the locked driver's-side door when her assailant makes his move, materializing out of the anonymous comings and goings in the parking lot to grab her wrist and make his demands. From the construction site along Old Gentilly Road, more than one of the men witness to the death of Delores Dye will first mistake this minuet—the man's hand to the woman's wrist, turn once, turn again—for an exchange between lovers, a quarrel perhaps, or a moment of affection. The distance obscures Mrs. Dye's age and its marked contrast with that of her assailant, a young man, variously described as eighteen or twenty-nine, with bushy hair or, as some would have it, braids. He is black, as are most New Orleanians; she is white. But this is a city long since accustomed to cross-racial romance, if not, in some quarters, entirely comfortable with it.

And then, never having begun at all, in a split second the dance was over. Perhaps Mrs. Dye kicked up a fuss and foolishly refused the young man's demand for her purse and her keys. Perhaps, in the tension of the moment, she had been unable satisfactorily to explain that her money was in her purse and her purse was in the trunk. Or perhaps her assailant had planned all along to pull a .32-caliber revolver from his left pocket and, with the nonchalance of a parent tucking a stray hair behind a daughter's ear, press it to the side of Mrs. Dye's skull and fire once, a clean kill that eliminates the closest witness to his crime.

But there are others.

"She just dropped to the ground," is how one of the gas-line workmen would remember it. "She just dropped out. She ain't kicked or nothing, just fell out."

Just as coolly, the gunman then proceeds to step around Delores Dye, her skull circled in its widening aura of blood and brain fluid. He slides into the driver's seat, fires up the motor, and, without so much as a nervous lurch or an impatient beep of the horn, glides slowly into the line of cars exiting the parking lot. The gunman's strategy is apparent: hide in plain sight, blend in, ease on out of the crime scene without causing a ripple in the macadam millpond of the supermarket parking lot. The implementation of that strategy, the finesse and composure, the icy nervelessness with which the gunman turns homeward-bound grocery shopper, border on the superhuman—or the subhuman, depending on your point of view. An impressive attempt at camouflage, except that it is utterly unsuccessful.

The workman impressed by how cleanly the gunman felled his prey is one of at least a half dozen witnesses to the murder of Delores Dye. Five of them will provide accounts comprehensive enough for police to take seriously.

Bobby Territo, young, white, and scared to death, was in a company pickup heading east along Old Gentilly Road when he glanced to his right and, so he claimed, saw the woman drop to the ground. "Damn, that nigger just shot that lady!" Territo remembered exclaiming. In court, he would apologize for the racial epithet, knowing full well, as would the prosecutors who called him to the stand, that his embarrassment only lent credibility to his account. Having yelped loudly and with his windows open, Territo was then appalled to glance in the rearview mirror and see that the Ford had slipped into the line of slow-moving traffic directly behind him. Trembling violently, certain he was to be shot, Territo sank down so low in the driver's seat that he could barely see over the dashboard or work the clutch, which began to lug badly, causing the truck to lurch and stagger, verging on a stall.

But then, without incident, the Ford passed him on the right, slowly skirting the construction site and heading for the turnoff onto France Road at the far end of the parking lot. One of the hard hats had the presence of mind to shout to the man at the controls of the crew's jackhammer, mounted on a long arm that jutted out from the glassed-in operator's cab: Swing the crane around, and bring it down on the Ford's roof, he yelled. But the operator missed the chance to pin the car, perhaps having thought better of using company equipment in a demolition derby, and the Ford passed the work site unimpeded. Now it veered right, onto France

Road in the direction of a famously pestilential labyrinth of brick boxes and damaged lives known as the Desire public housing project.

The call came a little before midnight, and it came from his father, which Lowell Dye found odd because, as is often true among fathers and grown sons, the wife and mother—Delores Dye—was the family switchboard, the communicator, the envoy and negotiator. Robert Dye had just heard from the police, or was it the coroner's office—someone in authority. "They have a body there. They think it might be your mother. And they think she may have been murdered."

There are different ways to deal with the unspeakable, and one way is to seek refuge in the mundane. For Lowell Dye, half awake but instantly beside himself with anxiety, that refuge lay in ragging his father for not calling earlier and, for the two of them, in faulting the goddamn police for taking so long to track them down.

In fact, the elder Dye had placed a call to his son earlier in the evening—it was unlike Dee to be AWOL—but Lowell and his wife, Jan, hadn't picked up. Robert put the steaks out anyway; they were salted and thawing on the countertop. Hours ticked by, and still no sign of Dee, no call to confirm the likeliest explanation, that she and a friend had stopped by the World's Fair, along the downtown riverfront. Like most government productions in a famously corrupt state, the exposition, then in its final weeks, had been a financial sinkhole touched by scandal. But it was a great hit with local residents, many of whom, like Dee Dye, had acquired season passes and used them regularly.

In fairness to the police, tracking down Mrs. Dye's next of kin had been complicated by her inveterate frugality. The same instinct that sent her to a discount chain like Schwegmann's had also inspired her to register the car with one of Lowell Dye's aunts who lived over the line in Jefferson Parish, the white-flight mecca of 1950s-era ranch houses that had crowded out the older wooden bungalows and doubles just across the Seventeenth Street Canal from Orleans Parish. The sales taxes were lower in Jefferson by a mill or two. There were savings to be realized. Twenty bucks a year? A hundred? The principle of the thing would have mattered more to Delores than the amount.

Witnesses had provided police with snippets of numbers from the getaway car's license plate, but when police cobbled them together and called the Jefferson Parish address to inquire about the woman listed on the registration, Mrs. Dye's relatives ducked what they thought was an effort to nip them for the evaded registration fee and suggested that the cops had a wrong number. Police thought better of disclosing that they were seeking survivors of a murder victim and continued their search until they reached Robert.

"Will you come with me?" Robert asked Lowell.

Lowell looked at the phone in his hand. Come with me? Come where?

"To identify the body."

Maybe it wasn't her, Lowell thought to himself. Right? Why would they need someone to come down and make an identification if they already knew who it was? Grasping at what shreds of hope could keep him from falling apart completely, Lowell stumbled out of the bedroom. Like every kitchen in New Orleans, his and Jan's had its share of plastic go-cups, the colorful customized beakers that Mardi Gras parade clubs—krewes, in local parlance—print with their names and insignia and toss into the sea of upstretched arms that wave like eelgrass along Carnival parade routes. He loaded a cup with ice, then filled it to the brim with Jack Daniel's.

It was about ten minutes from Lowell Dye's lakefront home near the Jefferson Parish line to the place where he had grown up and where his parents still lived, a squat brick house on Wildair Street. Dye honked. Waiting for his father to come out, he could contemplate the pocket park across the street, a neighborhood asset that had made their place action central for sports-minded friends of Lowell and his brother, Robert junior, back in the good old days before they were swept into the more structured rigor of high school athletics and college and work and women. Before Robert junior moved off to Florida with his bride. Before Jan and Lowell had been blessed with the birth of their son, Jason, little more than a year earlier.

The drive to the coroner's office was dead air, interrupted by spasms of chatter in which Robert Dye nursed the possibility that his wife had gone to the World's Fair. Or maybe the car broke down. Or . . . Lowell kept his silence. Soon the damp grid of empty city streets deposited them at the coroner's office, carved into one flank of the immense criminal courts building, the oldest and, in its way, most magnificent structure in a government complex that also included the city's police headquarters, the district attorney's office, and the sprawling, ever-growing collection of concrete bunkers that comprised the parish prison. Not the least remarkable thing about the Orleans Parish coroner's office was the sweet and fetid stench that wafted from the loading dock, a place visited both by body wagons and by the waste service that hauled away a big-city coroner's ample production of blood and tissue. It was the smell of human flesh, as unmistakable and matter-of-fact as the smell of garlic outside the back door of an Italian bistro.

But Lowell's more vivid memories, once in the waiting room, were of a fedora'd newspaper reporter, ordered by the city desk to keep the all-night vigil that might yield, in time for the bulldog edition, the identity of the Schwegmann's murder victim. That, and a weird bit of embroidery hanging on the wall, an old-time sampler with a slogan stitched into it that, in his state of mounting distress, baffled Dye completely.

"I kept looking at it—I'm reasonably astute, right?—but for the life of me, I couldn't figure out what it meant."

In due course, an aide intercepted father and son, and they were led out of the room and down a flight of marble stairs. It was the mixture of the ordinary and the very very strange that made the experience excruciating, the juxtaposition of the macabre and the intimately familiar in a pattern as distinctive as a fingerprint. And there was the suddenness of the exposure: the opening of a drawer, the slab rolling out from the wall and . . .

Two decades later the memory of it still knocked the wind out of Lowell Dye, turning his voice to a whisper: ". . . and baby, like, there she is. I mean, it's her."

The sheet had been pulled down to the dead woman's waist, exposing the white-and-blue patterned blouse. And sure enough, there was a toe tag on her foot, like in a cheesy TV drama. The entrance wound was appallingly tidy, a small caked hole in among the strands of gray-blond hair covering her left temple. The barbarity of what had befallen Delores Dye told in her closed eyelids, livid purple, the color of grape juice. It was as though she had been punched in each socket, except that the blow had come from the wrong side, from inside her skull.

Robert Dye was in shock, frozen in contemplation of his wife of four decades, the war bride he had met in a West Coast dance hall and who had followed him back to New Orleans. The woman who ran his drywall business and raised his sons. He could have stood there all night, lost in his thoughts. Or so his son feared.

Lowell could not take another minute of it. "I went, 'Dad, let's get out of here. Let's get out of here. That's her. Okay? That's her. Let's go.'"

In the car, they quibbled over whether to call Florida. Robert wanted to reach his other son. Lowell couldn't see the point in not waiting the few hours until dawn broke and his brother, a honcho with the National Park Service, would be up and about. The father yielded and stepped out of the car on Wildair Street, suddenly a widower and needing to be alone with his thoughts. Lowell was about a block from his own place when he realized that he could barely see. He would remember the strangeness of the sensation. He wasn't sobbing, nothing that cathartic. It was as if all his grief had narrowed to laser intensity and afflicted his eyes, only his eyes. They began to leak torrentially. A friend had come over to be with Jan in his absence, and it wasn't until the two women heard his car pulling in and opened the door and asked what had happened that he hit an emotional trip wire and fell apart completely. The sun had come up before the last of the shudders had coursed through his exhausted body and he fell into a fitful sleep.

"What can I say? She was the best friend I ever had in my life," Lowell would reflect years later, "the total loving package." He settled back on the sofa as he spoke, a bachelor again after a series of failed marriages, childless now that his only son was off at a boarding school in Arizona. "She wasn't a debutante; she never went to college," he continued. But Lowell had gotten his mother interested in reading: trashy novels at first, then serious ones; then he moved her into nonfiction—histories and self-help books and then the biographies that became her passion.

"How do you describe a woman who was wonderful and motivating and so totally worthy of your trust? I've been around too long. I mean, I haven't had it with my wives. I don't have it with my kid. To have that yanked away, it was . . ." He fell silent, searching futilely for the right word, which does not exist. He gave up and looked around for his drink. "It was devastating," he said quietly, sinking back into the sofa cushions.

Sons are meant to love their mothers, and Lowell Dye was devoted to his, awed by the saga of her childhood as part of a vast and patriarchal Mormon family that had migrated west from Illinois, not to Utah but to Wyoming. Of thirteen siblings, a half dozen were brothers who, amalgamating the 160 acres each could claim under the Homestead Act, put together a goodly chunk of Wyoming, near the Wind River Indian Reservation, and ranched it together. One of the brothers was a Marlboro cowboy. Literally. Good-looking enough to land a modeling gig with the cigarette company and see himself on billboards. And all of them were rodeo riders, talented ones. In time, they became well known on the circuit that included the Cheyenne Rodeo and the annual Pioneer Days blowout over in Laramie. That might have given Delores an edge when it came to picking a queen for those events—Lowell would never give up the photograph of her on horseback, a sash proclaiming her title—except that she didn't need an edge, not a big, good-looking woman like her. Big in all the right places, her husband didn't mind telling his buddies.

They met in California in '43. In San Jose, midway between the Alameda naval base, where she was working, and the camp at Salinas where he was getting trained for combat. Two kids—she had just turned twenty; he was twenty-three—trying to pack in a little living just in case the war had something else in mind for them. Within a year they were married, and after the war they came straight back to New Orleans, Robert's town, in time for the boys to be born there. Robert Dye did some college on the GI Bill (Tulane) only to get caught in the Korean War draft. After that it was time to get down to business. Their partnership was a natural one.

"She was a very resolute person and could do things that I was hesitant about," her widower would reflect years later. "I couldn't get on anybody, you know. But somebody owed us money, she could do it. She could haggle. And wheel and deal. She took care of all that. If I had to buy a new piece of equipment or a truck or something, she did it. Billing, payroll, she did it." And because she knew how to charge things against the company—new cars, improvements on a home that was also an office—the Dyes, Robert said, lived a little better than most folks would suspect you could on a business with a crew of laborers that never grossed more than $300,000.

Given the chemistry of his love for his mother and all that she stood for, the murder would have been enough to unhinge a son as devoted as Lowell, even a son past thirty, with his own wife and toddler to buffer him. But right from the start Lowell's grief was compounded by another emotion: guilt, and the self-reproach that came with it. Delores Dye's murder was, of course, sheer coincidence, the accidental intersection of two lives—an unsuspecting housewife and an armed desperado for whom any target would do, the more vulnerable the better. The irony Lowell Dye would nurse bitterly to his dying day was that his mother wouldn't have been anywhere near the Schwegmann's parking lot but for a secondary coincidence, one that took rise in her devotion to him.

Delores Dye was a creature of habit. For decades she had done her shopping, as well as her banking and most of the other chores related to the drywall business, on Friday, not Thursday. And the week of September 20 would have been no exception but for one thing. Lowell and Jan had made weekend plans. They were heading over to Gulfport, a couple of hours east on the Mississippi coast. A friend was getting married, a Saturday affair that, to be fully savored, would mean showing up Friday night for the rehearsal dinner and the looser, boozier good times that would follow into the wee hours.

Hearing of these plans, Lowell's mother had offered to take Jason, the grandchild she had yearned for longer than most Louisiana housewives are kept waiting, the grandson—the first of many, she hoped—that her Mormon upbringing had told her was not only her right but her obligation. Her dreams had been delayed, first by the lack of children from Robert junior's marriage, then by Lowell's perpetuation of his bachelorhood late into his twenties. At last Jason had been born in July of the previous year, and an elated grandmother had taken the baby on as if he were her own.

True to form, that very weekend she proposed to combine quality time with the baby's self-improvement. She wanted to try her hand at toilet training him. She knew to be tactful about it: "Do you think Jan would mind?" That was her question to Lowell during a phone call to his office earlier in the week. He chuckled over her solicitude. Mind? Who would mind having their kid toilet trained?

As the prospect of her weekend with the baby drew nearer, Delores had called Lowell a second time. Why didn't they plan to drop the baby off first thing Friday rather than waiting until after work? That would get them out of town earlier. Maybe they'd beat the rush-hour traffic. Lowell saw merit in the idea and was certain Jan would too. All that would be required was for Delores to move to Thursday the chores that she habitually did on Friday, a departure from routine that Lowell had not seen more than a half dozen times in as many years. And was Jan comfortable with the idea of the toilet training? Lowell assured his mother a second time that it would be fine. And Jason's grandmother had added a baby's potty seat to her shopping list.

She finished the banking first, two stops, two different banks: one to deal with the payroll account, one to draw weekend cash from the family account. From there, as far as these matters could be reconstructed, she drove out Old Gentilly Road, past the hodgepodge of fast-food joints and tire dealerships, past the leafy oak allée at the entrance to the Dillard University campus and the strict white-trimmed brick of Baptist Theological Seminary. The Schwegmann's was on her right. There were parking slips nearer the supermarket entrance, but it would not have been like Mrs. Dye to angle for one. She'd be damned if she'd see her Ford all nicked up with ding marks from doors swinging open. And so she circled around and pulled into a slip on the outer margin of the lot, a more isolated spot, less trafficked, and, as a young thug calculated with some interest, less likely to invite interference.

Most accounts of Mrs. Dye's final minutes would begin with the tussle in the parking lot or the gunshot, seconds later, that took her life. A high school student named Edward Williams provided a longer narrative, which began inside the supermarket. Williams thought he had noticed the woman as he paid for a bottle of Big Shot soda to see him through the long bus ride home. And he remembered a man lurking over by the sporting goods section, within eyeshot of Mrs. Dye as she cashed a check at the cashier's window. A black man, like Williams, and not much older. Or so Williams would tell police.

Williams had left the store and was killing time at the bus stop on the far side of the parking lot when he noticed the woman again, now pushing a clattering shopping cart. She emerged from the tightly packed rows of cars bunched near the store's entrance and pressed on toward a more isolated car, a big red Ford—or was it a Thunderbird? They were harder to tell apart in those days. Williams had popped open the Big Shot and was scanning the boulevard for some sign of his bus forging through the thickening afternoon traffic, when something drew his attention to the red car. It may have been the woman's scream, though it was barely audible above the jackhammers and diesel rumble of the construction crew laying pipe along a stretch of Gentilly that began maybe two hundred feet east of the bus stop.

Glancing toward the car, Williams saw that the woman had been joined by the man he had seen in the store. They seemed almost to be in a playful mood: the woman darting around the car, the man grabbing at her, like lovers playing hard to get before they fall laughing into each other's arms. And then suddenly it wasn't playful at all. The sound of a single shot rose above the background din, and Williams watched in astonishment as the woman dropped instantly to the ground.

The details of Williams's story would vary over time. He would contend that in the split second before the gun went off, the woman beat her assailant about the face and kneed him in the groin. That might have been consistent with Mrs. Dye's feistiness, but it might also require that a suspect in her murder have evidence of facial abrasions not placed there by the police themselves in the rough-and-tumble of the arrest. In any event, other witnesses reported no such lashing out by Mrs. Dye, and prosecutors made nothing of Williams's account of it.

With the exodus from the city gathering force and the pipeline work adding to the congestion, two or three cars might stack up at the parking lot exit before the first in line could make the right turn into the divided boulevard's eastbound lanes. To Williams's horror, that placed the killer on course to crawl past the bus stop, only a few yards from the bench where he sat with mounting dread that as witness to a murder, he would be rubbed out then and there.

The driver's-side window was open, according to Williams. And now his anxiety verged on outright panic as the gunman swiveled his head toward the bus stop and locked eyes with him, a look "of death," as the witness would recall from the stand. Williams shut his eyes and found himself muttering a prayer for deliverance. When he looked up again, it was to see the Ford's tail end, its brake lights popping on and off impatiently as the gunman nudged out into the prospective anonymity of passing traffic. Now Williams rushed to the woman's side, and, just before her eyes fluttered shut for good, Mrs. Dye had reached out as if to grasp his hand. Or so he claimed.

TWO

This much is also certain: that a little short of one a.m. Monday, a little less than eighty-four hours after the murder of Delores Dye, a diminutive, pipe-smoking detective named Pascal Saladino pulled up in front of a two-story fourplex at 2313 Desire Street and plucked five bags of garbage—plastic bags, dark green ones—from the curbside. These he bundled into the trunk of an unmarked car and carried back to headquarters, where they were opened and, amid much muttering and joking about the stench, inventoried. Bingo. A purse, a brown leather purse, and, scattered through the garbage, the credit cards, the driver's license, and a World's Fair pass, linking the purse to the late Mrs. Dye. Armed now with a warrant to search the downstairs right apartment, police circled back to Desire Street, a whole posse of them, enough to subdue an urban predator.

The day had begun like any Monday, which for Curtis Kyles meant it began early. As usual, he woke a little after dawn and lay still beside Pinkey, savoring a Salem and the quiet in the house before the kids began fussing and it was time to get up and take the older ones to school. A gray-blue haze still hung in the air in thin horizontal wisps, reminding him of good times the night before. Donald Ray Powell had come by, lured by the smell of Pinkey's ham hocks and by the wail of the Stylistics after they hauled the big JVC speaker right out onto the front stoop. Later on, Frank Price had turned up with his old lady. And then Johnny Burnes,

Kyles's brother-in-law, you could say, except that Curtis and Martina Burnes—everybody called her Pinkey—had never bothered to make it official. Not after the first baby. Not after the fourth. And now there was another one on the way, the swell of it just starting to show under the sheet smoothed over Pinkey's young belly here in the bed beside him. And of course, where you saw Johnny Burnes, you were going to see Beanie Wallace. He had come of age with Johnny and Pinkey, a lodger taken in by their mother and treated like another son. And being Johnny's age, Beanie had become his running buddy, his partner in a hundred capers—someone to keep an eye on, as far as Kyles was concerned. He and Beanie had drawn guns on each other not so far back. That had been patched over, Kyles liked to think. But you never knew.

A little beer for them that wanted it, a little weed. A lot of weed, to be truthful, Curtis being not much into the sauce but definitely a man who liked his weed and didn't mind doing a little dealing on the side if you needed some too. There had been dancing. Nothing too serious—a chance for the men to handle one another's women without anybody needing to get worked up about it. It was more in the spirit of the thing to leave the dancing to the little kids, show them a few steps, laugh at their imitations. Because mostly on these Sunday afternoons, at Curtis and Pinkey's or whoever's turn it was that week, the main event was sitting around and shooting the breeze—that and of course the food. Finally the hocks had been ready, and they were good. Better than good. Pinkey's always were. People figured it was the country in her. Pinkey's father still had some acreage up in Mississippi, where she was born, a hardscrabble farm tended by another of her brothers, with enough slaughter in the freezer to lay something in their trunk every time she and Curtis came up from New Orleans for a visit. And they came up a lot, a time or two every month if they could work it out.

Maybe they should have gone up that weekend. Instead there had been Brenda's stuff to move—Curtis's kid sister. They had decided to store it at their mother's apartment on North Dorgenois until Brenda and her husband could straighten things out with their landlord and move into a new place. The big pieces anyway. Let the landlord have the rest. But Brenda said she'd be damned if he could take the refrigerator. It was worth more than the back rent he was after.

Two days later, in the bedroom on Desire Street, Kyles touched his left wrist, feeling for the metal pin that held his hand together, hoping he could not find it. They had been hoisting the refrigerator up the stairs, Curtis on the downstairs end, his brother Larry on the up end, when it slid back on him, just a few inches, enough to grind his hand into the staircase wall. Curtis screamed, and someone budged the refrigerator forward again, freeing his hand. But the damage was done. You could see the pin right there, outlined against the skin of his hand like it was about to rip right through the flesh. The emergency-room people pushed it back in place. Kyles knew his wrist would be like this forever, but the pin was better than the bullet fragments it replaced.

Pinkey stirred beside him now. He caught the smell of her on the air seeping out from around the edges of the bedsheet, thought seriously about beginning the day as they had so many others, then thought better of it, and reached for another cigarette to smoke his yearning away. Let her sleep. That was her thing. He was the early riser, the one who got the kids off to school even when she wasn't pregnant.

He was at the sink rinsing a couple of cereal bowls and juice glasses when Curtis junior padded in—Chester, they called him—followed by Tyteannia, at seven the oldest. The radio deejay was promising another nice day: hot still, but not so damp, not like the summer of ninety-five-degree days and hundred-percent humidity that was finally lifting. From the weather they segued into the headlines, an item about low attendance and financial problems at the World's Fair and then some chatter about the Schwegmann's murder. Kyles's mother, Gracie Walker, had mentioned it over the weekend when he came by her place with his sister's stuff. Another murder. Oh, my, my, my. When would it all end, she had muttered. And wasn't this the Schwegmann's they all went to, the one just down Louisa past the project?

Curtis had calmed her with a hug. It was better than words. She was a talker, but sometimes it seemed like it was the tumor that was talking. It wasn't malignant, but, added to her many other frailties, one day it would probably kill her, doctors said. Curtis flinched at the thought. He revered this woman who had bundled her kids out of rural Mississippi by dark of night and brought them to a new life in the big city. There was nothing he wouldn't do for her.

He could only dimly remember his father, an abusive man, a boozer, given to abandoning his wife and kids for long stretches followed by violent, lusty homecomings and another baby. A man whose woman he messed with finally had put an end to Roosevelt Kyles Sr. with a shotgun blast to the face as he sat on the tailgate of a pickup eating a sandwich before heading back out into the fields to work. Or had the old man been discovered in the sack and dispatched as he rolled off the other man's woman, grinning sheepishly at her outraged husband as he died? The family's oral history came in a variorum edition. Either way, it was 1967. Kyles had just turned eight and was already long gone from Edwards, Mississippi, a small town about thirty miles northwest of Jackson, and the sharecropper/ wage-laboring world into which he was born.

Two years earlier, his mother had fled to New Orleans, a widow-to-be with the six kids fathered by a man she hated, two of them older than Curtis, three of them younger. Gracie had herded them onto a Greyhound and slipped away from Edwards without telling many people at all. They arrived in New Orleans in the fall of 1965, just ahead of Betsy, the worst hurricane in the city's recorded history.

For weeks water stood ten feet deep in some neighborhoods, inaccessible to the huge pumps and sluiceways required to drain a city built behind levees and below sea level. When the waters finally receded, Mrs. Kyles and her brood settled briefly in the Desire housing project, a misspelled homage to Napoleon's mistress Désirée. That association imbued the place with overtones of romance and yearning, but there was a more mundane reason why the name had flickered above the windshield of the streetcar that caught Tennessee Williams's fancy: it was, very simply, the end of the line, a low-lying tract backed up against a stagnant industrial canal that in a lifetime Blanche DuBois would never have had occasion to visit. In the early 1950s, as city fathers came to realize that there was federal money in housing projects, it had seemed like a fine place to quarantine the social undesirables who would qualify for occupancy.

The Desire neighborhood was an urban extreme, even by the standards of a city like New Orleans—a closed city, some said a dying city, where the no longer quite so rich haunted the moldering antebellum mansions along oak-canopied boulevards at the opposite end of town, and the very poor arrived by bus and streetcar to serve them. Desire, be it the project or the street, was all part of the same troubled patch, the Ninth Ward, as it was listed on the city police and political maps, a swampy, downriver area that had once been home to working-class citizens who were favored at least in one particular: the color of their skin. The blue-collar whites began to move out as the projects went up in the 1950s—first the Florida project, then, across a drainage ditch, the Desire. As the public schools were integrated in the 1960s, the trickle of people taking flight became a riptide, leaving the Ninth Ward to citizens favored by very little at all.

As Gracie Kyles settled in with her brood, one in ten New Orleanians lived in the projects—some 50,000 souls more or less, almost all of them women with too many children, a gulag of women and children enisled by poverty. No men. Not on paper, anyway. A man was expected to work, and if he could work, the woman had a means of support and didn't qualify for public housing. Men with the sinew for it worked the wharves, or—a lucky few—landed jobs on the oil rigs out in the Gulf: four weeks on, four weeks off. The rest washed dishes or swept out warehouses, their industry honored not with a paycheck sufficient to raise a family, but by banishment from the public housing in which poor wages had forced them to install their wives and children. And so the men bailed out on the mothers of their children or snuck into the projects at night and tried to keep their marriages alive after hours, which rarely worked for long. As a result of these policies, their sons grew up fatherless on the streets and needle-strewn courtyards of places like Desire.

It was not long before Gracie Kyles realized that she had to get out of there to have any chance of survival, any chance at all. A plumber named Tom Walker took her in, and in due course there were two more children, bringing her brood to eight. She kept the girls with her, and Larry, the youngest boy. Roosevelt junior was grown now, a man in his twenties with a woman and a place of his own. She farmed Curtis out to her sister Eva, a woman of means, comparatively speaking. Eva had a little store and a house she was making payments on over in Press Park, one of the first New Orleans subdivisions to be built with the Negro market in mind. It wasn't far away—walking distance to Gracie and Mr. Walker's place. Curtis was at his mother's all the time, but in the eyes of the rougher kids he encountered at school, project kids for the most part, the privilege of a Press Park address was something to atone for.

———

Kyles pulled himself out of his reverie. Now he had kids of his own, and if they weren't living in Press Park, neither were they living in the project. It was 7:50, time to bustle Chester and Ty out the door and down two blocks to Johnson Lockett School, not an unpleasant chore in fine weather, a chance to catch the air and see who was already up and about, sitting on their stoops or in the group always gathered out front of the corner store, with its stacks of cigarettes and a cooler full of milk and beer and soda pop. But it was late, and so Kyles herded the kids into his car.

Kyles's own schooling had been routine, which is to say that like many of his cohorts—a majority of them in the poorer parts of town—he had dropped out of high school after very few semesters and, for all practical purposes, did not know how to read. He hoped his children would do better; indeed, he hoped as much for Pinkey, whose skills were nearly as limited but whose ambitions were better focused. She dreamed of becoming a cosmetologist one day, a career path that required her to pass a state licensing exam. She talked of going back to night school to earn her high school equivalency diploma, a dream that became only more fanciful as one baby followed another.

On the way back from Johnson Lockett, Kyles pondered the thunkety, thunkety sound of a cylinder misfiring in his car's engine. So much for the time he spent fooling with it the previous Thursday in the repair shop where Johnny Burnes had a job and an absentee boss. He had been still tinkering with it the following morning, Friday, when Beanie had passed by in a big red Ford and given him a ride to Schwegmann's for some transmission fluid. Well, there was time enough to work on it some more, time being one thing Kyles had plenty of, now that the disability checks were coming through, relieving him of the monotonous routine he had known as a bricklayer. Eight lead slugs had drawn that part of his working life to a close, officially if not entirely. There were always offers to work off the books. Some of the metal was still lodged near his spine, the souvenir of an afternoon two years earlier when he had been followed into the shadows by a very anxious junkie, a junkie too unsteady to just settle for Kyles's jewelry and wallet and move on.

Back at the house after dropping off the kids, Kyles popped the hood

on the Monterey. He had backed it into the driveway alongside the apartment, a rusty red car with a cream-colored vinyl skin over the roof, a hole
full of wires where the radio once had been, and pictures taped onto the
dashboard of the three older kids in their school uniforms: Tyteannia,
such a pretty little girl and, at seven, already a mother to the babies; Curtis junior, his daddy's namesake, the serious one; and the third-oldest,
Elmeco, just like his old man. Impulsive, brooding, short-tempered. Everybody noticed it. Cutina was the baby.

Kyles was laying into the spark plugs with a socket wrench when a
neighbor drifted by—a young woman from across the street.

They were on the porch, standing around talking—Pinkey, Kyles,
and now another neighbor had dropped by with his baby boy—when the
woman from across the street asked if anyone was feeling the heat. Or
was it just her?

"The heat?"

"The cops. They're everywhere."

And so they were, Kyles realized, glancing around—men in street
clothes, but surely cops nonetheless. One of them in an unmarked car,
halfway down the next block toward Galvez Street. Another standing on
Desire at the Dorgenois corner, pretending to wait for the bus. Black
men, all of them, trying to blend into a black neighborhood and suc-
ceeding about as well as seal-skinned Eskimos on a Gulf Coast beach.
The neighbor had heard it was the Schwegmann thing, that they were
edging in on a suspect, someone in the neighborhood.

As a black man, as a black man on the wrong side of several laws,
Kyles inventoried his points of vulnerability. He would have had a hard
time producing a receipt for each and every household furnishing. That
was a fact. The smash-and-grab set—the junkies and burglars and purse
snatchers—knew him as a man willing to pay a halfway decent price for
the odd stereo amp or gold chain or microwave, hold it awhile, and then
unload it at a profit after it had cooled off some. But Kyles knew better
than to keep the really hot stuff in his house. Never keep your shit where
you lay your head. That had been his credo, a bit of advice picked up as
a boy from his mentor, a pimp actually, who first guided him onto the
streets, a man long since murdered.

And there was a brand-new revolver right there in the Monterey's glove compartment. Kyles had papers on it, albeit papers made out to his mother's address. There was a hunting rifle under the mattress so the kids couldn't get at it, but there's no law against hunting. No, the only real problem, as they stood there speculating on what these cops could be all about, was the dope inside the apartment. Pot and just a touch of cocaine and, if they really took the place apart, a stash of about $6,500 in legal tender. Enough contraband to give cops an excuse to bust them—and, with the cash, an incentive to pocket some of the evidence—but hardly worth this big a stakeout.

Or so Kyles told himself. As if to convince the cops he had nothing to fear, perhaps to convince himself as well, he fired up a joint right there in the driveway, and those so inclined stood around pinching it off one another's fingertips until it was gone and the passersby figured they'd be on their way. A little less than three hours had passed since Kyles took the kids to school. He had just tucked his head back under the hood of the car when, at 10:40 a.m. on a Monday morning in September 1984, the world as Curtis Kyles had known it for twenty-five years came abruptly to an end.

Instantly the police were all over him. Hands up, motherfucker. Up, up, up. Motherfucker.

More cops than Kyles could imagine, uniformed and plainclothes cops, and still more arriving now in squad cars, the half dozen closest to him all with their guns drawn and, as Kyles was acutely aware, "every one of them aimed at my head."

Now the commands turned to taunts. "Run, nigger. Run, you motherfucker. Run just like your daddy did." This from cops who hoped to startle Kyles into bolting, there being no mechanism in the rules of jurisprudence quite as efficient as a bullet to the skull of a suspect attempting to flee. For the crack of the judge's gavel, substitute the thud of a slug on bone, and let the public appreciate that they have been spared the cost and unpredictable outcome of adjudication.

Details stick with a man in these circumstances, handholds in a world that has begun to reel vertiginously. For Kyles it was the socket wrench, the wrench he still clasped in one of the hands that the cops, the whole barking pack of them, were ordering him to raise. Should he drop it into the motor and risk the clanging sound that might startle a raw-nerved rookie to open fire? Should he raise it slowly aloft? Should he raise it less slowly aloft and enjoy the satisfaction, a doomed man's final hurrah, of sending at least a couple of these assholes in search of reconstructive dentistry?

Kyles set the tool down gently on the engine block and instantly was sprawling on top of it as cops shoved him forward and jerked his hands behind his back to cuff them.

Babies are yowling from inside the apartment. The one in Pinkey's belly screams silently as cops push the pregnant woman up against the exterior wall with her legs spread. It feels like hours, the weight of the fetus pressing down so heavily that she   her cervix will split open then and there. Now the cops swarm inside, and the children's noise is drowned out by the thud of furniture and crowbars and slamming doors as the men tear the place apart.

Bingo. A .32-caliber Model 732 H&R revolver turns up under the stove, one of its six chambers empty, the other five containing bullets identical to the one tweezed by the coroner from Mrs. Dye's brain. And in a chiffonier—or chifforobe, as New Orleanians call them—bingo. A nasty little handmade holster fashioned of duct tape and shaped exactly to the contour of the revolver. A bedroom dresser yields bullets of varying caliber, a couple of boxes of them, and shoved under some Schwegmann grocery bags below the sink, there are cans of dog and cat food, the same brands that Delores Dye's widower would say she customarily bought. Dog and cat food galore, and not a dog or a cat in sight.

Among neighbors on hand as cops took Kyles down was a friend of Pinkey's named Sharon Whittington. Whittington's enduring souvenir of the arrest would be not a socket wrench, but another inconsequential detail: a man squatting on a stoop across the street, watching it all go down. What struck her as she slipped away from the chaotic scene unfolding behind her was his preternatural calm, like he was watching a movie, not a brother's arrest. Any other black man would be making himself scarce about now, with these het-up, half-scared cops all over the place. It offended her, and she said something to him. "What do you think you're doing, man, minding other people's business."

The remark went unanswered, which was answer enough. It dawned on Whittington that the man was high on junk, his mind canceled. She might as well be talking to herself, so she moved on.

She was scarcely at her own door before the manacled Kyles had been read his rights, frog-walked out to the curb, and shoved onto the floor in the backseat of a squad car. He writhed some, fitting himself to the drive-shaft hump, a maneuver that was met with kicks and cracks from a cop's billy club as a detective named Mike Rice piled in after him.

"And every time he hit me in the back, I'm thinking I can feel that slug"—keepsake of his mugging two years earlier—"inching closer and closer to my spine, and I'm thinking, Please don't hit the slug and paralyze me. Please don't."

The driveshaft was less trouble than an antsy cop, so Kyles quit his fidgeting and lay still for the fifteen minutes it took to drive over to the police headquarters on Broad Street, fast by the courthouse and the sprawling parish jail. But once inside, there was no accommodating his captors. They were too numerous, their modes of assault too various. Kyles was pushed into a straight-backed chair, his hands cuffed below the seat and behind one of the chair's rear legs. From there it got ugly, Kyles would claim, launching into an account of a routine police station working over that police would just as routinely deny. Fists and phone books flew at him, along with a fusillade of questions, he said. It occurred to Kyles that it was almost a game, a competition: which cop could care least about the strictures against brutalizing a suspect. Others worked out deeper grudges in which Kyles figured as a stand-in. He was every young black man on a nighttime street who had ever caused a cop to wish he'd followed his mother's advice and taken a job in the water department.

"One of them took his billy and put it here, in the center of my chest, and started pushing: 'Yeah, motherfucker. You killed the white lady, right? You killed her.' And I'm going, 'I don't know what the hell you all talking about. You *know* I ain't killed nobody.' Just screwing that billy into my chest until the chair has slid all the way across the room and can't go no further because it's up against the wall. That's when one of the detectives slugged me from the side—you know, punched my jaw. And then it was like they just wanted to take turns punching, hitting me upside the head, and like that."

Outside, the morning traffic streamed by the sealed glass-and-concrete fortress, oblivious to the unheard groans and shouts of the man in the sliding chair. Like any other lowborn black from a rough neighborhood, Kyles had never had any illusion that cops were his allies. The Desire project and the Florida project were seething and well-armed encampments patrolled by a better-armed constabulary. But his reception at headquarters that day in 1984 was something different, even for him. "I'm serious. I never thought they were . . . that they was just that racist. You know what I mean? It wasn't about trying to solve no crime. It was about trying to punish this black man. I think some of them was punishing me just out of hatred. And you know the most disgusting thing about it? They knew to hit me in spots where it wouldn't show so bad. Like right behind my ear, even though that did swole up pretty bad, or in the chest. Or they'll punch you right there, basically in the nuts, but not quite in the nuts. It was like every white cop in there wanted to hit the bull's-eye."

An open-and-shut case of police brutality? His lawyer, when Kyles finally got one, would caution that too much time had passed. The bruises Kyles pointed out as evidence of his ordeal could have been inflicted longer ago than the day of his arrest. And anyway, it would be his word against the cops, and the cops would just deny it.

The ghetto is good at keeping secrets, even from itself. "Don't ask, don't tell" was a Ninth Ward watchword long before the Pentagon took it up. But when it matters, the ghetto is a switchboard like no other, and it was inevitable that someone in the cluster of bystanders who watched Kyles's arrest go down would know someone who knew someone who knew to call family.

The first call went to Kyles's sister Brenda, the good-looking, hard-living woman her brothers had helped move temporarily into their mother's place over the weekend. Brenda was at work, so her mother took the call and, stricken with dismay, relayed word to the meatpacking plant across town on Magazine Street, where both Brenda and Lela, another sister, were working. Brenda called back on break.

"Your brother's been arrested," her mother began. "They say he killed a woman."

"What woman?" More to the point: "Which brother?"

There were three of them, all told: Roosevelt junior, the oldest;

Curtis; and then Larry; along with three sisters, not to mention the half brother and half sister who were Gracie's children by Mr. Walker.

Brenda, less than two years younger than Curtis, had always been the closest to him, in age and in spirit. Lela, eight years older than her brother and deeply religious, had been a more motherly figure in their lives, and for a decade that ended only the year before with her return from a sojourn in Jackson, Mississippi, she had been largely absent. Brenda found Lela at her workstation, splitting and quartering plucked chickens, placing the cleavered parts in foam trays to be plastic-wrapped.

The two sisters left work stunned, talking too much, trying to fill the void of what they needed to know and dreaded to find out. Maybe their mama had got it wrong, they told each other. But no, the message had not been the prattle of an ailing woman. From Gracie's apartment, Brenda called the friend who had tried to track her down in the first place, and pumped her for details. Curtis had indeed been arrested: murder, and not just any old Ninth Ward rubout. The realization crept over Brenda like a wave of nausea. This was the Schwegmann's murder, the white lady, the murder on the television news.

Brenda remembered the uneasy feeling it had given her the first time she heard about the killing, something so terrible at a store she had been to a hundred times. She remembered thinking to herself, I hope they get the son of a bitch who did that. Now it dawned on her that the son of a bitch might be her brother.

But why? It just didn't make any sense that Curtis would be behind something like that. Jack a car? Sure, Curtis had jacked his share. Deal some drugs? Yep, unless he smoked the whole stash himself. And there was no end to the trouble he could get into behind females. But an older woman like that? Older than his own mother?

Looking for any telltale sign of guilt or trouble, Brenda scanned her recollection of Curtis's behavior two days prior while he helped move her furniture. Nothing. Lela had also seen her brother over the weekend, at the birthday party she threw for her little daughter, Denise. Curtis had shown up at the apartment on Martin Luther King all full of beans, like he usually was. He had picked up his big sister and squeezed her until she squealed and made him put her down, her short, round body like a medicine ball against his wiry frame. Then after a while he had gone out to the curb to fool with her car antenna, which was hanging limp off the side where somebody had snapped it. Give him something to do. That was the best way to handle Curtis, she had found. And if it was something to do with a car, you could count on him to fix it, or at least try. His dream, he had told Lela, was to fix cars full-time one day, like Pinkey's brother Johnny did.

From their mother's place Brenda and Lela headed over to Roosevelt junior's—Juny, as they called him—to watch the news and try to make sense of what was going on. The apartment was already packed: Juny's woman and kids, friends of his, and now the two sisters. And all of a sudden the news came on, and there he was: Curtis, being led into the city's Central Lockup, the classic perp walk, with the perp, Curtis, trying to duck the cameras, looking down and away, like he was guilty as a motherfucker.

In the packed and smoky living room, some of the women began to cry, some of the men too, the ones who weren't cursing and muttering. And in the back of her mind Lela felt a terrible premonition taking form: They're gonna give him the electric chair. She shared her anxiety with Roosevelt. "I just know it." And there wasn't much he could do to allay her dread.

Now the newscast had moved on to other stories, and there was no enduring them. Roosevelt switched off the set and was on his feet. Pinkey. Where in hell was Pinkey? She would know something. Why hadn't she called?

Not that either of Kyles's closest sisters really had a lot to do with her. She was "street," in Brenda's unvarnished opinion. Hadn't they always known it would come to this, or something like it? They had been down on Pinkey right from the start. Too tough, too manipulative. Lela laid it on Pinkey's mother.

"Her attitude was a lot different from ours," Lela would recollect. "Our mama was one of those women, if she said be in here at six o'clock, you better be darkening that door at six o'clock." But in the end, there had been no stopping Curtis. When he fell in with Pinkey, he was "as green as grass," in their mother's somewhat naïve view, yet a boy of sixteen was almost a man, and what could you do about that? Well, for one thing, you could make damn sure he wasn't doing that girl under his mother's own roof. Gracie had made it a rule, and so Curtis found other places to bed Pinkey, and then all of a sudden there was a baby and then another and another.

But this was no time to say I told you so, no time to claim victory in so ancient a feud among the women in Kyles's life. Lela piled into Roosevelt's car along with too many others, and Brenda did the eleven blocks to the Desire Street place at a trot, past the freight yard with its acres of tracks and sidings, along the falling-down blocks of weed-choked empty lots and the rickety one-story cottages that were still standing, most of them raised high on sagging pilings ahead of the next storm or flood.

The Desire Street fourplex was a more substantial structure—a slum, to be sure, but something of an anomaly in the sea of smaller cottages, what with its looming second story and the cracked asbestos shingles that sheathed clapboard the landlord had long since grown sick of painting. Brenda could see it from two blocks away, and beyond it the patchwork of brick boxes, scores of them, a whole city of them, comprising the Desire and Florida projects. She arrived out of breath not much later than the car full of her family. The apartment, which occupied the right-hand half of the first story, had been entirely upended—drawers ripped out of dressers and clothes spilled onto the floor. Kitchenware was strewn about as though the oven had exploded, mattresses were split open, even sections of plasterboard had been hacked out of the wall, and presiding over her ruin, children at her feet, was Pinkey, in a state bordering on incoherence.

To every question, the same answer: "They arrested him. They arrested him."

Was she in shock, or as Kyles's sisters wondered, was this inability to communicate a smoke screen concealing something she could not bring herself to tell? The truth at least in part: she was totally wrung out. Pinkey too had been escorted downtown just after the arrest and questioned by police, a terrifying experience, only more so after her inquisitors made clear to her that not just Curtis's fate hung in the balance. Wrong answers could cost her her welfare check and perhaps even her kids. And so, feeling her way along the divide between saying too much and saying too little, she had portrayed her relationship with Kyles as far less than a marriage and, thus, her knowledge of his pursuits as sharply limited. And her household income, lest the welfare people have any doubt, certainly did not allow for such acts of reckless abandon as might result in impulse purchases of cat food. She left the police station dazed and exhausted by the rigors of the course she had tried to steer between loyalty to her children and treachery against their father.

With persistence, the two sisters got her going a little bit, pried from the shattered woman what they could about the arrest and what might have led up to it. Brenda did not entirely overcome her suspicions. "She just couldn't really give me any straight answers. And I'm like, 'Well, what did you do? How come you didn't call nobody?'" But then Brenda remembered. Maybe Pinkey was a little rough around the edges, but she had always been one to fend for herself.

It would be an eternity, nearly a month actually, before the vision of Curtis, there on the television screen, would be updated in Lela's mind by a glimpse of him in the flesh. Telephone contact from the prison tiers was severely limited in those days. Inmates had to write for permission to make calls, a process that took three or four days to churn through the prison bureaucracy, and even then could be denied by a moody guard. Someone, Lela can't remember who, had tipped her off that a court appearance was scheduled, one in a series of pretrial proceedings as the system ramped up to the main event. Without knowing quite what was going on, she made sure to be there, a small, round, scared woman sitting in the anonymity of the visitors gallery in an all but empty courtroom.

And then there he was—Curtis: shackled, bone-thin, a scarecrow in the Day-Glo orange jumpsuit that served to remind the accused that their claim of innocence until proved guilty was a technicality that had best not be asserted too arrogantly. Lela slipped into a seat closer to the table where her brother sat alongside a public defender. He sensed her there and turned to look. The sight of her was torment of an exquisite kind. She was the avatar of a world of love and comforts he had reason to doubt he might ever rejoin, yet in the very presence of this God-fearing woman he sensed reproach, a scolding for his recklessness over the years and his indifference to the laws of the land.

In the enforced silence of the courtroom, Lela shaped a question with her lips: Did you do it?

She mouthed the question again to be sure he understood her: Did you do it?

She had to know. Right there in the courtroom where someone else might hear his answer and crucify him for it, she had to know. He shook his head. But what did that mean? I didn't do it? Or did it mean don't ask me, not here.

THREE

Within hours of Kyles's arrest, John Dillman, the lead detective, had circled back to the parking lot with front- and side-view color mug shots of six young African American males, fresh shots of Kyles among them. Dillman parked his police car near the site where the construction crew was laying gas lines along Old Gentilly Road, and he called over one of the men whose names he had jotted down in the immediate aftermath of the murder four days earlier: Isaac Smallwood, black, thirty-four, a resident of Saratoga Street in New Orleans. Smallwood pulled off his gloves and stood in silence as Dillman produced the paired mug shots. The detective spread them out on the trunk of the police car, three to a row, one row on top of the other, trueing their corners with his fingertips before stepping aside to give an unimpeded view. Smallwood would know the type, know these boys for troublemakers. Dillman had put strips of white tape over the ID plaques slung over their necks, but this only underscored that these were booking mugs. The bush haircuts, the scraggly goatees, the fuck-you look in their eyes.

The detective was a piece of work of another kind: a wise guy, with a slicked-back pompadour, strutting around in a polyester suit and ankle-high boots like one of those TV cops on *Miami Vice*. John Dillman and Isaac Smallwood were from opposite sides of the tracks—a white cop, a black workingman—but sometimes when you looked over your shoulder at the generation coming on, these hopped-up, lost boys running wild in the streets, a black workingman and a white cop had more in common than they were accustomed to acknowledge.

Dillman glanced at Smallwood and then back at the pictures. "Any of them look familiar?"

Smallwood did not hesitate long. He pointed at the darkest of the boys, the one with the biggest Afro. There was another boy almost as dark-skinned, but the wisp of beard hanging off his chin didn't look right. Small-wood was pointing at the pictures of Kyles. That one. That's the one.

Dillman exhaled slowly and evenly, trying not to betray his satisfaction. He flipped the mug shot over and had Smallwood sign and date the back of it. Then he flipped the other five pictures, the ones Smallwood hadn't chosen, and the witness put his initials on each of those.

Next, Dillman drove his car a hundred yards to another knot of workers and asked for Henry Williams. An older man came forward, closer to fifty than thirty-five, black like Smallwood, but of another generation altogether. A light drizzle had begun to fall, so this time Dillman set up his traveling portrait gallery on the backseat of the police car—again in two rows, each containing three paired mugs—and asked Williams to take a look. Again the witness chose the shots of Kyles. Again Dillman had him sign those shots and initial the rejects.

Dillman was on a roll. This was going to be a piece of cake. He swept the mug shots into his palm with the smooth efficiency of a blackjack dealer who has just won one for the house, and thanked Williams for his trouble.

Did I pick right, man? Williams wanted to know.

Dillman's smile was his reward. Yeah, man. You nailed him. You done good.

Within a matter of several minutes Dillman had driven from the parking lot to a billboard company warehouse a mile or two farther east on Chef Menteur Highway, as Gentilly Road is known after the Danziger drawbridge lifts it up and over the spars and stacks of ships moored along the Industrial Canal. The billboard company, Naegele Outdoor, was the employer of Bobby Territo, the white teenager who had been stalled in eastbound traffic alongside the Schwegmann's lot when the shot rang out and the woman slumped to the macadam.

Dillman's luck held. The shadows of the warehouse yielded the scrawny, towheaded Territo. In the immediate aftermath of his brush with the dark side, as the red Ford LTD pulled away, Territo had retained his self-control long enough to dig a pencil stub out of the debris on his dashboard console and jot down the license plate number. Then he veered off onto the road's shoulder and fought back an impulse to vomit. Four days later, his confidence in the memory of what he had seen verged on cockiness. "If I was in the passenger seat of the truck I was in, I could have reached out and grabbed him. That's how close he was to me," Territo told Dillman. He had not reached out and grabbed anyone, of course. Instead, fearing the gunman might turn sideways and coolly blow his witness away, Territo had slumped down in his seat so far that he could barely see over the dashboard as the Ford rolled past him and took a right on France. Once again Dillman spread out his mug shots for the witness to inspect, and once again he came away with a signature on the back of Kyles's portrait.

Interestingly, Ed Williams, the high-school student at the bus stop who had claimed the lengthiest exposure to Mrs. Dye's final minutes, would decide when approached by police that he could not make a positive identification of her killer. It didn't matter. Dillman's hat trick of positive IDs made a fourth almost gratuitous. Ed Williams he could do without. But on reflection, he could see no good reason not to drop in on the young woman named Darlene Cahill, who had circled back to the murder scene to leave her name with police.

Black witnesses fingering a black man were what you wanted, and in Smallwood and Henry Williams, Dillman already had two. New Orleans had become a majority-black city in the scant couple of decades since the school system was integrated, and by an even larger majority, the perpetrators of crime in the city were black, as were most of its victims. But variety had its own persuasive power. Bobby Territo was probably going to be too skittish to make a powerful witness, too eager to convict a defendant he manifestly feared. Darlene Cahill would read differently in jurors' eyes. And truth be told, she had an allure of another kind not lost on a young peacock like Dillman—a saucy sexuality and, more specifically, as one impolitic cop had put it, a butt on her like a black woman.

Cahill was, like Territo, a young working-class white, more exactly, a "yat," to use local nomenclature for a New Orleans subclass known for its characteristic way of saying hello—"Where y'at?" With a toddler she was babysitting in her lap, Cahill had been in the passenger seat of a car traveling past Schwegmann's and on into New Orleans from the eastern suburbs when the couple tussling in the parking lot caught her eye. The sight was mildly intriguing, though surely not remarkable enough to interrupt the front-seat chitchat with her cousin Joni, the young woman at the wheel, nothing surely to compete with the topic of Cahill's impending divorce. But then suddenly the shot went off and the woman in the parking lot went down.

Within a few hundred hundred feet, Darlene and Joni found a break in the Gentilly Road median and made a U-turn that brought them back to the parking lot entrance and then directly to where the woman had expired. Cahill would not forget the sight: a white woman like you might have seen at church or in a good department store, with beauty-parlor hair, only more blond against the asphalt. One of her shoes, a pretty white sandal, had been knocked off, and it lay there on the pavement beside her bare foot. For some crazy reason the two young women decided to chase after the red Ford. Without stepping out of their car, they veered back toward the parking lot exit. But almost immediately their quarry had pulled off Gentilly Road to the right, leaving them trapped in the lanes of traffic feeding onto the Danziger Bridge and back out toward eastern New Orleans. Within a mile or so, they saw a pay phone and called 911. The dispatcher said the incident had been reported and suggested that they return to the scene and make themselves available to the officers. Police were already arriving.

So were the TV crews. After giving her name to the officers, Cahill was too flustered to want the TV people to stick their cameras in her face. Besides, her hair was a mess. But on the news that night, you could see her in the group of people milling around, the back of her head anyway, proof of her presence on the scene, though police and prosecutors would one day prefer to deny it.

"You go outdoors looking like that?" her mother had shrieked when she saw the news. "No wonder he's divorcing you."

John Dillman tracked down Darlene Cahill a day or two after rounding up his three positive IDs from the male witnesses. Just separated from the man she had married in her late teens, Cahill was living temporarily in her half of a shotgun double, as New Orleanians call the paired one-story apartments that are the city's most abundant architectural style. Shotguns are the Southern equivalent of railroad flats, each unit so long and linear that, in theory at least, a blast of bird shot fired from the front entrance can exit the rear unimpeded, assuming the French doors that typically partition the interior spaces are left open. The building belonged to Cahill's grandmother, who lived in the other half, in a neighborhood known by its most distinctive landmark, a big old ice-making plant, the vestige of a dying industry in the age of refrigerators and air conditioners. For reasons of his own, Dillman decided not to expose the young woman to his photo lineup. But on subsequent visits to her house—Cahill would contend it took a few—he persuaded her to testify, bringing to four the number of eyewitnesses who would point across the courtroom at Curtis Kyles and declare that he was the man who had killed the lady in the Schwegmann's parking lot.

Cahill made no bones about it. She was flattered by the attention— and not from Dillman alone. Lowell Dye, leading the family's search for justice and emotional closure, also came by to sit with her, to ask about his mother's final moments, and, implicitly, to ask her help in convicting the killer. There was a natural rapport between these two young people, a bond that was intensified by race and also by coincidence: the lawyer handling Cahill's divorce was a partner in Dye's firm. But Detective Dillman was the draw. She found him something of a hunk, with his slicked-back hair and broad smile. He had a way of making her think the feeling might be reciprocated.

"Come on, Darlene. I need you." The words stayed with her, words to catch a lonely woman's attention even if the need he was talking about was for her testimony rather than her body. She had resisted, coyly. And so Dillman upped the ante, reaching beyond romantic insinuations for the hot button: race. "Come on, Darlene. Help me take another nigger off the street."

And eventually she yielded. "It was like I was doing a good deed for everybody. For Lowell, I was doing a good deed. I was doing a good deed for the lady who lost her life. And the policeman—I guess I figured I was doing something for him too. I don't know. He was hot, a hot policeman, big, gorgeous looking. I guess he was playing the role, because he asked me out for drinks and stuff, even though I never went out with him."

Dillman's phone calls were somewhat clamorous events, announced by shouts and pounding on the partition between the two shotguns, given that the only phone was on the grandmother's side. But Dillman kept at it, Cahill said, calling frequently enough—"a lot of times just to chitchat and see how I was doing"—to keep her feeling wanted. "He's hitting on me. I'm loving it. Sure. I'm twenty-five. I'm getting divorced. My husband was the only man I'd ever been with in my life up until then, so hey, this was good."

Lowell Dye's obsession with the case against Kyles would have been intense even if he weren't himself a lawyer, and he did not limit his involvement to a visit with a reluctant witness. He had been the closest one to his mother, and now it fell to him to be her champion. His father would follow the case closely, but with a sense of stoic resignation that precluded any thoughts of meddling with the investigation. And Robert junior was off in Florida, ill-disposed by his obligations to the Park Service, not to mention his lack of training in the law, to get in Lowell's way.

Late in the morning after Lowell Dye identified his mother's remains at the coroner's office, he had waked from too little sleep as if from a nightmare, only to realize from a glance at the morning papers that it wasn't a nightmare at all. His mother's death was front-page news under a three-column photograph. Uniformed cops and plainclothes detectives stood around in a random configuration while at their feet, center left in the photograph, lay a corpse—his mother's corpse. It was shrouded, of course, a concession to public sensitivities that made only more shocking the dark, damp slick clearly leaking from around the end of the sheet that covered her head.

A son's horror was only compounded by the initial lack of information about the murder and any progress the police might have made overnight in solving it. When his repeated calls to the homicide division went unreturned, Dye found himself heading to the Schwegmann's parking lot. Maybe a cop would be there, someone he could talk to. Or a witness. Maybe he would arrive to find the perpetrator in flagrante—a man so stupid, a predator so habitual that he knew no better than to return to the scene of his last crime to stalk his next victim.

Instead, what Dye encountered was an eerie ordinariness, a few more guards than usual. Oh, yes, Schwegmann's was already on alert for the liability suit—a likelihood under any circumstances in a litigious town like New Orleans, a certainty when the dead woman's son is himself a liability lawyer. Dye's need, normal enough but certain to be wrenching, was to find the place where his mother died. With the front-page picture at eye level, as the press photographer's camera must have been, Dye tried to orient himself with the buildings and signposts visible in the photo's backdrop. It didn't work. Something was wrong, and he was preparing to give up on his attempt to reconstruct the scene, when one of the parking lot guards approached him, a woman named Miriam, concerned to know just what he thought he was doing.

When he explained himself, Miriam fell silent for a moment and then found the words to tell him that she had been on duty as his mother died. She gestured toward a spot several yards closer to the construction site along Gentilly Road. From this new vantage, the scene before him clicked into congruence with the newspaper photo in his hand, trued in every detail, from the angle of the background buildings to the streak of tar patching a crack that ran from a point near his feet. If further corroboration were needed, the pavement bore a second marker, as it would at least until the next drenching rain: the dark, faintly reddish stain of his mother's blood.

Dye's trip to the parking lot was only the beginning of a crusade that would last for years. Over the weeks that followed, he begged the district attorney's office to put him to work on the case, and when they didn't, when Cliff Strider, the lead prosecutor, finally told him, "Stay out of the way," he did not.

Dye decided to go after John Schwegmann for damages in civil court, and on his very first visit to the parking lot, began developing an argument that the place was inadequately guarded, despite repeated armed robberies—eleven in the previous three years, three of them in the month prior to the murder, according to police records. From conversations with Miriam and an examination of the time cards as employees clocked in, Dye decided that she had been the lone guard on duty in the parking lot at the moment of his mother's murder, though the usual complement was three. And as the time drew near for Miriam's 2:30 replacement to show up, she had driven her scooter over to the supermarket entrance to wait out the last ten or fifteen minutes in the air-conditioned interior, a contention Schwegmann's would challenge.

For a stickup artist haunting the lot, the unmanned scooter by the door and the uniformed guard's disappearance inside was a virtual all clear, in Dye's estimation, an invitation to strike. "And boom: out comes my mother, out of the store, and no security guards anywhere. Nothing." Even years later, an anguish would come over Dye's face as he re-created events in his mind as vividly as if they had happened only yesterday and he had been there in person. "He sees my mother, and fortunately for him, she's parked toward the back, middle back of the parking lot, so he just makes a beeline toward her and . . ." Dye's voice trailed off. He stared into the distance at a point a million miles beyond the walls of the comfortable lakefront condo where he was then living, alone with his memories. Eyes still in the blue beyond, his hand found the damp glass on the coffee table in front of him, and the feel of it seemed to bring him back into the room. A swig, and he went on with his story.

A customer brought word of the shooting to Miriam inside the store, and with her supervisor, she ran to the side of the dying woman. Dye recalled Miriam's words: "We could see that your mother was still breathing. I saw your mama's hand moving." These were details horrifying to a loving son but also vital to the lawsuit he was fixing to file, because the extent of the damages due her survivors would turn critically on whether his mother lived long enough to suffer, even for a very few minutes.

FOUR

It is the perverse genius of prison life that inmates become their own jailers, even their own executioners, leaving it to the guards to orchestrate the power struggles that keep prisoners at one another's throats rather than at the throats of their guards and wardens. Kyles had spent no adult time in prison, and his early brushes with detention had been limited to juvenile facilities—no bed of roses, but places in which the patterns of violence and recrimination, like the young inmates themselves, had yet to reach full flower. But any black man who grew up on the streets and in the pool halls of the Ninth Ward knew all about prison, the myth and perhaps even the reality, and everything Kyles had heard about it told him one thing: strike first or be struck; fuck people over or they will fuck you, but good.

Ordering a new arrival to strip naked, pull his buttocks apart, squat, and generally display himself to the throng of hooting, whistling inmates in the tier ahead is, of course, only partly so guards can be certain that he is unarmed. Kyles felt his testicles tighten but otherwise tried to keep body language from betraying his terror. To show fear was a lethal mistake, particularly for a high-profile catch like Kyles. His rap was at once cowardly and brash—the murder of a white woman. His perp walk had been televised. He might need bringing down a peg. And after all, connoisseurs of boyish men and manly boys were agreed: with or without his clothes on, this new one was a pretty piece of work.

Now Kyles was permitted to step back into his prison-issue togs and was being escorted onto the tier. The corridor parted the sea of prisoners into two pools. The cacophony was deafening—catcalls, wolf whistles, sexual propositions. But to his right, Kyles became aware of particularly aggressive and insulting taunts. Strike first, or be struck. And so to the guard, but loud enough to be heard all over, Kyles commented on the self-appointed reception committee. "There be some people hollering at me over there, some people that must know me," Kyles said, pointing with his jaw. "So put me in with them, okay, man?" And with that, Kyles had lurched to the right. It was a bluff, of course, a Br'er Rabbit improvising in this briar patch as fast as dread could fire the synapses of his brain. But it worked, and the guard yanked him back toward the more subdued left-side tier and pushed Kyles in among the three dozen inmates crowding a ten-man cell. He sank to his haunches with his back against the wall, on guard against every possibility while waiting for the moment of close and hostile scrutiny to give way to indifference or something like it.

"You done all right out there." The words were quiet, as if heard from a distance. But when Kyles glanced in their direction, it was to the man hunkered down next to him along the wall. He was a little older than the average run of the inmates, a vic, as Kyles would come to know him, a convict—someone who had already seen the notorious state penitentiary at Angola, the belly of the beast, and been belched back into the parish lockup while his case dragged through some phase of the appeal process. Orleans Parish Prison was high school—violent, callow, chaotic. Angola was prison life's postdoctorate, a more profound experience, a realm of deeper grievances and more permanent pain.

It would be a while before Kyles shook off his readiest assumption, that the vic was a chicken hawk putting a wing over the new boy's shoulder. But hawks could be played; hawks had their uses. And Kyles needed all the help he could get. He would come to know the inmate variously as Burl or William—Burl Carter or William Reilly. In prison it was easy to forget which was the alias, which the real name, and hard to find a reason why it mattered. Carter was a seasoned jailhouse attorney, the first in a succession of them who would inspire Kyles to take an active role in his own defense, even if that first meant learning to read. Of more immediate interest to Kyles was Carter's success in finding a way around the loggerheads that forced most of the jail population into two camps: predators and the preyed upon; masters and slaves; brutes and the bitches who, whatever their sexual preference, were forced to service them. Carter was no prude, but in terms of prison politics and the thuggish clique of five or six inmates who basically ran the place by terror, he had found a way to be left alone.

As they chatted briefly that first night, at one point Carter lifted a corner of his shirt just slightly, and Kyles saw the hasps of two shanks Carter kept in his waistband. Always. Awake or asleep. One was the broken-off chunk of a metal plate he had honed into a blade. He had fashioned the more deadly skewer by melting and reshaping the hard plastic handle of a toothbrush. Toothbrushes, being legal, were handy feedstock for the fabrication of much prison weaponry, some of it remarkably effective.

The trick was to keep these tools handy, and that could take guile. A strip search, for example, for all its coarse intimacy—or perhaps because of it—had acquired ritual aspects, mostly designed around the guards' aversion to physical contact with inmates in the dawning age of AIDS. Ordering a prisoner to strip, spread his buttocks, and open his mouth was, under most circumstances, an examination sufficient to establish that contraband was not being brought back onto the tier after a session in court or time spent in a downstairs visitor booth. As filigree, custom required the prisoner to shake out each item of stripped-off clothing while the guard watched. To keep a shiv from being confiscated, the key was to set your underpants down over it. Kyles watched one day as Carter showed him how. Come time to give them a shake, you picked them up with your thumb and middle finger, pinching the very tip of the blade through the cloth. The fabric would hang loose around the shiv like a magician's handkerchief, and even a fairly rough shake would send a tremor through the fabric without revealing the outline of the weapon inside.

There would be other lessons, few of them uplifting. Kyles had not been on the tier two days when the guards hauled him back down to the processing center and booked him with another murder, that of a sixty-year-old Honduran seaman named Charles Suazo. Suazo's bullet-riddled corpse had been found four months earlier amid the clutter of a ransacked home in the Gentilly neighborhood. Kyles well knew the detective division's proclivity for clearing their books of unsolved cases by trying to lay them off on suspects in fresh crimes, but this time they appeared to have something. Ballistics tests showed that the weapon used to kill Suazo was the same pistol that had been pulled from beneath Kyles's stove on Desire Street. It was a murder charge that in several weeks would be dropped as suddenly and summarily as it had been lodged. But ironically, it stemmed from a crime Kyles had heard something about—and not just on television—a crime whose rumored perpetrators were people he vaguely knew. That knowledge mitigated the dismay he felt at finding himself the focus of two murder raps at once. The prosecutors were using the gun to tie the suspect in the Dye case to the killing of seaman Suazo. But didn't that logic work in reverse? If the Suazo killer were caught, might that exonerate Kyles of the Dye killing?

A suspect better favored by social privilege or skin color would have been outraged by the possibility that he had been booked for a crime he did not commit. A white, or even a black with a middle-class background, might have expected legal precision in the state's response to the opportunity for prosecution presented by a Curtis Kyles. But his experience with the law had not led Kyles to such an expectation. He did not automatically assume that the state's maneuvering against him would be all that closely calibrated with anything he had actually done. There was a world of crime out there. From Kyles's experience, most of it was committed with impunity. A tiny fraction caught the attention of polite society, if that term could be expanded to include police, many of whom were criminals themselves or worked so closely with criminal informants that they had lost all sense of where the boundary between the two worlds lay. Then there was the pool of criminals. Police fished it for perpetrators to take the rap for the most offensive, or the most visible, crimes, the ones someone squawked about. Or so it seemed to Kyles. The law, in its Ninth Ward manifestations, had never been other than clumsy—a vague and corrupt presence on the horizon of the local economy, more like a thundercloud than a lightning bolt. Cops, if you could not avoid them altogether, were a harassment that you learned to allay with bribes of cash, drugs, or information they could use against someone else. Police would deny finding any cash at all in the Desire Street apartment—something Kyles's lawyers would one day mention by way of refuting the contention that he had traded Mrs. Dye's car for a quick $400 the day after he killed her. If he had, where was the money? Indeed, it would no more have occurred to Kyles to expect fair treatment from cops than to seek their help against someone who broke the well-codified rules of his own criminal dealings. For Kyles, a man well aware that he was vulnerable from many directions at once, the Suazo charge was as much an opportunity as a threat. And then suddenly it went away. It might have been a cause for jubilation. Kyles greeted the news with anger and disgust, certain now that police had stumbled upon inconvenient evidence, evidence that someone else had killed Suazo, evidence that would only confound the effort to convict their bird in hand—Kyles—of the Dye murder if they continued to insist on a link between the two cases.

After a night in a holding cell while he was booked in the Suazo case, Kyles was returned to the tier to discover that his bedding had been appropriated and the small stash of clothing and toiletries he had set on top of it was dumped on the floor. It was a test, and from the grin on the asshole's face now watching how he would handle himself, Kyles knew just who was administering it.

Strike first. Think about it later. A surge of dread swept over him at the sight of his tormentor, as well muscled as he was fucked up, with easily a hundred pounds on Kyles. Ironically, this was a "tier rep," one of the men entrusted by guards with special privileges and the political power that came with them—ladling portions of food and pouring juice, for example. The privilege was payment for the tier rep's more important service: ratting out inmates the guards wanted to isolate or otherwise punish. Kyles found himself "shaking like a '57 Chevy" in the face of his date with this destiny, but the only antidote was action. He hurled himself at the man.

For a split second Kyles was overwhelmed. Then it all came back to him, the accumulated wisdom of his years fighting dirty on the streets: the knee to the groin, the salty taste of the man's flesh as Kyles bit down hard and tore away a goodly chunk of it in a bid to snap his collarbone. With a shrieking sound, like a streetcar rounding curved track, the man had rammed him into the bars of the cell so hard that for a minute or more, unable to breathe, Kyles could only hold on to his assailant as the huge man ran about the cell bashing into this wall and that.

Kyles did not pretend to have won that first set-to, but neither was he crushed, as by all rights he should have been. And he came away from the encounter cautiously optimistic that every one of the men who had come to the bars of their cells to check out the commotion knew better than to mess with the newcomer on a whim. There would be other fights, though, constant fights picked by men angry at the sight of a bastard as cocky and defiant as Kyles, or dry in the mouth to feel his body, even if the part they were feeling was just the knobs of his knuckles in their gut.

As far as Kyles could see, Burl Carter was right. With few exceptions, inmates came in two kinds: whores and the men who escaped that fate by debasing other men and selling them for cigarettes. Kyles fought to be in the minority who could ignore this grotesque parody of free-world sexuality, the group who did not have to constantly restate their sexual dominance in order to go unchallenged through the rest of the week. But there was no escaping awareness of it: the screams from the showers, the dayroom gangbangs while guards looked the other way, the occasional scurrying of a stretcher crew to haul off a newcomer bleeding so profusely that rectal suturing or even surgery was required.

Kyles was better than a month into this nightmare, a month and a million miles from the world he had known across town, when one afternoon he was led down into the visitors room and treated to the tears and smiles of four women from that other time and place. His mother was the first to sit with him, weak from her own afflictions, weeping softly over his predicament. They had spoken only once since the arrest, a frustrating call from the tier's pay phone, in which he swore he had not killed the Schwegmann's lady, begged his mother to believe him, and finally wrested from her a promise that she did and always would. After his mother, Kyles sat with Brenda and then Lela. Pinkey had wanted to be last.

For a moment she simply gazed at him, rebuilding her recollection of what Kyles looked like without the busted lip and the blood-spattered shirt that had marked her last glimpse of him. Those were the things that had stayed with her, seen out of the corner of an eye after police pushed her up against the wall of the Desire Street building, kicked her legs apart, and told her that they'd bust her head open too if she didn't stare straight ahead. And so she had, gaining intimate acquaintance with a square-foot patch of sooty asbestos shingling while the weight in her womb pulled painfully against her groin muscles. The next sight of her unborn baby's father had been the televised perp walk, and then . . . nothing. A month of nothing. With the phone disconnected on Desire Street, not even a call.

She watched Kyles watching her. He studied her long, thin face, the hair heaped high on her head. He undressed her in his mind's eye, ran his hands the length of her body, imagining the softness of her breasts and thighs against the wiry firmness of the rest of her. She felt his eyes as if they were fingertips.

She loved this man. She could not deny it. And to those who knew them, their many children were testimony to that love and their stead-fastness as a family. The underlying truth was more complex. Because as much as Pinkey loved Curtis, she also loathed and even feared him, loathed the man who did not return to her at least several nights a week—and she knew better than to believe his lies about staying with his mother. She feared the man who slapped her now and again and who once, in a mo-ment as erotic as it was unnerving, had shown her his gun and said he'd use it if she ever left him.

A condition of deep despair had settled over Pinkey on the day of Curtis's arrest—his brothers and sisters finally gone, the kids bawling. She sat on the edge of the bed in the ripped-apart room, studying herself in the mirror: the lankiness of her hair, she was proud of that; her small breasts and the belly below them, already big and round enough to thrust her legs apart. What man would provide for her in this condition? Welfare would see her only so far. Everybody knew that except the welfare people. Her mother would help out where she could, and Johnny, and Curtis's sisters. Of course they would. But could they? And to make matters worse, she was the next thing from homeless. The landlord, a family friend who had seen Curtis and Pinkey into the Desire Street apartment four years earlier, had taken sick. That left management of the building to his son, a man who didn't take to her, by Pinkey's reckoning. He had been friendly enough with Curtis over the years. They'd hung out together every now and then, and she would hear them laughing in the next room. Now Cur-tis was gone, and the landlord's son wanted Pinkey and the kids out. "He didn't care where we was going. Just git." Maybe he figured that if he didn't roust Pinkey quickly, in due course he might have Beanie Wallace

under his roof as well. That he could do without. And indeed, whether
the landlord knew it or not, Beanie was already playing his hand. He had
come by. Not the day of the arrest—that had been him sitting on the stoop
across the street watching, the junkie Sharon Whittington wondered
about as she headed back to her place—but soon after. He had come on
to Pinkey like a long-lost lover home from the wars. Except that they had
never been lovers, no matter what Curtis thought. Brother and sister was
more like it. And if Beanie had been to war, it was with Curtis, the father
of her children. How fucked-up was that?

Beanie had put an arm around her and told her he had put together some
money, close to a thousand dollars, and he would take care of her. The
police had laid it on him, he said, something that Pinkey instantly wished
she didn't know and that she would certainly need to keep secret. He offered the world: an apartment across the river, a father for her kids, his
love and devotion. She knew where the love and devotion were coming
from, and she could do without it. Fat Head, she called him, always had.
It was a term of affection, but it bespoke a deeper truth. He never had
been her type. "I just didn't like him like that, and I never had." But an
apartment across the river, in Algiers, that was worth some discussion.
Maybe Beanie was right. Maybe the cops would be all over Desire Street
as long as she stayed on there. And then she came to her senses. Beanie?
A provider? She needed only to look at the tracks on his arm to know
where he stashed most of his ready cash. Her brothers were tight with
Beanie, their bunkmate during adolescence, but even Johnny had warned
her to stay away from him. And anyway, she had begun to sense that she
had an alternative. Tyrone Joseph was a neighbor of long standing, from
right across Desire. He had kids somewhere. Now and then she'd see him
with one or another of them on the weekends, but otherwise he was single, employable, with a job managing a fried-chicken joint, from what
she'd heard. It was not long before Pinkey found reasons to be sweeping
the front porch around the time Tyrone strode down Desire on his way
home from work, and that was reason enough for him to cross the street
and say something to her about Curtis, as common courtesy required.
The next time it happened, one of the kids started to bawl, so Pinkey said

he might as well come in while she dealt with the baby, and Tyrone had seen no reason not to. Pinkey would summarize the courtship this way: "Basically me and Tyrone started talking and conversating, and things moved on from that."

There in the jailhouse visitor booth, Pinkey and Curtis were real with each other, candid. She mentioned Beanie and Tyrone, that they had been coming around. She admitted it, without telling just how far things had progressed with Tyrone. Curtis knew a little something about Beanie, always hitting on Pinkey. He was not the first man who had taken an interest in Kyles's woman, nor would he be the last, but Pinkey had long since established to Kyles's satisfaction that she knew how to take care of herself. Tyrone was a different story. A good man, Kyles had to admit it—sober, and you made a little money managing a Popeyes fried-chicken outlet.

Kyles sensed that Pinkey was not telling everything, but then there had always been secrets, and God knows he had kept his share of them from her. Now she was grinning up at him, her smile lighting the dark beauty of her face. "Ain't none of them as good as you, baby. You know that, Curtis." Whatever happened, she seemed to be saying, was temporary. As soon as he got off—when, not if, he got off—she would be there for him. They were crying now, both of them. And it would stay with Kyles forever, how in the harsh light of the visitors room and through the blurry lens of his tears, Pinkey seemed to be two people, first one and then the other. The loving partner in all his dreams of sex and money and large living and all the pretty little babies they called their own—that was one Pinkey. And in the next instant, as his tears warped her face another way, she was the bitch his sisters had always warned him she was—rid of him finally, and not without a last laugh that would carry her out of his life and into the arms of another man, other men: exquisite revenge, now that he was caged and impotent, for all the times he had betrayed her.

Was it over? The possibility sent Kyles's mind spooling back to the beginning, to the very first time he had laid eyes on Pinkey Burnes. The attraction had been instantaneous. He thought she was, as he would put it, "the most beautiful little girl" he had ever seen. He also thought she was eleven, maybe twelve. Kyles was sixteen. Actually, Pinkey was only a year younger than he was, as Kyles would soon find out, but slight, like an elf, right down to the wink in her eye. She was at her mother's place on

Desire Street that day, the very building where Kyles would be arrested for murder nine years and many children later.

Everything in Kyles's being had told him to keep his hands off Pinkey Burnes. And where his being stopped talking, his sisters had started right in. Kyles knew what they were saying when they kissed her off as "street," but he saw the edginess as the tomboy in her, and he found it intriguing. A little game of touch football might get going on a playground or in one of the project courtyards, six or eight boys to a side, and the next thing you knew, Pinkey would run out into the thick of things, steal a pass, and weave her way around the bunch of them. That was okay. That was kind of cute. Then there was another side to her, the way Pinkey could influence other girls, even grown women, get them to do things for her. There was a power she had over them, and Kyles, who had some of the same sway over males with a few years on him, was disposed to admire it.

Once the age issue got figured out, there was still something that bothered Kyles more than anything his family had to say. Pinkey was Johnny's sister, and Johnny was his best friend, his main man, a relationship that flourished on the streets and in the corridors of Carver High—when they bothered to show up—but until that day had not led to Curtis's visiting Johnny's home and encountering his vixen sister. Kyles had a rule of thumb: "I didn't get involved with my boys' sisters. I didn't want them messing with my sisters." It held him back, but not all that long.

What was supposed to be going on the afternoon that Curtis first laid eyes on Pinkey Burnes was not Curtis meets Pinkey, but Johnny gets a shot at Pinkey's friend Janetta. Janetta was going to be hanging out with Pinkey that afternoon, and Johnny was crazy about her. Bringing Curtis over was just a way to keep Pinkey busy while Johnny made his move. The girls put up with them for a while, Johnny and Curtis smoking cigarettes, all four of them smoking cigarettes out by the curb, acting cool. And then the girls went back into the house and up to the Burneses' apartment to fool with their hair and talk about these boys—way too full of themselves, those two, but cool looking. Johnny and Curtis stood around a little longer, scuffing their shoes and smoking their cigarettes and jiving with this one and that one and anyone else they knew who drifted along Desire Street on foot or rode by in cars.

Janetta's going upstairs did not bode well for Johnny, but then Curtis noticed Pinkey peeking down from the apartment window. She'd steal a look, then disappear, the curtain moving ever so slightly where she had been. Then there she was again. After a while she came back downstairs to where Johnny and Curtis were hanging out, and she said something about going down to the store. Did anybody want anything? Now Curtis made his move. Yes, there was something he wanted, which was to walk down to the store with her, okay? Nothing heavy. Nothing nasty. Just a pleasant walk down to the store with this little lady who didn't know it, but she was completely curling his toes. Okay, she said. It's a free country. By the time they got back from the store—a couple of Cokes, cigarettes, a candy bar—maybe they weren't in love yet, but they were somewhere they had never been before, neither one of them.

In the days ahead, the rule about not messing with your boy's sister was not entirely revoked. There would be no kissing. No pawing. None of that. Not that day, not for a while. And if Curtis forgot himself, Pinkey was sure enough going to remind him. And yet, as Kyles would say years later, reflecting back on that time in his life and a woman he would come to think of less fondly, "It was just lovely, just being together with her." Lovelier, certainly, than Carver High. The two of them started cutting class, not that either one had ever been all that religious about showing up. They'd meet at a friend's place in Press Park, the subdivision where Kyles lived with his aunt Eva. The friend's mother worked a job, so the house was empty: TV, cigarettes, Curtis and his buddy turning on behind a little weed, trying to get Pinkey to get high with them.

They were not routinely beautiful, these two. There were better-looking women than Pinkey—Skinny, as her friends called her. And there were men who came a lot bigger than Kyles. But put the two of them together, and you had something very cool, almost dazzling: a matched set, Curtis dark and slight, with his deep voice and some of the Mississippi farm country still in it even after all these years in New Orleans; Pinkey leggy and as thin as a ten-year-old boy, with long, straight hair that was the envy of her friends.

It is the mid-'70s. Curtis wears his hair in an Afro as big as a swarm of bees. For footwear he is partial to the easygoing look of "low quarters," mainly because everyone else is into platform shoes. Low quarters and a pair of starched jeans with a crease sharp enough to shave the legs of the girl he's dancing with, which most of the time is Pinkey. And a designer belt. A decent belt said something about you, Kyles had decided. And so he got good at sticky-fingering Gucci belts off the rack at Rubenstein's and Maison Blanche, and the other stores along Canal Street that had begun to work a little fly style into the stodgy product lines the whites were no longer coming downtown to buy anyway.

Curtis had done some of his growing up in the back rooms of pool-table bars and the other places where his brother Roosevelt hung out. "Hip"—that was the name they gave Roosevelt because he had all the moves. And so Curtis became L'il Hip—a mascot to the older pool-hall dudes and to the women some of them worked, a boy Christ among the temple elders, a Little Anthony among the Imperials. Kyles was not just a mascot, however. Little Anthony's thing was singing falsetto. Kyles could shoot pool like a demon. Roosevelt did the hustling: betting a stranger that this little kid—Kyles looked about twelve until he was fourteen or fifteen—could ice them. Curtis kept his mouth shut, and the balls just kept dropping, one right after another. It was a knack he could scarcely explain. "I could watch you shooting and see the trick you used, and for some reason I could master it." Now, in Pinkey, L'il Hip had found his miss, his female peer, right down to her pint size and wiry frame.

On the dance floor you'd see people step aside a few paces to give them room, the two of them zoned out, off in another world. Or they'd show up at a waistline party, which got its name because the price of admission for girls was based on the size of their waists: ten cents an inch; 22 inches, $2.20. The boys got their chests measured and didn't mind puffing them out a little bit even if it was going to cost, which made up for the girls trying to suck in their bellies. The party hosts sold chips and soda pretty much at break-even prices. There was money to be made hosting a waistline party, but you made it by the inch.

It took about two months before they stumbled on the snake in their Eden. Because if Pinkey was Curtis's first love, she was definitely not his first woman. He was not going to go on forever without sex, and he said so, but Pinkey wasn't buying. For all her streetwise ways, she had never once let a man do what he wanted with her, and she was in no mood to rush things, not even for Curtis. She wasn't ready, she said. Maybe when she turned sixteen. And when Curtis whined and whined some more, she said that was it. If that was all he had in mind, it was over between them.

They separated for two months. And then, right on schedule, she turned sixteen. Some of her girlfriends threw her a sweet sixteen party. Curtis naturally turned up, partly to see if she was as good as her word. It wasn't the only reason. After two months, he was happy just to be with Pinkey again, and then, after everybody had gone, she made him even happier.

Still, she found ways to piss him off. There was her little friend Duane. Duane was a friend of the family, Pinkey told him, almost like a foster child they had taken in, a foster brother to Pinkey and Johnny Burnes. One in a series—Beanie had been another. Maybe so, but it still bothered Curtis, Duane always hanging around her like that. Being stubborn, Curtis decided to walk out on Pinkey once again, the second breakup in less than half a year.

One of Pinkey's girlfriends caught up with him a few days later and told Curtis there was something he needed to face. "You know," she began, "Skinny pregnant." Curtis took it under advisement. It wasn't true until he heard it from Pinkey herself. He'd goddamn well deal with it then. And anyway, how did he know the baby was even his? *Tonti*

Two days later Pinkey tried to get him to take her out: a dance at St. Mary of the Angels Church, over on North Tonti. Breakup or no breakup, Curtis was a sucker for a dance. But he wasn't about to go if he couldn't do it right, and seeing as he didn't have enough money to do it right, or even wrong, he turned Pinkey down. Anyway, there was another girl who had caught his eye, a friend of Roosevelt's. People were saying his chances were pretty good with her. She was interested. So he decided to fall by her house the night of the St. Mary's dance. They had settled down for some serious getting to know each other, when there was a knock on the door, another of Pinkey's girlfriends, an envoy. "Skinny outside. You better talk to her, Curtis."

Just then Curtis heard Pinkey call his name, and it was as if Roosevelt's friend had never happened. He went straight downstairs. Pinkey cried a little, tough as she was, thinking she was probably in this all alone. But Curtis surprised her, maybe even himself. He didn't give it a moment's thought. He didn't get angry at her, didn't panic. He didn't tell her to get rid of it or try to guilt-trip her about whether the baby was his, because from the tone of her voice, the look of her face, he had absolutely no doubt that it was.

Their first apartment, on Conti Street between Dorgenois and Rocheblave, was a shack of a place, without even a refrigerator (they used an ice chest). But it was their own, and Curtis and Pinkey remembered being content there, the music going, another couple over for the evening getting to know them a little bit, Pinkey four or five months pregnant and finally starting to show. She waves away the bottle that Curtis has been passing around. No booze for the little mama, not even a swig of the MD 20/20—Mad Dog, as it was more commonly known—her favorite. No pot either, except maybe in the sweet, sexy half hour late in the night after she and Curtis get naked and start getting into it. "She knew I loved her to smoke weed," Curtis would reminisce years later. But for now, the night is young, and the visitor—call him Lionel—has a proposition, something to pass the time, impress the ladies, take the measure of his new friend.

You know the church? The one over there on Rocheblave? You ever been in that church, man? You know they got a lot of stuff in that church, man—a piano and drum sets, guitars, all kind of shit, man.

Right away Curtis can see where this is going, and he has to hope it's just the bottle talking. Because from what he knows about him, Lionel is seriously into burglary, and it's beginning to look like he is taunting Curtis to see what he's made of, or, as Curtis puts it, "calling his hand."

Lionel lowers the ante: "We don't have to take nothing, man. Let's just go in there, check it out. Save it for a rainy day."

Pinkey has fallen silent. Curtis picks up on it, and when she gets a minute aside with him, she lays it on the line. "What are you listening to this shit for, baby? We got enough, Curtis. We got what we need. We don't need to be robbing no churches."

Of course she's right. But this isn't about money anymore. This is about manhood, about being down with a brother, being willing to share his danger and his risks, and outside of what goes on with the women in his life, it is one of the strongest and purest feelings that Kyles has known. Plus, this could be a ball, busting into that old church with all the instruments inside, wailing on those guitars like a couple of rock stars.

In the end, Pinkey comes along, though it takes a lot of talking her into it. And she never does get comfortable enough to stop saying it's time to go. And then all of a sudden it surely is, because in the distance they can hear sirens. Neighbors must have picked up on the rock star racket and called in the law. Quick, out the back door. No, leave the goddamn guitar behind. Over the fence and off into the night.

That was all part of the deal, teasing the beast, taunting him, and then, like picadors in a bullring, rolling under the rails to safety just ahead of the slashing horns. Jacking a car was the surest way into this rush: the thrill of the chase, the possibility of a crash, even flying bullets, but a foot chase would do. "The police would always give you a good run once you got their attention," Kyles said, remembering those last crazy days before the first of his children was born and he became a man.

In her seventh month Pinkey moved back in with her mother to wait for the baby. And even if she hadn't, Curtis would have kept his distance. Having a warm place in his heart for kids was not the same thing as wanting to see them born. No thanks. Not just now. Not ever. But even when he was apart from Pinkey, it was almost like there was an umbilical bond between them. Curtis bolted that day in early July when the contractions began to rack Pinkey's small body. But he felt them in his own gut, physically felt them, as if he were getting ready to give birth himself—a weird sensation, "like my navel was pulling."

He collected a friend, and they started to drive, anywhere, nowhere at all, right out of town and along the Gulf Coast to Biloxi, a Mississippi beach town a couple of hours to the east. In the night, Pinkey's mother helped her over to Charity Hospital, Huey Long's huge and meandering gray deco gift to a city busted flat by the Great Depression, the beginning and end point of the Kingfish's cradle-to-grave vision of cracker socialism at oil company expense. Kyles came back into town to learn he was the father of a baby girl, Tyteannia, born on the seventh day of the seventh month, in the year 1977.

Gazing at Pinkey, in the sterile cloister of the prison visitor booth, Kyles could remember like it was yesterday the moment when she told him a baby was coming. "My chest grew so big. My head swole; it was a beautiful thing to me." He'd stay with her. Sure he would. He had always told himself that he'd never leave his kids like his own daddy had done. "I knew they were going to mean everything to me." Now the question was this: Would she stay with him?

The guard was tapping on the wall of the booth, signaling for them to wrap it up. Kyles composed himself, pressing his palm against the glass as she did the same. "Just promise me this," he said to her. "Promise me that whoever take the cow, he also takes the calves. Okay? You promise me that?" Pinkey said that she would. She'd never run off with a man and leave their kids behind. She swore it.

cow & calves

FIVE

A white family, even a poor white family, can survive a Southern city in relative ignorance of the law, but no ghetto family is unfamiliar with arrest and indictment. If its sons have not personally experienced the nighttime roundups or the more targeted pursuit of shoplifters and joyriders, then the experience of neighbors provides a vicarious education. But even in this climate of uneasy familiarity with the law, a capital murder charge is a beast not everyone has wrestled with, and the Kyles family was initially at a complete loss on how to proceed. Indeed, they were uncertain if there was a role even available to them in the costly white man's game then unfolding.

They knew only that the stakes were terrifyingly high. Just nine months earlier, a young black man named Robert Wayne Williams had become the first Louisianan to burn in the state's electric chair since the U.S. Supreme Court's 1976 ruling reinstated capital punishment. Kyles's sister Lela Johnson well remembered that execution. Everyone did. In particular, she remembered the hush that had seemed to fall over black New Orleans when, after the usual rounds of delay and demurrer and amid the gathering hope that an event so often postponed would never really transpire, the community had awakened that morning just before Christmas, to find out it had.

Desperate for guidance, Lela remembered . . . Oh, if only she could remember—what was his name, the one who stood up for Curtis that other time? A decade earlier, when Curtis was sixteen—in fact, around midnight on the very eve of his sixteenth birthday—he had answered a knock on the door and been hauled down to police headquarters to be booked with rape. It had amounted to very little work for the lawyer who agreed to represent him, a case of mistaken identity.

But a dropped rape charge was a long way from capital murder, and it was a stretch, she was warned, to suppose that one lawyer's expertise could span so large a spectrum.

Instead, an older woman in the community versed in these difficult matters—Miss Clara, as they knew her—suggested that she try a downtown criminal defense attorney named Reed. Lela made an appointment through Mr. Reed's secretary, and one afternoon in mid-October she found herself weaving through the unfamiliar labyrinth of New Orleans's central business district, searching for a place to park. She wasn't quite sure what she would do if she found one. Days off from work—once to visit with Curtis, other times to keep her lonely vigil in the back of the courtroom during hearings on pretrial motions—already had pinched her finances, at best never robust. She had set off for her appointment with Reed literally without a cent in her pocket, and it would take a quarter just to work the parking meter. Maybe she'd get lucky and the meter maid wouldn't come by. And if she did? Well, so what. A ticket was like a bill. You put it in the coffee can on the kitchen table along with the others you hoped to pay someday.

In a mood not so many notches above despair, to find an empty space just then and, on pulling in, to discover the meter pumped full of coins—two hours' worth—would have been enough to turn a woman less religious than Lela to thoughts of divine intervention. "A sign from God" is how she came to think of it—encouragement, in any case, to press on. But the parking meter epiphany had been followed immediately by a setback. Mr. Reed had listened patiently and intently. Delivered of a recap of her brother's dilemma and an appeal for the lawyer's help, Lela had fallen silent, girding herself for what she knew might be the whopping cost of this important man's services. And indeed, the cost would be enormous, he told her, many thousands. And even at that, she was asking him to make a gift of his time and talent, because the family could not possibly compensate him for the hours he would have to put in. They would have to look elsewhere.

Lela did not cry. Tears or anger might have followed a slap in the face. This was a deeper blow, a punch to the gut, and when you cannot breathe, you cannot cry or curse. Lela composed herself as best she could and left the office in silence.

Within a week, time running out, the family, at Reed's suggestion, shopped criminal defense work's discount shelf and engaged a young lawyer named Martin Regan, an upstart but a lawyer willing to work with them. They would need five grand, he said. No less. And he would do the best he could with it.

That night the family gathered at Roosevelt's and chipped in. He put bottles on the kitchen table, and as they drank and yakked and wept and hugged each other, he set an old pillowcase into circulation among them. Sawbucks and fifties were pulled out of thin wallets and dumped inside. Someone upended a cookie jar of God knows how much in ones and small coins. Lela had gone to the bank earlier in the day and pulled out her life savings, about $100. Others had a bit more, rainy-day funds of uncertain origin that were produced as the liquor flowed and the sense of family solidarity thickened along with their tongues. Brenda had a fresh paycheck on her, a week's wages from the meatpacking plant. She signed the back, and that too settled into the pillowcase like a falling leaf. If she cashed it, she'd only spend the money, she joked. How she'd feed the kids in the next week was another matter, but there was no sense talking about it. Not right then.

Two or three days later, a delegation of them showed up at Regan's office, a room in a little warren of offices along a low-rent part of Tulane Avenue near the courthouse. They upended the pillowcase right there on the office carpet, and Regan counted out enough of it to know that if it wasn't exactly five grand, it was almost certainly all they could come up with. And Curtis had a lawyer.

Their first meeting, in a prison visitor room, had not filled Kyles with much optimism. There was something of the automaton about Regan, a vestige of his days with the army's Judge Advocate General's Corps,

Kyles decided. And the fact that Regan felt the need to maintain so rigid a façade did not bode well for developing the kind of collaborative rapport that would energize a defense. Neither did the logistics of communication. Even contacting his attorney required written permission, and weeks would pass without Kyles hearing from the man hired to save his life.

But then Kyles didn't expect all that much of Regan. A lawyer was something you had to have, and a paid lawyer was, so they said, better than a public defender. When it came to finding out what was really going on, Kyles looked elsewhere. An opportunity for more reliable feedback had presented itself at a motion hearing some weeks after Kyles's arrest, the first of several pretrial sessions in which attorneys for the state and for the defendant would argue before a judge, but not a jury, over such legal issues as the admissibility of evidence or testimony, the quality of the warrants that may have led to the searches that yielded these pieces of evidence, and so forth. For the lawyers, particularly the defense, it was a chance to intuit the opposition's theory of the case and the points of law and evidence likely to be mustered in support of it. For Kyles and some of those close to him, it was a rare chance—the first since his arrest—to touch, to whisper, to catch up, to exhort each other not to give up or be scared.

Judge Waldron's courtroom, with its de rigueur dark paneling and heavy wooden tables, was on the second floor of the vast gray Orleans Parish Criminal Courts Building, a still functioning mausoleum in a part of town where the only buildings of equivalent size—the old Dixie and Falstaff breweries—stood empty. Brush, even small trees sprouted from crevices in the crumbling brick walls of the abandoned breweries, and the blocks of modest worker housing interspersed among the breweries had lost ground to neglect, outright abandonment, or conversion to the uses of prostitutes, crack smokers, smash-and-grab guys. The courthouse itself was a monument to WPA style and to the frugalities of the Depression economics its construction was meant to relieve: only three of its four sides had been dressed out in granite cladding. The fourth side, turned toward police headquarters and the razor-wired grounds of Orleans Parish Prison, had been daubed with stucco, now chipped and discolored.

Johnny Burnes and Kyles's sisters—Pinkey also was with them that day—had gravitated naturally to the gallery seats closest to the defense table. Kyles was able to turn quickly and greet them with a faint smile, a sign of bravado more than optimism. But the sheriff's deputies shushed the group as the judge entered the room and gaveled the proceeding to order. During a break, Kyles tipped backward from the defense table and quickly hugged Pinkey and his sisters. The women attended to, Johnny leaned into his ear and whispered answers to the question that had been plaguing Kyles ever since his arrest, a question he had no need to put in words: What the hell was going on? Years later, Kyles would still recall Burnes's answer, encrypted instinctively against the chance that they were being overheard. "The coward done what he done," Burnes began, looking around to see if any of the guards were paying attention, "and then he done what he had to do."

"Coward" was not a judgment; it was shorthand, signifying that this was all about the Dye murder, not Suazo, not drugs. Killing a grandmother for no reason other than the convenience of robbing her was, in the eyes of the street, a coward's crime. Any man could be a coward. The term was neutral, referential. The same could be said of Burnes's subsequent observation: "and then he done what he had to do." What he had to do— what any man might do in similar circumstances—was to save his skin, and what was done to that end had been, of course, to set in motion the sequence of events that led to Kyles's present predicament. The killer had sold Kyles out.

But who was he, this coward who had ratted out Kyles? The old adage is true: there is no honor among thieves. Kyles knew several men— nearly as many as were present at his own dinner table the night before his arrest—capable of overdoing the robbery of an old woman and then pushing someone else into the path of infuriated police.

Burnes looked around once again to make sure his audience was limited to the old friend in front of him, and then he leaned forward again to rasp a final few words into Kyles's ear: "I should have let you kill the nigger when you had the chance." In hindsight, Kyles would remember this moment—not his arrest, not even his sentencing—as the most mind-blowing of his whole ordeal, and it is not difficult to imagine the numbing shock of what he had just heard.

Because there was only one man Johnny Burnes had ever kept Kyles from killing—after a drug deal gone bad—and that was their mutual acquaintance and sometime friend Beanie Wallace. Kyles had found reasons

to distrust Beanie over the years, even to loathe him, but the tensions between them had abated, and at their worst, they didn't explain why Beanie
would sell him out so completely.

But wait. Kyles reined in his thoughts and the runaway paranoia they
were engendering in him. There was another way to take Johnny's coded
message. Maybe it wasn't so much a report as a suggestion. Johnny was
no fool and certainly no saint. Here was a way, he might have been saying, to shape your defense and save your hide: blame Beanie. Let him take
the hit. Didn't he have a grandmother working for some sheriff's department somewhere? That was the word on the street. Beanie stood a lot better chance than Kyles of wriggling free of a heavy charge. He'd done it
more than once before.

Kyles wrenched himself all the way around in his chair to look Burnes
in the eye. He said nothing, then turned and leaned back toward the defense table. The most careful scrutiny of the defendant would have yielded
no clue, no tensing of the jaw, no drumming of fingernails, no clenching
and unclenching of an ungovernable fist. He sat there quietly, seemingly
at ease. But the sense of rage that swept over him was of a force greater
than any emotion he had ever known. It was the rage of a grackle Kyles
had seen fly through an open door and then hurl itself repeatedly against
a closed window, trying to rejoin the world. It was the rage of a muskrat
gnawing off its own leg in order to escape the traps Kyles's older brother
set out along Mississippi creeks when they were boys.

It was the rage of an inmate named Curtis Kyles who now, hearing that
a cousin and sometime accomplice of Beanie's was somewhere in the catacombs of Orleans Parish Prison, began maneuvering—unsuccessfully, as
it would turn out—to be transferred to wherever he was. He needed to
hurt the boy. Torture him. It would be vengeance at one remove, but it
was better than nothing at all.

Burnes's identification of Beanie as the man who had fingered Kyles
was shortly confirmed by the police themselves. As they were pleased to
disclose to the court, a good citizen had come forward with information
that led to Kyles's arrest, a citizen named Joseph Wallace, a man known
to his friends as Beanie. A good citizen was not necessarily a prig. Wal-

lace, after all, was a cohort of Kyles's, and Kyles was suspected to be a killer. But according to the police, Beanie had bought a red Ford LTD from the defendant in good faith on the day after the murder, only to have it dawn on him on the day after that, Saturday, that the red Ford might well be Mrs. Dye's. A relative had seen news reports that police were looking for a red Ford LTD, one with a missing hubcap. The one in Beanie's possession was missing a hubcap—and to think he had been seen in it the night before, joyriding through the French Quarter with a friend and their women.

Beanie had promptly called headquarters, turned over the car, and named Kyles. His motive was only more credible for being uncomplicated by any claim to civic virtue. Wallace was, he said, irate that Kyles had set him up like that, sold him a car so hot it exposed him to a bum rap for murder.

The gun, the holster, the cat food. Four eyewitnesses. Police had even turned up Kyles's fingerprint in Mrs. Dye's car. It was on a receipt, a supermarket receipt, from the Schwegmann's on Gentilly Road.

Martin Regan was going to be blunt about it. However often Kyles protested his innocence, the odds were looking longer and longer. The man didn't even have an alibi worth a damn. He had been working on his car. He had been picking up his kids at school. What good was that? He could have killed Mrs. Dye and still made it over to the school in time for the three o'clock bell that Thursday afternoon. And the receipt with the fingerprint, found in the dead woman's car! How could that be?

Here at least, Kyles came up with an explanation, however shaky. He had been working on his own car Friday morning, the morning after the murder, when Beanie came by—Beanie in an unfamiliar red car, now that Kyles thought back on it. Not that there was anything at all unusual about Beanie turning up in cars no one had seen before. Kyles knew better than to ask questions about them. Nor had he hesitated to hop inside when Beanie agreed to swing by Schwegmann's so Kyles could pick up a can of transmission fluid and some cigarettes. Inevitably, he had pulled out the cigarettes and fired one up on the ride back over to Desire Street. The receipt, Kyles suggested, had fallen out of the bag and onto the Ford's floorboards where the evidence technicians found it.

There were things about the story that worked for Regan in a strange sort of way. Kyles's very nonchalance about letting the receipt become litter was certainly not the mark of a man who had made off with the car after killing its owner. But then there was Beanie's equally flagrant nonchalance to factor in. If he was the killer, as Kyles and Johnny Burnes were urging Regan to argue, wasn't it even less likely that he would have driven the dead woman's car back to Schwegmann's on a trivial errand for Kyles the very next morning? Regan reviewed his options. Should he try to bargain? Offer to plead Kyles guilty? The state almost certainly would not settle for manslaughter. But a second-degree murder plea would at least limit the sentence to life. Kyles would not hear of it. And even if he had, it probably wouldn't have gone anywhere. The politics were all wrong.

That New Orleans just then was in the crosshairs of global media attention as host of the faltering 1984 World's Fair lent the case a special urgency, especially for those, such as District Attorney Harry Connick, who were charged with averting or at least mitigating civic disgrace. Add to that the pressure of electoral politics. Connick had only recently survived review by the electorate to win a third term, trouncing a black challenger in part by convincing black and white voters alike that he was tough enough to handle crimes as heinous as the one that had befallen Mrs. Dye just nine days before the vote. That juxtaposition of events energized the Kyles prosecution in ways that had not yet faded as Connick's people tore down their yard signs and peeled off their bumper stickers and the swank, silver-haired—and notoriously short-tempered—prosecutor got on about the business of his third term in office.

Harry Connick was a piece of work, a great showman, as prosecutors and politicians tend to be, even if the stage on which he found himself was not quite what he once had in mind. When not orchestrating a prosecution, Connick was a crooner, had been ever since high school. His prospects with the big bands had been cut short by service in World War II, but he had been able to indulge his love of music at least in part as proprietor of a record store that he and his first wife ran to put themselves through law school. After a stint as a defense attorney, in 1973 Connick had defeated the equally theatrical Jim Garrison, whose abortive efforts to prosecute a local business executive as the alleged ringleader of the Kennedy assassination had made the New Orleans district attorney's office briefly the wonder and the laughingstock of worldwide media.

Connick was a survivor. When first elected, he was the chief prosecutor in a city still run by whites. By 1978, a black man, Mayor Dutch Morial, had captured city hall; and, given the widening black electoral majority, there was good reason to think that every mayor who followed him would also be African American. The same calculus surely applied to the district attorney's office, but Connick defied the odds, ingratiating himself with the Morial political apparatus to win reelection three more times before ending a thirty-year career and retiring as the new century dawned.

A seasoned pro politically, as a musician Connick had been the consummate amateur, singing along to his own piano playing, now and then sitting in with local bands, regaling crowds at his fund-raisers. But serious opportunity and greater talent were channeled into his namesake, Harry junior, a child prodigy who by the late 1980s was a young man on the brink of international acclaim. The son's triumph would prove infectious, and Connick, late in life, would attempt his own nightclub career, a prosecutor by day, by moonlight a provincial Sinatra, snapping his microphone cord and shooting his cuffs in front of a jazz combo with a once-a-week gig at a French Quarter club.

Even before rekindling his musical career, Connick left the courtroom work to his assistants, an ill-paid, hard-driving group, mostly men, mostly white. In assigning assistant district attorneys to particular cases, Connick generally deferred to his chief of trials, Cliff Strider. And as the Kyles case ripened and came due, Strider had turned to one of his most aggressive young comers, a fellow product of the LSU Law School named Jim Williams. Prematurely balding but still filled with the fires of youth, in 1984 Williams hadn't yet been able to notch his pistol by actually condemning a defendant to death. But his colleagues well knew him as a man particularly hungry for blood, or at least for the smell of it coagulating in the veins of a man with fifty thousand volts of electricity passing through his body. By the end of the decade, that appetite would be sated several times over, and Jim Williams would enjoy a brief moment of fame as one of several tough-guy prosecutors in a national roundup put together by *Esquire* magazine. As a prop in Williams's portrait, the photographer would not neglect to include the miniature electric chair that adorned the prosecutor's desktop, the chair itself decorated with photo cutouts of the six men, all of them black, that Williams had pushed toward the hot seat by that time.

A white victim from a good and decent family—a woman at that—and a young black for a defendant, an animal spraying the Ninth Ward with bullets and jism with equal abandon, this was a case a hard-bitten prosecutor like Williams could be expected to relish. And then in an impulsive moment Cliff Strider had decided to step in too. A buddy had put him up to it. They'd been playing touch football on a weekend afternoon, as young lawyers were wont to do, and the talk had turned to the Dye case, the outrageousness of the crime, the importance of an effective prosecution. Strider did not need much convincing. Failure to convict Kyles would be a political fiasco. And he hardly needed to be told that bringing a predator like that down hard would burnish a first assistant's prospects, maybe even lead to a judgeship one day. Besides, this had all the makings of a cakewalk.

Regan's tangle with Strider and Williams was hardly a David and Goliath encounter. For the pittance he paid in salaries, Harry Connick got very few Goliaths. But Regan at first blush seemed to have no case at all. He would quiz the police technicians who had handled the physical evidence. That was routine. He could comb the edifice of eyewitness testimony for the cracks and fault lines that might jar loose a stone or two. But was there really much chance of it going anywhere? What was there to say in the face of the stolid laboring men, black men at that, united from the start in their view that the figure at the wheel of Mrs. Dye's car had been the one in Detective Dillman's collection of mug shots, Regan's client, Curtis Kyles.

Kyles had his own views of how to fight the case. Did anyone really think, for example, that a man as deeply involved with guns and ammunition as he was would have left a loaded pistol on the floor of his kitchen? With the kids crawling around—kids he demonstrably adored? Wouldn't he more likely have stashed it under the mattress along with the rifle police found there? It flabbergasted Kyles that anyone in his right mind would see the evidence from his apartment and the garbage bags out front as proof of his guilt. "Take any child in the ghetto—today, tomorrow, whatever—they know better than to be bringing shit around to where they live. We are taught from an early age. Like you see a purse laying around that's tore up, or something like that. Or you see a knife or something throwed in the bushes. You know not to touch that. Because that's been part of a crime. You are taught these things young. Just like you see a car with windows busted out and no tires, you don't go anywhere near it. You don't want your fingerprints on that. This is how you're taught. And the worst thing is to bring stuff like that around your house."

Understandably, Regan had cringed at the idea of drawing on Kyles's innate knowledge of the criminal mind-set in order to argue for his innocence of the Dye murder. We can't do it, he told his client. The one thing you've got going is a clean record. And now you want to tell the court that you know all about handling stolen goods? But if not that line of defense, what? And then it occurred to Regan. Maybe Johnny Burnes was onto something. Maybe the thing to do was swing for the fences. Don't just poke holes in the prosecution's evidence against Kyles. Don't settle for undermining confidence in the credibility of the snitch. Go all the way with Beanie Wallace. Make him out to be snitch and killer both.

The problems were obvious. One of them was that Kyles and Wallace didn't look all that much alike, from what Regan was hearing. Beanie was short and squat, they told him. Kyles was no Wilt Chamberlain, but he was skinny enough to look taller than he actually was. The other problem was motive. Beanie's explanation to the police—that he had ratted out Kyles as vengeance for sticking him with Mrs. Dye's car—struck Regan as patently absurd. So supreme an act of treachery over a stolen car? Streetwise kids played hot potato with hot cars all the time. Suspicions raised, somebody like Wallace would have known how to fob the car off on the next sucker as effortlessly as he claimed Kyles had fobbed it off on him. And when you started to run out of suckers, there were chop shops, dozens of them, all over eastern New Orleans. Kyles had filled in around the edges of Regan's knowledge of the criminal underground. As a teenager, like every underclass adolescent with a sporting interest in the occasional joyride, Kyles had carried a B-10 key, a kind of master ignition switch that worked on most every brand of car you'd care to borrow for a few hours. It was part of a young man's kit, as standard as a cigarette lighter and the rolled condom outlined against the leather of a well-worn wallet.

No, there needed to be something more to explain Wallace's breach of black brotherhood's ultimate taboo. And the motive Regan began to toy with was love. A love bordering on obsession: Beanie's love for Pinkey. There was something between them; that was easy to prove. The question was how far you could push it. Beanie had grown up as a virtual brother to Pinkey, a lodger in her mother's house, her brother's best friend—Johnny's "business" partner. As such, he was a familiar presence in the Desire Street apartment as well. Regan pressed Pinkey to tell him everything about her dealings with Beanie. But the best she could do was not all that compelling. Beanie hit on her from time to time. She acknowledged that. He'd done it the night before Kyles's arrest. She'd been alone in the kitchen, washing up, when he had come over to her, wrapped his arms around her, and pulled her rump against him. Beanie's patter had sounded more like whimsy than a proposition—"him saying things like, if I didn't have Curtis, would I be with him. Foolishness like that," as Pinkey put it.

"And I'm saying, 'Beanie, you better not let Curtis catch you like this.' But it's like he don't care. He didn't want Curtis to see him doing that, but if Curtis did see him, it was like he didn't give a damn. I'm trying to clean up my kitchen and he's hugging me and he's asking me that question—which is getting on my nerves—and finally, I guess I just said, 'Yeah, boy. If there wasn't no Curtis, sure it could have been you.'" And with that, she had twisted free of him, with a word of warning: "But you listen to me, boy, because there is a Curtis, and if he catch you like this, he gonna kill us both."

The best Pinkey had to offer, as far as Regan was concerned, was this: in hindsight, she had wondered if her effort to humor Beanie and get out of his arms hadn't "kind of lifted him up. That it was like something he had been waiting to hear. I guess he took it for 'go ahead'"—as though she had green-lighted her husband's betrayal. Regan caught himself. He was being played for a fool. Pinkey was telling him whatever she thought he wanted to hear. The interlude by the kitchen sink didn't green-light anything at all, because by the time of the Sunday night get-together, Wallace's call to the police was already a day old. It made it hard to believe something else Pinkey now told him: that Beanie said he had been paid a reward by the police for his help, more than $1,000—the money he offered Pinkey to move her to a new apartment across the river. The police flatly denied it, not that Regan took their word for gospel.

The attorney's skepticism about the honesty of his client's wife posed a dilemma. If he were to argue that Kyles was the victim of a classic love triangle, Pinkey might well be the key witness in a campaign to save his life. But Regan couldn't bring himself to trust her, and almost certainly the feeling was reciprocated.

After all, Pinkey had issues of her own to think about, above all the need to figure out how to keep her life afloat if Kyles did indeed take the long walk. She knew that Kyles wanted her to keep the family intact, keep the calves with the cow, not pass them out among relatives as had happened to Kyles in his own boyhood. With all that hanging over her, Pinkey was a woman eager to please. The police had taken her down to headquarters. God only knew what she had told them. During the pretrial discovery phase Regan had routinely demanded all statements taken from witnesses by police, but few documents had been forthcoming, and none at all bearing Pinkey's signature. The police were short of typists and stenographers, the prosecutors said; the records didn't exist.

There was another way to test Pinkey's loyalties, of course. Maybe there had been a time when she was sincere in her efforts to hose down the ardent Beanie Wallace, but Regan couldn't help wondering if changing circumstances had caused her secretly to reconsider. She had begun making herself scarce almost immediately after the arrest. Where the hell was she, anyway? Holed up with Beanie? For purposes of the case Regan was planning, that would not be a bad thing to establish.

A better-funded defense would have had professional investigators for this sort of mission. Regan, husbanding his limited retainer, looked to Kyles's sisters. Lela, for example, was dispatched to the Social Security office on a search that might shed light on Kyles's finances and on whether his physical disability—the bullets that had shattered his wrist and elbow and the one still lodged in his spine—might seem to preclude the parking lot tussle that had preceded Mrs. Dye's demise. Then Regan pulled Brenda aside and shared with her his hunch about Pinkey: that she was in league with Beanie and, in fact, had already moved in with him. Brenda's mission was to track her down. A quick check gave promise that Regan was onto something. The Desire Street apartment was empty, abandoned, a warren of dusty rooms littered with the detritus of a household not possessed of much worth hauling to life's next stopover.

From former neighbors along Desire, Brenda got an address for Pinkey on Louisa Street, not many blocks away. Both the promise and the limits of Brenda's competence as a private eye were quickly revealed. A knock on the Louisa Street door a day or two later did indeed scare up a glimpse of Pinkey, looking out at her from a pulled-back corner of the blanket she had tacked over the panel of smudged and sooty glass. Pinkey opened the latch and stepped out onto the stoop, leaving the door open behind her, and for a few awkward minutes—as the women spoke about this and that and how things were going—Brenda found herself peering over Pinkey's shoulder and down the shotgun's long hallway, sifting the static of Pinkey's many children for the sound of a man's voice or, better yet, a glimpse of Beanie. In due course, the conversation wound down, the only evidence harvested in support of Regan's theory being that Pinkey, in not inviting Brenda into the place, had denied her the opportunity either to prove or disprove it.

The fact of the matter—a fact Pinkey was understandably reluctant to share with Kyles or his sisters—was this: she was living with Tyrone Joseph. But the move had not gone unnoticed. There was a graveyard across the street, and one morning as Tyrone headed off to the Popeyes franchise he managed, there was Beanie, squatting on a patch of earth, just staring— the same stare Sharon Whittington had noticed as Beanie watched Kyles's arrest go down. Tyrone turned on his heel and went back inside the house and woke up Pinkey. She needed to know what was going on. Soon enough, Beanie started turning up at Popeyes—"didn't order nothing, didn't ask for nothing," according to what Tyrone told Pinkey, just stood there and watched him for a minute or two and walked out. Tyrone was unnerved enough to ask for a transfer to a different Popeyes. The next thing he knew, Beanie showed up there too, and a week after that the place got hit. As Pinkey told it, "Some guys came in and jumped over the counter and put a gun to Tyrone's head and robbed the till." Tyrone assumed that Beanie was behind the hit, maybe behind one of the masks the men wore, but he had no proof.

Johnny Burnes's detective services would prove more useful than Brenda's. It was with his help that Regan was able to reconstruct a list of

Kyles's buddies, several of them young men who had dropped by the Desire Street place as the music swelled and the booze flowed that final Sunday night. Their more valuable recollection preceded the party by three days. Three of them were prepared to testify, and so was Johnny, that on the evening just after the murder, Beanie had been seen sporting about in a red car—a Mercury in some accounts, a Ford in others—and that was a full day before, by Beanie's own account, he had bought the red LTD from Kyles. Burnes had another contribution to make, a memory suddenly much clarified by the knowledge that Beanie had betrayed Kyles to the police. At one point during the partying Sunday night Johnny had walked back into the kitchen to find Beanie alone there, squatting by the corner of the stove. At the sound of Burnes's footsteps, Beanie "raised up suddenly," Burnes said. Hours later, police would retrieve the murder weapon from behind that same corner of the stove.

The testimony of Kyles's buddies proved nothing, of course. Was it even true? Had Burnes invented the bit about Beanie squatting by the stove? Regan was in no position to be picky. Maybe they would plant a seed in jurors' minds, a basis for reasonable doubt. It was basically all he had, and here it was early November, with the trial set to begin before the end of the month.

SIX

On the night of Kyles's arrest, the common rooms of Orleans Parish Prison, erupting as they had in wolf whistles over the young man being perp-walked across the television screen and into the city's collective consciousness, were not the only place where interest in his looks and manner was acute. In a proper living room in a proper part of town, a young woman—a woman privileged both by the pallor of her skin and the advantages of a medical education—found herself riveted by the lead story on the evening news: a suspect in the Schwegmann's murder case had been brought into custody. Kyles's shoulders were hunched, his eyes cast to the ground precisely as if he meant to avoid her gaze and hers alone—which only deepened the young doctor's sense of having seen his face before. But where?

And then, with a shudder, it dawned on her. Sixteen months earlier, at the end of May 1983, Marylou Courrege, a physician at Charity Hospital, had joined colleagues for an evening of live music and libation at an Uptown jazz joint known as Tyler's Beer Garden. Shortly after midnight it had come time to pack it in, she decided, and the two women she arrived with, Nedda Handler and Marilyn Brown, had risen with her in sisterly solidarity to take leave of the others. They had reached the car, just a block down Magazine Street from Tyler's and around the corner on Valmont, when a young black man rose from a crouch, showed them a revolver, and demanded their purses and jewelry. They had readily given up their purses and were unfastening jewelry when the man bolted, apparently unnerved by passersby.

At the sight of Kyles on the TV news, Courrege had contacted her friends and then the police. Handler, an internist at Ochsner, a big private hospital, had joined Courrege at the home of Brown, an administrator at a dermatology clinic. As Detective John Dillman had done in developing witnesses to the Schwegmann's murder, police officers Steven Gordon and William Murray arrayed a photo lineup that included a mug shot of Kyles. All three women had homed in on him, but with varying degrees of certainty. Brown had no doubt he was the one; Courrege said the perpetrator had haunted her nightmares for fifteen or twenty nights but still declared her identification tentative. Handler demurred altogether, saying her memory of an encounter so fleeting and so long ago was not clear enough to be reliable.

It didn't make for a bulletproof case, but Strider and Williams could see no reason not to add three counts of armed robbery to the murders—first one, then two, then just one again—they already had laid on Kyles. It would prove an unexpectedly useful contribution to the rap sheet, both immediately and for the long term. The immediate use of the indictment for armed robbery was this: with a trial date for the Dye murder just weeks away, Regan could no longer fake the jaunty self-confidence that had seen him through the early hours of his attempt to mount a competent defense against capital charges. And so, before formally seeking a continuance from the judge, he had sounded out Cliff Strider. Would the prosecution be willing to delay? Strider was unsympathetic. Connick's number one man had made a high-profile career decision in thrusting himself into the case, and he wasn't about to let up for a minute, let alone weeks or months.

Of course, Regan was free to try his luck with Judge Waldron—continuances were pretty freely granted in death penalty cases—but Strider had a parting shot: if it came to delaying the murder trial, the state would proceed directly to try Kyles for the armed robberies. Did the defense really want to have three armed robberies on Kyles's heretofore clean record? Regan knew that he did not. Previous offenses would be inadmissible as evidence against Kyles while jurors tried to assess his guilt or innocence of Mrs. Dye's murder, but should he be convicted of it, come the trial's sentencing phase, one of his strongest bids to avoid the chair would be the lack of serious priors. And so on November 26, 1984, a Monday, Judge Dennis Waldron gaveled to order the first trial of Curtis Kyles for the murder of Delores Dye.

Lela would long recall the sense of dread she brought to the proceedings and the way that mood, perhaps the proceedings themselves, were mocked by the young children—Judge Waldron's children, she was told—scampering around the bench. "It was like, we just don't care about this man. He's nobody. He's a criminal sitting up here." That was Lela's reading of the statement implicit in making day care an adjunct to a murder trial.

Strider and Williams knew their stuff, and the trial seemed to go well for them. Witness followed witness, attesting that the man subsequently identified as Curtis Kyles had been seen at the wheel of the murdered woman's car—or, in fact, minutes earlier, pressing a gun to her head and firing once. Detective followed detective. Ballistics linked the weapon found in Kyles's home and the bullet found in Mrs. Dye's brain. Her personal effects turned up in his garbage. His fingerprint was on a Schwegmann's sales slip found in her car. Robert Dye, days away from a fortieth wedding anniversary he would now mark as a widower, was called to the stand to testify that the cans of cat and dog food present in such abundance in Kyles's kitchen—and without much evidence of a cat or a dog in the household—were the very brands and flavors that his late wife habitually bought.

And yet, less than thirty-six hours after opening arguments, a gasp coursed through the room as Judge Waldron declared a mistrial. The jury had found itself hopelessly deadlocked. A balance of seven to five in favor of acquittal had eroded to two holdouts against conviction, but two were all it took. The physical evidence—the gun behind the stove, the cat and dog food, things that police and prosecutors insisted were persuasive—had been largely dismissed, jurors said. "Even people who voted guilty thought the gun was irrelevant," a juror told reporters after the trial. "That very easily could have been wiped clean and dropped behind the stove." And the picture of Beanie Wallace that was circulated among jurors convinced some of them that the eyewitnesses could have confused him with Kyles. Strider and Williams announced that they would retry Kyles within a week, maybe two. As Lowell Dye muttered his disgust and stalked out of the courthouse with his father to phone Robert junior in Florida, Lela rushed up to Martin Regan to share a sense of relief bordering on joy. The attorney dampened her spirit. Jurors had not seen fit to convict her brother, but neither had they been able to acquit him.

It was easy to feel Cliff Strider's pain. With a black defendant and blacks on the jury, mistrials were always a possibility. But something had gone wrong. And if Strider couldn't claim a scalp in an open-and-shut case like Kyles's, he was going to look like an ass—the big shot chief of trials, Harry Connick's first assistant, shouldering aside Jim Williams, depriving him of a turn as lead prosecutor to make sure the job was done right. And then blowing it. The problem, Strider seemed to sense, was the snitch.

Sometimes it seemed like stool pigeons were more trouble than they were worth. Scumbags, all of them. Sometimes it seemed like the slack cops cut them just to keep their informants singing was worse than the crimes they helped solve. In so many ways the defense's theory was absurd: that an imbecile and a doper like Wallace could kill a woman and then, like a maestro, coolly orchestrate an elaborate frame-up that sucked in half the homicide division. Strider hadn't even interviewed Beanie before the first trial. That's what God made cops for. That was their world. But now they were all in this together: the cops and the prosecutors and the scumbags on the street. There was no way around it. Strider was going to have to rethink the case, bring Wallace in, get to know him a little bit, and plug whatever holes had caused the jury's faith in the state's case to leak out all over the courtroom floor. Judging from comments pulled from jurors after they deadlocked, the biggest hole was Beanie himself, his absence from the witness list. He was all over the case, both sides of it. The police had relied on him as an informant; without Beanie they might never have got to Kyles. And if he was central to the state's case, he was the defense theory in its entirety, yet no one had called him to the stand.

Strider knew one thing for sure. He would not be the one to call Beanie as a witness, no matter how much jurors were troubled by the void in the state's presentation. There were too many flies on him. And Regan, he knew, was praying for the chance to cross-examine the informant. Well, to hell with that. If Regan wanted a crack at Beanie, he'd just have to call him as a hostile witness for the defense. That's certainly what Strider would have done in his shoes, but for some reason Regan was holding back. The reason, as Regan would honorably reveal during the appellate phase of the case, was rooted in ignorance of the law. He was unaware that he had the right to call Beanie as a hostile witness. Regan wanted nothing more than to undermine Beanie's credibility, to catch him in some of the inconsistencies in the story he had told the police. But if Beanie was called by the defense, that would mean Regan was impeaching his own witness, something he didn't think the rules of evidence allowed him to do. Indeed, they did not—unless, that is, the court accepted Wallace as a hostile witness, a ruling that would free Regan to interrogate him more aggressively. Finally Strider and Williams had come up with a clever plan, a way to put flesh and bone to the name Beanie Wallace during the second trial without opening him up to cross-examination. The gimmick would be to parade Beanie in front of each eyewitness, make him stand beside Kyles right there in the courtroom, and invite the witnesses to say again which one they had seen at the wheel of the car. Of course they would stick with Kyles. They had already sworn he was the killer. They were invested in his guilt. But for the new batch of jurors, seeing the two men standing side by side would seem subliminally as though the identifications were being made for the first time and before their very eyes.

There was of course another possible outcome of ordering Kyles to do his little *dos-à-dos* with Wallace: the chance that Kyles would lose control of himself altogether and lash out physically at the man who had betrayed him. Like a cornerman coaching a prizefighter to pull his punches in a rigged fight, Regan would whisper beseechingly to Kyles before signaling, near the very end of the second trial, that it was time to stand and follow the prosecutor's instructions. "Don't become the animal they want to think you are, Curtis. Stay cool, man. Stay calm." It wasn't easy. Kyles would remember tensing his body rigidly against the temptation to turn on Wallace and bloody him right there in front of the judge and jurors, damn the consequences. The moment passed. A new eyewitness was brought to the witness-box, and once again Kyles was ordered to stand.

Was Beanie taunting him silently? Laughing at him under his breath? Goading him to do just what Regan had warned against? Without even looking at Wallace, Kyles measured the space between them like a sensor on a perimeter fence. But the claymore never exploded.

Just to be on the safe side, Strider decided to take out an insurance policy on his new strategy. Bringing Beanie into court may have eliminated any lingering suspicions that he, and not Kyles, was the black man driving Mrs. Dye's car out of the parking lot, but the parking lot wasn't the only place where people claimed to have seen him at the wheel of a red Ford LTD. There were Kyles's buddies to deal with. All four of them had been a problem on the stand, but in particular the two who put Beanie in a red car the very night of the murder. According to the narrative Beanie fed to the detectives, that would have been a day before he ever laid eyes on the LTD.

Kevin Black had been the first of them to testify, a clean-cut twenty-one-year-old with no record and a job as a security officer out at the airport. Thursday was his day off, and true to habit, he was watching his wife's favorite soap opera with her when Beanie pulled in behind the four-story apartment building where they lived on France Road. Beanie honked and yelled up, and Black came out on the landing long enough to get a look at the car Beanie was trying to unload. No thanks, man. No dinero. On cross-examination, Black would be unable to remember the name of the soap opera his wife always watched—one was like another, after all—but he knew what time it came on, so he was able to state with some certainty that Beanie's visit was between 3:15 and 3:30 that Thursday afternoon, less than an hour after a killing less than a mile away.

About three hours later, Beanie turned up in a red car on North Rocheblave, some ten or twelve blocks from Desire Street, at the home of Ronald Gorman. Gorman's bona fides were not in perfect order. He had been busted for marijuana and was once booked with armed robbery, he told the court, a charge that was lowered to purse snatching. This time the discussion got as far as price; Beanie was asking $200 for the car. Gorman said no thanks.

The next day at around eight in the evening, according to Donald Ray Powell, the third of Kyles's buddies to testify, Beanie came by his place, just down Desire Street from where Pinkey and Curtis lived. Under Regan's guidance, Powell made a clean breast of his priors so as not to give prosecutors the pleasure of ambushing him with them on cross-examination. Powell had done time for burglary and then a little more time for escape. But that was a while back. He'd been steadily employed at a soda-bottling plant for the past three years, which is maybe why the price of the red car had risen overnight. Beanie was asking $300, Powell testified. But he overestimated his market. Powell had just made a child-support payment and was feeling a little pinched. He told Beanie he didn't have the money to be thinking about buying a car, even at a bargain-basement price like that.

Johnny Burnes, the last of the foursome, testified to two encounters with Beanie, both on the Friday night following the murder. First he had seen Beanie on foot—no red car in sight—as Beanie approached the house on North Dorgenois Street that was home to the Burnes family and, off and on for several years, to Beanie himself. A little later he saw him in among the junked cars that had accumulated along one of the spurs of railroad track that were part of the nearby Illinois Central switching yard. While they chatted, Johnny watched Beanie take the license plate off one of the abandoned—probably stolen—cars and substitute it for the plate on the red Ford.

If the prosecution's case was going to hold water in the second trial, Kyles's buddies had to be exposed as liars, lowlifes. Black was the biggest problem, for being the cleanest. The others were rough customers and looked it. Black didn't even have a record. He was almost like a cop himself—at least that's how jurors probably saw him—with his airport security job.

As irksome to prosecutors as their testimony in the first trial was the confident manner of its delivery, a matter of tone and body language. Strider and Williams decided to do something about it. Just prior to their scheduled testimony at the second trial, Strider asked for a bench conference with Regan and the judge. Kyles's witnesses needed to be advised of their rights, he said. They needed to know that what they said on the stand could cue the district attorney's office to charge them as accessories to a crime they seemed to know so much about—be it car theft or the murder itself. Regan, predictably, was outraged. The prosecution had no more intention of charging these men than he did. This was intimidation, pure and simple. The witnesses were merely going to repeat testimony from the first trial. Why hadn't they been warned then? Because the state had no intention of prosecuting them, that's why, Regan said, answering his own question. But Judge Waldron, a former prosecutor himself, saw no choice but to yield to Strider. The state was saying there was a chance these men could be prosecuted as accessories. Well, of course there was. A chance, but a slim one. Waldron would be remiss in not informing them of their peril, however remote. He would read them their Miranda rights as if they were criminals who had just been picked up in a raid. There was no other way to handle it.

And so, one by one, the four of them—Johnny Burnes, Don Powell, Kevin Black, and Ron Gorman—were called into Waldron's chambers and, in the presence of counsel hastily assigned from the ranks of the underemployed attorneys who haunted the courthouse, were advised of their jeopardy and informed of their options. They could testify or they could refuse to testify on grounds of self-incrimination. As an enticement to the latter option, Waldron explained that such a refusal would simply remove their names from the case; jurors would be told nothing about them or of what they had said from the stand in the first trial.

In turn, the men pondered their options and each other, wondering who might cave, who would hang tough. It wasn't the first time an intimidation tactic had been tried on them. On the very morning of his testimony in the first trial, Gorman had gotten a wake-up call from Beanie—Joe Wallace, as he referred to him. Beanie came right to the point. If anyone was getting any ideas about trying to lay the Dye murder on him, he wanted it known that vengeance would be swift and not necessarily limited to those, like Gorman and Johnny Burnes, who were taking the stand for Kyles. Wallace, it seemed, had been involved romantically with one of Ron Gorman's cousins, Valerie Brown, a young woman they all knew as Noonie. If he got sent upriver, he "was gone take her up with him," Gorman was warned, to a place where "she wasn't gonna get no dick and he wasn't gonna get no pussy." Gorman called the police to report the threat, and he told Regan about it, but the attorney, although tantalized by what it said about Beanie Wallace, had not encouraged Kyles to think there was much they could do with this latest development. Beanie could be guilty of countless crimes, he pointed out, but they might not be admissible even if he were to testify—which didn't look likely to happen. The crime that mattered was the murder Kyles was accused of.

In the end, Gorman, Powell, Burnes, and Black stood up to the prosecutors and agreed to testify again for Kyles. But the state's ploy had worked like a charm. Their stories, told a second time from the stand, were unchanged, but the self-possession that had heightened their credibility in the first trial was shot, just as Strider had calculated it would be. To Regan, his once strong witnesses looked visibly shaken—"scared to death." In his closing argument, Jim Williams would exult in the tactical success. He reminded jurors how "strange" Kevin Black's demeanor had been on the stand: "I couldn't get him to look at me." Burnes's experience on the stand was further undermined by frustration. He was certain he held the key to Kyles's cell. In his sly and insinuating way, Beanie had all but boasted about killing Mrs. Dye and laying it off on Curtis—at least that's what Burnes was prepared to say. But every time he started down that path, the prosecutors would cite the rules against hearsay and cut him off. If the court was going to hear anything from Mr. Wallace, they would hear it from Mr. Wallace himself, the witness they declined to call. In place of the declaration he wanted to make, Burnes was confined to muttering yes or no answers to narrowly tailored questions.

Kyles didn't have to testify at all, of course. No defendant is required to, and indeed Regan had kept him off the stand during the first trial. But well into the second day of the second trial, Kyles had risen from the defense table and walked the few yards to the stand, a hundred sets of eyes drilling into his back, twelve more pinioning him from the jury box. The challenge was to keep his legs moving, to move his legs smoothly enough to conceal his nervous excruciation.

After asking Kyles his name and confirming that he was, indeed, the defendant in the case, Regan got right to the point. "May I ask you, did you in fact kill Mrs. Dye?"

To which Kyles had replied, "No, sir. I didn't."

The "sir" was important. Regan had told him that. And then Kyles remembered to look openly at the jury as he answered the question. It was easier than looking into the gallery, at Lela and Brenda. Pinkey was there somewhere, Kyles supposed, though he couldn't spot her, and of course the Dyes, both of them, the old man and the son. He was just as glad the other son lived out of state and had chosen to spare himself the agony of the trials. Kyles could feel the hatred, but when he thought about it, he could also feel their pain.

Putting Kyles on the stand was a risky call. In the first trial, it had seemed like a risk not worth taking. Who knew how a man like Kyles would handle himself once the prosecutors started poking at his sore spots on cross, goading and taunting him. The man had no record to speak of, but clearly he was from the criminal class. The prosecution would do whatever it could to get at that. But Regan sensed he had to play every card in his hand. After all, Kyles's familiarity with the underworld had already slipped out. That was the downside of witnesses like Gorman and Powell—men with records who frequented the defendant's home—however helpful their testimony about seeing Beanie in the red car might have been. And Kyles had some explaining of his own to do. Maybe the rifle was for hunting, but what about the boxes of .32-caliber bullets, bullets that did not fit the rifle or Kyles's legally registered .25-caliber pistol.

That had been Regan's point of departure once he got Kyles on the stand. The bullets, Kyles explained, were collateral that Beanie had provided against a sum of money Kyles had loaned him—so was the rifle police pulled out from under his mattress. Regan did not quiz Kyles at great length. It was more a matter of showing that he had nothing to hide. Because in the end it was his word against the informant's. And in order to seem honest, Kyles had been brutally honest, going so far as to reveal from the stand something many in his family had never known: that simultaneously with raising a large family with Pinkey, he had maintained a relationship, a childless one, with another woman who kept him away from the Desire Street place as many as three, even four nights a week. Jim Williams had pried it out of him during his cross-examination, but it was a tactically shrewd confession. To the defense's contention that Beanie was mad for Kyles's wife had been added the running room Beanie might have needed to pursue his infatuation—and, for the jilted Pinkey, a motive to show him a little encouragement.

———

Every other issue of the case having been exhausted on cross-examination—the gun; the garbage; who wore his hair in a curl, who in a bush; who had picked up whom to drive to Schwegmann's for transmission fluid and cigarettes, and when—it came down to pet food. Having first established that Kyles and Pinkey had about $250 a month to spend on groceries and had shopped on the day of the murder, Williams continued with his cross. In Kyles's answers it was possible to hear jauntiness give way to irritation and then flag in the face of a gathering doom.

WILLIAMS: You testified that you went to the Schwegmann's store and bought some food?

KYLES: Yes, sir.

WILLIAMS: You bought some cat food and some dog food?

KYLES: Yes, sir. I bought it.

WILLIAMS: Why did you go buy all that cat and dog food?

KYLES: Because I have a cat. I have a bunch of cats running round there.

WILLIAMS: There's a special reason why you bought so much cat and dog food on that Thursday?

KYLES: Yes, sir, because it was on sale.

WILLIAMS: It was on sale. How do you know it was on sale?

KYLES: Because I was looking at it.

WILLIAMS: You were looking at it?

KYLES: Yes. I saw it.

WILLIAMS: Okay. So you're saying that Nine Lives cat food was on sale?

KYLES: Yes, sir.

WILLIAMS: Kozy Kitten cat food was on sale?

KYLES: Yes, sir.

WILLIAMS: How do you know it was on sale?

KYLES: Because they had a little sign there that said three for such and such, two for such and such at a cheaper price. It wasn't even a dollar.

WILLIAMS: There was a sign where?

KYLES: In the Schwegmann's Supermarket.
WILLIAMS: You're sure about that?
KYLES: I'm positive . . . It wasn't big. It was a little slip. It was a
            little bitty piece of a slip like this that they had on the
            shelf . . .

The trap was sprung. It remained only to call one Edwin L. Arce-neaux, Schwegmann's advertising manager, and establish that on September 20, 1984, Nine Lives cat food had not been on sale, nor Kozy Kitten, nor Kalkan dog food. Indeed, none of the brands that Mrs. Dye habitually bought—and, at least on the day of her death, that Kyles had decided his pets might like too.

All told, the second trial, like the first, lasted barely two days, a snap of the fingers. On December 7, late enough that Friday night to have missed the early runs of the papers that would hit the streets the next morning, Kyles's peers filed back into the courtroom and announced that they had been able to reach a verdict. Curtis Kyles had killed Delores Dye, a crime of murder elevated to the first degree by its commission in the course of another crime, armed robbery. Judge Waldron listened impassively as the foreman read the verdict and then polled each juror in turn to be certain that the consensus was unanimous. That nicety attended to, he scheduled for the following morning the testimony that would precede a decision on Kyles's proper punishment—life behind bars or death at the hands of the state executioner. With that, he sent the jurors back to their hotel rooms.

The morning dawned with a bright, if chilly clarity that mocked the somberness of the proceedings. So did Kyles's wardrobe. "They had him all prepped up in his little white shirt and yellow sweater and khaki pants," Lowell Dye would recall. But it was not enough to offset what Dye took to be Kyles's deepening sense of despair. "During the guilt phase, Regan had him trained: 'When I ask you questions, you look right at the jury,'" Dye concluded. But now, with his life in their hands, Kyles, like Kevin Black before him, could not meet the jurors' eyes. It made him seem skittish, evasive, as though the façade of quiet confidence that had seen him through two murder trials had disintegrated under the weight of the verdict. "And that hurt him big-time," Dye was not sorry to note.

In a defense favored with deeper pockets, psychologists and criminologists would routinely have taken the stand to argue that Kyles deserved pity as a victim of the poverty and violence in which he had been reared. Instead, Martin Regan tapped family—in particular the patriarchal oldest brother, Roosevelt Kyles—to make the same points. Earnestness would have to substitute for expertise. Kyles, his family stressed, had been beaten repeatedly by the aunt who took him in and reared him; and he had suffered the trauma of losing his father. (It seemed best not to mention the less than ennobling circumstances of that death.) His record heretofore had been clean. He deserved to live, even if the rest of his days were to be spent in prison.

For their parting shot, the rhetoric of the prosecutors carried them well beyond the case at hand. Kyles must die, Jim Williams shouted, not just in penitence for the murder of Delores Dye but for the broad social pathology that he seemed to embody. "Let's strike this man out; let's start this community back," he implored the jurors. "What I'm asking you to do is to return a capital verdict against this man and let that be a message . . ."

Regan by now was on his feet, objecting to the flagrantly improper politicization of the case and demanding a mistrial. Waldron sustained the objection, but the move for a mistrial was denied.

Jury deliberations had lasted three hours and then four, when they foundered on a question of law: If Kyles were sentenced to life in prison, what chance was there of parole or any other abbreviation of his time behind bars? It did not take an expert to see that this was a jury mustering its nerve for the final assault on the second thoughts and moral inhibitions that can make ordinary men and women reluctant to impose the death penalty. In Louisiana, for all practical purposes, the answer to their question was that a life sentence was accurately self-describing. It would carry no possibility of parole. But Judge Waldron—whether out of scrupulousness or, as the defense would contend, improper support of the prosecution's agenda—saw fit to offer a more ambiguous reply. The jurors filed downstairs and reassembled themselves in the jury box to hear his opinion. In essence, Waldron told them, it was not a question he could answer; it was beyond a judge's ken to anticipate what the future might hold. The implication, some jurors concluded, was that the only sure way to punish Kyles for life was to end that life here and now. Thrown back on their own intuitions in this matter, the jurors returned to their deliberations only to lodge another request minutes later. They wanted to review the crime-scene pictures, the collection of photographs that graphically documented the physical manifestations—the livid eyelids, the bloodied skull—of death by a bullet to the brain.

It was enough. Within an hour, word coursed through the courtroom and out into the hallways and down to the TV trucks at curbside that a decision had been reached. And in short order, as the jurors filed through a smaller door adjacent to their courtroom seats, another, larger stream of humanity flowed through the courtroom's main entrance: anxious attorneys, curious bystanders, Robert and Lowell Dye, the benumbed members of Kyles's family, print and television reporters, and sundry bailiffs, sheriff's deputies, and courthouse hangers-on. The massive wooden doors swung shut, sealing the courtroom from the last vestiges of the sunset streaming through the corridor's smoke-stained windows, and at Judge Waldron's behest, the foreman announced the jury's recommendation: death by electrocution.

There was a hiatus of perhaps two seconds' duration—a moment in which time froze and with it Kyles's pulse. Then the blood geysered back up into his brain to crest against the bony arc of his skull, and the room exploded in pandemonium, a tumult of shrieks and wailing and curses punctuated by the impotent thunder of Waldron's gavel. Roosevelt had coped with his grief by transmuting it to rage and thoughts of vengeance against Beanie. Pinkey fell into a numb silence, frozen in every part of her body except her tear ducts. Lela would remember simply dropping her head in despair as the foreman announced the penalty. It was the judge's droning elaboration of the sentence—that under the laws of the state of Louisiana, the people had opted to strap Curtis Kyles into the electric chair at the penitentiary at Angola and cause electrical current of fifty thousand volts to pass through his body until his heart ceased to beat—that defeated her utterly. She would remember stifling her sobs, the tears leaking soundlessly down her face, and two women, adjacent to her in the visitors gallery, turning to each other and whispering, "That must be his mama, right there." In fact, Gracie Walker had stayed home, too trou-bled by what was happening to a beloved son to be able to endure his trial. When Lela summoned the courage to look at Curtis, it was to see a little smile on his face—Kyles's way, jaunty in the face of sheer terror and the hubbub around him, of staying strong for his family, she decided.

The media bolted from the room to report the outcome. Now Lowell Dye and his father found themselves, by their own account, two of perhaps a half dozen whites in a crowd of what seemed like a hundred het-up blacks. It did not soothe the junior Dye to remember taunting remarks that he insisted had followed him around the courthouse during the trials: "Oh, poor little Lowell, lost his mama." Things like that. Or the time—he swears it—that he was followed into the men's room in an act of in-timidation.

"Sit right here. Don't move," Lowell ordered his father. And with that, he edged toward the aisle in search of someone in uniform to provide father and son with an escort to their car. To his relief, a white deputy had sized up the situation almost immediately and was moving toward them. As they were led out of the courtroom toward the broad flight of stairs that would take them to street level, Lowell Dye's lasting impression was of Kyles's brother—the one who had been sworn in as Roosevelt Kyles—standing in the middle of the corridor screaming and sobbing, sobbing and screaming some more: "You're dead meat, Beanie. You're a dead man." Or words to that effect. "I mean screaming it, just screaming," Dye recalls, still awed years later by the black man's volcanic rage. "And I went, 'Ah, Dad, let's get out of here.'"

SEVEN

Delores Dye's undoing was the 150th murder that year in New Orleans, a neat round number attached to a very random crime. Nine months earlier, one of the new year's first murders had been of another sixty-year-old woman. And she too had been dispatched on a Thursday by a single bullet to the brain, one that entered through the eye socket rather than the temple, a difference of inches.

In other respects the death of Patricia Leidenheimer differed from that of Delores Dye. For one thing, Leidenheimer had been murdered in the middle of the night in her home at 414 Thirty-eighth Street, a proper two-story structure of brick and shingling in a proper middle-class neighborhood out near Lake Pontchartrain, the city's northern shore. And the bullet had been .25 caliber, not .32. Both pellets would be retrieved from within the brainpans of the women they killed, having lodged in mid-trajectory without exiting the skull.

Mrs. Leidenheimer, a divorcée, had been sleeping on the living-room couch, as was her custom. Her thirty-three-year-old daughter, Cathy, was in a ground-floor bedroom to the rear. Cathy woke up around three a.m. that January 26, to the heavy tread of men in the house, upstairs and down. To her horror, she then heard the sound of a gunshot and a body slumping to the front-hall floor. She did not need to tell herself to lie still in the hope that the intruders would remain unaware of her existence. A diving accident some years earlier had left her paralyzed from the neck down, barely able—once silence settled again over the house, telling her the men had gone—to work her special phone and call for help.

Police arrived to find the front door ajar and Mrs. Leidenheimer prostrate on the floor, inanimate except for a gurgling sound as she tried to breathe. The initial assumption was that she had slipped and cracked her skull lethally on the doorstop, an antique clothes iron that now propped up her head. Only after she was rushed by ambulance to Charity Hospital and x-rayed did doctors find the copper-jacketed pellet in her brain. At 6:30 a.m. they gave up on emergency measures and pronounced her dead.

Mrs. Leidenheimer was, somewhat halfheartedly it seemed, the proprietor of a French Quarter antiques shop. Her colleagues and competitors along Chartres Street thought of her as a lovely soul, if not much of a businesswoman. Her son, Carey, recently had heard her say she was ready to dump the store and retire, if only she could get back the $10,000 in improvements and fixtures she had just put into the leased premises. She kept almost no records of her stock-in-trade, jewelry and old silver services for the most part, which she sometimes brought home to polish. That made it impossible for police to get far on their first hunch, which was that some of her wares might have been the object of a burglary turned murder and might now be circulating among the city's pawnbrokers.

There was every reason for Mrs. Leidenheimer's survivors to suppose that the police would be strongly motivated to solve this case and see the killer brought to justice. A friend of Mrs. Leidenheimer's, her neighbor just three doors down the street, was none other than Henry Morris, the police chief—a lame-duck police chief, destined to leave office at the end of the year, but a force surely to be reckoned with. Homicide assigned the case to a detective named Ray Miller, and he worked it doggedly, at first to little avail. The few leads he got went nowhere. One of them, conveyed in the intimate tone in which middle-class whites discussed their exasperation with the servant class, was from a Leidenheimer neighbor who, as the mother of a former city prosecutor, assumed she could count on an abundance of fellow feeling from the detective she buttonholed. She wanted Miller to know about a housekeeper who had been passed on to her after working for Mrs. Leidenheimer—a disaster. No sooner had she hired her than the household account went all kerflooey. When confronted with her employer's concerns, the housekeeper got sullen and, some months later, up and quit. Another, better-focused tip was from the dead woman's estranged husband, George Leidenheimer. He wondered if the killer might not be a white boy who he believed was responsible for neighborhood pilferage. Someone mentioned an elderly black who had been Mrs. Leidenheimer's yardman for a while—but he turned out to have died. Detective Miller pursued these tips as far as they took him, but it wasn't very far at all.

On February 7, thirteen days after the murder, the police fielded a call from a woman named Valerie Brown. Only later would they come to know her as Noonie, Beanie Wallace's sometime girlfriend. She identified herself as a former housekeeper for Mrs. Leidenheimer. No, she knew nothing about the murder, she said, but she wanted police to know about a threatening phone call she had just received. The caller had been a Negro, as she put it, Ms. Brown being black herself. "I know where you work," the man had said, "and I'm gonna rape you and kill you and Cathy Leidenheimer too." Then he hung up. Police promptly put a tracer on Brown's line, only to discover that the same day it kicked in, the phone company had cut off her service for nonpayment.

For Detective Ray Miller, the Leidenheimer case had meant a continuing series of bum tips and dead ends as winter gave way to the glory of springtime in New Orleans and then the city's summertime swelter. Miller's inability to announce a break in his probe had not expelled murder from the minds of New Orleanians, however. In July and August the city treated itself—as well as tabloids and wire services—to the spectacle of the Mintz murder trial, in which the adulterous scion of a prominent furniture-store magnate somehow managed to sow reasonable doubt in the minds of jurors as to whether he had murdered his wife in order to replace her with a comely mistress. The defense insisted it was suicide. Mrs. Mintz had shot herself through a pillow as she lay in bed with her husband, they contended. Why a suicide victim would be concerned to muffle the shot with a pillow and how that pillow managed to walk into an adjacent room and conceal itself among sofa upholstery was left to the jury's imagination, which evidently was vivid. Aaron Mintz walked.

But on September 11, with the less-glamorous Leidenheimer case out of the headlines, Detective Miller caught a break. An informant—identified on police records only as "an unidentified negro male"—called the homicide division and started talking. Detective Louis Berard was on the desk. What did the caller know? "Fuck, man. I'm telling you who did it." The caller went on to describe a young man about twenty-one years old, maybe twenty-four at the outside. He cut grass and pruned for Mrs. Leidenheimer. Another yardman tip? Berard knew better than to signal his disappointment. Keep the snitch talking. That was rule number one. Don't question what he's saying. Ask him how he knows what he's saying.

The caller's information was, by his own admission, secondhand. In the wee small hours of January 26, the yardman had shown up at a joint called the Famous, a hot black disco in a polyglot stretch of commercial establishments—an auto parts store, a Chinese take-out window, a failed movie theater—on one of the arteries that rushed one-way traffic from the suburbs safely past the Ninth Ward's rougher purlieus and on downtown. And before the yardman made his rounds—high-fiving his buddies at the bar, calling for a drink—somebody had seen him slip into the men's room and scrub what had to be blood off his hands. Next he was overheard trying to sell pieces of silver. What kind of things? Berard wanted to know. A chain, brooches, and the like—things that Berard knew to be among items stolen from the Leidenheimer house. Got a name for us?

Sure, mister: Joseph Wallace.

Ray Miller came on duty to find a memo from Detective Berard rehashing the call, and he routinely fed the name, Joseph Wallace, into the police computer, a primitive animal by the standards of the emerging info-tech revolution, but a generally reliable way to keep track of aliases, addresses, and the disposition of prior offenses. Sure enough, Miller got a hit: "Joseph Wallace, n/m [negro male], b: 3/2/62. aka: BEENIE [*sic*]; res: 620 N. Robertson." The record showed an extensive rap sheet, including a guilty plea to manslaughter four years earlier for which Wallace had served a notably gentle sentence: less than two years at Angola. As of the previous June, he was a tractor driver mowing fairways at the New Orleans Country Club, his last known place of employment.

Miller picked up the phone and called Carey Leidenheimer. Leidenheimer didn't remember his mother ever mentioning a yardman named

Joseph Wallace, but he said he would ask around and get back to the detective. Miller then took a ride over to 620 North Robertson, only to discover that there was no 620 on North Robertson Street. It was a fake address. Three days later Carey Leidenheimer called back to say that he had been unable to get a bead on anyone named Joseph Wallace in connection with his mother's management of the Thirty-eighth Street household. There were canceled checks made out to a Joseph Brown, but nothing that bore the name Joseph Wallace. That same morning—the Friday before Mrs. Dye would be murdered—Miller swung out to the New Orleans Country Club, one of the last redoubts of the old racial order in a city giving ground to integration. Joe Wallace? Beanie? Someone on the grounds crew remembered him, but too dimly to know where he might be found. He hadn't lasted long on the country club pad: a few days, and then he had been fired.

Stymied once again, Ron Miller didn't get around to writing up the latest installment in his continuing investigation of the Leidenheimer case until the following Thursday, September 20. And so, even as he hammered out the two-page update of his efforts over the previous nine days, other detectives were rushing down Old Gentilly Road to the Schwegmann's parking lot, where another sixty-year-old woman had been gunned down in broad daylight. Miller's report was officially directed to the attention of Sergeant James Eaton, the chief of the homicide division. But like every update of an ongoing murder probe, it was posted on a clipboard for review by other officers as they came on duty and brought themselves up to speed on developments that might be pertinent to their cases. It is possible to conclude from their later trial testimony that neither Eaton nor the homicide division's other Detective Miller—Johnny Miller, Beanie Wallace's handler—bothered to read Ray Miller's posted report. If they did, they would have realized that the informant about to be so useful to them in the Dye murder was wanted in the Leidenheimer murder—was indeed the prime suspect. Keeping up with "dailies" filed by brother detectives was a job requirement sometimes observed in the breach. But Kyles's lawyer at a later trial would cross-examine Johnny Miller with a different possibility in mind: that Johnny Miller read Ray Miller's suspicions about Beanie Wallace, either as they were posted or soon after, and decided to keep his mouth shut. After all, Beanie was Johnny Miller's man on the street, his eyes and ears, however dirty his hands. You worked a long time to develop that kind of relationship, and you did not lightly toss a snitch aside. If another detective could put Beanie away for the Leidenheimer murder, so be it. But until then, Johnny Miller would not want to give up a good thing. Moreover, confidential informants were promised confidentiality. Police ethics cut both ways. And so it transpired, some forty-eight hours after Detective Ray Miller posted his report on the Leidenheimer case, that his chief suspect, Beanie Wallace, was cozying up to Detective Johnny Miller, having arranged a midnight rendezvous on a Ninth Ward street corner that initiated a mutual effort to put Curtis Kyles away forever.

Contacting Johnny Miller was not the last time Beanie Wallace had picked up a phone and sought to influence the outcome of the Dye case. There was the threatening phone call to Kyles's witness Ronald Gorman on the morning Gorman took the stand in the first trial to say that he had seen Wallace sporting about after the murder in a red car believed to be Mrs. Dye's.

Not seeing a way to put the information to much use in Kyles's defense, Martin Regan had routinely instructed Gorman to call the police and get the matter off his chest. Gorman was put through to Pascal Saladino, the detective who had snatched the garbage bags from in front of the Desire Street apartment the night before Curtis Kyles's arrest. But that was sheer coincidence, and anyway, Gorman hadn't called to talk about Kyles, at least not exclusively. Saladino, whose pipe and mustache reminded more than one local police reporter of Simenon's Inspector Maigret, settled down to listen. Along with reporting Wallace's threat, Gorman claimed to have information about a different murder, the Leidenheimer murder, though he didn't know the victim by name, only by her address. His cousin Valerie Brown—Noonie to her friends—had once worked there. The day after the murder and burglary at the house on Thirty-eighth Street, Gorman told the detective, he heard Beanie Wallace prattling on about it, indulging in the combination of bad nerves and boastfulness that his associates had come to expect from him in the aftermath of a crime caper.

Getting into the house, Wallace was pleased to say, had been a snap.

He simply swiped and copied Noonie's key, the one Mrs. Leidenheimer gave her housekeeper. The killing itself was preemptive, as Wallace explained it, a way of heading off the trouble that was sure to come when Mrs. Leidenheimer opened her next bank statement and found out that he had got hold of her checkbook some weeks earlier and forged several checks to Joseph Brown, one of his aliases. Gorman even knew where Beanie went to cash them: a convenience store on Franklin Avenue near Capdau Street. Its owner—Mr. Pete—knew Noonie well enough to honor her weekly paychecks, drawn, of course, on the same Leidenheimer account.

Pascal Saladino puffed on his pipe. The detective had been around the block enough times to know that if there was no honor among thieves, there was even less honor among police informants. Here was one rat ratting out another. For all Saladino knew, Gorman could have murdered Mrs. Leidenheimer himself. But Saladino also knew better than to assume that Gorman was making it all up. As the conversation proceeded, he had revealed details only the killer or killers could possibly know: that Mrs. Leidenheimer was shot in the face; that a television set was bustled into the front hall but then left there, as though the murderers changed their minds and thought better of making off with it—details so telling that Saladino signaled in his write-up of the interview with Gorman that he was leaving them out of his report to keep them fresh for future tests of witness credibility.

The information also was kept out of Martin Regan's hands, whether by design or a convenient failure of communication between law-enforcement officials and the defense. So what Regan knew, he knew from Gorman, a man he could not entirely trust. After the threat against him and his cousin, Noonie, Gorman was gunning for Beanie, trying to implicate him in the Dye murder. That tended to undermine Gorman's credibility with Regan, just as his criminal record tended to undermine his credibility with jurors. What Regan couldn't know, because prosecutors didn't tell him, was that in the eyes of the police, Gorman's credibility was very high—that indeed, he had provided all the evidence needed to convince them that Beanie Wallace, the linchpin in their case against Kyles, was the murderer of another sixty-year-old woman dispatched not many months earlier with a single bullet to the brain.

Gorman's chat with Saladino occurred on the very day that jurors in the first Kyles trial despaired of reaching a verdict and Judge Waldron declared a mistrial. Eleven days later, with Kyles now convicted and jurors a half hour into deliberations that would condemn him to death, Beanie Wallace was arrested on three counts of forgery for dipping into Mrs. Leidenheimer's exchequer. Three days later, in a taped interview with Detective Ray Miller, Wallace owned up to the Leidenheimer murder itself, deviating from the account relayed by Gorman only to insist that his accomplice had pulled the trigger. Wallace conceded that he had put a towel over Mrs. Leidenheimer's head and shoved her upstairs at gunpoint in a search for valuables. But when he got back downstairs, Wallace told the detective, it was the accomplice who argued for killing Mrs. Leidenheimer so she couldn't identify them.

"I tried to stop him," Wallace said, "but he took the gun from me and made me go out of the house. After I got outside, I heard one shot. He came out, and we left. He told me he had shot the lady in the face. It was my gun, but I didn't shoot the lady. He did."

The story rang hollow—a trapped killer's maneuver to lessen his legal liability. But it hardly mattered. Mrs. Leidenheimer's death was murder in the first degree, a murder committed in the course of another crime, in this case burglary. And when it came to such an act, Louisiana law drew no distinction between triggerman and sidekick. Wallace was no less vulnerable to the death penalty than if he had committed the murder all alone.

At one point, Ray Miller interrupted the narrative of events he had been drawing from Wallace and asked, "Why are you telling me this?"

Wallace's answer was childishly naïve. "Because I don't want to get the charge that I killed the lady."

But maybe Wallace knew something—or someone—that Detective Miller didn't. Because Harry Connick's prosecutors never would see fit to charge Wallace or anyone else with the murder of Patricia Leidenheimer, contending that a confession, in the absence of physical evidence, was not enough. And even after the checks made out to Joseph Brown turned up in the late Mrs. Leidenheimer's bank statement, and Pete Breaux, the convenience-store operator, confirmed cashing them for Noonie Brown's boyfriend, Wallace was simply released to the custody of his police department handler, Johnny Miller, and never even prosecuted for forgery.

Wallace had been useful to the police. Kyles, on the other hand, was available to take the rap for an embarrassing lapse in public safety. Besides, he had already been convicted. And just to make sure, he was about to be convicted again, this time for the armed robbery of the three women outside the Uptown jazz joint. It was an afterthought, to be sure, now that the death penalty had been secured against him, but not without its uses. For one thing, a conviction would clear the books of a festering unsolved crime. For another, you never knew when a few extra priors on Kyles's record might come in handy.

Before Connick's shop could proceed, in early January a Jefferson Parish courtroom was witness to a freelance effort to lengthen Kyles's record, if not his sentence. Kyles was red meat, and the flies had found him. To divert attention from her client, the defendant in a parking lot armed robbery out along a stretch of suburban strip malls and drive-through daiquiri shops, an attorney named Yvonne Hughes had encouraged the young man to contend that he merely waited in the car while an accomplice held a gun on two women cornered in a furniture store parking lot and relieved them of their purses. The gunman's name? Curtis Kyles.

And so it was that a month almost to the day after he was sentenced to death, Kyles was taken in shackles to Jefferson Parish and led into the courtroom of Judge Jacob Karno. Kyles and her client looked alike, Hughes argued—both in their twenties, both black—and with the Dye conviction already on the books, not to mention his indictment and pending prosecution for the armed robberies outside the Uptown jazz joint, Kyles had a demonstrable penchant for relieving women of their purses at gunpoint.

A man so thoroughly in the clutches of the law could be expected to defend himself halfheartedly, if he defended himself at all, but it would take more than the convenience of an available scapegoat for Hughes to make her case. Jurors didn't buy it. Hughes's client was sent upriver and Kyles back to Orleans Parish Prison.

By February, Cliff Strider was ready to try the Uptown armed robberies, or thought he was, but so was Regan, and this one he felt sure he would win. Very simply, it was impossible for Kyles to have committed the crime, physically impossible, he would argue. The reasons why would be contained in Kyles's medical records stemming from a comeuppance two years earlier that had damn near ended his life.

It was a Sunday night in November 1982—November 14, for the record. Pinkey was home with the kids on Desire Street, three underfoot, another on the way. Curtis was off in the night somewhere, there being in the human condition no guarantee that heartfelt devotion to the kids and even their mother will blinker a wandering eye.

From the stand during his trial for murder, Kyles had confessed to an infidelity with a woman named Pat. The truth was, he had something going on the side all through his years with Pinkey. No extra children, so far as he knew, but always another woman. Or two. Prosecutors would try to make something of this, brandish it as evidence of a moral turpitude that made murder simply the next stop on the streetcar line. The reality was that Kyles held steadfast to the arrangement he had struck with Pinkey, both financially and sexually. He was there for her, perhaps several nights a week, and he made no effort to rub her nose in his tomcatting when he wasn't. He was discreet. Of course, now and then she would find out anyway, catch a name, hear about Kyles's latest from one of her girlfriends. She knew how to run these bitches right out of his life, but there was always a next one, new or recycled. After Kyles came home late or not at all, Pinkey might mock him for the way he let women lead him around by the dick. Once, she had slapped him, and when he swatted her back, she had called the police. But as a general rule, when it came to Curtis's women, she knew better than to ask for details.

On the night of November 14, as Kyles would recall it, one of his boys had fixed him up with a lady friend in exchange for putting the evening on wheels. Kyles had the car, the buddy had the women, and the two couples had been making time at an apartment in the Desire project when Kyles was swept with a wave of what might be called—though perhaps not by Kyles—ennui. All of a sudden he just wanted out of there. To paper over any inconvenience caused by this lapse of gallantry, Kyles told his buddy he could keep the car for the evening, drop off the woman spurned, do the town with the other one. In fact, to avoid exposing Pinkey to one of those noisy homecomings—the sound of women's voices, a car door slamming as he clambered out onto the Desire Street curb—Kyles had them drop him off several blocks away, at a point where he could cut through the project on foot to get home.

"So I'm walking, and I had been drinking a couple of beers, so I just stopped on the side of a project building and went to pissing," Kyles remembered. It was a moment of sweet relief. He laced his fingers behind his neck and stared up at the starless sky as his bladder emptied. Maybe he had made a mistake letting go of a ready woman. Well, he could always get back to her. It was then that he noticed out of the corner of an eye that he was not alone with his idle thoughts, and that the barely visible figure he was not alone with had a gun in his hand.

Instinctively Kyles reached for his own revolver, and that's when it hit him: he had left the gun in the glove compartment of his car. The realization would gall Kyles as often as he thought back on this moment, which would be for the rest of his life. "That was the first thing that burst into my mind: Boy, why did you leave that gun?" The second thing that occurred to him was that he knew the man standing there in the shadows, knew him for a friend of Jackie's, one of the finer women Kyles saw from time to time, knew him for a junkie, Jackie's junkie friend. Junkies were the walking dead. Kyles knew that. But there was always a chance the junkie would recognize him too, break into a big smile, lower the gun: "Sorry, man, I didn't realize it was you." But that's not what happened. That's not what Kyles heard. "Nigger, don't move. Give it up." That's what Kyles heard, and he knew the junkie was talking about the gold around Kyles's neck and wrists. "I said, 'Man, you can have all this shit, you dig?'" And with that, Kyles held out his arms, made a show of stripping off his wristwatch and thrusting it toward his assailant.

Kyles was, to say the least, vulnerable: unarmed, unzipped. But he was also making rapid calculations. "Being raised in the street, you know one thing: if you can get close enough to him, you can challenge him. That's the stupid mentality you was brought up with, but that's what kicks in at a time like that: never let nobody take nothing from you." And so, as Kyles pretended to pull off his jewelry and thrust it toward his assailant, he inched closer to the man, hoping to jump him. The hope was quickly abandoned.

"So I'm starting to ease up toward him, and that's when I saw the fear in his face and realized that even though he had recognized me, he wasn't going to let it go. Because, see, there's a code: You don't pull a gun on a person unless you're going to use it, all right? If the first words out your mouth isn't, 'I'm sorry, I mistook you for someone else,' if you even just stand there and pause a few minutes and just look, then it's a full-out play."

Kyles had got within maybe six feet of the gun when the junkie sensed his strategy, took a step back, and opened fire. The first bullet went through the hand that Kyles raised as he made a lunge for the weapon. He was batting at the gun with the now limp and useless hand when he felt another bullet mulch the bones in his elbow. Kyles turned and ran, taking another couple of bullets in his back before throwing himself over a fence and collapsing on the sod alongside a small frame house that abutted the housing project. Now Kyles could see his pursuer rounding the fence and coming toward him. "He knew he had to finish the job. If he let me live, I was coming back."

Somehow Kyles found it in him to writhe and twist until he had eased himself in behind the low brick piers that raised the frame house maybe a foot and a half off the ground, but the junkie had no trouble finding him. He stood there now, just a foot or two away, visible from the shins down, and Kyles was wild-eyed as the man bent over, bringing the gun within an inch or two of his prone and bullet-riddled body. Waiting to die, Kyles counted back, trying to inventory each bullet wound he had sustained—the wrist, the elbow, one to the pelvis, two to his back—hoping upon hope that there had been six, but counting only five. The gunman bent over now to deliver the coup de grâce. He clicked the trigger, clicked it again. Damn!

The air rushed out of Kyles's lungs in a surge of relief. The sixth shot must have missed. But then there was nothing to do but watch helplessly and in horror as the man dumped the empty casings out of the revolver and prepared to reload. "I'm looking at this man. I can't do nothing. He's like three feet from me, and I'm watching this guy shoveling bullets in. He's dropping some of them, trying to shove them in, because he had this big old coat, and they're loose in the pocket. And the next thing I know: boom boom boom boom boom boom—he fired six more times. I don't recall if all of them hit me or if he was just shooting out of fear, but

I heard all six shots, and then he broke and ran, and I'm just laying there, left for dead."

Three days later Kyles came to in a hospital bed. He could dimly remember people coming out of the frame house as he lay under it screaming in pain. Kyles would be forever grateful that they ran back inside to call the police, who in turn produced an ambulance. He recalled somewhat less gratefully that the Samaritans also saw fit to relieve him of his wallet and what little jewelry had not been offered up to the junkie before the bullets started to fly. But then Kyles was not one to be surprised by the depravity of life, not as he had experienced it growing up in the Ninth. He reflected for a moment on the ethics of a household robbing what was not quite a corpse. "It was a cutthroat neighborhood," he said simply.

One of Curtis's sisters placed the call to Pinkey late on the night of the shooting. He was alive, but barely, in the trauma unit at Charity Hospital. Pinkey could scarcely believe what she was hearing, not because it was impossible to imagine, but because she had imagined something so very like it in a dream two or three weeks earlier. In the dream, she and Kyles were walking on a street when a man ran up and pumped five or six shots into him. Even after telling Kyles about it that night, weeks before life imitated her nightmare, she couldn't seem to shake the horror: "She used to cry when I got ready to leave, because it spooked her that much. And I just thought she was out of her mind or just trying to keep me home." Now it had come true.

Pinkey made it to Charity the next day, time enough having passed for her anxiety to mutate into rage. She arrived in the trauma unit freely cursing Kyles and all his women, because she was sure that was how it had come to this, and of course she was not far wrong. With tubes running in and out of his every orifice like vines claiming a derelict house, Kyles stared back at her wordlessly.

"I was talking to him kind of bad," Pinkey would recall. "He was hooked up to the heart machine and the breathing machine. Tubes in his mouth and in his nose—all kind of little stuff he was hooked up to. I felt like unplugging him. That's what I told him. I felt like unplugging him." Instead, during the couple of weeks before Kyles could leave the hospital, she fell somewhat grudgingly to what little she could do for him. She would wash his face, brush his teeth, and scold him again and again for having nothing but balls where his brain was supposed to be.

Kyles left the hospital with his arm in a sling and a portion of his liver in a medical biohazard bag destined for the hospital incinerator. His hand and his elbow had been bolted back together with metal screws he would carry to his grave. There would be another legacy of his run-in with Jackie's junkie friend. He now qualified for a disability check. In the eyes of the government, he was too badly maimed to lay brick, though the reality was, he could lay brick pretty much as well as ever, provided he was paid off the books in cash.

As for the junkie, Kyles's candor about so much in his life did not extend quite that far. "I went looking for him," he said one afternoon years later, as though about to begin a tale of retributive justice as brutal as the attack that provoked it. But instead, he stopped himself short. "And that's all we're going to say about that."

In preparation for the armed robbery trial, Kyles directed Regan to his medical records as their best defense. They would show that at the time the women were held up, he was still recovering from the mugging memorialized by the bullet he carried near his spine and the copper pins that held his hand and elbow together. His arm was in a cast in those days. He was hobbling around on a cane. And if jurors didn't accept the claim that he was physically incapable of the crime—or, in any case, highly unlikely to be out on the streets taking on young women three at a time—then surely they would note that none of the robbery victims, all three of them medical professionals, had mentioned anything to police about their assailant having his arm in a cast. To mount an ironclad defense, all it would take would be the doctor's notes on his initial treatment and continuing rehabilitation. Kyles wanted them subpoenaed. Regan assured him that Judge Waldron would fulfill the defense's request for them without recourse to legal coercion. Whatever the reason—and a much darker theory would immediately suggest iself to Kyles—the key medical reports turned up missing as the case came to trial. And when Regan went after the doctor of record, he had left the area and could not easily be served.

So it fell to Kyles's family, his brother Larry and sisters Brenda and Lela, to take the stand and describe Kyles's ordeal—the bone graft, the pins and screws in his arm—and to try as best they could to put dates on the period of his incapacitation. They meant well, but in all likelihood the defendant's orange prison jumpsuit and shackles spoke more eloquently under the circumstances. In any case, jurors soon returned with a verdict of guilty. Lela erupted right there in the courtroom. "You done picked up a man and charged him just so you don't have to go out and look for the one that truly done this crime," she would remember howling. And with that, she grabbed her change purse from the gallery bench beside her and hurled it toward the judge. Instantly the room exploded, guards screaming at the sisters to sit down, the judge hammering with his gavel.

Delivered of her castigation, Lela slumped into her seat, sobbing. She would remember glancing toward Curtis and seeing the look on his face—the look of a man with a noose tightening around his neck, combined with a look of dismay over his sisters' outbursts. She read the words on his lips: "Y'all just sit down." Brenda said she had never seen him look so hurt, even when he was sentenced to death. The death sentence had marked a terrible but dignified defeat. Now it seemed as if prosecutors were just toying with him, laughing at him, as they convicted him of a crime in a part of town he scarcely ever visited, under conditions that seemed to rule out a cripple as perpetrator.

The court adjourned with a request from jurors that deputies escort them safely past the Kyles family, seething there in the visitors gallery. Kyles was returned to Orleans Parish Prison, now serving for each of the three robberies a concurrent fifteen-year sentence, or whatever portion of it might have elapsed by the time the state tired of the appellate process and strapped him into the electric chair.

PART TWO

EIGHT

It was typical police-blotter fare. A Sunday morning wrap-up of the weekend's mayhem: three men dead in unrelated shootings. Another long, hot summer had set in, the summer of 1986. The life of a fifty-two-year-old night clerk had been canceled by a stickup team at a convenience store over in Metairie, a bedroom community across the city's western border. A bullet-riddled corpse (male) had been scraped up off the railroad tracks near the big Illinois Central switching yard in the city's Ninth Ward. Another Metairie resident, little more than a boy, had gone down in a fight out along the lakefront. Sometimes it seemed like every teenager in New Orleans and plenty more from the suburbs made the lakefront scene on a Saturday night, the lowriders cruising along the manicured strip of land between the towering levees and Lake Pontchartrain, the small, brackish sea that defines the northern border of New Orleans. And when they spotted friends or a place to park or got tired of cruising, they'd angle their muscle cars toward the seawall and party, one car right next to the other for miles, doors open and radios turned up loud, the kids in clusters—black, white, Hispanic, Asian—strutting their stuff and passing joints, if they weren't in the backseat necking.

In the parish prison dayroom, an inmate put aside the newspaper and looked over at the man with whom he was sharing the Sunday morning quiet. Cigarette smoke hung in the humid air. The heat of the day lay ahead. "The man that ratted you out. What was his name—Wallace?"

Kyles looked over and took a pull on his cigarette. "Wallace? Banks. I know him as Banks."

"Joseph Wallace?"

"They call him Beanie."

The man glanced over again at Kyles. "He's dead."

Kyles took the section of *The Times-Picayune* thrust toward him and began picking his way through the three-column crime wrap-up. He had had two years to work on his reading, two mind-numbing years in parish prison waiting for his appeals to run their course before the state could send him on his way to the penitentiary at Angola, to death row. You couldn't watch TV all the time, though there was little else in the way of rehabilitative programming offered by the prison. Just by sticking his nose into books and magazines, Kyles was beginning to get the drift of words on paper. The headline was straightforward enough: THREE KILLED IN AREA SHOOTINGS: MAN BOOKED IN BRAWL SLAYING. Kyles pressed on into the smaller type: "Two Metairie men and a New Orleans man were shot to death in separate incidents Friday night and Saturday and one person has been booked with murder, police said. Joseph Wallace, 24, 2088 N. Dorgenois St., was found dead Saturday night between railroad tracks and a house at 2887 Law St." Kyles jumped over the intervening paragraphs about the two killings the reporter had deemed more important— the Metairie holdup and the lakefront killing—looking for details about Wallace. "Wallace's body was found by New Orleans police called to investigate a report of gunshots on Law Street at 6:50 p.m., police said. Wallace was hit twice in the head and once in the abdomen, said John Marie, police information officer. No witnesses, suspects or motive were known, he said. The slaying is being investigated by Detective Melvin Winnins."

It took no imagination for Kyles to see Beanie go down. He knew the train tracks as well as he knew his own block. They were a pedestrian short-cut between Desire Street and his mother's place on North Dorgenois, a desolate terrain of shattered bottles and used condoms and termite-ridden railroad ties that had been tossed into the underbrush as they were replaced. He could picture the Law Street houses fast by the tracks and hear the rumble of freight cars, long miles of them, being banged together or pushed off onto sidings.

Kyles admired the thoroughness of the hit: the bullet to the stomach, the two shots to the skull. He hoped the belly shot came first and that Beanie had at least a few minutes of agony before the skull shots finished him off. He savored the thought of it: Beanie lying there on the track bed knowing that he's dying, the blood oozing through the fingers of the hand he has clapped over the hole in his gut. Then the sound of the insurance shots to the skull, and the killer quickstepping out of there, his footsteps crunching on the track-bed gravel and fading in the distance. For one brief moment, Kyles was happy, almost ecstatic, as happy as prison allows a condemned man to be. And then he was thrown into a mood more like despair. Because Wallace's death, however pleasing to contemplate in its particulars, was also the death of Kyles's best hope for sloughing the Dye murder off onto someone else, onto Beanie. For that to work, Kyles figured, first they would have to nail Beanie for the Suazo murder, or maybe Leidenheimer's—why not both? But there was no prosecuting a dead man.

The murder of the Honduran seaman was the key. Kyles had been certain of that ever since he learned that the bullet fatal to Charles Suazo had been fired from the same gun that killed Mrs. Dye. Cops had seen the link and read it backward. They had charged Kyles—before apparently thinking better of complicating a high-profile open-and-shut case like the Dye murder with this second slaying from the city's lower depths. Suazo, after all, wasn't even white.

Prosecute the Suazo murder, and you could nail Beanie, Kyles had come to believe. But the Suazo murder, like Leidenheimer's, had gone mysteriously unprosecuted, perhaps for the same reason: protecting a high-value snitch.

Kyles could recall Martin Regan's attitude toward his theory only with bitterness. Regan had dismissed the idea of stressing the Suazo link to the Dye killing—the ballistics match. Maybe it would have implicated Beanie in both murders, but there was just as good a chance it might all come back on Kyles, Regan had warned. Well, maybe it would have. Maybe it would have led to the worst possible outcome for Kyles. Maybe he'd have been convicted and sentenced to die. Imagine that. Now, with Beanie dead, there was little chance at all.

It got worse. Kyles put down the paper and went to the phones. After the usual rigmarole—a call placed and a call returned—he got through to Pinkey's parents' house. The strangeness of that conversation would stay with Kyles—the things said and the sense that things weren't being said. "You could hear crying in the background, a lot of whispering and shushing. And from that I kind of understood that it had something to do with Johnny." Indeed, within a day or two, Johnny Burnes had been charged with Joseph Wallace's murder.

Pinkey conveyed the news to Kyles in a later phone call, and Kyles felt a wave of love for Johnny, his avenger. But he ain't done it, Curtis. I'm telling you. He's up in Bassfield, Pinkey remonstrated. To Kyles, it didn't matter where Johnny was, or what his alibi was, or even if he had killed Beanie. What mattered was that Beanie was dead and that Burnes was on the right side of cosmic justice, if not its agent.

Days later, Burnes's father would drive Johnny down from Bassfield and hand him over. Police claimed that he had gone up into Mississippi to hide out. Johnny would claim—and a couple of witnesses would back him, including a man he did some work for that Saturday—that he had been there all along. The alibi didn't spare him an indictment. It didn't spare him conviction. His only respite was that jurors saw fit to reduce the charge from second-degree murder to manslaughter. The toxicology report showed that Beanie was so drugged up on the day he died that he would have been as crazy as a man with his clothes on fire—a mitigating circumstance. Johnny had dropped him as you would a mad dog, jurors seem to have concluded.

As a matter of strategy, Connick's prosecutors chose not to stir up questions about Wallace's role in the Kyles case. They assigned a simple motive to Burnes for killing the informer: a drug deal gone bad; dishonor among thieves. The media weren't so sure. They couldn't resist theorizing that Wallace's rubout was a long-fused act of vengeance. Wallace had scoffed at the street's ultimate taboo. He had ratted out a brother. He had ratted out a black brother to a racist police force. And the black brother he ratted out was blood: Johnny's sister's old man, the father of all those kids, kids who shared Pinkey's blood. Which meant Johnny's blood too.

Kyles's views on the subject were more complex. In the first place, if Johnny Burnes was in Mississippi when Beanie met his fate alongside the railroad track, then Johnny's charge was bullshit. But if, for purposes of discussion, you allowed that Burnes did pump three slugs into his long-time partner, Kyles had reason to doubt it was all about him. Vengeance on the cosmic plane did not require that Beanie's treachery at the time of the Dye murder would haunt Johnny's every thought. The Dye murder was two years old. That was an eon in the life of a junkie as far gone as Beanie, and from what Kyles had been able to tell, Johnny was pretty far gone himself by then. They were into a hand-to-mouth existence, from what Kyles had heard, a jittery rhythm of quick hits and equally quick fixes. Foresight had been reduced to a matter of an hour or two, and hindsight had lost any hold over them at all.

According to the narrative worked up by police, the incident began with Wallace and a friend dropping in on Johnny to conduct a little business at the house he was renting on Law Street, a brick bunker of a place on an odd little wedge of land. It was pushed up against the railroad embankment on one side and surrounded on all sides with a wooden stockade fence six feet tall.

Wallace goes in alone, according to the police. His friend is waiting in the car, when the next thing he knows, Burnes is standing in his doorway with a pistol drawn, ordering him to come inside too. The men settle around the kitchen table. Burnes is not happy. The dope they've brought is shit. Beanie has ripped him off, and Burnes wants his money back. Tension is escalating to the breaking point when Burnes is momentarily distracted by someone at the door. At that, Wallace and his buddy bolt out the back, Burnes on their heels, and jump the fence onto the Port Street side of the triangular lot. Wallace yells to split up, and they peel off in different directions. Burnes stays on Beanie, and within fifty yards or so, Beanie's blood is soaking the gray-black stone of the railroad bed and a neighbor is on the phone to police.

How crazy had things gone in the world of Beanie Wallace and Johnny Burnes? Pretty far, given that the best character witness Burnes could summon for his sentencing was a woman grateful that six years earlier, he and Wallace had only shot her through the jaw rather than kill her in the course of murdering her lover. Beanie had wanted to finish her off too, but Burnes had talked him out of it, the character witness said. That was the incident that had cost Beanie a manslaughter conviction, though he had been out in the blink of an eye—eighteen months—further proof, as far as Kyles was concerned, that the police would always look after a snitch. Soon Burnes, for killing a killer, had been sentenced to twenty years at hard labor and, as the twentieth century gave way to the new millennium, he would still be dreaming of parole.

Even Pinkey had never been quite sure how Beanie Wallace came into their lives. Trouble with his mother? Or maybe the Wallace household had simply swelled up to where a neighbor like Mrs. Burnes, with an extra bed and a willingness to take in a neighbor's adolescent son, was a godsend to be met with gratitude, not questions. Johnny was friends with Beanie. Maybe he just started staying over and never left. He bunked with another of Pinkey's brothers, Claude, in what they called the patio room, just off the kitchen. Maybe some money changed hands. Maybe not. It could be like that in the Ninth Ward, and etiquette meant not inquiring too deeply into other people's business, even when their business was your business, as, in due course for Pinkey, Beanie's was.

When Curtis first took up with Pinkey, he didn't know Beanie. He knew *of* Beanie, and what he knew of him—a pastiche of street rep and boasts and rumors—made him reasonably sure he didn't want to know him any better. Kyles called it ear hustling: the process of tuning in on the grapevine without ever asking a pointed question, without ever letting on you were listening. He'd hear about something that had gone down, a robbery, a holdup, a beating, a killing, and from the way people spoke of it, rarely letting on who they thought might be involved, Kyles would come to his own conclusions. And with some frequency, the dude behind some of the wilder capers Kyles was hearing about seemed to be Beanie Wallace.

The word on the street was that Beanie had connections with police—a grandmother with a job as a sheriff's deputy. Kyles didn't really need more reasons to dislike Beanie Wallace, but Beanie provided them anyway, and soon enough he was providing them firsthand. With Pinkey under Kyles's roof and Beanie living with Johnny, it was inevitable that their paths would start to cross, and quite regularly.

In the best of times, junkies were a drag. And by the early '80s Beanie was a junkie. It started with powder, but everybody did a little powder now and then, this being the high noon of cocaine's vogue. (Crack hadn't come along yet, and freebase was too much work.) Like a million poor boys before him and some rich ones too, Beanie moved from cocaine to speedballing, the coke/heroin mix that livened up the heroin while bringing gravitas to an otherwise dipshit high like cocaine. After speedballs started to wear thin, you still had choices to make, but you were going to want a needle either way. And if your choice was to shoot cocaine, you were going to need a lot of money, which Beanie didn't have. By about 1982 he was a straight-up heroin addict—unless you counted the jones for Pinkey, which had also started to claim him. From what he told her, a boast that probably did not overstate the truth by much, he was pumping $400 to $500 a day into his arm. Other boasts were verifiable: there was the time Beanie, in the talkative phase of a heroin high, started regaling Pinkey with details of an overnight burglary that turned violent and then deadly. When Pinkey signaled skepticism, Beanie told her to turn on the TV news. Sure enough, there it was: a murder out by the lakefront matching Beanie's story in every particular, the Leidenheimer murder, as Pinkey would come to realize. Horrified, Pinkey had scarcely dared look at the gloating junkie on the sofa beside her. He knew his secret was safe with her, and it was. She knew more than she wanted to know about Beanie Wallace, certainly more than she would ever consider telling police— which, in strict adherence to the mores of the society she lived in, was nothing at all. Even if she wanted to pull the plug on Wallace, police, from her experience, were an unreliable way to do it. Besides, Beanie was capable of revenge. The reason Beanie's cousin was in the parish prison as Kyles arrived there was because Beanie sold him out after they co-authored a burglary. At least that was the word on the street. And as far as Pinkey knew, Wallace had offed his own stepfather, a small-time renovator, after the man took him in and taught him the business, a business whose profits Beanie decided he would prefer not to share. Pinkey told the story this way: "Beanie started self-contracting the jobs, bringing some of the workers and stuff with him. And the stepfather came up dead." The imperatives in Beanie's life could be summarized as succinctly. "He would smile and joke with you, and he would blow your brains out," Pinkey said. "He needed money for that dope."

Addicts were a fact of life. You learned to work around them. Kyles's boyhood mentor, Big Slim, had lost it to scag. So, for a time, would Kyles's brother Larry. Kyles's thing was weed. Weed and a little wine or beer. Not even that much liquor. He dealt powder of various descriptions, but somehow he never developed a taste for it. You learned to be wary of junkies. You watched your back around them, but there was no writing junkies out of the picture. After all, desperation has its uses, as Kyles found when it came to warehousing hot goods until he could fence them. Another use for junkies was that you could get them to do your dealing for you. That was about the only reason Kyles had much truck with Beanie once he got to know him. You could sell Beanie a fix at cost. To pay for it, he'd move three or four bags, sparing you the need to risk the street yourself. But it was bound to go bad between Curtis and Beanie, and in due course it did.

By June of '83 it had reached the flash point. You could call it a $150 misunderstanding, except that everything was completely understood. Johnny Burnes and Curtis had come by some cocaine and also clickem juice, a chemical that could be added to reefer to make a much crazier high. "I put that in Johnny's lap," Curtis recalled, "and Johnny put the cocaine in my lap, because neither one of us messed with that type of drug, so it was strictly a selling thing."

Beanie got wind of their score, and soon enough he had come around, angling for a little piece of the action. Of course he was a few bills short just then and also in urgent need of a fix, but here was the deal: Spot him three bags of the cocaine, and he'd be back in no time, with heroin for himself and cash for Curtis. Then he'd settle down and deal another six bags, just to show how grateful he was to be fixed. The bags were "corner bags," a little wedge of cocaine in the corner of a plastic baggie sealed shut with the edge of a playing card heated with a match or lighter. Corner bags went for $25 apiece, and sure enough, Beanie was back in about two hours, high as a kite but with $75 for Kyles as promised.

Phase two did not go so well. Kyles gave him the six bags, $150 worth of coke. Unfortunately, in saying he would be back in no time, Beanie was as good as his word. "He became a no-show," Kyles said, "and that's when all the problems started arriving." A couple of days later Kyles ran into Beanie and got the usual sob story: Beanie had been robbed. Kyles knew the game, knew this was bullshit. He also knew better than to say so, because that would be both a threat and an insult. The rules were unambiguous: "You don't threaten no street person. Not until you are ready to hurt them." Instead, Kyles played along with the lie: "I'm sorry you got robbed. But you know, business is business, so when are you going to have my change?" Beanie promised the money the next day, and Kyles let him go.

Jump to Saturday night. The better part of a week had passed, and still no sign of Beanie or the missing $150. For reasons now lost to memory, on that Saturday night Kyles dropped in on Johnny Burnes and his woman, the one they called Vee, for Veronica. They were at Burnes's parents' place, and seeing as the old folks were up at the farm that weekend, they had the house to themselves. They were sitting around talking, Kyles and Johnny and Veronica, when there was a knock on the door. It was Beanie, a grin on his face, a brown paper bag in his hand.

The grin went away at the first sight of Kyles, and the situation unraveled quickly from there. What Johnny sensed but Curtis didn't—not yet—was that Beanie wasn't carrying a can of beer in the paper bag. It holstered his rod, a snub-nosed .32, a paper bag being the readiest place you can carry a gun, short of walking around with it drawn. There was no small talk, no how-de-do. One glance at Kyles, and Beanie began muttering about how he didn't have the fucking money and didn't know when he was going to get it. Now Kyles picked up on it, as Johnny had right from the start. Something was not right with Beanie: "I'm looking at him, and I said, 'What's that look in your eye, bro?'"

"C'mon, y'all. Just step outside." That was Johnny cutting in, and it was a signal to Kyles that this could get ugly, that Beanie was packing. "He was letting me know exactly what time it was." Thus alerted, Kyles stepped into the bedroom to grab his jacket, which he hung over one shoulder. As he stepped out onto the patio, Beanie whipped his gun from the paper bag. Kyles let the jacket slip from his shoulder, and the .45 it had concealed was aimed at Beanie's ample gut.

Johnny Burnes was quick. He threw one arm up and hit Beanie's .32, knocking it onto the ground. With the other hand he swatted Kyles's gun, which went off, lodging a bullet in Mrs. Burnes's back door. Enough of this shit. Burnes bolted back inside as the sound of the shot echoed down the back alleys and died away.

Beanie, disarmed, had the presence of mind to grab the cylinder of the gun still in Kyles's hand, which effectively froze the trigger. The two men struggled inconclusively for a minute or more until Kyles managed a rabbit punch to the testicles, and Beanie dropped to the ground, his face contorted in a scream that would be silent until he could resume breathing.

Now Kyles took charge. "I'm gonna shoot him. In my mind I'm gonna shoot him. He owes me the money, and I'm a-shoot him." His logic was crude but unimpeachable under the code of the streets. He pulled the trigger. The revolver jammed. He pulled it again. Same thing. Beanie sensed redemption, pulled himself up off the ground, and scrambled inside the house and out onto the street faster than Kyles had ever seen so plump a junkie move. Kyles was not unaware of the absurdity of his situation. To be lethally armed was no guarantee that the weaponry actually worked. But having gone this far, he realized there could be no turning back. And so, ignoring Pinkey's entreaties, that same night Kyles set to stalking Beanie Wallace with no other thought in mind than his violent elimination.

Beanie's theft was unconscionable, and it was brazen; and for Kyles, looking bad—weak, ripped off—was not just insulting, it was dangerous, a provocation to strangers in the street. "It makes cowards try you," Kyles said, thinking especially of the occasional evenings he still spent dealing pot in the Florida housing project. "It makes the buyer think they can try you." Kyles knew his duty, but he did not embrace it with any relish. "Don't get me wrong," Kyles continued. "I'm hanging tough, but I was scared to death. I really didn't want to do it, but I knew the code."

In search of Beanie, Kyles prowled the gray areas. "This is the type of person Beanie was, like a shadow or a ghost." To catch a shadow, you went to shadowland: the shooting galleries, the drug dens, the empty houses on the fringes of what passed for human habitation, their floors glittery with broken glass and used needles. Abandoned houses, they were called, and properly so, not because nobody lived there, but because the people who did had themselves been abandoned—or had abandoned themselves—to drugs and decay.

Kyles's blood oath to take Beanie's life was twenty-four hours old when a visitor accosted him in his home—his mother-in-law, Dorothy Burnes, the woman who had reared Beanie like a son. Kyles knew to start with apologies, and he did so sincerely, because by his code, by any code, to have done your business in the home of a village elder, to have horrified the neighbors and left a bullet hole in the door as your calling card, was an act of utter disrespect that had to be atoned for. Mrs. Burnes wasn't interested in apologies, however. She wanted peace. That said, she turned on her heel and walked out of the apartment her daughter shared with Kyles. The next night, she contacted Kyles by phone and told him to get on over to her place right away. She didn't tell Kyles that Beanie was already there, but when Kyles showed up not too many minutes later, it came as no surprise.

Mrs. Burnes sat the two of them down like a couple of ten-year-olds who had tied firecrackers to her cat's tail. "I mean she threatened us. She cursed us. She called us her two babies, and like that." And when she got done talking, she made her babies start talking. Beanie copped the junkie's traditional plea: how he had to have it, couldn't help himself, hardly knew himself anymore, didn't mean no harm. Kyles's position was this: "I just don't want him around me." (He said it to Mrs. Burnes, as if Beanie wasn't even there.) "Because if he do it once, he do it again. And I'm not going to let this happen again."

Mrs. Burnes looked at him, her eyes iced over with scorn, and then she turned her head slowly and evenly and looked at Beanie the same way. With that, she dragged her purse across the table to where she could reach inside and pull out $50 in loose bills—two twenties, two fives. She threw them down on the table in front of her, like chump change, threw them down without looking at them. As if to say: You assholes were going to kill yourselves over pieces of paper? Beanie got the message. He fished in his pocket, came up with $22, and threw that on top of the fifty. That made $72, just shy of half the $150 that Beanie owed Kyles for the six packets of powder. Kyles was expected to eat the rest, but he was philosophical. "I came up short, but that was cool. I didn't really want to kill nobody."

With the cash on the table, the woman made them both swear that the foolishness was over. The terms of valor had shifted for Kyles. Instead of this being about defending his honor, now it was about keeping his word to a woman he should and did respect. It didn't entirely cancel the obligation to bring vengeance on an enemy, but it definitely complicated things.

Beanie started staying out of Kyles's way, and Kyles stayed away from Beanie. They ran into each other maybe three times over the next half year. On the street, at parties. Kyles knew better than to let his guard down. No more leaving his rod in the glove compartment of a loaned-out car. He was always armed now, and he knew Beanie was too. In some ways, not running into Beanie was more nerve-racking than having him around. At least when he was around, you knew what he was up to. That didn't mean Kyles had any desire to spend the holidays with him.

It would be Kyles's last Christmas as a free person, the last for fifteen years, but of course there was no knowing that. They decided to go up to Bassfield to Pinkey's family farm—Kyles and Johnny and a whole posse of their friends, so many that they chartered a coach: "Me, Claude, Larry, Denny, and others I can't rightly recall. Seven guys, maybe, and eleven or twelve girls."

They got to Bassfield for Christmas, and most of them stayed right through New Year's. And somewhere along in there, Beanie turned up. Mrs. Burnes had invited him. At first it got to Kyles: "I had a hard time sleeping, knowing he was in the next room." But after a couple of nights and nothing had happened, the tension started to ease. On New Year's Eve it broke, and in the general mood of revelry and brotherhood that the evening brought on, Beanie had fallen in with Kyles and the others as they drank their wine and smoked their smoke and laughed and made time with the women. Came the witching hour, the men stepped outside to fire off their guns, and the feeling of bonhomie was such that they started swapping, trying out one another's weapons—"just to see what the person next to you was working with," as Kyles put it. The good vibes extended even to Beanie. "I just went over to him. 'Here,' I said. 'Shoot this one.'" In return, Beanie handed his to Kyles, and the two of them stood there, saying little, firing bullets into the night sky. It was like a huge weight had lifted. Or like you're lying in bed with a sinus full of snot, and all of a sudden you feel it open and start to drain, and for the first time since you can't remember when, you can breathe again.

NINE

Kyles had run out of money and he was running out of time. Martin Regan's $5,000 retainer was long gone, even before the spring of 1985 and Kyles's trial for armed robbery of the young women outside Tyler's Beer Garden. Regan stood by his client anyway, through an automatic review of the capital case by the Fourth Circuit appeals court. Regan's final recourse in the state system—an equally automatic appeal to the Louisiana Supreme Court—was a few months in the offing when, in the early months of 1987, Kyles made the trip upriver to get ready to die. Angola was going to be different from Orleans Parish Prison. Angola was the big time. Not necessarily more violent than OPP—few places were—but different. Regimented. A study in closely regulated oppression, in contrast with the chaotic hellhole he had known in New Orleans.

Kyles had tried to rise above it. He really had. He had studied Burl Carter's example, listened to his lessons on how to avoid the fray. He had tried to apply them, and he had failed. A turning point was his reckoning with the change in Pinkey's life. She had moved in with another man— no matter that he had told her to. By February or March of 1985 his illusions about her fidelity had become harder to sustain. "When I called, her voice would be different. Then my sisters started letting me know:

'You got to keep it real, Curtis. Her life don't stop here.'" They broke it to him slowly, fearful that he might crack from the stress he was already under. She had found a man who took the calves along with the cow, just as he had hoped she would, but somehow the thought of it, now that Kyles had a name and a face to put to his successor, had been the final humiliation. "If I didn't accomplish nothing else in my life, I just wanted to be there for my kids. My kids were my world." Now another man was raising them. Well, not Tyteannia. Lela had taken her in, but the rest of them were under Tyrone Joseph's roof. Kyles wanted to hate Pinkey for it, but his loathing turned back in on him. It was as if he had nothing left to live for.

Louisiana does not recognize common-law marriage, though by any definition that was the nature of the union between Martina Burnes and Curtis Kyles. The sundering of it, a direct consequence of the Dye murder and Kyles's incarceration, was tantamount to divorce. In the very different world inhabited by Mrs. Dye's survivors, sometimes it seemed as though a similar rash of schisms and misfortunes had flowed from her death, among them Lowell's breakup with Jan. Kyles had seen another man coming; he had sanctioned Pinkey's decision to move on with her life, however painful that would prove to be for him. Lowell Dye, by contrast, was caught completely by surprise. Maybe his grief had blinded him to Jan's emotional needs or left him too distracted to do much about them. Whatever the reason, the separation came like a bolt from the blue.

Two and a half years had passed since the murder when, in April 1986, Lowell Dye woke up to the realization that Jan—Dr. Lassen's comely daughter, the mother of his only child, the woman he had coached through court-reporting school and proudly squired through his world of cocktail parties and club sports—was moving in with another man. Yes, he was an investment banker; yes, he drove a Mercedes—but in so many other respects the betrayal mystified Dye as much as it pained him. "He was forty-three; I'm thirty-five," Dye would recall. "But he looked like he was fifty." Balding, skinny, and, most preposterous of all to Dye, who knew his wife could only pretend to the same enthusiasm, an opera buff. As far as Lowell knew, there was nothing wrong between him and Jan. They never fought, and he had just won the first big settlement of his career. A brand-new

BMW graced the garage. They were fresh back from a ski vacation with friends. "We were on a roll, baby."

Whether it was the receding hairline or the lack of country music in the household, within two months Jan's relationship with the investment banker had expired, and she was willing to give Lowell another try. Dye acquiesced, but with conditions: she could visit; she could be over a lot; but she needed to have her own place. "The fact that you had an affair is one thing," Dye told her. "The fact that you moved out of my house and moved in with another man and three hundred of my friends know all about it, that's a big deal; that's a little bit tough for me to handle. Right?" At first the arrangement seemed to be working out. Three months had passed when a friend pulled Dye aside and told him what, in hindsight, seemed as inevitable as the original affair was unexpected: Jan was interested in someone else, a lawyer this time from one of the big, prestigious firms, a guy more her age. That was it. In the ensuing divorce proceedings, Dye wound up with custody of their child. Jan moved to California with her future husband. What Dye came to think of as Jan's revenge would be delayed, but it would be exquisite.

Stripped of his own sense of fatherhood, Kyles abandoned himself to some of the worst of the jailhouse thuggery and racketeering: the dope game, as he called it; the sex game, buying and selling flesh, not for his own delectation—Kyles was unable to adapt his sexual preferences to the prison menu—but as a means of profit and a way of maintaining control. "Basically, all the goodness just up and left out of me," he would say in summarizing this time in his life. It was a descent that smacked of self-annihilation; yet, perversely, it sealed Kyles's reputation among other inmates as someone not to mess with. That held for guards as well—with occasional exceptions. His most serious run-in with his jailers came just before he was due to be transferred to Angola. A boy had been raped on the tier—a punk, in Kyles's estimation. Nothing unusual about that. But the boy's parents got wind of it and demanded some kind of official response. Kyles was among a cadre of thieves and buggerers—the cream of the tier's power elite, in other words—hauled in for questioning by a special investigations team seeking the rapist or rapists. Kyles was outraged. "You got no business calling me up here," he told the investigators. "You know how I play it. You know I don't participate in that type behavior."

"You participate in whatever we say you participate in," one of the guards shot back, whereupon in the corner of his eye Kyles saw the man's foot coming at him. Instinctively Kyles managed to grab the flying foot and drive the man back against the wall. Within seconds, but not before Kyles bruised the kicker's lip, two guards had jumped and hog-tied him, and in no time he was on his way to the prison office to be booked with assault on a police officer. He did not stick around long enough to find out what consequences might have flowed from that infraction, because suddenly, early in 1987, there came the day when the state of Louisiana signaled it was ready for the long since "state-ready" inmate named Curtis Lee Kyles.

Kyles knew better than to pack the muscle shirts he had dyed mauve and yellow with the chemical fruit drink he ladled out to other inmates after becoming his tier's "juice boy." The word was that the only clothing tolerated at Angola was gray or navy blue. Kyles had a few such items, though he had seen fit to relieve the drabness of them with monograms he sewed into the fabric, a minor fad at OPP that the fashion-conscious Kyles found diverting. Besides blue and gray, the only other colors that mattered at Angola were black and white. OPP had been a black prison, even blacker than the city. The guards at OPP were white and mostly racist, as far as Kyles could tell, but even the stupidest of them knew better than to bait the inmates gratuitously. Angola was different. It had been a slave plantation in the antebellum era, and without appreciable changes in the lives of its resident population, it remained one after slavery gave way to a system of inmate labor gangs available for hire under the guns of their guards.

By the mid-twentieth century, adjustments were being made. Forced labor by the general prison population—death row inmates were exempt, even if they wanted to work—had been reviewed after a group of Angola inmates slit their Achilles tendons in protest against it. It was hard not to take that seriously. Once cut, the tendon—the long one that rides from the heel up under the calf—shrivels and retreats uselessly into the leg, permanently crippling the self-mutilator. Additional reforms had been in the works since the mid-1970s, when a federal district judge named E. Gordon West despaired of inducing Angola to heal itself and put the vast prison farm—then generally regarded as the most violent penitentiary in America—under the direct supervision of his court.

More slowly in fact than on paper the place began to change. The old Angola had been a Hobbesian nightmare ruled by inmate trusties only more malignant than the guards whose favor they curried in order to maintain the shabby privileges of their office. Rape and the knife had been the ward heelers of penitentiary politics, and every aspect of life, from where you sat to when you smoked or showered, was political. But now, under West's successor, U.S. District Judge Frank Polozola, the trusties, officially abolished, had melted back into the prison population like a death squad slinking away after regime change in a tin-pot Central American dictatorship. Under the Polozola reforms, the guards would have to actually run the place, no longer leaving the task to inmate proxies.

The guards were overlords of a manor on which many of them had grown up, as had their fathers and grandfathers before them. Their ancestral cottages, clustered right there on the prison grounds, stood trim and neat behind picket fences that mocked the concertina wire enclosing the inmates' world. Now to the caste of these white rustics was restored responsibility for the power that had been vested in them all along. The culture of violence was too entrenched to end overnight, of course, but now the onus was on the guard if an inmate's injuries were too egregious to be easily patched up in the prison sick bay—or not bad enough to warrant a declaration of death by suicide or heart failure and a trip to Angola's hillside boneyard.

What did not change, indeed it seemed only to deepen among the guards, was the bitter and fearful racism in their dealings with the majority of Angola's five thousand inmates who were black. In the old days, before the guards' power was subject to review, the racism had been reflexive, abrupt, and inarticulate. Now it grew sly and more guiltily self-aware in ways reflecting Polozola's upgraded rules of accountability. New Orleans was a Caribbean port. Angola, a hundred miles or so upriver, was the Deep South, Klan country, a region reverent in its admiration for David Duke.

The three-hour trip to Angola by prison van took Kyles past Baton

Rouge and on to St. Francisville, a picturesque town where weekend tourists stopped for lunch or an evening in a guesthouse before driving off for a look at a stately home, perhaps the one where John James Audubon wintered as drawing master to the young belles of a planter's family. At a junction a few miles north of town, a stretch of macadam cut off to the left and coiled for twenty miles through the Tunica Hills, an uninterrupted wilderness of washes and vine-choked gullies as hospitable to copperheads and water moccasins and mosquitoes as it was hostile to any inmate foolish enough to think he could outrun a pack of bloodhounds. At last, the road bottomed out on the verdant floodplain formed by Angola's even more impregnable border—a huge and sweeping arc of the Mississippi River—and the gates to the vast prison complex hove into view.

Kyles was not alone that day. He shared the van with a biker named Clarence Smith. Smith had been convicted of killing a federal witness, a heavy offense by any standard, but Smith was white. Confounding what Kyles had heard about Angola's austere clothing regulations, Smith was permitted to hold on to the clothes he brought with him. Kyles was proved wrong again in his assumption that at least his own blue and gray threads would be keepers. The guards stripped him of everything, every color except the color of his skin, and that, they reminded him, was not a fashion asset. It could be partly covered by blue and gray, but in Kyles's case it would be prison-issue blue and gray. There were other differences. At OPP, prisoners pretty much kept their own hours. If you slept late and missed breakfast, that was your problem. At Angola, at least on death row, the lights came on at five a.m., and beds had to be made military-style, the sheet and bedspread tucked tight around the two-inch mattress, the blanket—one only—folded at the foot. Death row was, of course, the regulatory extreme. The death row inmate was afforded a one-man cell but confined to it twenty-three hours a day, a condition inmates from the general prison population experienced only during isolation—"lockdown," as it was known at Angola, a punishment of varying duration for infractions of prison rules. Death row inmates were fed on trays pushed through a transom in the door to their cell. General population inmates ate in dining halls. The daily hour death row inmates were allowed outside their cells was generally dedicated to a stroll in the small caged yard off the row, maybe some layups or lonely jump shots—there was a basketball and hoop out there—and then a shower. Men who had made friends on the tier might spend some of their hour cross-legged outside the friend's cell, playing chess, perhaps, which would become Kyles's passion, or just shooting the shit face-to-face rather than shouting to an unseen conversationalist elsewhere on the tier. But these cell-door chats required the indulgence of the guard on duty, and in any case, many of the men were no longer capable of socializing, if ever they had been.

Angola was organized into a series of "camps" spread out across its thousands of acres. Death row, in those days, was at Camp J, but Kyles's first days at the penitentiary were spent on a reception tier, as chilly in winter as it would be sticky and bug-ridden in summer, and this posed a problem. In warm weather the bullet in Kyles's back merely ached. In cold weather it was like a tiny shaving of dry ice exhaling frigid vapors that coursed the length of his spine. And where his wrist and elbow were held together with screws, circulation was shot; the limb went numb. In hindsight Kyles could be mordant about his problems of adjustment: "Here I am, fixing to be fried, and I can't even keep warm."

There wasn't a lot to do in prison at first besides lying in bed, but the warden had managed to bedevil even this simple comfort with odd rules. One of them was that any prisoner who saw fit to lie down between five a.m. and lights-out seventeen hours later had to keep one foot on the floor. And so there Kyles lay, one foot on the floor, the rest of his very skinny body numb and shivering and wrapped in a blanket—a blanket that was supposed to be folded at the foot of the bed, a passing guard reminded him, whipping out a ledger to write up the infraction. It was the first of countless write-ups that would fatten Kyles's dossier over the years, most of them trivial, some not so trivial. The next step after a write-up was a disciplinary hearing. A captain and a lieutenant presided, and Kyles was assigned an inmate counselor. Inmate counselors were a relatively recent innovation, another of Polozola's reforms.

The counselor recommended that Kyles plead guilty to the crime of wrapping himself in a blanket. Remind them that you are new to the system, the counselor suggested. Keep from getting another write-up for thirty days, the magistrates said, and the problem would go away.

But not the cold. Within the month, Kyles was caught again, this time in a deep sleep induced by the soothing lump of breakfast grits in his

belly and the nimbus of his own body heat trapped beneath the offending blanket. The timing was inopportune, coinciding as it did with a tour
of the cellblock by a guard captain and his retinue. Kyles was threatened
with some time in solitary—the hole—a place he knew better than to
want to visit. Because the one thing the hole was not was solitary. Unan-
nounced visitors dropped by—guards seeking to ensure that the hole would
be an unforgettable experience for even their most hardened charges. But
this time the threat of solitary was a bluff, the sergeant confided to Kyles.
At a disciplinary hearing three days later he learned his real punishment.
It was time to move from the reception tier to death row, and Kyles was
being assigned to its most racist tier, Tier A, a white supremacist bastion
overseen by a contingent of guards more than willing, Kyles had been
warned, to look the other way if the Aryans saw fit to take an uppity black
down a peg or two.

Kyles knew to be apprehensive. In any prison, there was as much to
fear from guards as from inmates. Here the two were united in an unholy
alliance against blacks that was uglier than either faction could have been
on its own. Officially, Louisiana had not had a lynching in half a century.
But that was true only if you accepted the proposition that Angola was
somewhere else, and from what Kyles was coming to realize, it kind of
was. He had not been there six months when word spread that an inmate
in another camp had been found strung up by his bedsheet from a basketball hoop in the yard. The official postmortem—suicide—was not without imagination, it being virtually impossible to leave the tier with more
than the clothes on your back, let alone a bedsheet, and entirely impossible to bring off anything so elaborate as a basketball hoop hanging under
the watchful eye of the armed guards in their turrets overlooking the yard.

Still, as his transfer approached, Kyles's more immediate concern
was not the guards, but the supremacist cabal that, partly for the vicarious pleasure of the guards, partly by exploiting their indifference, had entrenched itself on Tier A. He knew his first days on the tier would be a
test, a gauntlet he'd have to run if he was to establish himself as somebody not to be fucked with. He did not come with expectations of the
overt violence that had punctuated the long days at OPP—the rapes, the
fights, the knifings. They would be difficult to bring off in an environ-
ment as closely patrolled as death row. The racism at Angola, like other

kinds of oppression, was a subtler beast, a war of nerves without clear winners, only survivors. The losers paid not with their lives, but with their self-respect, and the unluckiest of them—there was one man this far gone on Tier A—spent their days staring into stainless steel prison mirrors and talking only to themselves.

Kyles had his OPP training to draw on. And so, upon arriving at Tier A for the first time, he managed a quick tour of its full length before yielding to his escorts and letting them lock him in his cell. It was reconnaissance and a challenge rolled into one. Which inmates would meet his gaze? Which ones would look away or pretend they weren't looking at all? (Everybody's looking, Kyles knew from OPP, especially the ones pretending not to.) Instinctively, Kyles was trying to read the politics of the place, trying to spot the alpha inmate, the gorilla, as inmates call him, the one who runs the tier. Kyles looked for the gorilla's hard glare and the silence that always accompanies it. And there it was, or so he decided, emanating from the visage of a man soon to die, Wayne Felde. In figuring him for the tier gorilla, Kyles figured Felde wrong, but it would be a while before he realized it. Felde, of course, was white. So were most of the tier's twenty-five inmates, and Kyles's arrival did not improve the racial balance. There were four blacks on the tier before Kyles arrived and four after he moved in, because the night just prior, a black man named Leslie Lowenfeld was taken out to be prepared for execution. Kyles got his cell.

The black inmates were not uniformly welcoming. Keith Messiah, later a friend, had nothing to say to Kyles on that first quick tour of Tier A. He eyeballed him in silence. And Tracy Lee was not much more sociable. But cell 12 housed "this little biddy something," as Kyles would describe him, "about five five, and the man weighed about a hundred and five, but a nice little build on him and long plaits down almost to his chest, two plaits." This was Dalton Prejean, a cop killer from Opelousas. Prejean, barely in his twenties, was much the youngest inmate death row had seen in a while, but he had packed a lot of living into his brief sojourn as a free person. Also a lot of dying. For killing a man who attacked his sister, Prejean was sentenced to "juvenile life." Normally, juvenile life would have kept Prejean behind bars until he reached twenty-one, but the gallant nature of a killing in defense of a sister allowed for his release at seventeen, just in time for him to rise to the defense of another sibling. This go-round, it was Prejean's brother who was getting the shit kicked out of him, and the shit kicker was a state trooper. Prejean pulled his brother's gun out from under the seat of their car, and suddenly the trooper was not moving anymore.

Prejean took to Kyles immediately. "Hey, man. What's up?" Words of welcome. No eyeball games, no bullshit. An alliance had been struck that would nourish Kyles until the day, the second most painful day of Kyles's many years within the system, that Prejean was strapped to a gurney and fatally poisoned by the state of Louisiana, the electric chair by then having given way to lethal injection.

Locked in Lowenfeld's old cell, Kyles arranged his few toiletries and books and snapshots as the others, in sequence, took their "shower hour." While waiting for his turn, Kyles noticed that some of the inmates were carrying cups with them as they passed his cell on the way to the showers. Now, as Kyles made the same trek, Prejean thrust his cup through the bars and asked Kyles for hot water. Hot water? Prejean pointed Kyles toward the end of the tier and an electric burner and a kettle the inmates could reach through the bars to make instant coffee or bouillon. It was a minor revelation to Kyles about the way things were going to be on Tier A. As the whites trundled one another's cups up and back from the hot-water pot, it wouldn't have occurred to them to take Prejean's even if he'd asked—especially if he'd asked. Now the ordinarily unsociable Keith Messiah wanted some hot water too, and so did Tracy Lee, loner inmates who had not previously given much thought to the possibilities of mutual assistance.

Kyles didn't mind playing water boy for the brothers, and when he finished his shower and passed by Prejean's cell, the mood of sociability was extended. Prejean offered him a spoonful from his stash of instant coffee. If Kyles's kaffee-klatsch was partly calculated to provoke the whites, he had read the tier correctly. After the lights went out that night and the idiotic chattering of the wall-mounted TV sets in the corridor gave way to conversations from cell to darkened cell, Kyles picked up that they did not at all like the morning's show of solidarity among the blacks. "That nigger didn't ask us for no water," one of the whites said, loud enough for Kyles to know he was meant to hear. "See how them niggers stick together." From his cell, Kyles could not resist a comeback. "You know, I'm hearing this now, but y'all didn't ask me about no water. Y'all walked past my cell like it was contagious. So I'm gonna play it like y'all playing it." Of course it was not really about water. Or coffee, for that matter. As far as Kyles could figure, it was about the kind of hatred that comes over a white man when he has lost his final illusion and realizes that he won't do any better in life than the biggest loser of all, a death row black in a state like Louisiana.

The nighttime carping had not flared off the tension. The next morning, it erupted into something like open war—or the pathetic and stunted simulation of it that a place like Angola allowed for. A knock on the wall of Kyles's cell was followed by a word of friendly advice from the man next to him. "Let me pull your coat to something." It was Felde, of all people, revealing himself not as the gorilla Kyles had judged him to be, but a decent man who, though white, would become a friend to Kyles, almost a confidant, before he was taken away and electrocuted. "They'll be throwing batteries before long," Felde warned.

The first whiff of trouble was the sight of a particularly white son of a bitch at large in the corridor outside the cells, even though another man, another of the Aryans, was still completing his shower hour. Two men out of their cells at the same time meant a guard was complicit. Kyles mused on the guard's possible motivations: a shared thirst for revenge against the blacks? Sheer boredom? For reasons not yet clear to Kyles, the inmate coming down the tier had equipped himself with paper bags for his stroll—two of them, the big shopping bags they gave out at the prison canteen. From these bags, in short order, he produced screw-cap instant-coffee jars. At first glance their contents appeared to be original: instant coffee, albeit hardened and lumpy. Then Kyles caught the aroma. It was shit, human feces, its vileness enhanced by two additives—bleach and floor stripper, a floor stripper so caustic that it was meted out to prisoners in capfuls by a guard under orders not to move on to the next cell until he had seen the inmate dump the capful into a diluting bucket of water and then upend the bucket onto the cell floor and start swabbing. As with all prison regs, there was a way around this one, and so inmates slowly augmented their arsenals of waste and bleach and stripper in anticipation of just such a day as had dawned that morning on Tier A.

The immediate focus of the attack was not Kyles. Any black man would do, in this instance Tracy Lee. Lee returned fire, splashing his own jars of shit in his assailant's direction, followed immediately by the concussive thud of prison warfare's most basic ordnance: radio batteries, the big ones, size D. The defensive maneuver was well practiced, if new to Kyles. Pull your blanket up, Felde hissed. And in no time Kyles had popped the batteries out of his radio and joined the other blacks who were lobbing them into the corridor from behind duck blinds fashioned on the fly by pulling a handful of bedding chest-high.

Evidently the white dude had been so confident of surprise that he did not expect a counterattack. Now he found himself beating a retreat toward his cell under heavy fire, his flight made perilous, and also ridiculous, by the slippery brown puddles all along the way. He was trading epithets and a couple of D batteries with Prejean when the guard realized that his boys were not at the top of their game on this particular morning and he'd have to reassert the rule of law if the whites were not to be humiliated. He ordered the roving inmate back to his cell, which meant passing in front of Tracy Lee's shit-stained domicile and a final fusillade of batteries, two of which caught the white in tender parts of his person.

A battery fight was typical of the absurdity of life on death row, as Kyles would come to know it. Here were men, facing the ultimate sanction for crimes as monstrous as society could identify, reduced to squabbling like schoolyard brats. Not that the prison system took their disruptiveness lightly. Tracy Lee knew his fate. Even as alarms sounded through the camp and a goon squad of a half dozen guards stormed into Tier A, he bundled together a few things and prepared himself for the hole.

Kyles would follow some months later, after an altercation over the TV. Kyles wanted it on. Another inmate had seen enough, notwithstanding his well-developed flare for drama. This was a killer, after all, whose partner had cross-dressed as a female hitchhiker to lure the driver they murdered to his ruin. The hole reminded Kyles of an oversized cemetery crypt, a windowless chamber beyond a steel door a half foot thick. The bed was a concrete slab not quite long enough for him to stretch out on. No mattress. A blanket, but only during the nighttime hours. Kyles's first visit was for three days, pending disciplinary action for the shouting match over the television.

No aspect of life on death row is quite as appalling as the vertiginous acceleration of time as an inmate approaches his date for execution. The hole was an antidote to that—one of its more persuasive discomforts, Kyles found, being the sense that time had stopped altogether. That and the silence. For hours on end—or was it days?—Kyles would hear nothing at all. Then a sudden burst of sound, the sound of a prisoner shouting out his own name. But why? The sound of a door slamming and then, again, silence. The silence reinforced the sense of isolation, and with it came a feeling of extreme vulnerability—to the guards, to the chill basement air, to the demons that lurk in a lonely man's mind. Kyles thought of many things in the darkness of the hole: his kids, already so much less frequent in their visits now that he was upriver; the slick warmth of a woman's vagina; the hatred he felt for Beanie Wallace. The kids were the worst of it, not being with them. Or worse yet, being near them but not near enough.

Back when Kyles was still in parish prison, when his sister Lela was babysitting the older kids at her apartment not so many blocks away, on one or two occasions—Christmas Eve 1985, most memorably—she had been able to get word to him that they would be standing on the Broad Street overpass above the expressway that formed the western boundary of the prison complex. And sure enough, there she was, with Tyteannia and Chester, and little Meco as well—a treat for Kyles that was reciprocated with something equally memorable for the kids: the sight of their daddy's hand clutching a white washrag and waving it at them from one of the upper windows of the high-rise jail. Meco would never forget it—or anything else about the father he had known for four years before he was snatched away. Now the man had been replaced in Meco's mind by a set of disjointed recollections: the sight of him being led into the visiting room, the smell of his cigarette breath through the wire mesh of the visitor booths, the tears welling in the corners of his eyes even though he was a father and fathers weren't supposed to cry.

The first Christmas at Angola would etch itself in Kyles's prison memories just as poignantly. A charitable group called Trim the Tree Fellowship arranged to give presents to inmates' kids on their behalf, and Kyles filled out the application form by asking if Meco, then just about to turn eight, could have a Big Wheel tricycle. Christmas morning, there it was. Pinkey put the boy on the phone: "'Dad, Dad'—he was hollering at me—'I got the Big Wheel, the Big Wheel, Dad.'" Then Meco handed the phone back to his mother and made her hold it out into the room so his father could hear him riding, and Kyles's eyes watered over at the faint sound of the wheels rolling across the linoleum as the little boy circled round and round the room, a lifetime away.

How had it come to this? The hole was good for one thing—the profound contemplation of what had gone wrong. Not least of the ironies that occurred to Kyles as he surveyed the wreckage of his life was this: in the eyes of the wider world, he might be a creature of society's lowest depths, but as a child, his struggle had been to convince his peers that he was not pampered by privilege, that he was just as tough as the project kids.

Eva, the shopkeeper aunt who took him into her Press Park cottage, could not be called a socialite, but she had at least a couple of nickels to rub together. She also had a mouthful of gold caps, one of the first people Kyles knew to affect a fashion that would later become so commonplace. Other metallic appurtenances augmented the distinctiveness of Aunt Eva's presence: a back brace and an aluminum walker, mementos of an unsuccessful run-in with a back surgeon who had convinced her he could repair a disk that had bothered her ever since a car crash some years earlier. She needed help around the house and store, and Curtis was it. "She just loved Curtis, I don't know why, out of all my mama's children. And he got anything he wanted," his sister Brenda would recall. "Oh, she did for us too, but there was just something about Curtis." He would whine about her "whuppings." Do something wrong, out comes the belt or an extension cord. But even at that she was softhearted. In Brenda's words, "She would chastise you and tell your mama on you, but what she called a whupping was nothing."

Over time, Kyles came to know a darker side of his aunt. Through the usual pastiche of gossip and overheard remarks that carries family legend to the next generation, Kyles sensed that in her day, this now hobbled and irritable creature had been quite a number. Whether she first sold her charms by the hour, as Kyles suspected, or played all along for higher stakes, in due course she had snaked her current husband and his money away from a previous wife, and as Kyles came to understand it, in the course of the uncoupling, the other woman wound up dead. The means to that end had been a technique probably less familiar in Cleveland, Eva's home at the time, than in New Orleans, where voodoo was still enough of a presence to leave young Curtis frankly unnerved by this tidbit from his caregiver's past.

Kyles's aunt and her lover had first secured a pair of the "in the way" wife's panties—more precisely, panties stained with menstrual blood. A chicken's foot had then been stuck through a photograph of the woman and the whole gris-gris wrapped in the panties and buried in the ground. Whatever role voodoo played in all this, within days the woman had sickened. Within months she was dead, and Aunt Eva and her old man beat it out of Cleveland with enough of an insurance settlement to set themselves up in the Press Park house and start their little store. In Kyles's view, Eva's crippling at the hands of her surgeon had been penance for the murder as surely as the talon-pierced snapshot and the dirty drawers had caused her predecessor's death. But fate's vengeance was not complete.

Kyles and his uncle were fishing one afternoon in the Industrial Canal—the very same waters Lowell Dye and his brother fished as kids, with lures and rods acquired at the nearby Schwegmann's—when Kyles, by then in his early teens, put it to his guardian. "Uncle," Kyles began, "what happened to your first wife?" Instantly uncomfortable with the question, the man scolded Curtis for his nosiness and evaded the question with a glib reference to the woman's terminal illness. Kyles cut him off: "No, I mean, what did you do to her?" Again the man took cover in an account that Kyles knew did not jibe with family legend, at least not the version of it that circulated in hushed tones among the adults when Eva and her husband were not around.

Within a week of that conversation—and Kyles saw it as payback— Eva's husband had plowed his car into an 18-wheeler in the maze of roads that snaked through the factories and junkyards just east of the Industrial Canal. For his deceitfulness, the man would lie in a body cast for months. Kyles did not entirely escape the hex himself. Along with the many chores assigned by his aunt, it fell to him to nurse her invalid husband. The memory was not a pleasant one. "I washed shit off that man for the better part of a year," Kyles would mutter decades later, still repulsed by the experience.

Whatever role voodoo played in the dark of her nights, Aunt Eva's Christian faith was her mainstay, and one of her disciplines was church. In fact, she was something of a Holy Roller, and there was no way Curtis was going to get out of going with her. He'd break free of her to sit with the kids his age—that much she allowed—and before the first reading from the Gospel, he'd have snuck out into the churchyard to roll dice with the other boys.

The bigger issue was curfews. Maybe 8:30 made sense during Kyles's grade school years, but then Curtis started to grow up and the curfew didn't, which made breaking it a point of pride. If he was home by 8:30, by 9:45 he was back out the window and all over the neighborhood, trying to show the Bucktown Gang, as the local bloods called themselves, that he might be a squirt with a country accent, but he wasn't a squirt with an 8:30 curfew. At least not one that he paid much mind.

There were other ways to be down with his boys, not a real gang as much as a loose confederation of rowdies into petty theft and vandalism. Now and then they'd jack a car and joyride all over town, tripping on the sphincter-tightening rush that came with the sight of a police cruiser, or the sound of one whooping through the night with its dome light flashing like a disco strobe.

In hindsight, Kyles would come to see his uncle as wiser than he first realized. The man had gotten his, however diabolically that insurance settlement was obtained, and then settled for it, at least feigning the life of a proper burgher for the rest of his days. Thus, a man Kyles did not much like—even before it fell to him each day to sponge excrement off his broken body—stood sentinel in Kyles's moral landscape over a better road not taken. As for the road Kyles actually took, the one that wound through minefields of escalating violence and eventually landed him on death row, ironically, he would come to see the most revered of all his brothers as the one who started him on his way. It all began with a gun.

Roosevelt had one, of course—a .22 pistol. He was a man, well into his twenties. Kyles was eleven when he started to take note of it, and like any kid brother whelped in poverty's machismo culture, he wanted one too. Roosevelt said no, but Kyles swiped it a few times and then a few times more. Yielding to the inexorable, Roosevelt stopped saying no. What he said instead was this: If you're going to show it, you need to use it. And if you're going to use it, you need to know how.

At first it wasn't even about showing the weapon. Just knowing he was armed was like magic to Kyles, a source of latent power that in later years brought inner peace and a Zen focus to the tricky business of re-lieving the well-off of their wallets and the less well-off—and sometimes extremely testy—of whatever they were offering in trade for their next fix. Roosevelt's recommended training regimen began badly. Cops surprised Kyles and a friend as they took potshots at pigeons nesting in the eaves of an overpass near the Press Park house. The boys were fingerprinted, and they spent a couple of nights in juvenile detention. And then sud-denly it wasn't just pigeons getting a look at Kyles's gun, and the conse-quences were potentially far more grave.

Kyles's route to school carried him to his mother's place, where he picked up a couple of his sisters, and then past the projects. With his dap-per togs and the sisters in tow, Kyles would have been a provocation un-der any circumstances. But residence in private housing marked him as fair game for all manner of retaliation. Schoolyard fights were common-place, or they might break out blocks before Kyles and his sisters reached what could be called a place of learning only if its lessons were not looked for in books. Fights often started with catcalls or stone throwing and ended at the point of a blade. Kyles had always fought back, sassed back, punched, kicked, repaid his foes in whatever currency they carried. Partly it was his temperament. But when temperament faltered, there was al-ways his mother.

Gracie spent much of each Sunday in church, but she saw no practi-cal application of Christianity's basic precept. To turn the other cheek was to show weakness, and such a display guaranteed continuing harassment and testing. No, the Golden Rule was in effect, but it was not a prescrip-tion for peace. "Do unto others" meant giving as good as you got. And if her own kids shied away from their tormentors, Gracie beat them herself until they went back out into the street and avenged the honor of the household—singly or, if need be, collectively. "One fights, you all fight," was her mantra. And Kyles took it to heart.

On one particular day, Curtis, then still eleven, had been walking to school with Brenda, a year younger, and Ann, who was eight, when five boys jumped him. Instantly Brenda and Ann were upon them, biting and kicking and getting punched in return. The odds—five on three—gave the Kyles/Walker kids no option other than to cut and run, but it was a feint, a strategic retreat. A half hour later Kyles, now armed with Roosevelt's .22, reached Carver Middle School. He wasted no time and made no particular effort to conceal what he was doing. Almost at once, two of the boys who had jumped him lay wounded in the schoolyard and Kyles was slipping the .22 into his belt and heading for the gate. His arrest followed by a few hours.

The authorities asked for juvenile life, a sentence—the same one Dalton Prejean drew for killing his sister's assailant—that would have kept Kyles incarcerated for the decade before his twenty-first birthday. Unexpectedly, Carver's principal came to the eleven-year-old's defense, explaining that the boys from the project had struck first and that Kyles had been motivated as much as anything by the obligation to defend his siblings. Kyles was put on a kind of juvenile probation, and because the incident was not followed by any other conviction—a rape arrest, yes, but not a conviction—when Kyles reached his majority, his record was expunged, or so he had been promised.

You never could be sure, though. Martin Regan had seemed oblivious to the schoolyard incident, and Kyles surely had not chosen to bring it up with him, but as he pondered his past from the silence of Angola's hole, he wondered if the appellate attorneys he now needed so desperately would find out and be repelled by this evidence of a misspent and sometimes violent youth.

Press Park was, for the most part, a study in social aspiration, not fully realized propriety—a labyrinth of bungalows favored by families determined to maintain a toehold in the black middle class. It was a neighborhood of driveway basketball hoops and little kids scooting around on jazzy bikes, Kyles among them long after most boys his age had decided they were too cool for bikes, even jazzy ones.

But within Press Park's grid of almost suburban conformity, one house caught the boy's eye, a house where women came and went in unusual abundance, some of them fine-looking women, too fine not to be spoken for. Kyles was maybe twelve when he first started noticing that house and the women in it. The older boys told him what was what: the women were whores; the dressy dude was their pimp, Big Slim. Slim was an old-style pimp—the red velvet trousers; the black leather boots, ankle high; the requisite Cadillac, and one not nearly as ancient as the ten-year-old wrecks by which other Press Park males signified that they had finally put something together in this world of tribulation and denial.

"He didn't live in the Press Park house. That was just where he was housing his women," Kyles came to realize. And the women didn't trick there either. That's what hotels were for: the big downtown hotels for conventioneers or, closer at hand, the "Oriental spas" and by-the-hour motor courts out along Chef Menteur Highway—before that thoroughfare gathered up its skirts, had done with such diversions, and made a flat-out run through the snake-filled swamps and on across the state line into Mississippi.

Kyles and his buddies decided to rob the house where the pimp kept his women. For the older ones, the thirteen- and fourteen- and fifteen-year-olds, it was more an act of penetration than of plunder. The concentration of so much feminine flesh, at once available yet entirely beyond their reach, was more inspiring than any material goods these women might possess. For Kyles it was a chance to be down with his brothers. He was the one tapped to pop the window, slip inside, and open a door for the others. Then he played lookout while they ransacked the place. It was a junior role in the partnership, but for his trouble he got a cut of the cash they found stashed here and there, and in a jewelry case tucked back of a shoebox in one of the closets, they found something else: a big old diamond ring. He got that too.

A few days later Kyles answered a knock on his aunt's door. If he had harbored any illusions that a pimp, being an outlaw, would not report his losses, these illusions were instantly dispelled. There stood Big Slim, not just threatening to turn Kyles in but, in fact, flanked by two cops. "That's when I realized the pimp had police power," Kyles said. Apparently, Kyles had left a fingerprint on the window he had pushed in. Police matched it with the set of prints they had taken from him when he was hauled down to juvenile detention for shooting pigeons.

There in the doorway, Big Slim struck a tone of sweet reason. "I understand the hustling game," he said, "but the ring I got to have." Kyles noticed that he was staring into the barrel of the pimp's revolver. "That this man threw down on me in front of the police, that's when I knew he was serious," Kyles would recall. The whole episode cured him of any real appetite for burglary. There were better hustles. Slim was living proof, and Kyles began tailing the man, trying to learn his secrets.

The pimp's portfolio was well diversified. "He had a pool hall, a barroom, and a little store, and by him seeing me following him, observing everything he was doing, he started letting me come in. Basically I was his little protégé, sitting back watching how he conducted himself. He'd look out for me, and if there was a package that needed to get picked up, he'd give me twenty-five, thirty dollars, and I'd just go get it." The packages, of course, contained contraband, heroin more often than not, and a tyke of twelve or thirteen was too young to draw much in the way of reprisal if the police caught up with him, which in Kyles's case they never did.

The cash was nice, but Kyles would also accept payment in kind. Along with the Ph.D. in street smarts that he earned just from hanging out with someone like Big Slim, Kyles kept himself in pool games and, before too long, women. The ones Big Slim looked after were crazy about the little boy with the smooth hands and the all-night hard-on, and Curtis was crazy about every last one of them who would give him a turn. Some of the lessons he learned from Big Slim were how not to do things. With women, Big Slim's technique was unsubtle. "He scared them into doing what he wanted." Kyles tried the opposite: "I always thought you should sweet-talk 'em." But other aspects of Slim's approach bore close study. "I always thought of myself as a ladies' man, all right? So I would observe this pimp and always wonder how he can maintain this many women, how he was able to fool them, you know, to go out there and sell their selfs and neglect their kids for him." Kyles's observations gelled in an informal taxonomy of sexual hustlers. From his experience, they came in three varieties mainly, four if you counted their acolytes. "See, you got wannabes, and then you got pimps. Just like you got a player and then you got a real gigolo. See, a player he just go out and fuck for nothing. But a gigolo, he gonna get some ends."

The ends—money—was also in pimping, but Kyles knew better than to compete with Slim. He would settle for being a player, with maybe a little gigolo thrown in for the women who wanted it that way. Kyles could always use the money, and opportunities were not lacking. Girls got into schoolyard fights over Curtis—hair-pulling, face-scratching, tit-jabbing fights, according to Brenda, who found her brother's magnetism somewhat mysterious. "As his sister, I just couldn't see what it could be about him, a skinny little something like he was then."

And then all of a sudden the family Lothario was in way over his head. A girl at Carver High was raped, right there in the schoolhouse, with kids passing in the corridor outside the storeroom where it happened, a knife at her throat to keep her quiet. A day later, when the principal got wind of it, he hauled her into his office and demanded her assailant's identity. Giving way to sobs, she moved her hands above her head in the outline of a bushy Afro. That was all the principal needed to put the finger on Kyles, a troublemaker and a wiseass from way back, with the biggest Afro in the schoolyard.

"I was one of the bad little kids always getting into trouble," Kyles recalled, "so the principal, when she described the big bush, automatically he thought it was me."

It happened to be Kyles's sixteenth birthday, a Friday, and it began cheerfully enough. Kyles cut school and accompanied his aunt to the hospital for one of her treatments. It was 1:30 in the afternoon by the time they got back, and Eva gave her nephew some money and told him to go buy something for himself. En route, Kyles ran into some regulars in the Bucktown Gang who made their own contribution to the birthday fund: a joint, Kyles's very first. Years later in prison, with some work still ahead of him in the businesss of learning to read and spell, Kyles would jot down his recollection of that inaugural high: "I smoked a whole joint that day and found out that peoples were giving me the wrong impression about how weed would blow your mind, all it did me was made me tide and hunger, along with making everything seem funny and the day went by in a beautiful and funny way."

To avoid the constraints of Eva's curfew, Kyles had talked her into letting him stay the night with his mother and his younger siblings over on Dorgenois Street, which is where the day became less beautiful and funny. It was a little after one a.m. when Kyles heard a knock at the door and, through the peephole, saw no fewer than five uniformed police officers.

The cops were cagey. They asked for Kyles's brother Larry. Not home, Kyles said. But then, worried that Larry might be in some kind of trouble, he slipped the chain and opened the door.

"So what's your name, boy?"

When he said Curtis, "Man, they just swarmed all over me."

Kyles had been in the lockup maybe three nights when police brought in the girl to ID her assailant. She made no bones about it. A different boy had raped her. Same do. Different dude.

They actually knew each other, she and Kyles—from the daily parade that streamed out of the Florida project and down Desire to Carver High, and it wouldn't be long before they knew each other quite a lot better.

In the darkness of the prison hole, Kyles thought of her now, the feel of her, the chewing-gum smell of her breath on his ear. God, what he wouldn't give to have some of that now, just to know she was beside him there on the hole's slab of a bed, a voice in the darkness, a landscape of warm flesh to lose himself in, like wandering the soy fields and creek bottoms he could dimly remember prowling as a little boy in Mississippi. He wrenched his mind away from such thoughts, as he had trained himself to do. Dwelling on the unattainable was crazy-making. He knew that. Better to stay focused on present circumstances. Because if he was honest with himself, they could be worse. And so to banish the girl from his mind, he made his thoughts roam coarser landscapes nearer to hand, and for no particular reason found himself thinking about an inmate who had followed him from parish prison to Angola, not someone he knew well enough even to know his real name.

Kyles had been in the yard in back of death row one morning during his shower hour, shooting hoops by himself, when he heard someone yelling from a line of inmates heading out into the fields. Yelling his name and waving at him, the voice barely audible in the distance. And two weeks later, that pathetic attempt to connect with someone the inmate barely knew had been followed up with another ritual of prison sociability: through the wire mesh of the yard fence, a second inmate from general population got a minute or two with Kyles and told him that the brother from New Orleans had asked after him. Rules forbade conversation of this sort, but if no rank was on hand, the guard grunts would let it go. The Orleans inmate was in the infirmary, Kyles learned, and might appreciate some smoke.

Sure. Kyles could spare a couple of cigarettes. He found an orderly willing to complete the transaction—in exchange, of course, for a smoke or two for himself—and in due course the requested cigarettes were coursing through the vast web of the Angola underground. The next day, the orderly, Jackson Renwick—"Action Jackson" to the inmates who knew him as purveyor of their food trays and towels and laundered clothes—checked back with Kyles. He had delivered the cigarettes. "But, man," he said, "I don't see how in the hell your boy be smoking cigarettes anytime soon."

Kyles looked at the orderly, waiting for him to go on, and Renwick described what he had seen: a full body cast, the inmate's arms suspended in slings, the white plaster sheathing uninterrupted from his neck to his thighs, except for the gaps cut away below the waist to allow for bodily discharge.

It had been a while before Kyles crossed paths with the man again. This time he had passed just outside the chain-link fence that defined Kyles's world and paused for a moment to briefly recap the ordeal.

His undoing had been his own temper, a fast-growing weed amply irrigated by a field sergeant's spit. Everyone knew the sergeant, or knew of him, a man whose habit and pleasure was to salivate liberally when he spoke and to speak so expressively and at such close range that the spit and phlegm were sure to fly in the prisoner's face. The inmate had put up with it for a moment, then stepped back out of the line of fire only to have the guard close in on him again. And when a comment from him did nothing to end the spritzing, he clocked the son of a bitch. A mounted guard fired a warning shot overhead, and the inmate dropped to the ground, as every prisoner knows to do under these circumstances. Instantly a passel of guards was upon him, and he was hog-tied and hauled to the hole. The guards broke one of his arms the first night and took turns whipping and stomping him, he told Kyles. The first arm was in a sling but not yet a cast when they came back the next night and broke the other one. There was no keeping track of the ribs as they shattered, now one, now another; now, with a particularly well-placed kick, maybe two or three at once.

Kyles imagined the sight of him, hanging from the ceiling in his full body cast like a ghost on a front porch at Halloween. He thought about him until he didn't want to think about him anymore or ever again. Kyles hadn't clocked a sergeant to earn his trip to the hole, but he was certain it was only a matter of time until the guards burst in on him with their stun sticks and their steel-toed boots and their meaty fists and began to beat him. For being black. For killing a white woman. For something to do. Judge Polozola might have ended the worst abuses, but guards still found plenty of room to work out their grudges, and not just in the active imagination of an inmate getting a little loopy in lockdown. Then suddenly—two days? three days?—into Kyles's stay in the hole, there they were. At the door. Not orderlies. Orderlies brought food or had some other reason to be there. Guards—idle, menacing. And now the man hollering his own name was Kyles, aware suddenly why others had done it. It was instinct, a pathetic last declaration that someone had passed this way. If he came up missing, maybe someone would have heard him and sensed what went on. It was an impulse as ancient as prisons themselves and the tradition of men notching a name or their initials in the wall as testament to an otherwise forgotten life. The guards told Kyles he was being taken to the infirmary for a checkup. Kyles, much too loud, still in the faint hope that someone would hear: "Infirmary? What for, man? I ain't going to no infirmary. I ain't hollered for nobody to come take me to no infirmary." And then the hole's door swung open, and Kyles was being bustled along windowless corridors, this way and that, and now into the harsh fluorescence of—of what? An interrogation room? A torture chamber? Kyles looked around him at the steel frame of an examining table and the glint of devices mounted on the wall, tubes and needles and dials. An infirmary after all. The checkup was routine at the end of a spell in the hole. Just to be sure, in due time, that a death row inmate would make a healthy corpse.

TEN

Not all the guards were antagonistic, Kyles found, and not all the free people who visited the row were guards. Kyles had not been at Angola very long when he encountered a strange woman named Helen Prejean—in no sense a relative of Dalton's and not yet delivered of *Dead Man Walking*, the book about an Angola inmate that would make her famous. Prejean was a white woman born to a comfortable family in a fashionable suburb of New Orleans. Improbably, she had become a nun, and like Saint Peter, she was a fisher of men, plying the deep waters of death row for those in need of spiritual reinforcement. She did this while also working as a liaison between the row and the community of lawyers, mostly based back in New Orleans, who fought the death penalty by helping these men with their appeals. Prejean had the approval of prison authorities to arrange meetings with inmates who might need guidance, be it spiritual or legal. And so there came a day when Kyles, more interested in the legal than the spiritual side of Sister Helen's ministry, found himself seated across from her in one of the camp's visitor booths. He found Prejean a bit eerie, to use his word, perhaps in part because she was so entirely immune to the chivalrous manner in which he clothed his curiosity about most any woman. If Angola was going to allow Kyles to spend time with one, did it have to be a woman so transcendently indifferent to the funky side of life? But Kyles welcomed the assistance she hoped to provide him. God knows he needed it.

In September 1987, almost exactly three years after the murder of Delores Dye, Kyles got word that his last recourse within the state appellate process had been exhausted. The state supreme court had rejected Martin Regan's arguments for a new trial as routinely as they had been filed. And a month later, when a request for a rehearing of the supreme court proceeding was likewise rejected, Regan stood ready to apologize one last time for his failure to spare Kyles the legal catastrophe that had engulfed him and to withdraw from the case for good. In subsequent years, Regan would overcome terrible personal tragedies, including incapacitating illness among his children and the death of their mother. As the proprietor of a successful firm, he would develop a penchant for mixing more routine defense cases with humanitarian legal work, in particular a massive and ultimately unsuccessful suit seeking to wrest billions from the New Orleans–based Freeport-McMoRan gold mining company on behalf of tribal Indonesians. But he would never overcome his anger at what he saw as dirty tactics by the men who prosecuted Kyles. Nor would he shake the guilty sense that he had failed his client. Over the years, he would cooperate readily with Kyles's new counselors, a role mainly limited to testifying to his own incompetence as a young and very green attorney.

To assist Kyles in finding a successor to Regan, Sister Helen put him in touch with a newly minted lawyer named Nick Trenticosta. Raised Catholic in the same New Orleans suburb as Prejean, Trenticosta also had found focus in the strain of radical activism that rocked young people in the 1960s and 1970s, churchgoers and secularists alike. Trenticosta had been a social worker around the New Orleans public housing projects and was moonlighting as manager of Tipitina's—an Uptown music and dance hall famous as the final home of the late piano legend Professor Longhair—when he decided that the next step beyond trying to connect the poor with competent legal assistance was to provide it himself. On the spur of the moment, during a drive back from Angola, where he had assisted a video crew making a documentary about death row, Trenticosta stopped in Baton Rouge and picked up an application packet for the LSU Law School. That was in January 1984. He enrolled the following September, the very month of the Schwegmann's murder. His ponytail and radical critique of the social and political establishment precluded a mainstream legal career and the riches that might eventually flow from it. Instead, Trenticosta had become involved with the Loyola Death Penalty Resource Center, a two-way transaction that, on one side, helped inmates with their often futile appeals and, on the other, gave law students and upstart staff lawyers hands-on experience in an area of practice many cared about passionately.

Kyles's first take on Trenticosta was skeptical. He had seen enough young crusaders by then to worry that for some of these kids, death penalty work was more a romance than a profession. And Trenticosta, not yet having tried his first case, was decidedly wet behind the ears. Worse still, Kyles figured him for a government man. The Resource Center operated with a public subsidy. That might make him at best a seat warmer, someone attached to the case just to draw a salary. Did it also mean he was cut from the same cloth as the police and Harry Connick's crew? "It was scary," Kyles said—the thought of entrusting himself to such a lawyer. Trenticosta explained that he would help steer Kyles through the appellate courts as his case manager, but they'd be looking for another, more seasoned attorney to actually argue the case. Kyles really had no choice but to try to get enthusiastic about Trenticosta. A wet-behind-the-ears lawyer was better than no lawyer at all, and with Regan no longer available, Kyles knew to take what help he could get—somebody, anybody, willing to shove a stick into the legal machinery now clicking smoothly into place as the state of Louisiana prepared to execute a convicted killer.

Justice seems to pivot on happenstance and coincidence, not less so than some of the crimes it is supposed to redress. If Mrs. Dye had not opted to break with routine and do her shopping on a Thursday instead of Friday, in all likelihood she would have lived to old age. Had Darlene Cahill left home a few minutes earlier or later, had she and her cousin Joni decided to stop for cigarettes and coffees after packing the baby into the car and heading into town, she would not have been available to Detective John Dillman to point an accusing finger at the man police had arrested for Mrs. Dye's murder. A young legal secretary named Sheryl Bey might have found her way to Curtis Kyles's assistance through some other sequence of contingencies, but it is just as possible that she would not, given her orientation toward civil law, the field in which she would make her career once she completed law school and escaped the secretarial pool. But on this particular February afternoon in 1988, as Bey left Loyola Law School and headed back downtown to her typewriter at Phelps Dunbar, her thoughts were on criminal procedure, the topic of the day's lecture by a professor she esteemed enough to have met with him for a few minutes after class. In fact, as she would recall years later from the vantage of a plush corporate law practice in Jackson, Mississippi, "I was feeling kind of charged about criminal law that day. God knows why."

Phelps Dunbar, one of the two or three most established white-shoe law firms in New Orleans, then occupied an elegant warren of offices some thirty stories above Poydras Street in the Texaco Building. The glistening black office tower was one in a row of monuments to petroleum that had sprung up along Poydras in the late 1970s as the machinations of the OPEC oil cartel and the soaring price of crude briefly gave New Orleans and other oil-patch cities the delusion of boundless, perhaps permanent prosperity. It was a kind of euphoria more familiar to Riyadh than to the gentry of a fading river port that, in fact, had reached its economic high-water mark in the 1850s. Before the Civil War took it all away, cotton and sugar fortunes had made New Orleans the richest city per capita in the United States. The 1970s reprise was not to last, as speculators behind the construction boom and the bankers who backed them discovered the hard way. In 1984, the year of Mrs. Dye's murder, the bottom fell out of the oil market, and the New Orleans economy toppled and sank like an offshore platform in a category 5 hurricane.

Old money survived the cataclysm, as old money generally does. The rich retired to their luncheon clubs to cluck over those less well insulated— the upstarts now bolting from New Orleans and dumping over-leveraged mansions on the market, with dismaying effect on local property values. Farther across town, the men with whom Curtis Kyles had once laid brick pondered ways, not all of them legal, to supplement their unemployment checks.

As Sheryl Bey returned from law school that afternoon and prepared to settle back into her secretarial duties at Phelps Dunbar, an intra-office memo happened to catch her eye: an appeal for volunteers within the firm willing to work pro bono on a death penalty appeal. Come one, come all. Louisiana provided a public defender for indigent men and women facing criminal prosecution, a kind of assistance Kyles had not had to accept, thanks to what his family scraped together and stuffed into the pillowcase they presented Martin Regan. But Louisiana did not see fit to provide death row inmates with continuing counsel once they had exhausted their options on direct appeal and their cases, like that of Kyles, moved on to what was called collateral review, in the federal courts. There, among other issues, the rules of proper procedure might be debated, perhaps even the constitutionality of the death penalty itself—arcane, philosophical considerations far removed from the hurly-burly of criminal court and the usual preoccupations of the defense lawyers who made a living there. This lack of competent appellate counsel in Louisiana was a problem, and in 1987, the year Kyles arrived at Angola to await execution, the federal courts had decided to do something about it. The upshot, the so-called Special Committee on Death Penalty Post-Conviction Representation, was devised by the state supreme court in collaboration with the federal Fifth Circuit Court of Appeals, which ruled over Louisiana, Texas, Mississippi, and Arkansas from an art deco mausoleum on Camp Street in New Orleans. It does not impugn the motives of either court to suggest that the Special Committee was born as much of frustration with criminal attorneys trying to master appellate work as of compassion for death row inmates. The courts had had it with the antics and energies— sometimes well-meaning, sometimes not—of criminal defense lawyers thrust into appellate work. Although shiny suits and theatrical flair are the signature traits of sometimes very talented criminal defense lawyers, the glare of even the shiniest suit most likely brings little illumination to the nuances of constitutional law that are the concern of the appeal courts. The inspiration of the Special Committee was to dragoon private firms into this arena. To make sure the burden was sustainable, the court stipulated that it would fall only on sizable firms, defined as those with twenty-five attorneys or more. The catch was that in New Orleans, as in most cities, big firms meant firms, Phelps Dunbar among them, that were better versed in corporate than in criminal law.

A petite woman of thirty-one, with black hair and big glasses, Sheryl Bey reread the memo. It was not as if she had time on her hands, what with the secretarial duties and her belated tilt at law school. She had become a mother as a teenager and, now married to an aspiring professor of anthropology, was beginning to think about adding to the family. But a death penalty case—that could be fascinating. A life at stake—perhaps not much of a life, but a life nonetheless. Bey could only wonder what it would be like to meet a killer. And who would her teammates be? There were some fine people at Phelps Dunbar, even if the pressures of the law didn't always showcase their most endearing personality traits. And then there were the outright creeps, men and women whose most venal instincts were laid bare by the pressures of their profession and the gnawing fear that a classy sheepskin on the wall and an overmortgaged house in the suburbs was no more than mediocrity's temporary disguise.

What the hell. Pumped by her meeting that afternoon with the professor of criminal procedure, Bey folded up the memorandum and resolved to sign on. It was not an impulse that swept the firm. Indeed, in the following week not one attorney, be he a well-heeled partner or struggling associate out to show the world, found room in a busy schedule for charity work on behalf of Curtis Kyles. It was time to lean on someone to lead the charge, and the someone that Phelps Dunbar found to lean on, one of the few partners with a smidgen of criminal defense work on his résumé, was an Uptown patrician with a good ol' boy's way about him named George Healy, Bunky to his friends. Healy was in his fifties, an affable, clubbable father of five with a taste for hunting and fishing and long lunches over good food. With unfeigned reluctance he agreed to take the case, assured that it would be an intermittent task of a few months' duration and that Sheryl Bey, the woman who would be working with him, could take dictation and retype a brief with the best of them.

If Curtis Kyles had been the millionaire owner of a jack-up rig damaged by a clumsy maintenance boat plying oil tracts out in the Gulf, he could not have done better than George W. Healy III. Indeed, though Bunky Healy's specialty was admiralty law—the law of the maritime world—Kyles could not have wished for better counsel on a range of corporate issues in which advantage accrues, as it often does, to an attorney who combines legal competence with an unstained pedigree and reliable social graces. In New Orleans in the 1980s, as for decades before, that meant a white male, a resident of one of the leafy streets in some proximity to Audubon Park, a graduate of Tulane University and, in Healy's case, of the Tulane Law School as well. A law degree from Harvard or Virginia would not have been held against him, provided the prodigal returned directly from this broadening exposure and did not bring strange views back with him. For Healy, the time away had fallen between college and law school, and it had taken him to war in Korea with the navy. He had been a New Orleanian ever since, the son of the editor in chief of *The Times-Picayune*, the city's newspaper, whose publisher in those days, Ashton Phelps Sr., was by inheritance the Phelps of Phelps Dunbar.

But if your dilemma was a murder conviction and a date with the electric chair was staring you in the face, you might have had second thoughts about Bunky Healy, however grateful that a man accustomed to high fees was working for you for free. Because not only was murder well outside the range of his specialties, but Healy had a secret, known neither to Curtis Kyles nor to many of Healy's colleagues. It was not just that he was a proponent of the death penalty, with no faith whatsoever in the claim of innocence maintained by his unsolicited client. It was that, having inadvertently frustrated the public's lust to take the life of a killer the last time he handled a case like this, Healy felt he owed one to the people of Louisiana, and the simple and obvious way to repay that debt, Healy had decided, was to deliver Curtis Kyles to the executioner "on a silver platter."

Healy's sense of obligation, he would confide toward the end of his career, had been incurred some ten years before he took on the Kyles case—a pro bono venture into criminal law on behalf of another indigent defendant, also a black man, whose victim was a white woman, albeit a white woman decades younger than Mrs. Dye and not of her ilk at all. Healy's client in the earlier case had been obliging enough to lead police to his victim's corpse, in a Dumpster out back of a fried-chicken joint—Jim Dandy's fried-chicken joint, to be exact—at the seedy downtown end of New Orleans's grand residential boulevard, St. Charles Avenue. And the man's spirit of cooperativeness had not ended there. He also confessed. Twice. And he signed both statements as beaming cops looked on.

He had boasted to his girlfriend—who described him as a sex maniac—about the particular pleasure he felt watching the white girl die. But—and this was the gist of his defense—when it came to the actual snuffing, the honors had gone to a buddy of his, not that it made much difference in the eyes of the law.

Healy would have been forgiven for undertaking a perfunctory defense, and that's exactly what he provided. But even a perfunctory defense could not avoid the possibility that his client was not quite right in the head. And so Healy hired a psychiatrist to explore the issue, and that's where he got more than he bargained for. The psychiatrist turned out to be something of a sophist. The clearest evidence that the man could not be held accountable for the death of the girl in the Dumpster was that he had owned up so freely—and so often—to putting her there. Both confessions were suppressed, and Healy's client was found not guilty by reason of insanity, a courtroom victory that was less a source of pride than an embarrassment to a hard-line conservative like Healy. On a fluke, a guilty man had gone free. Now Kyles was Healy's chance for atonement.

A review of the trial record and of the state supreme court opinion denying Kyles's appeal gave Healy no reason to think he would disappoint the state a second time. Due process demanded that Kyles have his shot at higher levels of appeal, but it was an open-and-shut case if ever there was one. Healy had no doubt that his client was, in his words, "guilty as sin." That much seemed clear. The procedural details, for both Sheryl Bey and Bunky Healy, were going to be a matter of learning by doing, and they were not above asking for help. One source of it, they were told, was a nonprofit organization called the Capital Defense Fund, an advocacy group supporting appeals by death row inmates in Georgia and Alabama. The CDF people agreed to sit down with the pro bono team from Phelps Dunbar. The case might last more than a few months of off-and-on effort, they cautioned. Maybe as much as a year, but that was the outer limit. Bey and Healy came away with the sense that their entanglement with Curtis Kyles would probably be of about six months' duration, an expectation that Healy would remember bemusedly some six years later as he prepared to fly to Washington as part of a larger team arguing for Kyles's life before the highest court in the land.

As a first step down a road longer than they knew, Healy and Bey interviewed people associated with the case: Kyles's sister Lela, Martin Regan. They also were put in touch with the Loyola Death Penalty Resource

Center, the local analogue to the CDF, where Nick Trenticosta had begun handling the basic paperwork of the Kyles case while waiting for a pro bono big shot like Healy to come forward and take charge of the final appeals. Now it was time to meet the client himself.

That Healy, an attorney since he was a young man, had never before set foot in the state penitentiary at Angola was one measure of the divide between criminal and civil procedure. He and Sheryl Bey went together that first time, along with a young woman from the Capital Defense Fund as their escort into a land far from the luncheon clubs and downtown towers where Healy was accustomed to doing business. Angola's death row would later be moved closer to the main administrative office, not far from the prison gates, but in those days it was still deep within the eighteen-thousand-acre penitentiary. Once there, Healy and Bey reported to the camp office, as required. One gate led to another, which opened onto a fenced walkway leading to another set of gates, three of them this time. Each had to click shut before the next could be opened. Death row was the last in a series of cellblocks. The visiting station was an antiseptic metal box in which the prisoner confronted his guests through metal mesh, both sides of it appointed with metal coffee cans half full of sand for the smokers. And there was a lot of smoking.

On the long drive upriver from New Orleans, Healy had been prey to anxieties, well concealed behind his shambling gait and raconteur's drawl. Admiralty law was not without its buccaneers and cutthroats, but there was no provision in its penal codes leading to the extremity in which a man like Kyles now found himself. Healy had to wonder if he could be entirely safe in the company of someone with nothing left to lose but his life. These concerns, ridiculous to Healy in hindsight, dissipated on first encounter with the inmate, his feet shackled, his hands cuffed and bound to a chain around his belly. A new, more realistic concern now supplanted Healy's fears for his physical safety: that Kyles would scoff at him because of his dearth of experience with capital cases, perhaps more emphatically because, as an envoy from the upper reaches of New Orleans society, he might epitomize everything a black man like Kyles had learned to hate and envy.

That concern was not groundless, but it would be a mistake to suppose that Healy and Kyles, a bourgeois white and a working-class black, would necessarily be oil and water. The reality was that their respective social strata were too entwined in a place like New Orleans not to have struck an accommodation of sorts over the generations. Middle-class blacks, with their cheeky ambitions and disrespect for the old social verities, were the wild card at that juncture in an evolving racial history—a source of dismay and lamentation at both ends of the social spectrum, and most especially among middle-class whites, whose incomes and some of whose privileges the upstarts not only coveted but stood soon to usurp. But Healy and Kyles, in their way, were familiar with each other and others of their kind—as master and servant, as boss man and laborer, as home-owner and yardman, as toddler and nanny. Not that there was no chance of tension or hostility. A man of Healy's breeding would have seen it in a maid's sullenness or a laborer's muttered curses, an attitude problem that could surely bedevil an attempt to build lawyer/client rapport. Here again, any such fears proved unfounded. Kyles was almost courtly in his etiquette toward the strangers now beholding him. Full disclosure required Healy to confess that admiralty law had better acquainted him with ship-ping magnates than with murder convicts. Kyles could appreciate the self-effacing modesty of that statement while also regretting the truth be-hind it: that the white man's system of justice had evidently been afflicted with a twinge of guilt over what had happened to him, if not quite enough of a twinge to actually get him a lawyer who really knew criminal law. The visit lasted about an hour, time enough to go over the facts of the case, and Kyles was able to steer Healy and Bey toward some of the documentation they would need to review. Kyles let on that as Regan faded out of the picture, he had taken it on himself to petition the court for paperwork he thought pertinent to his case. This was worrisome to Bey and Healy. They asked him not to do so again without first consulting them. In exchange, Bey promised Kyles that she would forward him copies of everything they dug up. They left Angola that first time sharing a sense of relief—not just because the gates were in their rearview mirror but be-cause things seemed to have gone reasonably well with the penniless killer now on Phelps Dunbar's client list.

Was he guilty? Did he do it? The issue hadn't come up during the long drive home, silence on the subject attesting partly to its irrelevance in ap-pellate work. A presumption of innocence may be the bedrock of American jurisprudence—and it does not necessarily expire when a jury renders its verdict—but at the appellate level, the processes of justice are of equal or even greater concern than their outcome. An appeal lawyer's focus, only more so when the lawyer is working for free, is the law itself and the community of professionals who share faith in it. In a capital case, the role of the appeal lawyers is to examine the mechanics of law that have driven a case thus far, checking for points of abrasion or possible malfunction—ratcheting this, oiling that—before the engines are gunned a final time and the condemned is carried up over the horizon line and into the great beyond. As far as Healy was concerned, in convicting Kyles, the people had spoken, and from what he could tell, they had spoken clearly and well. Bey was of less conservative inclination, still alive to the drama of injustice undone by doughty legal idealists. But even she had not been able to shake the suspicion that she was looking into the dark, somewhat shifty eyes, if not of the triggerman, then almost certainly of someone in some way involved in Mrs. Dye's demise. There was just an awful lot of evidence tying him to the crime, she thought, and the defense argument had seemed desperate and scarcely provable: that a romantic rival, now dead, had somehow planted that evidence and manipulated the police. Bey would never fully shake her doubts. Ironically, Healy, the death penalty advocate, would reach a different view of Kyles, though it would take him a while to get there.

Bey and Healy's approach to the task was the mark of their inexperience in criminal defense work. Civil lawyers build cases at a leisurely pace that allows for exhaustive, some would say spectacularly fussy, attention to the facts. A well-prepared civil lawyer handling a product liability case involving, say, a fire-prone electric blanket, will know almost as much about the device—the fabrics and insulators involved, the conductivity of the elements used to carry electricity—as the engineers who designed and manufactured it. The devil is in the details, as the saying goes, but so too, happily, are the billable hours it takes to master them. Criminal defense work is necessarily more selective, elliptical, and discretionary in its relationship to fact. For one thing, there isn't the luxury of time. For another, there are limits—usually sharp limits in the case of violent crime, the preponderance of which is committed by indigent defendants—on the amount of money available to the defense. But as it turned out, the habits of civil law would well serve Bey and Healy as they set about un-packing the Kyles case and putting it back together again.

The summer of 1988 fell into a productive rhythm. More interviews with Kyles led to one with Johnny Burnes, by then housed in a state prison near Bogalusa. Bey and Healy also contacted a lengthening roster of family and associates they were counting on for insight into the tangle of lives—Pinkey, Beanie, Curtis, Johnny—from which Mrs. Dye, a complete stranger, had been subtracted. Pinkey was the conundrum. She had moved on, and yet she hadn't. She had taken up with Tyrone Joseph fully and quickly enough to have named Kyles's fifth child—born a few months after his conviction—Tyra, in Tyrone's honor. And she had gone on to have a sixth child, a daughter named Jean, with her new man. And yet, from a sprawling subsidized apartment in the Desire housing project, she still maintained a modicum of financial independence by taking in other single mothers trying to get by on welfare, as she was, and she spoke of one day reuniting with Curtis. Or was that just the chatter of a woman indulging his lawyers with speculation on a scenario that she could confidently assume would never be fulfilled?

And then Bey and Healy were slapped in the face with a reminder that in one crucial particular, criminal law is not at all like civil procedure. At summer's end, a bland-looking letter conveyed word that Judge Waldron had set a date for Kyles's execution: November 7, less than two months away.

Death was never not present on death row. It was a ubiquity, like the buzz of a fluorescent tube. Like the tube's buzz, it could be tuned out some of the time, even a lot of the time, only to surge back into consciousness. Kyles had been on the row not long at all when he heard the screaming and the blubbering and the scuffling feet of the guards forcibly carrying Leslie Lowenfeld, the very inmate whose cell he occupied, to the chair. No one wanted it to go like that, not the executioner, not the inmate—least of all the inmate—not even the guards. Almost as much as you hoped for a reprieve, you hoped to go with dignity, Kyles felt, and you didn't know until the end which way it would be for you. Now it looked like he was going to find out.

One of the torments of prison life, of course, was the boredom. A corollary unpleasantness is that time passed so slowly it seemed to be moving backward. An interminable four years behind bars, counting both the parish prison and now Angola, had turned Kyles into an old man among boys the age he was when Mrs. Dye was murdered. And now, at twenty-nine, on the verge of becoming a youthful part of Angola's middle-aged population, he seemed to be looking at the end of his days. Suddenly prison time was no longer a sluggish bayou; it was rapids. Kyles would remember the onrushing execution date like this: "Your mind be running all different directions. You don't want to go to sleep, because when you wake up, the next day will be here. And within seventy-two hours of your date, the sun starts to rise and set in the same hour." To shut his eyes was to see Lowenfeld writhing against the guards grasping his limbs. To open them was to see the metal bars that trapped him, like a hog ready for slaughter at the farm up in Bassfield. Panic made his imagination perfervid, and he began to fantasize about hurling himself bodily against those bars, shattering his skull and rib cage so as to force them through, then somehow making a run at the guard station. On a television movie one afternoon he had seen a cop grab a bad guy by the Adam's apple and twist it once. Instant death. In the dark of his cell that night, Kyles fingered his own throat, probing for a grip he could use on any guard who tried to stop him. So what if he failed? A bullet to the brain was preferable to Lowenfeld's terminal thrashing. Quicker, more manly. "I was thinking about all the dirty tactics I know," Kyles would recall. "I reflected back on animals, how they fight to survive, and I said to myself, Just let the animal out, the animal in you. Just tear up out of here, Curtis. Just tear up out of here and make them shoot you."

Back in New Orleans, Bey and Healy hunkered down with a criminal defense specialist from Loyola Law School, a professor named Gerard Rault, and under his tutelage began frantically trying to pull together the paperwork to petition the state supreme court for a stay. Bey remembered the division of labor: "Bunky was the leader. I was the Trojan, and the Loyola Death Penalty Resource Center would provide us with old briefs that I would pull the law out of." Bey, still a secretary, also had the less glamorous task of handling the phones and doing the typing, while the three of them—Bey, Healy, and Rault—took turns dictating the substance of the petition. By midnight Bey would be exhausted to the point of tears. "That's how I handled things," she said, reflecting on her inaugural and, she assumed, final death penalty case. "I talked through tears and wrote through tears and typed through tears and researched through tears."

Within days of the execution date Kyles was moved from his usual cell, number 8, to the number 2 cell, the one most convenient to the tier's exit. He began to sense other inmates avoiding him, as if they could smell death on him and feared infection. "You might have your cup on the bars and want to ask them for some water, but they just move past the cell real quick." In place of the more accustomed camaraderie now denied him, Kyles found himself the focus of evangelists from within the prison's general population, groups of two and three and four with permission to minister to a man about to die. "They don't have the right words to say, because no one knows what to say to a condemned person," Kyles discovered, but he was patient with them and tried earnestly to lose himself to their Sunday school visions of penitence and forgiveness. It didn't work. "You can't block out reality." At least Kyles couldn't. "Reality is the clock ticking."

In its final stages, the anxiety was fully palpable. "I don't know if you ever bumped your nuts or anything, but the pain just caves in your heart, and you get this hard thumping in your head. You want to cry, but you can't. You want to break down like a little kid, but at the same time you're trying to hold on to some type of dignity. That's what I was taught. I kept trying to tell myself, Curtis stay strong. You're not going to go out like no pussy." Finally Kyles let down his guard and turned to another inmate down the row, a risky proposition in the macho world of the tiers, even if that inmate was the genial and pint-size Dalton Prejean. Kyles confessed his fears, his doubts about the competency of his lawyers, his dread. Prejean looked quizzically at Kyles and then burst out laughing. Kyles felt a flash of hatred for his confessor that verged on violence, then settled back into himself on the assumption that Prejean had finally cracked up. But no, Prejean had simply seen it all before, many times in his eight years on the row. "Man," he began, "you don't have the slightest idea what you're talking about. Y'all get two stays before any of this amounts to shit, and you haven't had one. You get two stays, man. Then they kill you."

About thirty-six hours before Kyles was set to be burned in the state's electric chair, the stay came through—as Dalton Prejean knew it would—and Sheryl Bey burst into tears once again. Word of the stay, by phone from Healy, melted Kyles like a hot bath. He wallowed in his sense of relief, felt sphincters loosen and blood flow to extremities he had forgotten he owned. And then, like a man who has dozed off in the tub and snapped out of it to find himself shivering in tepid water, he was wrenched wide-awake. A stay meant only this: another countdown had begun, and the hands of the clock already were starting to spin.

ELEVEN

November 18, 1988. It would have been a memorable day in the life of Sheryl Bey even if it hadn't marked a turning point in the Kyles case. November 18 was the day she was scheduled to take the ethics portion of the Louisiana bar exam, at noon. And so Bey stayed home that morning, cramming in a last few hours of review, trying to make up study time lost to the manic effort to spare Kyles his date with the executioner eleven days earlier. She was almost out the door when the phone rang. It was Healy. After much to-and-fro with the district attorney's office, Jack Peebles, a former first assistant now handling appeals for Harry Connick, had agreed to make the Kyles file available. At three o'clock that very afternoon. Healy told Bey she'd better be there.

By now Bey was well and truly hooked on the Kyles case. That first brush with the executioner had had a powerful bonding effect on lawyer and client, and not on Bey alone. Whether Healy realized it or not, Bey could tell that he too, her fatherly partner, was warming to the young man from so far to the other side of the tracks that some of their time together was spent learning his language and customs—the difference between plaits and braids, for example, or between a bush and a curl. The ironies amused Bey. Here was Healy, the gravel-voiced death penalty proponent, beginning to toy with the possibility that his client was not only ill served by the processes of law but possibly innocent of the crime for which he had been sentenced to die. She could see it in the time Healy was allotting to a case that not only stood to pay him nothing but was costing him the generous fees he could be earning from other clients, as the firm would soon begin gently, and then not so gently, to remind him. And here was Bey, at some deep level offended by the death penalty itself, and yet—though she was inclined to keep this to herself—still torn by the possibility that if anyone deserved the ultimate sanction provided for in Louisiana law, it might well be Curtis Kyles.

She had whipped through the two-hour ethics exam in what felt like twenty-five minutes and—more prayerful than confident that she had passed—jumped into her car and shot over to the four-story fortress of glass and whitewashed concrete that was the domain of Harry Connick and his assistants.

There were still some snags. Peebles wouldn't let Bey look at the grand jury testimony that had preceded Kyles's indictment four years earlier. Grand jury testimony was a separate matter, and the proceedings were sealed. But in other respects Bey found her adversary forthright, gallant even, if not quite as soigné as the singing DA for whom he worked. A well-fed Texan who had found his way to the prosecutor's office via Tulane Law and a stint in civil practice, Peebles provided Bey with a bowl of popcorn as she spread out the files on the office floor and settled down cross-legged to the task of picking through the case against Kyles. There was no reason to expect surprises. Bey found herself browsing desultorily in the stack of documents, transcripts, affidavits, arrest reports, and the like, setting each page aside as soon as she got the gist of it. Peebles had said she could copy what she wanted.

Now and again she'd come across something perplexing, a list of license plates, for example, evidently copied from cars that were parked in the Schwegmann's lot as the supermarket closed for the night that fateful Thursday. She didn't remember any testimony about a list of license plates. But then she remembered Kyles's car, the effort by Strider and Williams, late in their presentation, to insist that it had been present in the parking lot, the huge photo blowup they had propped up on a courtroom easel purporting to prove it, though the photo showed little more than a patch of the vinyl roof a few cars away from where the photographer was standing. Presumably Kyles's license plate was on the list. Bey set it aside for copying.

But what was this? One batch of documents was readily identifiable as statements police had taken from witnesses and persons of interest—Isaac Smallwood, Bobby Territo, Henry Williams, Pinkey Burnes, the whole lot of them. As best Bey could remember, Regan had routinely asked for this type of material before the trial began, only to be told that it did not exist, had never been transcribed. This would bear close inspection, though Bey could presume that most of what she'd find would match the testimony these same people gave on the stand.

In one envelope she found a cassette tape—no accompanying transcription, not even a label that meant anything to her, just a tape. She hadn't thought to bring a cassette player. Maybe Peebles would be so kind? He dug one up for her, a cheap, stripped-down model with no headset, but it worked. Peebles lumbered off, and when he was far enough away to have restored her privacy, Bey slid in the cassette and hit the PLAY button. Traffic sounds. Static. Men's voices, but for the first few inches of tape the background din made them unintelligible. Now she could pick out words. "You don't have to put them in a bag; we'll take them like that . . . let's go across the street."

Coffees to go?

The accent was that of a white man, working-class. From the boom of his voice Bey guessed that he was wired, a microphone concealed under his shirt. Which probably meant he was a cop, a detective. But who was he with? A man—a black man, to judge from the accent. But who? "He's supposed to be bringing me some papers."

WHITE MAN: Who?
BLACK MAN: For the car, dude. He's going to get the papers changed into my name. That's what he supposed to be doing. He didn't get them to me yet.
WHITE: What's his name?
BLACK: His name Curtis. See, his mother-in-law . . . I stay with his mother-in-law, right?
WHITE: Okay.

BLACK: 'Cause I'm his brother-in-law's partner and so they took me in. And by them taking me in, I don't know why he's sold me the car, but I went with him yesterday, though, in the parking lot, at Schwegmann's . . .

Bey dived for the volume control, amazed by what she was hearing, eager that Peebles not know what she had turned up. The black man was BeanieWallace. It had to be, no doubt in an early encounter with his handler on the police force.That would be Johnny Miller, the detective. How was it possible that they had never been told about this tape?

As blandly as she was able, Bey asked Peebles if she could make a copy so as not to waste time on it now. Again Peebles obliged. Before the afternoon was over, Bey had worked through the rest of the file methodically, conscientiously. But by then she was a picky eater, staring down vegetables, waiting for dessert. Once home, Bey threw everything else aside, left her husband and son to fend for themselves, and tore into the tape. The weekend was upon her, and by Bey's estimate, she played portions of the cassette more than a hundred times over the next forty-eight hours, sleeplessly trying to tease a clear transcript from the muffled exchanges, the bursts of static, the honking traffic. By Sunday night she settled for what she had: twenty-six typed pages, the conversational backdrop to a nighttime drive around some of New Orleans's rougher neighborhoods, a couple of cops working a snitch named Joseph "Beanie" Wallace.

Detective Johnny Miller, as he would later elaborate under questioning by Healy, had connected with the informant at about 10:30 on the Saturday night after Mrs. Dye was killed. And for a while they sat on a stoop along Claiborne Avenue, one of the city's grand thoroughfares, or at least it had been before the forces of progress roofed it with an elevated stretch of Interstate 10. What had been the city's most vibrant and storied Creole neighborhood was now a blighted district of abandoned shotgun houses, closed theaters, upstart nightclubs, and chain convenience marts like the one across the street where Miller and Beanie—Sergeant James Eaton would join them in a bit—picked up their coffees to go.

Beanie was in pale green surgical scrubs, as Miller would recall, with his hair in a plastic shower cap while a chemical process, a Jheri Curl, set in. Beanie's story went like this: The night before—Friday night, some thirty hours after the Dye murder—Kyles had phoned Wallace to see if he might be interested in buying a car, a red Ford LTD: $400. When Wallace showed up at the Desire Street apartment, Pinkey directed him to an intersection a couple of blocks away, the turnaround where the Desire Street bus reached the end of the line and, after roosting for a while in the billows of its own idling exhaust, lurched forward and headed back downtown. Sure enough, there was Kyles with the red car.

Kyles with the car, trying to fob it off on Beanie? Bey hoped she was hearing lies. But if the whole yarn was a fabrication, some of it was well thought out. Wallace even had an elaborate backstory to explain Kyles's willingness to unload a car on the cheap. His rationale for dumping the car was that he bought it for Pinkey, only to have a falling-out with her, and now he'd be goddamned if she was going to have her own car. Take it, man, he told Wallace, and I'll bring you the papers tomorrow—or so went the informant's story.

Celebrating the purchase he'd been suckered into, Wallace and a buddy then picked up some women and headed downtown, whooping and hollering and guzzling Friday night beer at the wheel of a big red Ford LTD, unaware that it was also red-hot. "That is what pissed me off," Wallace told Miller, establishing a motive for his own act of treachery in ratting out Kyles. "We could have got busted." And of course there was another consideration: Wallace wanted his $400 back. By then Sergeant Eaton had joined them: "You're not going to lose your $400, I guarantee you that," he reassured the informant as Wallace led them first to the car, then to Desire Street, where he pointed out Kyles's residence, and finally to the Schwegmann's parking lot, just to ease Eaton's concern that everybody was talking about the same Schwegmann's, the same murder.

Like photographic film in the developing soup, the significance of some of what Bey was hearing would take time—months, even years—to come clear. But certain exchanges strongly suggested that maybe Martin Regan had been onto something with his theory—a notably unsuccessful theory—that Beanie had more than fingered Kyles: he had framed him, and maybe even murdered Mrs. Dye.

For one thing, on tape Beanie seemed to be saying that the night after the murder, Kyles had fished Mrs. Dye's handbag out of the parking lot shrubbery. But hadn't her bag been locked inaccessibly in the trunk of her car—indeed, hadn't she been killed for failing to hand it over? Bey rolled the tape back a few inches and tried again to make out the words as Beanie walked the detectives over to the shrubbery.

JOHNNY MILLER: Right about here? Huh? What's that?

A traffic sound, perhaps the roar of a truck accelerating behind the Schwegmann's lot, had drowned out the banter between Eaton and Beanie, and Miller wanted in on a joke that had left Eaton chuckling.

MILLER: What's that?
EATON: He said his garbage goes out tomorrow. I said, if he's smart, he'll put it in the garbage. He said he ain't that smart.

Maybe it was nothing more than that, a joke. But Bey could not help remembering that Mrs. Dye's handbag and identification papers had indeed been recovered from a garbage bag on the curb in front of Kyles's house, a day after this conversation and not many hours after Beanie dropped in on the Sunday night soirée.

And then, after Johnny Miller wanted to know whether Kyles generally carried a gun, there was this exchange:

BEANIE: He got a .38 and he got a .32.
MILLER: Where's he keep 'em at?
BEANIE: He keeps one on him at all times. See that's why I say, if you can set him up good, you can get that same gun.
MILLER: You'd help me?
BEANIE: Fucking right, if you'd get my money back.

Twenty-four hours later, unless he was lying about it on the stand, Johnny Burnes had seen Beanie squat down beside the stove in Kyles's kitchen, and the next morning the Dye murder weapon was found right there. Was Beanie delivering on his suggestion that they "set him up good," or had Burnes invented the memory to deflect attention from the father of his sister's kids?

Bey was thunderstruck. Maybe this wasn't just a snitch ratting out a suspect to collect a reward. This could be a snitch orchestrating the whole probe: telling cops not only what the evidence might be, but where to find it. And in the case of Sunday night's garbage, it hadn't even been put out yet. Might that not also explain the mysterious delay between the fingering of Kyles late Saturday night and his arrest on Monday morning, thirty-six hours later? Police would contend that they held back out of concern for the safety of Pinkey and of Kyles's many children in what might have become a violent takedown. Skepticism about that explanation would eventually give way to scorn among Kyles's lawyers. When were police ever so conscientious? With a murder suspect in their sights, why didn't they begin a round-the-clock vigil and nab Kyles on Sunday as he went about his business, frequently leaving the Desire Street place unaccompanied by Pinkey, the children, or anyone at all?

The tape proved nothing. But that didn't matter. What mattered was that it might engender reasonable doubt. No wonder the police did not come forward with it during the trial's discovery phase four years earlier. Bey caught herself: Did they deliberately suppress evidence of a frame-up concocted by police and an informer? That was a pretty drastic accusation to level at officers of the law. Maybe the failure to disclose was inadvertent. Maybe the cops really did feel hamstrung by the lack of typists they had complained of at the time of the first trial. But still, evidence was evidence, and this was a powerful find. Maybe even grounds for a new trial. And having heard the tape, what jury wouldn't contain at least a couple of members plagued by the possibility that the condemned man was not guilty?

The witnesses' statements to the police also proved intriguing, if not in ways as startling as the tape. At first blush the witnesses were consistent. Every one of them described the killer—the man in the getaway car—as young and black. But the police had never let on how much they varied on the details. Did he have an Afro or braids? Like most of the witnesses, Bobby Territo had described braids—"reggae braids," he called them, adding that the car had passed so close to his that, were he not sinking down into his seat in terror, "I could have reached out and grabbed his hair without stretching." But on tape Beanie mentions Kyles's trademark "bush." Plaits and an Afro weren't the same hairstyle, not even close, as Kyles had patiently explained to Healy. The witnesses could be forgiven their deviations from one another. They were doing their best to recall details noted under conditions of stress and dread. But what was Sheryl Bey to make of Detective John Dillman? From the stand, he had described the range of variation in the witnesses' descriptions of the killer as inconsequentially narrow: a little more than three inches' difference in height, a few years' difference in age. But here was Henry Williams describing a short, stocky man, five four, maybe five five, and close to 150 pounds, while Kyles was razor thin, a 125-pounder just shy of six feet tall, according to the police who arrested him. Dillman had to have known that. He took down some of these statements.

Handwritten notes of a conversation that lead prosecutor Cliff Strider had with Beanie were only more suggestive of manipulation, especially if compared to the tape transcript. The notes had to be Strider's heart-to-heart with the informant after he called him in and rethought his strategies following the abortive first trial. You had to hand it to Beanie. He knew how to deliver, with or without Johnny Miller there to prompt him. The night of that first encounter, the night Wallace met up with Miller and Eaton, he sang like a canary without once mentioning Kevin Black as he led the detectives to the car, to Kyles's house, and to the Schwegmann's lot. Not once. Johnny Burnes, yes. Pinkey, sure. Kyles, of course. But no Kevin Black, the most effective of the defense witnesses— the one who claimed to have seen Wallace in Mrs. Dye's car immediately after the murder, when Beanie offered to sell him the LTD for $200.

That Black had proved an effective witness in the first trial was clear from the pains Cliff Strider and Jim Williams took to disarm him in the second, with their empty threat of prosecution. It was clear from the notes that Strider had quizzed Wallace about Black, asking questions that seemed to have worked on the informant like a cue card. Altogether absent from Wallace's earlier account, in the evolving updates Kevin Black was now strapped into the story of the car like a crash-test dummy. Where was the

Ford hidden the first time Beanie saw it? At the Desire Street bus terminus, as Beanie told Miller and Eaton? No. In Strider's notes from his conversation with Beanie, the car was now stashed at Kevin Black's. Who helped carry the groceries up into Kyles's kitchen? Kevin Black. And when it came time to fetch Kyles's car from the Schwegmann's lot, who was added to the passenger list of those who drove Kyles over to get it? Kevin Black.

To look back over the transcript of that second trial was to understand how useful Wallace's adaptable memory had been. If any of his accounts were true, then some of them were lies, and prosecutors should have known better than to hang their case on him. Instead, Williams and Strider seemed almost to draw inspiration from Wallace's inventions. Bey leafed through the transcript of the second trial until she came to Kevin Black's cross-examination. The prosecutors had shoved Wallace's story right down his throat.

> STRIDER: Isn't it true that between 2:15 and quarter to three [Kyles] came by your house and dropped off that red car?
>
> BLACK: No, sir.
>
> STRIDER: Isn't it true that he asked you to give him a ride to his house, which you did?
>
> BLACK: No, sir.
>
> STRIDER: In your car?
>
> BLACK: No, sir.
>
> STRIDER: Isn't it true that after you gave him a ride to his house, he, Curtis Kyles, called Johnny Burnes on the phone?
>
> BLACK: No, sir.
>
> STRIDER: . . . You got in the backseat of Johnny Burnes's car, Mr. Wallace got in the backseat of Johnny Burnes's car, Johnny Burnes got in the driver's seat, and Curtis Kyles got in the passenger seat, and all four of you drove to Schwegmann's parking lot?
>
> BLACK: No, sir.
>
> STRIDER: . . . and got Curtis Kyles's car, which was already parked there . . . ?
>
> BLACK: No, sir.

STRIDER: Sir, could I remind you that there's a law in this state and it's called perjury.

Regan had objected. Regan was sustained, and jurors were advised to disregard the whole exchange. But the damage was done, the scenario planted in their minds. And for that, Strider had Beanie to thank.

Wired as much on sheer excitement as on her morning coffee, Sheryl Bey bustled through the doors at Phelps Dunbar that Monday in her crisp size-four business suit and went straight to Healy to tell him what she had found. Healy was not a man given to hyperbole or hysteria, but in the deepening concentration he brought to reading the tape transcript, and in the arch of an eyebrow as he quizzed her about what else was in the file, Bey realized that she was not alone in the belief that the new material could turn the case on its ear. Whatever their personal views about Kyles, they had stumbled on a treasure trove, an appellate lawyer's El Dorado, and it was now a professional priority of the highest order to make the most of the disturbing new material. It might not prove Kyles innocent, but it did strongly suggest that evidence had been suppressed and manipulated in ways that cost him a fair trial. The case might be pro bono, but the stakes were now much higher; professional reputations were on the line.

Immediately Healy and Bey set themselves to the considerable task of integrating the new material into pleadings seeking to avert Kyles's second date with the executioner, in the spring of the coming year. One merely technical detail could be attended to quickly: a check of the list of license plates from the Schwegmann's parking lot to make certain Kyles's vehicle was among them. Curiously, it was not.

No wonder prosecutors had ignored the work of a couple of police officers who routinely jotted down crime-scene license plate numbers. If Kyles's plates weren't on their list, that was hard to square with Wallace's claim that after killing Mrs. Dye, the defendant had taken off in her car, leaving his behind because it wouldn't start—a claim Wallace had embellished by saying that Kyles had asked for a ride back over to the parking lot the next night to pick it up. It also undercut the prosecution's claim that Kyles's car was visible, if just barely, in their blown-up photo of the parking lot shot within an hour or two of the murder.

The lack of clerical support from Phelps Dunbar for the pro bono team was symptomatic of a deeper tension within the firm. Here were Bey and Healy with a man's life in their hands, yet Bey was forced to double as the team's typist. "Phelps Dunbar never permitted us to make a full-time commitment to the Kyles case—ever," she would recall. For Bey that meant carrying a sixty-hour workload for paying clients, plus law school at night and squeezing in the Kyles case after hours and on weekends. The work was pro bono, but she and Healy opened a file on the case anyway to keep track of the time they devoted to it. Uncollected attorney fees exceeded $150,000 when they stopped bothering with the bookkeeping. In the end, by Healy's estimate, the appellate work for Kyles was worth about $400,000, of which he would one day recover only $100,000 in expenses through a federal program he twigged onto belatedly.

Phelps Dunbar's disregard for Bey and Healy's ordeal was matched by outright disappointment within Bey's own family that she was wrapped up with this dubious character named Curtis Kyles. Bey grew up in Los Alamos, "a good, guilty Catholic girl," as she put it. Her father was not directly involved in the Manhattan Project, but he would have felt at home with the team that made the atom bomb. He wrote computer programs to guide subsequent generations of weaponry and, as his daughter would drily observe, was "terribly sad when the cold war ended."

As the holidays approached, Bey was so torn by the Kyles case, her other obligations to the firm, and her father's displeasure that she sought pastoral counsel from a Monsignor Reynolds at Saint Patrick's, a few blocks down Camp Street from Phelps Dunbar. Saint Patrick's was a church conservative enough to be still celebrating Mass in Latin twenty years after Vatican II. And yet, as he had on other occasions in Bey's life, Reynolds cut right to the quick of her dilemma. "He was, like, 'Do what you think you need to do and what Curtis needs you to do.' And at that point I was able to tell everybody, 'Leave me alone. I will do what I need to do,'" Bey said, still grateful for the simple clarity of the priest's guidance.

Her priorities affirmed, Bey drove herself forward, and on the first workday of the new year, January 2, 1989, the team from Phelps Dunbar presented itself in criminal court, the venue where it all began, to tell Judge Waldron that the case against Curtis Kyles must be reopened. Their omnibus filing was in the form of various petitions. One sought a second stay of execution—without which the rest was academic. They then wanted an evidentiary hearing to review the new material disinterred from Harry Connick's files and make it part of the record of the case. The further goal was a new trial.

It took Judge Waldron four days to say no to everything, five days more for the state supreme court to reverse him in part. In light of the new evidence, the justices ruled, Kyles could have his evidentiary hearing, a process in which witnesses again would tell their stories from the stand and physical evidence would be combed piece by piece to assure its relevance and that it had been properly come by. Errors and inconsistencies that cut to issues of substance in the case, if any were found, would be the basis for a retrial.

In deference to the eminent admiralty lawyer from Phelps Dunbar, a chastened Judge Waldron conducted the hearing piecemeal, a day or two at a time, from late in February until the first of June 1989, usually on Fridays, when Healy's other clients were preparing for the weekend and less clamorous for his services. At the end of the process, Bey and Healy handed the court a brief summarizing the argument in favor of a new trial.

Martin Regan could be credited with the basic theory of their defense: that Beanie not only framed Kyles, he killed Mrs. Dye. But Regan had had no more than intuition to guide him, and the testimony of rattled witnesses who claimed to have seen Beanie in a red car hours after the killing. On appeal, Regan had centered his argument unsuccessfully on technical flaws and improprieties: that informing Ron Gorman and Kevin Black that their testimony might subject them to prosecution had amounted to witness intimidation; that the search of Kyles's garbage was not supported by a proper warrant. In Cliff Strider's closing, the inflammatory references to the city's high crime rate—and his exhortation to jurors to "send a message" by convicting Kyles—were clear violations, as was Judge Waldron's failure to strike them when the defense objected, Regan had argued.

Now, with the tape transcript, the witness statements, and other material they had unearthed, Bey and Healy could move beyond technical flaws and buttress the heart of the case Regan tried to make: If Wallace wasn't himself involved in the murder, how was he able to steer Detectives Miller and Eaton to the exact location in the parking lot where Mrs. Dye went down? With other witnesses testifying that the killer had cornrows, what would a jury have made of Wallace's description of Kyles on the tape as a man with his hair combed out in an Afro? And with Beanie on tape suggesting that the officers search Kyles's garbage for Mrs. Dye's effects—strong evidence that he was preparing to plant the purse there—hadn't police testified that the search was not based on a tip? Then there was the matter of the murder weapon. As police discovered in searching his apartment, Kyles was in the habit of hiding firearms under his mattress to keep them out of his young children's reach. Why then would he have stashed a loaded pistol at toddler level behind the stove, indeed at the very corner of the stove where Wallace was seen squatting down on the evening before Kyles's arrest? That was just the beginning. Healy and Bey went on to itemize numerous missteps by Regan and to argue that in the aggregate Kyles had been denied his constitutional right to effective counsel.

In Healy's view, proper procedure required Waldron—as the judge presiding over evidentiary hearings ordered by the state supreme court—simply to have forwarded the brief and transcripts of those hearings to the higher court. Waldron chose a different course, one that seemed to reek of contempt not just for the defendant but for the appellate process itself: Rather than defer to the supreme court, he issued a judgment dismissing the new evidence as insufficient to warrant a new trial. That done, he set another date for execution.

That particular ordeal was Waldron's last hurrah. The return to his jurisdiction exhausted Healy and Bey's obligations to the Louisiana court system. Now they could look ahead to the no less daunting challenges of collateral review by federal judges.

The date would be stayed again, but this time there was less certainty of that, and with Healy out of town on an admiralty case—he was president of the national association of admiralty lawyers at the time—the work fell to Bey. It quickly became clear that Phelps Dunbar's indifference to the pro bono labor on the Kyles case had given way to outright impatience, and over at the Death Penalty Resource Center, Nick Trenticosta was verging on the panic mode that necessarily set in as the appellate process unwound and an execution drew near. As the center's director, it was Trenticosta's role to coordinate student support for the whole roster of pending death penalty cases, homing in on one or two in particular as they gained urgency. And the Kyles case was definitely gaining urgency.

On one of Bey's phones, Trenticosta was screaming at her that she had to give the matter her full attention. Fuck Phelps Dunbar. Yes, she could recycle a lot of the work from the first petition, but it had to be adapted and updated or she would only insult the court. On another phone was a Phelps Dunbar partner to remind her that working herself to the bone on the Kyles case after hours would not be an option this time. There would be no after hours. She had a deposition to take and a vessel inspection to complete, with the first of them scheduled for five p.m.

TWELVE

Prisons stake their first claim on an inmate's attention by how different they are from the free world, the real world. After a time the thing notable about Angola to Kyles was how completely it replicated the full spectrum of free-world pursuits, albeit in twisted and shrunken forms.

Kyles's Casanova complex found diminished expression in the correspondence he kept up, mostly with women he would never meet, his efforts still limited by his fragile literacy. In answer to whatever needs of their own, a sorority of lonely hearts from around the world contact death row inmates and enter into relationships by mail. Cards become letters. Letters give way to gifts and visits, and some of these relationships even culminate in marriage—unions whose principal appeal for the unincarcerated pen pal, it has been suggested, is that they can never be consummated. Kyles settled for the occasional gift of money and the momentary relief of his boredom that came with the postcards and letters. They were certainly an improvement on the hate mail. Kyles got plenty of that too, also from strangers, men and women who drew some satisfaction from heaping vitriol on a black man convicted of killing a white woman. Kyles learned to spot and discard these letters almost as soon as he opened them or, in the case of the regulars, even before.

In his stable of more supportive correspondents, one woman in particular intrigued him, a Brit named Claudette. She was a mountain climber—"a breath of fresh air" in the drabness and tedium of Kyles's cell—and her cards were postmarked from all around the world. She'd mention her next stop to Kyles, and he would write on ahead so there'd be a letter waiting for her. In a letter from Switzerland she told Kyles that she had been injured in a climbing accident. Kyles wrote the hospital more than once, but his letters were returned to sender. He then tried her address in England. No reply. "So I let her go."

Angola's recognized clubs and sports leagues and prayer groups were only the most obvious extensions of free-world social custom, but they were largely off-limits to death row inmates, and Kyles had nothing to do with them. What spoke to him was the prison underground and the way it mirrored so much of what he had known on the outside: greed, lust, vengeance, the itch to subjugate and hold sway over others, and, above all, the opportunity for material gain. It was testament to the indomitability of the human spirit, Kyles supposed, allowing as well for the indomitability of sin. This was not to say that he was a theological man, a Bible banger, though there were plenty around bidding for him to join hands with them. He tolerated their visits to the row, and he was not against joining in with them when they asked if he would like to pray. But even with the crucifix he had tattooed on his right forearm with ballpoint ink and sewing needles, religion was not Kyles's game, and neither was politics. His lifelong awareness of racism and its sidekick, poverty, did not turn him toward Angola's ideological poles—not toward the Panthers, in any case no longer quite the force they had been a decade earlier, or the black Muslim movement in which many an ex-Panther had found refuge. If pressed, Kyles would mutter that both groups seemed closer to the problem than to a solution, each too badly infected with the racism they deplored. But Kyles didn't sound as though he had subjected the question to close analysis. He was a survivor, an adapter, and an opportunist. His gift was being able to read people in their particularity and play them to his advantage. Politics was a generalist's game; it just got in the way.

Kyles's calling was commerce—to give hustling a dressed-up name. He traded in contraband, drugs mostly, but also radios—the big Super 2 models General Electric made, radios powerful enough to pick up the

New Orleans stations that, for city blacks at Angola, were a staticky lifeline that kept them closer to sane. The goods changed with the shift of his
market from the Ninth Ward to Angola, but the impulse to work it had
not. Kyles was an inveterate trader, a poster child for capitalism's primal
force. Prison forced him to be more resourceful than before, but he could
think of no better way to pass his days.

It was small wonder that his first exposure to the wage earner's life,
as a teenage dropout, quickly impelled Kyles toward an entrepreneur's
existence. The atrocious public school system in New Orleans guaranteed the city's labor pool an annual infusion of illiterate and ignorant
young people sufficient to keep wages abysmally low—a system pleasing,
perhaps, to the captains of industry and commerce, but deeply alienating
to a young man trying to get by. A baby on the way had not instantly
made a grown-up out of the seventeen-year-old father-to-be, but to Kyles
it seemed like a good enough reason to quit school once and for all and
try to find a job. He signed on as a gravedigger at one of the city's vener-
able cemeteries. His mother was proud of him: a city job—almost a church
job, if you thought about it. It wasn't hard work. The dead mix easily into
the alluvial silt that loosely underpins New Orleans and the rest of the
Mississippi River outwash southeast of Baton Rouge. Families wealthy
enough to be dismayed by the hastiness of nature's embrace slid caskets
into aboveground crypts of stone or masonry or brick. The subjects of
Kyles's attention were not so fortunate. A day or two into the job, he received an unexpected lesson in the economics of his new profession when
a couple of his co-workers unbolted the lid of a casket interred a few
hours earlier. The body, unboxed, was dumped back into the gravesite
and covered over. The casket was rinsed clean and restored to the under-
taker for resale to the next grieving family looking to do right by the
dearly departed.

It spooked Kyles. You did not have to partake of Aunt Eva's voodoo
hoodoo to wonder if the dead might not be capable of revenge. The living too might be expected to take offense. "People who had spent all this
change trying to send their loved ones off, give them a proper burial—it
was disrespectful," Kyles would conclude. He stayed on the job through
the end of the first week and the beginning of the next. On that Tuesday,
Kyles tendered his resignation. A check was waiting for him on Thursday.

The look in the paymaster's eye told him what did not need to be spoken: that it would be best to keep his mouth sealed tighter than any coffin known to the trade.

Kyles's next stop was a sewing factory on Dauphine Street that cranked out khaki uniforms. He was what they called a bundle boy, moving around the workroom distributing clothing parts—a batch of back pockets, two dozen fly zippers, buttons, whatever—to this bench or that one. For his own pocket: a check for $135 every second week, which was nothing, even then.

The Conti Street apartment where Curtis and Pinkey played house waiting for Tyteannia to be born was within walking distance of Canal Street and the city's downtown. Before the big department stores followed the whites out to the suburbs, Canal had been the grandest shopping boulevard in the South and probably the widest as well. The lanes of traffic flowing to and from the river were divided by a vast median strip, or "neutral ground," as New Orleanians have called it ever since the days when the upstart Americans and the original French settlers lived in armed camps on either side of Canal, encountering each other to transact their business only on that long patch of turf dividing the two worlds. In more recent years, the face-off had been racial. The sit-ins of the 1950s were at lunch counters along Canal. Now the bespoke haberdasheries and jewelry stores that blacks picketed for permission to enter had given way to black-only outlets the likes of Soul Train Fashion, discount camera and stereo stores, and cheap shoe stores. On the sidewalks, burnoosed black Muslims sold incense and genuine African artifacts, not all of them fabricated in warehouses on the edge of town.

Canal's down-market drift did not make it uninteresting. The big hotels were on Canal, which made for an abundance of tourists and conventioneers, and by night it was a gateway to the sanctum sanctorum of New Orleans tourism, the French Quarter. Partly for sport, partly out of need, Kyles was good for the occasional jostle and jerk, relieving a passerby of a gold neck chain without his prey quite realizing what had gone down. And there were pockets to pick. At least until Pinkey's belly got too big, Kyles tried without success to get her to work with him as a lookout. What he really wanted was for her to shill, cut in on folk walking by, get them to stop a minute, and give her a light—whatever—while he slipped a wallet from the man's back pocket or ran his hand lightly through an open shoulder bag. Pinkey could stop traffic. No doubt about that. But she wouldn't do it, not even for Curtis.

With the duties of fatherhood impending, drug dealing took a more serious place in Kyles's home economics—pot, mostly, Valium when it came his way. Nothing heavy. Kyles also got known as a fence, someone who would take your hot stereo component or stolen wristwatch or snatched chain, hold it a few days, and, with luck, unload it at a modest profit in cash or trade. Drug dealing was the art of knowing what Curtis called the hot spots, the junctions—street corners, levees, pocket parks— where users with money in their pockets bumped up against the boys with a little something stashed in the shrubbery nearby, provided you knew how to ask for it. The guiding principle was simple as far as Kyles was concerned: don't get greedy.

That had been Big Slim's undoing: greed. By the late '70s, Kyles's mentor had lost the steady hand it took to run girls and deal drugs; he was ravenous for more. Within a few years, more would mean crack, but Slim did not live that long. More—toward the end of his days—meant heroin. Slim had always dealt it. Now he dealt nothing but, and as his own habit blinded him to fellow feeling for others in the same business, greed carried him farther and farther into turf where he was not welcome. In due course, as Kyles summarized it, "he had went all the way bad." At one remove, Kyles watched the man's downward spiral and took notes. "Competition started brewing, and he tried to get into the whole scenario, the whole game. He wanted to run the dope game, the whore game, basically everything. But the thing is, you don't want to step on nobody's toes. Joe Blow over here, selling dope like he's always been selling dope: don't put your clientele in his district. Slim did that, and Joe Blow had him killed." Cut down in an eviscerating burp of automatic gunfire, Slim was left to bleed to death on a curbside out in the city's eastern suburbs, a lesson to those who knew him and to those who had only heard of him. For Kyles, the lesson was this: "Whatever you good at, stay there, because you will bring on enemies if you venture somewhere else. As long as you stay in your own backyard, you're cool."

Kyles was twenty the year Big Slim went down, and Pinkey was pregnant again, with their third child. Curtis junior, known to all the world as Chester, had been born little more than a year after his big sister, Tyteannia. Their brother would be born twelve days after the onset of the new decade. Kyles named him Elmeco after a gunslinger from a western that he admired, a man as fast on the draw as he was fast with women. The children, and the intensity of Curtis's love for them, had encouraged him to try again to find legitimate employment, and about a year earlier, after a stint working a three-a.m.-to-dawn shift bending metal at a steel fabrication yard along the Industrial Canal, he found it laying brick.

The 1970s oil bubble, then in the dizzying final hours before its equally dizzying collapse, had made a whole generation of New Orleanians start to feel rich. Subdivisions pushed farther and farther out into the swamps beyond the Desire housing project and the Industrial Canal as blacks and blue-collar whites alike, newly enfranchised in the middle class and finally able to give up the city's older neighborhoods, if not the parish itself, sought to enshrine their good fortune in brick and mortar. As a result, much of Kyles's work was residential. "Basically, we was bricking homes. We went in exclusive residential areas and built miniature mansions. Then every now and then we might brick a wall to a shopping center, you know, so it was good pay. By the time I got to be a layer, I was making about ten seventy-five an hour."

The problem was that decent pay wasn't steady pay. A rainy week left Kyles stranded, so he kept up his connections on the street, dealing grass and pills and coke. One eye out for the cops, he kept two eyes open for jackers—younger boys, mostly, who preyed on the nickel-and-dime dope dealers much more mercilessly than the law. His hustling was intermittent. "It wasn't a regular thing for me. Say I'm short of money—like, say, we want to get together and do something or go out of town. I'd go out two, three times a week, eight to twenty bags a night. I could put together four, five hundred dollars, just to have a little extra."

They were on Desire Street by now, thanks to the landlord's willingness to take Pinkey back into the building where for a time she had lived as a child. Kyles worked a "cut," one of the gaps between buildings in the Florida project, a short walk from his door. It was a bustling scene once you knew how to read the vacant stares and laconic comments of people who just seemed to be standing around. The people out on the curb were steerers. Somebody looking to score would state his business—coke, weed, heroin—and the steerer would point his chin toward whoever was holding what, point his chin without saying much, if anything at all. And when the cops came by, the whole casbah—steerers, dealers, buyers—could barrel back through the cruiser-proof cut into the labyrinthine wilds of the Florida project, where no cop in his right mind would willingly venture on foot. It had been like this as long as Kyles had been dealing, and, as far as he could tell, it would be like this as long as he dealt.

Fencing stolen goods was also a craft he picked up from Big Slim. Kyles started small and prided himself on the way he was soon able to leave the thievery to others. "A lot of the guys were pickpockets, snatching purses. Basically I was legit. Some guy might jack a guy out of a belt or a certain pair of shoes, and if they couldn't fit into them, I'd buy them and just hold them until I could find somebody who could wear them. I'd make an extra ten, fifteen dollars. It really started from there." The strategies became more intricate over time and the goods more valuable, but the economics remained straightforward enough. "I'd go looking for the drug users, and I'd tell them, 'Look, if you get something hot—some watches, chains, a microwave or component set or whatever—I got a little extra cash, 'cause I know you need it, and you know, I just might break you off a little bit.'" By component set Kyles meant a stereo system, one of the basic units of exchange that passed through his hands as a fence. "No matter how good it is, ain't nobody gonna buy it for more than seventy-five dollars, because they know it's hot. But if I offer the dope addict that stole it a hundred and ten dollars, he gonna come looking for me." To pay $100 for a stereo too hot to sell for $75 was Kyles's way of "breaking you off a little bit." Kyles could be generous and still make a profit by simply waiting for hot goods to cool. "You can sit on it as long as you want to, because eventually somebody gonna need a component set. So instead of them paying two ninety-nine, you'll give it to them for like a hundred and seventy-five."

One challenge was storage, a deep freeze in which to keep the goods for a while. Here again Kyles borrowed a page from Slim's playbook: "Don't shit where you sleep." It was the wisdom behind Slim's refusing to tolerate his women bringing their tricks into the Press Park house. "He was a serious pimp. He was the type of pimp that kept his nose clean. Nothing come into that house." Before Kyles moved Pinkey back onto Desire Street—and more strictly after the household began to fill up with kids—to store his wares, Kyles looked again to junkies and to the abandoned houses in which they sold and shot their wares and nodded off in the company of their own kind. Kyles would cultivate the most reliable of the regulars, put him in his debt, help him with a fix when it really mattered, and generally turn a business relationship into something like veneration on the part of the junkie for this very together Curtis dude who always had a few bucks to see you past a rough patch. In exchange, Kyles would ask the junkie for a simple favor: to stash some of his fenced goods and guard them. Guard them with your fucking life, my man, and if they are gone in the morning, so are you.

There was another reason why a dope house was a good place to stash stolen goods. In the pecking order of the police department, narcs considered a professional interest in jacked merchandise a tad demeaning. In a raid, and they were not infrequent, a self-respecting drug cop would look for drugs, period, walking right past the microwave with the store tags still on it or the six stereos that might otherwise have seemed five too many for even the most ardent music lover.

Music and weed. They would carry over into Kyles's Angola enterprises as his basic commodities, albeit in slightly diminished form: needle-thin joints instead of corner bags; $40 GE radios instead of $200 stereos. But as in the free world, the trafficking was bound up with the social relationships that underpinned it, on the supply side as well as the demand side. From the start of his Angola years, Kyles's family had dominated his visitor list, but he never involved them in his business pursuits. There were other visitors for that, women Kyles had romanced in his Desire Street days—none of them named in this book—and over time, they began to bring more into the visitor room than fetching smiles and the lusts and memories they stirred in Kyles. Nothing happened in prison without the complicity of guards, but in due course, familiarity between Kyles and his keepers began to breed the necessary accommodation, depending on who was on duty that day. A few minutes of contact in a corner of the room required special dispensation, but it was time enough, between the hugging and the kissing, to relieve a visitor of the wad of heroin or hashish in a knotted condom lodged in her vagina. Or she could remove it herself and pass it to Kyles if there was a wire mesh between them. The trick then was for Kyles to get back onto the tier without the usual strip search, but there were ways, and in the privacy of his cell, almost dizzy from the womanly scent of the contraband's casing, he would roll needle-thin joints of drug-dusted tobacco.

Such a product, more rolling paper than pot, went for $4 or $5 a smoke at Angola in those days. With $50 worth of marijuana, Kyles could gross $600. But the trade was heavily taxed. There were the guards to take care of, both before and after Kyles had lovingly relieved his perfumed mules of their burden. And circulating his wares required additional complicity, which also came at a price. By the time the guards were cut in and the merchandise transported—usually by an inmate counselor or an orderly—to prisoners permitted to mingle with Angola's general population, the $600 had been whittled to $300.

Dealing pot was a natural outgrowth of Kyles's deep pleasure in the drug. The radio business was something new to master. About once a month he'd take delivery of a GE Super 2. A cooperative guard was his middleman, a link with someone on the outside willing to accept payment via a "draw slip," the equivalent of a personal check drawn on an inmate's prison account. The Super 2 arrived by return mail at a cost of about $55, shipping included. It could be unloaded for $125 inside the pen.

In time, Kyles's reputation preceded him. He was surprised to discover just how far. He was in the prison pharmacy one night, a privilege, like phone contact with legal counsel, that guards had only limited power to deny. Kyles was making his purchase when an orderly he didn't know said loud enough to freeze him in his tracks, "Aren't you the one at Camp J with weed?"

Kyles's denial was instinctual. "What you talking about?"

But another inmate caught his eye and signaled with a nod that Kyles could accept the orderly's remark for what it was: an overture to a deal. Soon enough, the orderly was a central part of Kyles's distribution network, in exchange, of course, for a piece of the action.

Kyles's family visitors—Lela and Brenda, his mother, Pinkey and one or another of the kids—brought something infinitely more valuable than drugs. Their love was sustaining. It was also exquisite torture for Kyles to watch his kids grow up through the wire mesh of a visitor booth, just beyond reach of his arms and lips. Little Meco, a four-year-old when Kyles was arrested, was now in grade school. And Tyteannia was becoming a young woman. Kyles would never forget the visit when that dawned on him, along with the realization that her childhood was passing without a father, just as his had. She had been so uncharacteristically bashful that time, all fidgets and distraction as she sat across from him in the visitor booth, burdened with something she needed to say but didn't know how. Finally, guessing what was up, he eased into the subject of menstruation, and Ty found it in her to pick up on the cue and tell him her news.

By the early part of 1990, with Kyles now in his third year at Angola, Pinkey began to fade away. She just couldn't take it—not the six hours up and back by car or with the other inmate wives on the Saturday morning bus from New Orleans, not the emotional wringer she went through on encountering Kyles. Tyrone was not the problem. He never felt the need to run Curtis out of her life or her thoughts, not even after he and Pinkey had a baby of their own and little prospect of having to deal with Kyles's return. In fact it was Tyrone, pushing good sportsmanship to champion levels, who cooperated with Pinkey in her desire to be photographed in the nude in provocative poses, a roll of snapshots for Curtis. Kyles delighted in them, of course, though as care packages go, he knew it was at least as much a taunt as a tease.

Even under the terrible burden of the brain tumor that would kill her, Gracie Walker twice a month settled into Lela's or Brenda's rattletrap car for the long drive to Angola, a ritual that continued after Alzheimer's had emptied her mind of speech. As the interval since the previous visit lengthened, her daughters would notice Gracie clutching more anxiously at a toy animal, a stuffed rabbit that in her mind, or what was left of it, had become a surrogate for her beloved Curtis. When she could still talk, she would sometimes give voice to every parent's deepest hope, that she would die before any of her children did. And Kyles would chuckle darkly and point out that when it came to him, her chances of seeing that wish come true were not very good. But then she began to fail badly. Her decline coincided too neatly with the ramped-up legal campaign to save her son, and Kyles fell prey to a superstitious sense of guilt. It was almost as if he were sucking the life right out of her, that she was giving it up to save him.

A health crisis also struck Delores Dye's survivors in the late '80s. Robert senior, her widower, had checked into one of the big private hospitals in New Orleans for an overnight battery of tests after noticing he was having trouble urinating. The next morning, the doctor showed up all smiles to report that everything was fine. "You're in great shape. I hope I'm in the shape you're in when I'm your age." That kind of thing. Relieved by the good news, Dye showered and dressed and called his son to come get him. "So I'm waiting for Lowell to come, and I see this guy coming down the hall in a suit and tie, and I think it's him, Lowell. I'm leaning against the rail. So this guy comes up to me, leans against the rail next to me. He doesn't say good morning, all he says is, 'My friend, I've got bad news for you; you've got cancer.'" Dye deflected the shock by assailing the doctor's bedside manner. "Don't put me in front of the firing squad and ask me if I want a handkerchief over my eyes and a last cigarette," Dye groused. "Take me out to the sunroom or something. Sit me down, get me a cup of coffee, and break it to me gently." When Lowell Dye showed up moments later, he was equally abrupt with his own pronouncement. "You're out of business," Lowell said to his father. "Right now." Losing one parent was enough. That very day, they called the big construction companies who used Dye as a subcontractor. Within weeks, as Dye underwent chemotherapy for bladder cancer, his workers finished off his last job and Robert Dye closed down his business for good.

By the end of the century Dye would still be going strong, plastic prostheses where his hips had been, but still active and alert. Gracie Walker, however, was ten years dead. Kyles would still choke up at the memory of this time. The family tragedy was compounded by his brother

Curtis Kyles had an irrepressibly wandering eye for the ladies, but his relationship with Pinkey Burnes, the mother of his five children, remained the stabilizing center of his world until it was suddenly upended by his 1984 arrest for murder. Here, in happier times, Kyles and Burnes socialize at a Ninth Ward neighborhood function.

A year before the murder, Lowell Dye presented his parents with their only grandchild, Jason. The family's joy was shattered by Mrs. Dye's murder not long after they had gathered for this photograph. Absent on this occasion was Lowell's brother, Robert junior, who had moved to Florida.

In the immediate aftermath of Mrs. Dye's murder, New Orleans police had cordoned off the crime scene in the sprawling parking lot of a popular New Orleans supermarket.

Mr. Dye would testify that the cat and dog food found in some abundance in the Desire Street kitchen was suspiciously similar to brands Mrs. Dye was accustomed to buying for her pets. A marketing executive of the Schwegmann supermarket chain disputed Kyles's contention that he had loaded up on pet supplies because the products were on sale.

Cited as evidence that Kyles had bustled Mrs. Dye's groceries into the Desire Street apartment after killing her were Schwegmann shopping bags stashed under the kitchen sink. But given Schwegmann's huge market share in New Orleans, it was not hard to argue that such bags were as common as cockroaches.

In adolescence, Pinkey Burnes and her family had occupied one of the upstairs apartments in the Desire Street fourplex. She and Kyles would take over the ground-floor unit on the right as their nursery began to fill up and were living there on September 24, 1984, when police descended on the place and arrested Kyles as he tinkered with his car.

At the suggestion of an informant, three days after the murder police seized garbage bags set outside the Desire Street apartment. Mrs. Dye's purse and personal papers were recovered from one of them, providing police with grounds to arrest Kyles the following morning.

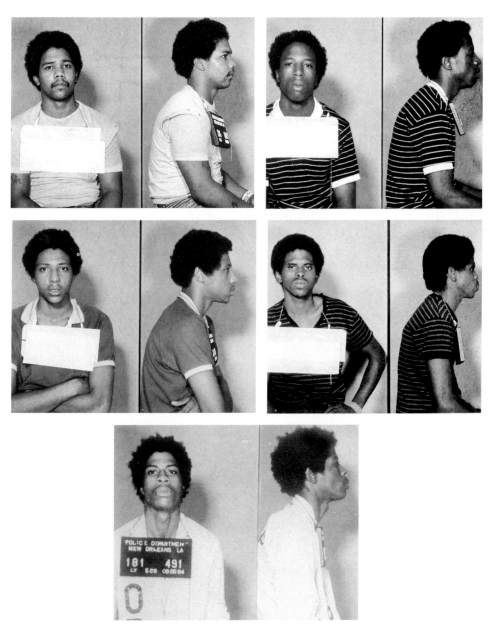

The case against Kyles pivoted on identifications made by eyewitnesses who picked him out of a photo lineup developed by police detectives. These anonymous mugshots, plucked from the nightly parade of young men arrested as suspects in crimes of all descriptions, were grouped with similar front and side views of Kyles. Within hours of Kyles's arrest, three men claiming to have seen the murder of Delores Dye were shown the photo lineup and declared him the killer.

September 24, 1984: New Orleans police detectives Johnny Miller (left) and John Dillman escort Kyles into custody following his arrest on Desire Street for the murder of Delores Dye. Kyles would remain behind bars for the next fourteen years. Both detectives would leave the police department before his retrials, Miller to become a bodyguard to movie star John Goodman, Dillman to become a private investigator and crime writer. (Photograph © 1984 The Times-Picayune Publishing Co., all rights reserved. Used with permission of The Times-Picayune)

Though never brought to the stand, police informant Beanie Wallace figured at the heart of both the defense and the prosecution theories of the case. Kyles's desperate hope was to prove that Wallace had murdered Mrs. Dye and then framed him in order to pursue his sexual obsession with Pinkey Burnes.

A prosecutor and skilled politician by day, New Orleans district attorney Harry Connick never abandoned his dream—later realized by his son, Harry Connick Jr.—of becoming a big-time jazz singer. Here, late in his career, Connick moonlights at Maxwell's Toulouse Cabaret, a French Quarter nightclub. (Photograph by Matt Rose © 2003 The Times-Picayune Publishing Co., all rights reserved. Used with permission of The Times-Picayune)

Prominent New Orleans maritime attorney George "Bunky" Healy (center) guided the Kyles case through the appellate phase that led to the reversal of Kyles's conviction by the U.S. Supreme Court. On the occasion of Kyles's release in 1998, Healy and Kyles were joined by Sister Helen Prejean, the anti–death penalty activist and author of *Dead Man Walking*. Prejean had encountered Kyles on Angola's death row and put him in touch with Nick Trenticosta, a young New Orleans attorney who would also figure prominently in his defense.

Death penalty attorneys Nick Trenticosta (right) and Denise LeBoeuf (second from left) convinced courtroom superstar Mike Fawer to argue the Kyles case pro bono. With them is LeBoeuf's sister, investigator Marie Campbell, whose close scrutiny of crime novels written by the lead detective on the case led to a dramatic moment on the witness stand that threw witness identifications into doubt.
(Courtesy of Denise LeBoeuf)

A young man of twenty-five when arrested for murder, Kyles was a grandfather before his release. Following the inconclusive fifth trial in 1998, defense attorney Denise LeBoeuf shared a moment with Kyles and the grandchild born to his daughter just weeks earlier. (Courtesy of Denise LeBoeuf)

Roosevelt's accident. Roosevelt was working under a car when a jack failed and it fell on him, crushing his chest and permanently debilitating him. And Larry began to lose his struggle with drugs. It would be more than a decade before he got straight. But none of this matched Kyles's grief at Gracie's living death. In her honor he added a large tattoo to his growing collection, a vaguely Egyptian-looking image that the prison tattooist called African Queen. It entailed a variation on the usual prison tattoo technique. Instead of using needles and ink from a ballpoint pen, the tattooist lacerated Kyles's flesh with small razor slashes and then rubbed them with carbon paper until the dark purple was permanent. "My mama was the only thing, man, helping me to survive that whole ordeal," Kyles said. "Every two weeks, man. She was making it every two weeks. Even though half the time she didn't know where she was. Brenda and Lela, they tore their cars up coming here." Kyles finally put a stop to it, convinced that the trips were killing Gracie, and six months later she was dead. The irony was not lost on Kyles. As much as he fed off of her, she had lived for him. "I was the only thing that kept her strong."

In time Kyles was able to forgive Angola much of what he went through. He could credit Terry Mayeaux, the most obnoxious of the guards, with progress toward a less bigoted way of dealing with black inmates. He could see beyond his own fear and the disgust with which he viewed the white brotherhood on Tier A. After all, compared to Orleans Parish Prison, with its gangs and rapes and free-floating violence, death row had some of the serenity and orderliness of a monastery. But the affront that Kyles was never able to forgive Angola was the way he was treated when Gracie died.

They sent a chaplain to tell him, a pasty, balding man who reminded Kyles of John Lithgow, the actor. Kyles paid little notice as the chaplain arrived on the tier that afternoon and began working his way along the row of cells, a word for this inmate and the next delivered in the empty, ritualized manner favored by the profession. "I didn't have no kind of belief in the ministers and preachers that came around the row," Kyles would observe drily. "I figured they was just doing it because they couldn't preach or practice nowhere else." Finally the Lithgow look-alike ran out of digressions and stood before the unsuspecting Kyles. Still, he beat around the bush. "How are you doing, Curtis? Have you been reading your Bible?" That kind of thing.

"I don't know whether he just couldn't face me, or if it just wasn't important to him," Kyles would reflect. "Then he went to quoting stuff about how God does things for a purpose. I'm paying attention to him. I'm respecting him because I know this is what they do. Then he went into detail about how sometimes God brings things when you least expect it and we just got to prepare for the worst. That man called my brother's name, then he called my sister's name, my older sister—I'll never forget this—and then he called my mama's name, told me she had just passed."

If this was meant to ease Kyles into his grief, it failed completely. Infuriated by the man's roundabout manner, Kyles blew up. "I told him to get the fuck out of my face and let me get on the phone and call home." He reached Lela's house, and when she answered in tears, he knew the truth and hung up with scarcely a word. Unhinged by his own mix of grief and guilt, Kyles kept it together by making a request that quickly took on the force of an obsession: that he be allowed to attend his mother's funeral. And for a week the warden played him along, letting him believe the matter was "under review." But as Kyles would later come to understand, death row inmates were never allowed home for family occasions, however serious. Finally the guard boss, Captain Pete Arnold, came in person to Kyles's cell to tell him his request had been denied. Going to the funeral, even under guard, was a security risk. It would not be tolerated.

Kyles wept and argued and raised his voice and wept some more. But the venting was not enough. He had to get out of his cell. Right away. Now. Whatever it took. He played a trump and demanded to phone his lawyer. From the look in Arnold's eye, Kyles knew the guard captain saw the ploy for what it was—"like he was reading my mind," Kyles would recall. But Arnold also knew the rules. Calls to legal counsel could not be refused, no matter how wild-eyed the inmate exercising the privilege. "Don't give me no trouble," Arnold said. "I've had enough trouble this week." A turnkey was summoned, and Kyles was sprung.

Arnold's suspicions were quickly confirmed. Whatever Kyles thought he was doing, this wasn't about making a phone call. He was yielding to the blindest and most futile of the compulsions that come to substitute for reason in the prison setting. He had got out of his cell. No matter that he was still locked in a concrete-block bunker in the middle of the most securely guarded prison in Louisiana. He was out of his cell.

And now, with equal conviction, the guards realized that they had better put him back in it. Quick, before this man, now pacing here and there, shouting and crying, started acting any crazier or more recalcitrant. There was a science to it, a technology of electrified prods and shields that—in the era before the electric chair yielded to lethal injection—gave guards the heady power that came with administering a foretaste of the horror ahead. Helmeted and squatting behind their shields, a squadron of three of them advanced on Kyles, zapping him again and again with their prods until he could smell his flesh burning, and his brain began to ring like a gong. Now they closed in on him, close enough to slam him up against the wall and pin him there with their five-foot shields. He knew better than to put his hands against the shield, because its edges also were electrified. Instead, Kyles raised his arms into the air, but the guards were not ready to accept a surrender, not without first rewarding themselves with a few moments of satisfaction.

Za-zapp. Za-zapp. That was the sound the prods made, in Kyles's rendition of the incident. *Za-zzapp. Za-zzapp. Za-zzapp.* An angry, snarling sound, as Kyles attempted to re-create it, which was unusual for him. Because while Kyles often talked about his anger and other strong emotions, he rarely gave vent to them in conversation years after the moment he was describing. *Za-zapp:* the sound of a stun stick wrapped in cloth so it wouldn't leave a telltale welt. The cell door slammed shut, and Kyles fell to the floor as if something had snapped.

Two weeks after his mother's death Kyles woke up to find that the left side of his face had gone numb. His eye on that side would not stop leaking, nor would his salivary glands, to judge from the pool of spittle that seemed to well up in the corner of his mouth, now drawn downward on that side in a permanent sneer. Doctors figured it for Bell's palsy, a neurological condition. Kyles's own circuitry had gone bad, more likely from accumulated years of stress than from any particular application of the stun stick. The condition entitled Kyles to be ferried once a month to Charity Hospital in a prison van. He was becoming desperate, certain now that he was going to lose the long legal struggle with the Louisiana executioner and that his only options were suicide or attempted escape, which in all likelihood amounted to the same thing. But so what?

Another piece of metal had found its way in among the fillings and bridgework in Kyles's mouth: a handcuff key. Don't ask how he came by it. It was as much a talisman as a tool, but alone in the back of the locked van, Kyles would sometimes spit it into his shackled hands and give the key a try. Just to be sure it still worked.

THIRTEEN

Bey and Healy's wall-to-wall approach to reassembling the Kyles case meant that every witness and item of material evidence was worth a second look—a commitment to thoroughness that would serve them well, if slowly. An investigator had little trouble tracking down Isaac Smallwood, Henry Williams, and Bobby Territo. Johnny Miller, John Dillman, and other detectives and police specialists had been duly subpoenaed to appear at the evidentiary hearing and regurgitate their rendition of the Kyles probe before Judge Waldron. Regan, cast in the complicated role of having to assert that he had been incompetent as Kyles's counsel, humbly agreed to do just that. Every state-level option expended, Healy and Bey had then digested and refined this wealth of material as part of their appeal to the federal court presiding over the Eastern District of Louisiana from a gray-granite palace on Camp Street in New Orleans.

One of the eyewitnesses, Darlene Cahill, had proved elusive, and the federal appeal had been filed without her. No matter: Healy and Bey had not expected her to make much of a difference. It was more a matter of leaving no stone unturned, of completing a checklist, an exercise that dragged on for three years and might have been abandoned altogether, except that one day in the spring of 1992 their investigator turned up a Darlene Cahill living across Lake Pontchartrain in a bedroom community known as Slidell. Was she the Darlene Cahill who had testified against Curtis Kyles?

No. But she knew the Darlene Cahill they were looking for.

Could they have her number?

No. But she agreed to pass along a message.

The wrong Darlene Cahill—the woman reached by phone in Slidell— was the former sister-in-law of the woman they were looking for. By coincidence, both the Cahill boys had married Darlenes, one more successfully than the other. The teenage marriage of the eyewitness was unraveling at the time of the Dye murder, and in short order, so would much else about her life. She had long since reverted to her maiden name, Darlene Kersh, and by the time Healy's investigator tracked her down, was living in Kenner, out by the New Orleans airport. The other Darlene Cahill had played coy with the investigator, but she wasted no time getting on the horn to her former sister-in-law. This was juicy stuff. "Darlene, it's about the murder trial," Cahill told Kersh. "This guy wants you to call him."

Kersh felt a spasm of anxiety, but she took down the number. She assumed it was someone in Harry Connick's office, no doubt one of the prosecutors who walked her through her testimony years earlier. She put the phone aside and lit a cigarette, glancing now and then at the number she had jotted down. When the cigarette was gone, she lit another and reached for the phone. She punched in three numbers and was about to add a fourth when she put the phone down again. Her heart was beating so fast that her throat ached. She breathed deeply, ten deep breaths. She was going to make the call, but for reasons neither Healy nor Connick could have known, it was going to take some doing.

The '80s had not been easy on Darlene Kersh. Like many another good-time girl grown a little older, Kersh had slipped deep into the sauce, then found cocaine, then crack. When drug dealers began to compete with the landlord for their share of her unsteady income, she had entered into a nomadic existence punctuated by fitful decampings in the night as back rent came due and eviction loomed. In due course she was back where she started, at her grandmother's place in Gentilly, around the corner from the icehouse. The hard knocks were not Darlene's alone. One morning she looked in on the old woman and found her dead on the floor, an apparent heart attack. A sister was booked with manslaughter for killing her boyfriend—"accidentally," in Kersh's view—and was packed off to prison for seven years. And then one night the man in Kersh's life didn't come home. He had been rubbed out execution-style by a hooligan duo from New Orleans. It turned out to be a case of mistaken identity, but the dead man's family blamed Kersh. It was always like that when a black man messed with a white woman—nothing but trouble, they said, and they refused to let her attend her lover's funeral.

Indeed, Kersh's luck was so rotten that she came to wonder if it wasn't retribution. Because, along with her crack pipe and her ever-evolving set of apartment keys, Kersh had carried a gnawing secret ever since the brief moment in which Detective Dillman and the prosecutors made her feel a little bit important. And the secret was this: she had lied on the stand—lied about being able to identify Kyles; lied about being able to identify anyone at all as the killer of Delores Dye. And the guilt she felt for doing so had only worsened as her love life carried her over the color line and she came to understand that black men, perhaps even Curtis Kyles, were human.

Now, with the phone message from her sister-in-law, she knew it was time for atonement. It was time to have done with the lie. That was clear to her, but it made the call, in prospect, no less terrifying. What would they say, these happening young DAs and cops who had jollied her into their camp? They would hate her. They would call her a nigger lover. She had heard that before. Would they also come after her legally? Would they prosecute her for perjury?

It was Good Friday, 1992, and much of downtown New Orleans had bailed out early and headed home for the Easter weekend. At Phelps Dunbar, Healy let his secretary go and then stayed on to attend to some loose ends in another case. And so when the phone rang, he picked it up himself: a curt hello in place of the more professional salutation—"Phelps Dunbar, may I help you?"—that was expected of the secretaries and receptionists.

Still assuming she had reached the DA's office, Kersh identified herself, and then, as though releasing a terrible poison, she seemed to vomit into the phone, a torrent of words that she couldn't stop or didn't dare to. "Look, you're not going to like what I'm getting ready to say, but I'm going to say it because I been holding it in all this time: I lied. I lied . . ." She took a sharp breath and then, stunned by the echo of what she just said and the huge sense of relief that came with saying it, plunged on. "I lied. I lied. I could not tell if it was Curtis," she would remember saying. "I could not tell who it was who done it. I just knew it was a black man, and that's all I'm gonna tell you. You can hang up the phone right now, but I'm telling you, I lied, I'm not lying any more. This is it. I'm finished with it."

There was a silence, a frozen moment. For Darlene Kersh it was the gap between the blinding flash of a Fourth of July firecracker high above the Mississippi and the bone-jarring boom that follows. The explosion she awaited would be the anger of the man on the phone, disappointed and disgusted as it registered on him that she was betraying the cause, that she was no longer trying to keep "a nigger off the streets."

For Healy, of course, the eruption was altogether different, if not less stunning. Lawyers wait a lifetime for a "Perry Mason moment" like this. Healy knew better than to try to make much sense just then of what he was hearing. The woman was too upset, too much in the grip of her catharsis. Gently, so as not to scare her off, he told Kersh that everything would be all right, that in fact he was very happy to hear her say what she had just said, and that they should get together and talk some more. He set a date and made her promise to come down to his office to discuss the matter. On the chance she might need coaxing, he took her number. With that, Kersh hung up, still assuming she had spoken to one of Connick's men, but a decent and forgiving guy, as prosecutors go.

Her mother came along for the interview with Healy, and it was not until they were sitting in his office that Kersh, still wretched with anxiety but determined to press on, came to realize that he was Kyles's attorney. The irony of it all was not lost on her. "Mr. Healy must have thought he'd died and gone to heaven," she would reminisce a decade later. Healy, of course, was delighted by what he was hearing, and cagey enough not to show his excitement. But as they settled in for a talk, Kersh started to break down altogether, and Healy feared he might be losing her. "Look, Mr. Healy, I'm scared. I'm very scared. I'm scared that this man, this Curtis Kyles, will get out and come after me. Revenge. I'm scared his family will do it, if he doesn't. Someone's gonna get revenge on me for this horrible thing that I done."

But Healy had ways of dealing with anxious witnesses, and he proved adept at calming Kersh. As she sat there, he called in a stenographer and drew up an affidavit in which the young woman acknowledged coming forward to recant her earlier perjury and stated that she feared revenge by the defendant or his family. Somehow, knowing it was there in writing, over her notarized signature and on file in a lawyer's office, eased Kersh's fear of being disappeared in the night. At least this way, it seemed to Kersh, her killer's motive would be known. Maybe that would forestall such a fate.

Kersh was more than just an eyewitness recanting an identification. There were, after all, three others still pointing the finger at Kyles. Much more important to the defense was her account of how she felt maneuvered by police and prosecutors into making that identification. A recanted identification was an inconvenience to the state. Testifying that she had somehow been coaxed into giving misleading testimony was potentially explosive, grievous enough to throw the state's other stratagems into question and undermine the verdict itself.

What became clear in more measured conversations with Kersh was that, though she and her cousin had injected themselves aggressively into the crime scene by peeling into the Schwegmann's parking lot and then chasing off after the killer as he left in Mrs. Dye's car, Darlene came reluctantly to her role as an eyewitness prepared to make an identification in court. It took more than John Dillman's visits with their heady undercurrent of romance. The problem was that she really didn't get a good look at the killer. She had broken her glasses several days earlier—sat on them; $150 down the drain—and was blind without them. And so Dillman upped the ante, she claimed, with his appeal to racial solidarity: "Come on, Darlene. Help me take another nigger off the street." And there was no resisting that one, not in New Orleans in 1984. Not for a young woman like Darlene.

Kersh, like Kyles, was born in 1959. Which is to say she was reared in the middle of the most convulsive adjustment of the racial order to have befallen New Orleans since Reconstruction: the integration of the public school system. And no class of whites—certainly not the Uptown aristocrats on the federal bench who decreed an end to Jim Crow—felt more directly threatened by legal parity with blacks than whites of low-to-middling means like the Kershes. These were the people who would actually share classrooms as well as workplaces with the newly enfranchised African Americans, though in many cases not for long. Within ten months of Kersh's birth, a little girl named Ruby Bridges became the first black child to run a gauntlet of spitting, cursing, shrieking white parents and enter the doors of a formerly all-white New Orleans public school, William Frantz Elementary. The Frantz parents turned out in platoons for an entire year of razzing and obstructionism before admitting defeat. By the end of the decade, many of them had bolted not just from the public school system but from the city itself, continuing a migration to the suburbs that would reduce the population of New Orleans by about a quarter from its 1960 peak and shift the racial balance until two of every three city residents were African American, a group that had been a numerical minority as late as the 1950s.

White flight did not necessarily allay the racial animosity among those who had turned tail on the city. Forty years later, as the New Orleanians who stayed put were rewarded by soaring housing prices and a cultural magnetism that was drawing young artists and musicians and tourists from around the world, the nearby expatriates still muttered about the city they had known, and indulged among themselves in the fashion of wishing the worst for the place it had become. Suburbia's ultimate vengeance was the election of an ex-Klansman named David Duke to the state legislature, followed by the support of a majority of the state's white electorate in his failed 1991 bid to become governor.

Darlene Kersh was nursed and reared on that kind of static, and it had taken its toll. "I was brought up prejudiced," she would freely confess. "I didn't hate black people, but I didn't associate with no black men or women. That's just how it was. We was just prejudiced." The flip side of racial animosity was a supremely high regard for the authority figures the working-class whites counted on to protect the shrinking privileges that came with pale skin. "Policemen was just something that I looked up to. They were like just a step below God to me. They never did any wrong. They were right. They were the people who protected you."

Whether or not he was aware of her reluctance to testify, Lowell Dye had soon joined with John Dillman in double-teaming Kersh. He had wanted to know about his mother's last moments, mostly out of compassion, but partly because the possibility that she had lingered, that she could have been resuscitated, would figure importantly in the civil suit for damages that he was readying against Schwegmann's. In Lowell, Darlene Kersh saw a bereaved son desperate for details he could cling to. Had his mother suffered? Had she fought her assailant? Dye's need to know these things was touchingly authentic. But his and Dillman's contact with the witness had the ulterior effect of deepening the bond between the young white woman and her tribe. In hindsight, as she came to grips with her bigotry and with the perjured testimony that had helped put Curtis Kyles on death row, Kersh would tell herself that she had been "immature," "ignorant," a creature of her times, as she surely was. But back in 1984, her decision to testify looked very different to her, more like a civic duty.

What seemed to push Kersh past her qualms and second thoughts was Dillman's assurance that the evidence already in hand was conclusive even without her testimony. She came away from her encounters with the detective convinced that the police had found Kyles's car in the parking lot after the killing and had traced the license tag to him, something Healy and Bey now knew to be untrue. Mrs. Dye's groceries had turned up in Kyles's kitchen, Kersh was led to believe, though the failure to find Mrs. Dye's fingerprints on any of the canned goods would leave this allegation at best unproved.

Because of her skittishness, perhaps, Dillman had chosen not to risk exposing Kersh to the photo lineup that he used in developing the other eyewitnesses. Whether she was blind without her glasses or merely bashful, he didn't need another tentative ID or, worse yet, no ID at all. Instead, on the day she was scheduled to testify, as Kersh recalled, Dillman met her at the district attorney's office adjacent to the courthouse.

"I went up there to whatever room he told me. It was me. It was Dillman and some other guy that I think was his partner at the time. Mike somebody. We went into a room, and there was another guy. I think they might have told me he was a prosecutor. And they had an easel up with white paper on it with a drawing, and they said, 'Look, Darlene. This is the courtroom. You ever been in a courtroom?' And I was like, 'Nnooooo . . . I don't know nothing about it.' And they said, 'This is where the judge will be, and we'll be right over here, looking at you. And here's where Kyles will be—no prison jumpsuit, regular clothes. And when the prosecutor asks you their questions, you just describe exactly what happened. And when he says could you describe him, you say, 'Yes, that's him.' Point to him, in this direction over here, and say, 'Yes, that's him.'"

It was an account that Dillman and Kyles's prosecutors would strenuously disown when confronted with it years later. But even with a script in mind and all the support and coaching from the hard white men fighting crime, Kersh said she had still been troubled by her uncertainties. Out in the hallway, waiting to testify that first time, she found herself chattering nervously with other people she assumed to be witnesses. A deputy rode herd on the group, in part to discourage just such conversations as this, but at one point, with the deputy beyond earshot, she asked the two men sitting next to her, "You sure it's him? You saw him and you're sure it's him?" And both men, both of them black, assured her that Kyles, their own kind, was the killer. Finally she was called to the stand, and at the culminating moment in her testimony was asked to identify the man she had seen kill Delores Dye. "Point to him, in this direction over here," she remembered being told. "Point over here and say, 'Yes, that's him.'" Which is exactly what Kersh did, rising from her seat and pointing into the blurry swirl of color and shadow before her, a young woman trying to please.

Before Darlene Kersh left Healy's office that first time, he yielded to a hunch and put her through a photo lineup of his own devising. Unlike the lineups that John Dillman had spread out on the trunk and seat of his cruiser for Smallwood and Williams and Territo—but not Kersh—this one included mugs of Beanie Wallace, front and silhouette, along with Kyles and three or four young black men chosen at random from the parade booked nightly in Orleans Parish. Kersh studied the lineups, trying to transport herself back in time to the parking lot and the sight of that man standing over Mrs. Dye's corpse—not all that much higher than the roofline of the car he was about to drive off in. She could see the plaits in his hair, the vague black blur that was his face. The exercise was really a matter of idle curiosity on Healy's part. Kersh's usefulness to the defense now hinged not on the accuracy of an identification she made years earlier, but on her acknowledged inability to have made any identification at all. After a pause, Kersh pointed her finger at the pair of mug shots that most closely resembled the blur graven in her fading memory. "Turn it over," Healy said. She did so. The name on the back was Joseph Wallace.

FOURTEEN

Judge Carolyn King was not one to waste her time. Not on the Kyles case, not on any case. She did not have time to waste. The federal Fifth Circuit—based in New Orleans, but also presiding from Houston, where King lived—generated upward of two hundred opinions per judge, per year, four a week on average, making it the first or second busiest circuit court in the nation. And with four vacancies on the bench in the early '90s, that workload was heavier than ever. A dissent was a lot of work, particularly for King, who was known among her colleagues—insofar as judicial etiquette allowed for any criticism at all—as capable of long-winded opinions. At any length—and her Kyles dissent would run close to seventy pages, twice the length of the majority opinion—dissents were most often exercises in futility. The court has spoken; the majority has ruled. Which is to say a dissent was often an intellectual self-indulgence, when not a complete waste of time.

Kyles's defense in criminal court may have been threadbare, but the appellate work on his behalf was verging on exhaustive. Having played every card the state court system allowed them, Healy and Bey turned to the federal court system. On November 2, 1990, seven days ahead of Kyles's latest date with the executioner, the U.S. District Court for Southeastern Louisiana had obliged with a stay—Bey's reward for the harrowing few days when she had Trenticosta screaming in one ear and a Phelps

Dunbar partner yelling in the other. But in June 1992, just weeks after Kersh came forward to recant her trial court testimony, that same court denied a motion to reopen the case.

Healy and Bey were running out of options. All that remained was the U.S. Fifth Circuit Court of Appeals and beyond that the all but impregnable fortress of the U.S. Supreme Court itself. Their argument to the Fifth Circuit played out primarily along two axes. One was that Kyles had been the victim of ineffective counsel at his original trials. Regan himself had acknowledged his youthful shortcomings. The other, more dynamic argument was that the state had not met its constitutional obligation—as affirmed in the pivotal 1963 Supreme Court ruling *Brady v. Maryland*— to turn over all pertinent evidence in their case against Kyles, even and most especially evidence that tended to cast doubt on his guilt. This was the mother lode of material Bey had unearthed, including the Beanie tape, the list of license plate numbers (notably lacking Kyles's plate), the statements taken by police from witnesses. Another year had gone by when, in the spring of 1993, two of the three members of the Fifth Circuit panel reviewing Kyles's pleadings decided they were groundless. Any aspersions cast on Kyles's original counsel were dismissed out of hand by King's colleagues, Judges Patrick Higginbotham and Edith Jones. Martin Regan had done as fine a job as could be expected given the "overwhelming" force of the evidence against his client. And on the *Brady* issue, even if prosecutors had turned over more of the evidence Kyles's lawyers claimed to be exculpatory, even if Regan had possessed the witness statements, the tape, the list of license plate numbers, it would not have made a difference, certainly not enough to undermine confidence in the jurors' decision that Kyles was the killer and should be put to death.

Judge King pondered the opinion, envying her colleagues only their certitude. She had read it a dozen times, when it became clear to her that she could not let it go unanswered. The doubts raised by the new evidence just would not subside for her, and in them she glimpsed an appalling possibility: they had nailed the wrong man—an angel, certainly not, but the wrong man had been snatched from the streets of a New Orleans slum and now faced Louisiana's executioner. She would dissent as forcefully as she knew how, not because there was any chance of dissuading her colleagues. Their work was done as hers began, a process that would delay release of their opinion by months. No, King was writing out of conscience, but above all on the chance that if the case were to reach the only court higher than hers, one or another of the nine U.S. Supreme Court justices would weigh her words and find them persuasive.

King went to work on the case. Or rather the case went to work on her, taking over her office as spring turned to summer in Houston. Desktop, credenzas, the floor itself—for weeks on end they were carpeted with stacks of paper large and small, drawn from what by then was the voluminous file of briefs and transcripts, police memoranda, photographs, witness statements, and citations from case law. Most federal appeal courts worked from an appendix culled from the district court record, a synopsis of key documents and rulings in the case. But not the Fifth, and in this Kyles was exceedingly lucky. The Fifth used the full record, including even the state court proceedings and all their supporting documentation. King would be able to rethink the case ab ovo, rather than simply assess the interpretations of evidence made by lower courts. By June she found herself crawling on all fours among the papers on her carpet as she sought out the connections and contradictions that would become her argument.

Given the ideological litmus tests that would bedevil the selection of federal judges by the turn of the century, it's easy to forget that there was a time when the men and women warming the federal bench did not necessarily bear the brand of the President who put them there, in King's case Jimmy Carter. There was no small irony in later hearing King's dissent dismissed as the ravings of a Carter liberal. For one thing, she was and intended to remain a Republican, as she made clear to the Carter envoys who sounded her out about a Fifth Circuit appointment in January 1979. And that said, she reminded them that she was happily ensconced in her work as a securities lawyer, a civil specialty about as far removed as the law gets from the tenor and consequences of a murder case.

King—née Carolyn Dineen—had grown up Catholic in the Tipperary Hill section of Syracuse, New York, a part of that upstate burg so Irish that city fathers eventually yielded to repeated vandalism of the Tipperary Hill stoplight by putting it upside down. The emerald-green lens then enjoyed pride of place above the red one, a target of repeated stonings by local hooligans. The stonings stopped. The Dineens were reasonably well set up—lace-curtain, not shanty, Irish. King's father would serve as state insurance commissioner under Tom Dewey, the GOP white knight whose reputation as a governor and mob-busting federal prosecutor carried him in 1948 to victory over Harry Truman—on the front page of the *Chicago Tribune*, if nowhere else.

Carolyn Dineen left Yale with a law degree as well as a first husband, an ambassador's son from among her classmates. Their shared ambition was not unlike the one that a decade earlier had carried another scion of eastern privilege, George Herbert Walker Bush, to Texas. Carolyn and Jim Randall wanted to make it on their own, which meant putting some distance between themselves and families that, as King would observe, "were willing and able and anxious to tell us how to live our lives." Bush chose Midland and the "oil bidness." The Randalls studied the map of the United States with one criterion in mind: a place outside New York City where it would be possible to pursue a sophisticated corporate practice. And so it came to pass in August 1962, the ink barely dry on their law degrees, that the Randalls blew into Houston in a six-year-old Chevy station wagon.

Seventeen years later, as the Carter presidency entered its final months, King found his people persistent. The President was interested in appointing a woman to the Fifth Circuit's western half, centered in Houston. Gender aside, what prompted their go at King, they explained, was her long service as chief financial officer of Houston's United Way. Jimmy Carter was big on community service. King traced her own commitment to volunteerism back to her father. "You should tithe your life," he had instructed her. "It's even more important than tithing your money."

Federal judgeships are for life, a prospect that was clearly daunting to a forty-one-year-old in love with securities law. The Carterites' last-ditch pitch was that King try it for a decade. There'd be time enough after that to go back to her practice. She acquiesced, and so it was that an Irish Catholic Republican woman from the Yankee North found herself installed on the bench by a Southern Baptist Democrat. By the time the Kyles case came along, King, by then divorced from Randall and remarried, had overstayed her decade by another four years, and she would still be on the bench a decade later. She could be pigeonholed only as a centrist.

She had, for example, joined many a judicial majority over the years in opinions that upheld the death penalty. But with Kyles, soon enough she found herself fighting tooth and claw to avert that fate.

She was ably assisted. King assigned the case to Brent Newton, one of four clerks in her service. Though his views would moderate over the years, giving way to a sneaking suspicion that some crimes were egregious to a degree that did not rule out the death penalty, in her clerk King had herself an outright foe of capital punishment. Fresh out of law school at Columbia, Newton had been lured to Texas by George Kendall, of the NAACP Legal Defense Fund, to work on the case of James Russell. Russell would become the forty-first Texas inmate to be executed after the practice resumed in the 1980s. (By the end of the century, that number would have risen to 239, and Texas would claim the dubious distinction of the highest per capita rate of state-sanctioned execution in the world.)

From work with the Legal Defense Fund, Brent Newton went on to clerk for Judge King and, soon enough, to the case of Curtis Kyles. Even before King fully acquainted herself with its peculiar and disturbing combination of evidence presented and evidence withheld, Newton was on fire with the conviction that justice had miscarried for Kyles and that it was up to his boss to do something about it. To Newton, for example, it was as obvious as it was outrageous—in his words, "a very big deal"— that police had eradicated the writing on a Schwegmann's receipt in the course of tests that would produce the only verifiable Kyles fingerprint in the entire case. The receipt had been found on the floor of Mrs. Dye's car. That police had not photocopied the receipt before subjecting it to the nitrate tests that bleached away all trace of the ink was strong evidence to Newton that they had not wanted it to remain legible. Why? Because it did not support their contention that this was Mrs. Dye's receipt—and as such, an ironclad link between Kyles and the killing.

Kyles, after all, had never denied riding in the red car—in hindsight surely Mrs. Dye's. Beanie had shown up in it on the morning after the murder and taken him to the supermarket to buy cigarettes and transmission fluid. A two-inch stub was about what you'd expect for the purchase of cigarettes and transmission fluid. But how could it be Mrs. Dye's receipt, when by all accounts she had bought several bags of groceries— a week's worth—on the day of her death, purchases that would have generated a receipt more likely two feet than two inches long? This one wasn't long enough even to account for the cat food. Equally disturbing was the amount of evidence that—whether by design of the prosecutors or the incompetence of Kyles's trial attorney—never found its way into his defense: the witnesses' statements; the list of license plates; the tape of Beanie's encounter with police, a snitch playing pied piper as he lured detectives along a trail that would take them to Mrs. Dye's car, to the parking lot where she had died, and finally to Kyles himself, to his apartment and to the gun.

Regan could not have specified each of these items during the trial's discovery phase; he didn't know they existed. Under the *Brady* rule, it was up to prosecutors to produce them voluntarily. But like any defense attorney worth a damn, Regan knew to ask for the witness statements. These were not forthcoming, police would later claim, because they hadn't been transcribed. Even the prosecutors did not have them in time for the trial, the state later contended, blaming the lapse on "slow typing" and a shortage of police transcribers.

King had no trouble making a mockery of that argument. The statements recovered years later by Sheryl Bey had been signed and dated by the witnesses who gave them to police within a day or two of Kyles's arrest, and the typing had been entirely professional. The state can't have it both ways, King thought to herself: either these documents were discoverable, or the dates on them were fraudulent. In her dissent, she would put the matter more elegantly, perhaps a bit sarcastically: "I simply cannot accept the proposition that the various typed documents were backdated and signed after trial," she wrote. And even if Cliff Strider's interview with Beanie was memorialized in longhand—an account of his role curiously at odds with earlier versions he offered to police, and energetic in its effort to entangle defense witness Kevin Black in the murder's aftermath—it was still legible and could have been photocopied. And the tape? Who needed a transcriber? Its contents could have been divulged to the defense or anyone else with a cassette player to slip it into.

When it came to Kyles's constitutional rights, not all the blame lay with the state for suppressing evidence. King broke with her colleagues decisively over their respect for the quality of counsel Martin Regan had provided his client. The decision not to call Beanie Wallace to the stand, or even to interview him in the course of preparing for trial, could not be called tactical, in King's view. It was incompetent, as Regan himself had conceded—a blunder based on a young attorney's misunderstanding of the law. Regan's mistaken belief was that he could not call Wallace to the stand as a witness for the defense and then proceed to pick apart his testimony to show its lies and internal contradictions—could not, that is, impeach his own witness.

It astonished King to think that a lawyer with a man's life in his hands could have been this ill informed. The solution to Regan's dilemma, as Cliff Strider feared he might realize, would have been simply to establish that Wallace was a hostile witness and grill him as an adversary. How could Wallace have been other than hostile, given the defense theory that posited his ambition to get rid of Kyles in order to enjoy the favor of the woman who had carried Kyles's five children. King stopped herself for a moment, allowing her hindsight speculation to take her in another direction. Suppose Wallace, once called to the stand, had simply clammed up, opted to take the Fifth. Well, Regan could have used that too, King decided. Prosecutors contended that Wallace was merely acting the part of a "good citizen" in cooperating with police. Why, Regan could have challenged the jury, would a good citizen need to invoke his constitutional right against self-incrimination?

And anyway, King reasoned, the inconsistencies in his testimony could have been laid bare in other ways, if prosecutors had not illegally withheld the tape and the statement Wallace signed in the wee hours of Sunday morning after leading Detectives Miller and Eaton on a midnight tour of the Ninth Ward. After all, Wallace wasn't the only hostile witness at Regan's beck and call. He could have played John Dillman and Johnny Miller against each other to question Dillman's contention that he had no idea Beanie had been in and out of Kyles's home all Sunday afternoon and had been the one to suggest that the cops search Kyles's garbage. What the hell. Regan could even have called Strider as a hostile witness for the defense, a dramatic and unusual maneuver, but it would have been entirely permissible once Regan saw the notes of Strider's session with Wallace—as he surely should have.

As King knocked the case around with Newton, chasing one hypothetical and then another, she was indulging a decidedly unjudicial love for what she called lawyering. She was playing what-if, imagining herself in Regan's shoes, trying to argue the case better than he had. It was a game that pushed the boundaries of proper appellate review, though the issue of a counselor's effectiveness—raised by Kyles's post-conviction team—required at least some of it. The rest came from King herself, the symptom of a mid-career elevation to the bench that this former securities lawyer hadn't been at all sure she wanted to make.

Such was her absorption in the case that despite her heavy workload—its demands only compounded just then by an accident that had made an invalid of her husband—King foreswore the common practice of letting a clerk draft the entire opinion for her review and signature. Instead, along with everything else on the docket, she and Newton reserved at least a few minutes every day to hash out their latest insights into the Kyles case and develop strategies for rebutting the majority view that he had no grounds for a retrial. Once they reached consensus, Newton would hazard a draft and King would revamp it, sometimes a little, sometimes a lot.

Their work was done by the last of the summer, as was Newton's clerkship. Several weeks would pass before the Fifth Circuit formally handed down its opinion against Kyles, accompanied by King's dissent. The hiatus in Newton's professional life looked like a good time to get married, and in early October he found himself passing through New Orleans en route to Alabama to show his intended around Auburn, where his parents were teachers. On a whim, he exited Interstate 10 and tracked down the Schwegmann's parking lot, epicenter of the case that had taken over his life for so many weeks. With photographs of the crime scene still firmly in mind, it was not difficult to triangulate the spot where Mrs. Dye went down. Newton stood there a moment or two, letting the events of that day nearly a decade earlier wash over him. Still lost in his thoughts, he strode across the parking lot and into the supermarket on a beeline to the pet food section. Sure enough, there were the standard-issue price markers on the edges of the shelves beneath the different brands—Alpo: four for 99 cents; Puss 'n Boots: three for a dollar—just as Kyles had described them. Kyles's memory was accurate, Newton noticed, uncannily so. His mistake, horrible in its consequences, pivoted on a preposition. The pet food was not *on* sale; it was *for* sale, at the prices marked.

The Fifth Circuit opinion was promulgated on October 14, 1993, days after Newton's stop-off in New Orleans. The single most resonant construction in the entire dissent was its second sentence. It was a purely personal admission rather than an argument of law, a rhetorical flourish by Judge King. But in light of her high position and her strong record, it would constitute a turning point in the long post-conviction phase of the people's case against Curtis Kyles: "For the first time in my fourteen years on this court—during which I have participated in the decision of literally dozens of capital habeas cases—I have serious reservations about whether the State has sentenced to death the right man."

In his cell at Angola, Kyles tore into the ruling, shipped up to him by his lawyers in New Orleans, and reread that sentence over and over again. Concerned about his morale, Healy and Trenticosta had steered him past the majority view to King's invigorating dissent, and he tried hard to share their excitement. She wasn't declaring him innocent, but here was a judge—a federal judge—as much as saying that he should not have been denied a retrial, that the doubts about his case were more than reasonable. It was grounds for optimism, unless he thought about it a little harder. And then suddenly there was nothing protecting Kyles from a sense of despair as abysmal as despair could get. Because once you wore out the giddy feeling that came with a new ally, there was this: even with a Judge King on the case, even with her support, the Fifth Circuit had ruled against Kyles, stripping away the next to last barrier between him and the executioner.

Sometimes it seemed clear that Angola was getting impatient to see the last one fall too. Healy would remember the phone call in the middle of the night, the sense of panic in Kyles's voice. The guards had moved him. Without provocation or cause, they had moved him down the tier to the number 2 cell, the one near the entrance, where the condemned were stashed in the days just prior to execution. He had a stay? Tell it to the boys in the death house, they told him. Orders were orders.

It had not been easy finding Healy. His daughter Mary Marguerite fielded Kyles's call at their house in Uptown New Orleans. But her father was away, and it was eleven o'clock at night when the paging service tracked him down at the Coastal Club, a fancy hunting camp way over by Louisiana's Texas border, where he was weekending with his wife. Healy called home, got the message, and called Kyles, who described the situation. "You got to straighten this out," Kyles demanded. "Now." Healy obliged. He got Judge Waldron on the phone, and Waldron got through to the Angola warden, and not soon enough a placated Kyles was being led back to his accustomed cell, uncertain whether he was the victim of harassment or of an appalling bureaucratic glitch.

Judge King's heartfelt doubts about Kyles's guilt had the force of a battle cry, except that the battle appeared finally to be lost, not joined. The U.S. Fifth Circuit, for all King's objections, had ruled against Kyles. There was a last option, and of course Healy would exercise it, but you almost had to ask yourself, Why bother? Along with thousands of appeals on every conceivable matter of civil and criminal law, virtually every death penalty case eventually floated up to the U.S. Supreme Court. From that number, the court chose to hear at most a handful in a decade, those being cases in which the court saw not just the possibility that justice had miscarried, but that substantive points of law needed clarification. Healy made a point of keeping Kyles informed. He fired off a petition for "cert," he told him, using law-office shorthand for certiorari, the process of seeking review of lower court proceedings. By then Kyles knew the system well enough to sense that the maneuver had a last-days feel to it. And another development contributed to his feeling that the case had run its course: Sheryl Bey was moving on, leaving New Orleans to launch her career as a full-fledged civil lawyer up in Jackson, Mississippi. Kyles would miss her.

Other changes were adding to Kyles's sense of anxiety, changes on the home front. Tyteannia had moved out on her mother and was with Lela now. That wasn't a bad thing, not at all, Kyles told himself. Lela was a rock, and Ty, at sixteen, almost a young woman. But what was going on with Meco? The details were hard to come by. Kyles's family spared him bad news as a matter of unstated policy, but he had learned to read the nuances in a caller's tone of voice and to aggregate hints and details dropped here and there over time—an application of the same "ear-hustling" skills that, as a teenager, kept him in tune with the street and its scandals. Finally Pinkey mentioned that she had shipped Meco off to the family farm in Bassfield to live with one of her brothers. And after a time, Kyles came to understand that the Bassfield school had booted him right back to New Orleans, dismayed by the proclivity for hooliganism and bad company that inspired Pinkey to get the twelve-year-old out of the Desire project in the first place.

It dawned on Kyles with frightening clarity: "Meco thought that what a man was, was me. Everything he heard about me, he tried to become it." Flattering, perhaps, but also terrifying to Kyles. On the phone they'd talk about it, insofar as possible. "You ain't me" became Kyles's message; "you're Meco." His dread was not that Meco would emulate his flash and criminal pursuits. That was inevitable to some extent for any Ninth Ward boy with the moxie to become a man of standing. What, after all, was the alternative? A minimum-wage job in a sewing factory? The father's inescapable dread was this: that Meco, in seeking to live up to his father's rep, would push well past it. And there was only one station stop beyond death row.

Sheryl Bey's departure from New Orleans threw Healy together more regularly with Nick Trenticosta—the young staff attorney from the Loyola Death Penalty Resource Center—but perhaps not regularly enough. It irked Healy that Trenticosta had sometimes begged off on court appearances during the latter stages of appellate review, leaving Healy to shoulder the burden alone. In fairness, Trenticosta had his hands full putting out legal fires as they flared and faded, scorching one or another of the several death row inmates whose cases he monitored. But it was perhaps inevitable that there would be tension between the two men, poles apart as they were in style and political values, and neither one of them ego deficient. In many ways they were diametric opposites: Healy the old-school conservative seeking to redeem the honor of law by fastidiously emending its errors and abuses; Trenticosta, the fast-talking radical, clearly open to the proposition that the whole system was rotten and that a case like Kyles's laid bare its disgrace. Somehow, they collaborated on the petition for cert, fired it off, and turned to other matters.

Six months passed. The date was April 25, 1994; Healy's secretary announced the call: Jack Peebles from over at Harry Connick's office.

Healy picked up the phone. "Congratulations," Peebles began. If it was the DA's office calling, it had to be something to do with the Kyles case. "Congratulations for what, Jack?" Healy tried to imagine. "We just heard from somebody at the Justice Department," Peebles continued, and without ado, he got right to the point: "They granted your writ."

"That can't be," Healy replied. But Peebles was not a man given to practical jokes. Just to be sure, Healy rang up Trenticosta. "I just got a call from Peebles, Nick. He says we've been granted cert." Trenticosta shared Healy's skepticism and thought he knew the source of Peebles's confusion. "Right. We've got a favorable ruling, but it's a state writ, Bunky—state supreme court, not federal." Some minor matter, he assumed, unresolved in the case's earlier trajectory through the state system, had finally been dealt with. To confirm his suspicion, Trenticosta swiveled his office chair around to his desktop computer and logged on to the U.S. Supreme Court site. But there it was—roundabout in its archaic grammatical constructions, yet at the same time laconic: "Supreme Court of the United States No. 93-7927. Curtis L. Kyles, petitioner. On consideration of the motion for leave to proceed herein in forma pauperis and of the petition for writ of certiorari, it is ordered by this Court that the motion to proceed in forma pauperis be, and the same is hereby, granted; and that the petition for writ of certiorari be, and the same is hereby, granted."

Trenticosta made the call to Angola. Kyles had overcome his initial skepticism about the young lawyer, about young lawyers in general; and Trenticosta, much closer to Kyles in age and, from his work in the projects, better able to fathom where Kyles was coming from, had developed an easy rapport with the death row inmate. Kyles could hear the excitement in Trenticosta's voice. He could also hear something else, the conscious restraint, and he knew it for what it was: a lawyer trying to keep a doomed client's hopes from soaring too high.

Cert was nice. Cert was rare. But all it meant was that nine justices were willing to take a further look. So too had the justices of the U.S. Fifth Circuit Court of Appeals, and the U.S. District Court and the Louisiana Supreme Court and before that the Fourth Circuit Court of Appeal in Orleans Parish. And Kyles was still in Camp J waiting on a date with the executioner that wouldn't be broken. He knew all that without needing Trenticosta to remind him. But there was no sense trying to be too cool about what had happened in the U.S. Supreme Court. When a slim hope is your only hope, it is as huge as certainty.

Whether or not a visit to the U.S. Supreme Court would come to anything for their client, for Trenticosta and Healy and the other lawyers attached to the case it brought bragging rights. Trenticosta had never been anywhere near the Supreme Court, and Healy, for all his eminence in the field of admiralty law, had never argued a case there. Suddenly each man was a potential stumbling block in the other's path to that high distinction. Trenticosta's ambition was buck naked, as far as Healy was concerned, and his belated if quickening interest in the Kyles case miffed the senior lawyer who had sacrificed so much to it for so long. Where had Trenticosta been when Healy needed him?

"Nick never came to any of the evidentiary hearings, all that spring. He didn't come to the argument at the Fifth. He said he had an execution to worry about, and I wasn't too pleased. But once the writ was granted, he decided he was taking charge, man."

And in short order Healy had the distinct impression that he was being frozen out. To work with them on the brief that would be submitted to the Court in advance of oral arguments, Trenticosta engaged the services of a New York Law School professor named Tony Amsterdam—a brilliant figure in criminal defense work and also merciless, as Trenticosta would discover, in subjecting early drafts to the meat grinder of his editing and critique. Brilliant the professor might be, but he definitely lacked the courtliness a Southerner like Healy expected in a fellow barrister. When Healy found himself in New York on other business, he called Amsterdam's office and introduced himself as Kyles's lawyer to the anonymous assistant who picked up Amsterdam's phone. "Kyles?" the assistant asked quizzically before setting Healy straight. "That's Nick Trenticosta's case." In any event, Amsterdam was too busy to come to the phone and never did call Healy back.

What rankled Healy even more was that when the brief was finally done, Trenticosta filed it without bothering to secure Healy's signature as attorney of record. The other shoe was not long to drop: a decision on who would get to argue the case. Clearly Trenticosta did not yet have the credentials or the training to appear before the highest court. But he could reasonably argue that Healy was no better qualified for criminal defense work's ultimate challenge. Healy was not quite ready to concede the point. And neither was Sheryl Bey. Pregnant with her second child, she happened to be in New Orleans representing her Mississippi law firm in a civil case. For old times' sake she dropped by Phelps Dunbar to see friends and kibitz on some of the tactical wrangling over who should do the honors. Healy and Trenticosta were present, as was Gerard Rault, the criminal law specialist from Loyola they had hired to advise them. Healy had left the room for a few minutes when Bey made a last-ditch appeal on his behalf. He's perfect for this case, she reasoned. "He's an incredibly good narrator; he brings such emotion and life to it." She was quickly reminded that narrative panache wouldn't count for much at the Supreme Court level. The Court would be looking at issues of law, not the facts of the case. They'd need a theoretician, a legal scholar, Trenticosta argued, not a storyteller, however effective storytelling might be in other phases of a criminal case. By all accounts—and Bey quickly fell in line—the man for the job was a Columbia professor named Jim Liebman, a legal prodigy still in his forties but already one of the nation's ranking experts on death penalty law. Healy took his lumps and agreed to carry the flag for Liebman on a visit to Angola. Kyles was initially reluctant. Healy had got the case this far—a hell of a lot farther than Martin Regan, the other lawyer to whom Kyles had entrusted his life. Kyles had faith in Healy. He wanted to stick with him. Healy talked him out of it. "They say Liebman's the best, Curtis."

To allay his own qualms, Healy looked in on Liebman the next time he was in New York. They had lunch together at the Columbia faculty club along with Charles Black, an admiralty law guru and, as a great hero of Healy's, someone he was delighted to meet. By the end of the session, Healy's impressions of Liebman were also highly favorable. The man was unmistakably a great student of the law and a dazzling speaker.

To work with him on the brief, Trenticosta tapped a young Loyola Resource Center staffer named Denise LeBoeuf. Like Trenticosta, Denny LeBoeuf had migrated to the law in a roundabout way. Born in Detroit and reared in New York, she had drifted to New Orleans in the late 1970s because she had a sister there and because, from all reports, the jazz scene was a sweet one. She was working as a bartender—and, frankly, worried enough about her drinking to realize it was time to quit—when she enrolled at Tulane Law School.

LeBoeuf was bright and extraordinarily passionate about her work, but as talismans go, her involvement in the case did not augur especially well for Kyles. She had cut her teeth on death penalty work with the Dalton Prejean case, and Dalton had been executed. Simultaneously with the Kyles case, she would nurse along the Antonio James case until his execution in March 1996.

The division of labor on the brief was natural and entailed no dispute: Trenticosta would handle issues of law. LeBoeuf would marshal the facts of the case—would "crawl all over the facts," to borrow a phrase that had stayed with her from her law school days. "Stay with the paper"—the printed record of the case—that was another mantra she would hew to. And as Judge King had discovered, by now there was a huge amount of it.

The eyewitnesses were still the hydra that had to be slain if Kyles was to escape the death house. Even with Darlene Kersh's perjury exposed, there were Isaac Smallwood and Bobby Territo and Henry Williams to contend with, each describing a slightly different killer but unanimous in their contention that the man in the red car was the defendant they had studied now twice from the witness stand. Jurors were bound to be impressed by that consensus, but LeBoeuf, something of a scholar of human cognition, was convinced it could be attacked. "The common sense, man-in-the-street notion of memory," she had come to believe, "is that you have a sort of video recorder up in your head, and if you can just access it, you can replay it and compare the picture of, say, the man killing Mrs. Dye with a line of possible suspects. And bingo! you pick your perp." Her readings in the cognitive sciences and contact with experts in the field had convinced LeBoeuf that common sense, in this regard, was nonsense and that the reverence for eyewitnesses among police and prosecutors was antiquated—"a hundred years behind the times." Memory, as LeBoeuf saw it, is not a recording device, it's a construct, and very much hampered by stress. For good reasons: "When we are afraid for our very lives, as we are when we see something as shocking and horrible as somebody killing someone a hundred feet away, the old snake brain at the top of the spine takes over. Remembering faces is not a survival skill that's going to keep you alive. Running fast, freezing, fighting—those are skills that keep you alive. And none of the chemicals that flood your brain to trigger those reactions assist in creating memory. Just the opposite: they impair memory." And then of course there was the egotism of memory. Having glommed on to a suspect—whether legitimately or through coaching of the sort Kersh said she had experienced—Territo, Smallwood, and Williams had an investment in their choice, one that would only deepen in successive courtroom exposures to Kyles.

Denny LeBoeuf picked apart the witness statements, studying the inconsistencies Healy and Bey had spotted, with an eye out for ones they might have missed. In the aggregate, the killer was tall but also short; his hair was braided and also in an Afro; he was a teenager and a man in his late twenties. Where was the monolithic unanimity in all that? LeBoeuf was only more tantalized by the evidence suggesting that Kyles had been framed. She deconstructed the tape of Beanie with his handlers by lining it up against his subsequent statement to police and the notes of Strider's heart-to-heart chat with him between the two trials. The contradictions were blatant; the protectiveness police had extended to their informant was extravagant and, in LeBoeuf's view, despicable. Finally, she and Trenticosta had something to show to Tony Amsterdam, their editor.

His reaction was devastating: They were whiny. They were data shopping. To thunder and cajole, to argue and contend was to impute to the nine justices of the U.S. Supreme Court an inability to see the truth themselves. Amsterdam slashed the brief by half and told LeBoeuf and Trenticosta to rewrite the part that he deemed salvageable. And hurry up about it. Time was running out. He wanted a just-the-facts approach, a weave of fact so seamless that you could not see the threads.

Much of the task was synthetic, pulling together disparate tidbits long since part of the record, but then LeBoeuf stumbled across something that amounted to a fresh discovery. She would not forget the moment.

It was late spring in New Orleans, which only partly accounted for the evening temperatures, a swelter that in most parts of the country would betoken the height of summer. It was worse on this occasion because LeBoeuf was working late, very late—up against Amsterdam's deadline—and the office building's central air-conditioning had kicked off for the night. Her brow beaded with sweat, a cup of coffee gone to room temperature at her side, LeBoeuf was bent over the bottom drawer of a file cabinet, scanning Beanie Wallace's rap sheet for the umpteenth time. LeBoeuf knew a thing or two about rap sheets. She had worked as a public defender, after all, and she knew as well as any cop the number codes and the different crime categories they denoted. Wallace's rap sheet was, of course, a fulsome one. This was a man who had been investigated for murder—Leidenheimer, if not Dye—and had done time for manslaughter. In other cases, the dispositon of the original charge against him went unreported on the rap sheet, a strong suggestion, as LeBoeuf interpreted it, that his role as a snitch spared him any follow-through.

And then, in among the lesser felonies that she had scanned so often, paying more attention to the charge on the right side of the printout than to the time and place of the offense printed on the left, LeBoeuf spotted an address she had not noticed before, an address she recognized: 5300 Old Gentilly Road, except it was written as one word: "5300OLDGENTILLYRD." That might explain why nobody on the defense team spotted it before, LeBoeuf thought to herself. It was, after all, a place much better known to all involved in the Kyles case as, simply, Schwegmann's. The crime: theft and possession of stolen property—a purse snatching, one that had not escalated to murder. The date: June 1984.

It was, as LeBoeuf would come to think of it, a eureka moment: here was the man who had fingered Kyles, haunting the very premises on which Mrs. Dye had been killed, and he was committing a crime that, at the outset, was identical. What galled LeBoeuf as much as anything was her confidence, from her days as a public defender, that the cops had known about this all along. "It's the first thing a cop does—run the rap sheet. They do it before they date a woman!" LeBoeuf added, remembering a case in which she had proved that to be true, greatly humiliating a hostile cop who had been called to the stand.

LeBoeuf grabbed a phone to share her discovery, then put the receiver down again. It was two a.m. Nick would be asleep. In the sweaty quiet of the office she settled back to think about the implications of what she had learned, and her delight in her discovery curdled into anger. "It kills me to this day," she would say years later. "Johnny Miller ran Beanie Wallace's rap sheet in 1984. And if *I* could figure it out, I know Johnny Miller figured it out. He knew that Beanie had been arrested at the site of Mrs. Dye's murder. And yet, knowing what he did, he let an innocent man rot on death row for fourteen years."

Kyles, perhaps not quite as innocent as LeBoeuf wanted to believe, took the news of her discovery in stride, his sense of encouragement about his case undercut by the bitterness engendered in him by the system's devilishly lethargic awakening to the truth about the man who had framed him. But Kyles was no longer the passive recipient of his counselors' ministrations. Slowly, over time, he had begun to get the drift of the lawbooks he ordered up from the prison library or borrowed from jailhouse lawyers on the row and forced himself to scan. Words became sentences, and sentences began to yield ideas and concepts, and in due course Kyles was even writing down his thoughts and theories about his case. He became convinced that one idea he had mastered might even make a difference in the brief LeBoeuf and Trenticosta were preparing, so he told them about it: that his arrest and the evidence pulled from his home were the outgrowth of a process so tainted—Beanie's conniving relationship with the police—as to preclude reference to any of it in a court of law. His arrest was, in the imagery of the law, "the fruit of a poisoned tree," and should be annulled, Kyles argued. He would see a reflection of his idea in the brief that was finally polished and submitted to the Supreme Court of the United States of America. It would be a source of quiet pride to Kyles for the rest of his life.

FIFTEEN

The oral argument before the Supreme Court was scheduled for November 7, 1994, a Monday. Late in the previous week, Jim Liebman set aside his work at Columbia University, took the train from Penn Station, and checked into the anonymity of Washington's Hyatt Regency, on New Jersey Avenue—a quiet, balding hotel patron in search of the perfect solitude he needed to immerse himself utterly in the case at hand. It was his ritual, a process of intellectual distillation, of pacing about, of talking to himself and thinking aloud until he had an answer for every conceivable question the justices might pose. Liebman toiled, his labors interrupted only by infrequent calls for room service and more frequent, sometimes urgent calls for last-minute research by the team in New Orleans. As the hours ticked by, minute-long exegeses got boiled down to ten seconds, and two-sentence replies were compressed to a clause or even a phrase.

The argument was not the problem; it could be rehearsed, memorized, reduced to rote—except that you needed versions of it in varying lengths. One would be a continuous thirty-minute spiel, rhetoric enough to fill the allotted half hour in its entirety. To be allowed the privilege of delivering a monologue of that length was not grounds for optimism. It might better be considered a strong predictor of failure. Perhaps, in the history of the Court, there had been a petitioner so spellbinding that the

justices sat for thirty minutes in enraptured silence. More likely, Liebman realized, an uninterrupted presentation would mean simply that he
had failed to engage the justices intellectually, and that foretold an affir-
mation of the legal status quo rather than a petitioner's challenge to it.

Questions would mean that the justices were alive and listening, but
questions could also be an attorney's undoing. Liebman, who had clerked
for Justice John Paul Stevens as a young man fresh out of law school, had
seen Antonin Scalia, the Court's most thunderous right-winger, deliberately sabotage an argument he didn't like by posing questions so numerous and so niggling that the petitioner couldn't make his case. But
politics was not everything. Ruth Bader Ginsburg, a justice more patient
with death penalty appeals, could also be talkative, Liebman had noticed.

And so in the isolation of his hotel room he paced and talked to himself and paced some more. Liebman did not anticipate indifference. His
greater fear—a fear so keen it racked his sleep and knotted his stomach—
was that the justices would take deep offense at the strategy he had hit
upon, a line of argument quite tangential to the brief drawn up by LeBoeuf
and Trenticosta and honed to such perfection by Tony Amsterdam.

Any attorney came before the justices of the U.S. Supreme Court as
a supplicant, not as a peer. And though there were lawyers mighty enough,
and frequent enough in their visits, to count on collegial indulgence if
they tested the protocols of the Court, Liebman—at least at that point in
his career—was not one of them. And yet, in addition to the Court's consideration on behalf of his client, he would be asking a huge favor on his
own: permission, in essence, to radically overhaul the theory of the defense. It would take time to elaborate his new vision, almost the whole
half hour—if only he could get away with it.

Once Liebman had been approached by the team in New Orleans,
his decision to argue for Kyles in Washington had been clinched by the
fact that the brief—the hard work of a case, as he modestly put it—had
already been completed. But his signing on had been conditional. He reserved the right to review the entire case file, and having done so, he
came to a daunting conclusion: the brief was off base. Intelligent as it
was, and well crafted, it was fundamentally and, Liebman thought, fatally
flawed. What LeBoeuf and Trenticosta had done, in Liebman's view, was
to look too eagerly to Beanie in their effort to shift guilt from Kyles.

There was no more convenient substitute for the role of culprit, but in essence that would be asking the Court to choose between bad guys, and that, Liebman knew from his year clerking for Stevens, was something the justices generally found distasteful. The object was not to convict Joseph Wallace, but to establish reasonable doubt about the conviction of Curtis Kyles, Liebman reminded himself. And as for the ineffectiveness-of-counsel gambit—the argument that Martin Regan was not up to the task of defending his client—Liebman decided to drop it altogether. It was a weak argument at best, at worst a commonplace invoked so routinely on appeal as to have lost all impact except in the most outrageous cases.

It might be a delicate matter, Liebman realized, easing LeBoeuf and Trenticosta away from the strategy they had worked out so painstakingly in the brief. But it had to be done. As the alternative, Liebman saw his best shot as an assault on what the prosecution had always identified as the great strength of its case against Kyles: the eyewitnesses. Discredit the eyewitnesses—those who hadn't already discredited themselves, like Darlene Kersh—and the whole case began to wobble and fall apart.

Not that Beanie could be ignored. He would haunt Liebman's presentation as much as he had Regan's and the brief by LeBoeuf and Trenticosta. But it would not be as a figure seen bent by the kitchen stove or staring blankly from across the street as Kyles was cuffed and thrown into a squad car. No. The discrepancies in the witness testimony—pivoting as they did on the size of the perpetrator, on his hairstyle, and on the vantages from which these features were glimpsed as he tussled with Mrs. Dye and then eased off in her car—made it possible to put Beanie at close proximity not just to the cover-up but to the murder itself.

As the Supreme Court date drew near, the New Orleans contingent had flown up to New York to put Liebman through his paces. A moot court was arranged in a room at New York University, with Trenticosta among those playing judge and various of Liebman's and Amsterdam's law students in attendance. A moot court is a dry run, a dress rehearsal, but that does not make the questioning less than brutal. And with Trenticosta on the bench, Liebman could not help wondering if his decision to abandon the fundamental drift of the argument as briefed would inspire animosity. To his relief, the team saw merit in his approach, or at least fell in line without kicking up too much of a fuss. Picking apart the witnesses' testimony from the stand with the sharp prong of contradictions within their statements to police held great promise, everyone seemed to agree. But would the justices let Liebman get away with it—junking the script implicit in the briefs and essentially rearguing the case?

Aside from requiring that he be permitted to review the complete record of the case, not just the brief, Liebman had made one other request of the defense team as they recruited him, and that was the chance to visit with the man whose life was at stake. He did not know whether he would like Kyles. He did not necessarily need to like Kyles, but he needed to know him at least a little if his presentation before the justices was to move beyond abstract argument and gain the vitality of flesh and blood. Liebman had appealed cases without meeting his client, but he did not like to do it. He had also appealed cases in which he did not like the client, or the client did not seem to like him. It was a kind of bad chemistry that made the job more difficult, though perhaps not as difficult as representing an abstraction he had never met at all. And so it was, not many weeks before he would stand before the justices and bargain for Kyles's life, that Liebman hopped on a plane for Louisiana to discover just whose life he was trying to save.

Denny LeBoeuf met him in Baton Rouge for the scenic drive to St. Francisville and the final half hour through the hummocky barrens that divided Angola from the free world. As the car barreled along, LeBoeuf filled her visitor in on aspects of her client that could not have been apparent from the court record—his steadfast devotion to his kids, for example. To LeBoeuf it was one of the more striking things about Kyles, the way he managed to remain a father to them even when most of the fathering was by phone. God knows it was hard keeping up a relationship that way, and the visits were even less frequent than the phone calls—maybe two or three times in a year. But Kyles kept plugging at remaining a moral presence in his kids' lives, LeBoeuf had noticed, and the text of many a sermon was his own catastrophe.

"I'm in here because of the company I kept," he would tell them, touching on a recurrent theme. "I was a fool because I saw the trouble, I saw these guys wasn't no good, but I said give everybody a shot. You see somebody going down the wrong path, get away from them."

Another of Kyles's themes was the importance of family and keeping together. "Look at me," he'd tell them. "Look at how I hurt for you all." And if he found out about trouble among them, between Chester and Meco most likely, he'd warn the offender about how terrible he'd feel if the roughhousing turned dangerous, or even deadly, and one or the other of them had to live with it for the rest of his life.

And when all else failed, he'd just show them the shackles on his hands. "Even if this screen wasn't between us," he'd say, "I still couldn't touch you like I want to. You all are standing right there—*right there!*—and I can't touch you." And by then he'd have given up fighting back the tears. "That's what bad company do to you. It makes you hurt for your family."

Liebman noticed that LeBoeuf seemed genuinely to like the man she was describing. His own expectations were somewhat tempered by experience. Death row was not tenanted with angels. The men who wound up there, if not brutes on arrival, were often brutalized by what lay ahead.

Finally they reached Angola, the very name of the place redolent of Africa, the ancestral homeland of all too many of the prison's five thousand occupants. Liebman's revulsion with the death penalty was principled and rooted in law, but the racial bias in its application had personal resonance for a man whose wife and son were African Americans. Death row had been moved since the time of Bey and Healy's initial trek to the remote wilds of Camp J. Now it was right inside the prison gates, and soon LeBoeuf was introducing Kyles to the attorney from New York. They were fortunate in having a man of his caliber, she told Kyles, reiterating what Healy had said in graciously stepping aside. Liebman had clerked for a Supreme Court justice. He knew his way around that world, she told Kyles. Liebman would remember being pleasantly surprised by Kyles, by his intelligent interest in his case, by his receptiveness to Liebman's strategies for arguing it. And like others who had put themselves in Kyles's service, Liebman would remember being struck as much as anything by the gentleness of the man the state portrayed as a monster.

On the night before the Supreme Court date, Liebman emerged from the clutter and stale air of his Washington hotel room to have supper with the New Orleanians—LeBoeuf was there, Trenticosta, Healy—an evening edged with anticipation but genial enough. Liebman got up the next morning nauseated with anxiety. The case was not the problem. He knew the case cold. But would he be able to present it? It was the business of asking an indulgence of the justices, of signaling somehow, as he plunged into his case, that he was going to need time to explain himself, a chunk of time unfractured by questions hostile or friendly. Kyles had done ten years, seven of them on death row, and now it all came down to a half hour.

The Kyles case was the second hearing scheduled that Monday morning, and Liebman knew the wait would be torment for him. In search of peace, he headed up to the Supreme Court library, a study in leather and mahogany and silence that he remembered fondly from his days clerking for Justice Stevens. He also remembered the young woman at the librarian's desk, familiar and easy to be with, a touch of déjà vu that helped Liebman put himself back together. There in the serenity of the library he remembered a trick from his days in student theater back at Stanford, and he set about imagining himself not as a law school teacher a bit dry-mouthed in anticipation of an infrequent appearance before the nation's highest court, but as a seasoned regular in this august hall of justice. It was a method actor's approach to litigation, Strasbergian and complete. If Brando had morphed into a raging wife beater in *Streetcar*, Liebman could channel Clarence Darrow, presenting himself as a colleague of these justices, one with them in a shared mission to defend the Constitution and the laws that flowed from it. He would comport himself suavely, as though confident that they would see merit in the nerve-racking departure from procedural orthodoxy he was about to commit.

Now the moment had arrived. He glanced at his watch and at fifteen minutes to the hour left the library. He arrived in the chamber—visitors to the Court are always surprised by its modest size—just in time to witness a fleeting crisis not at all likely to sustain his hard-won composure: an exchange of angry whispers between Healy and Trenticosta as to which of them would have the privilege of settling his behind into the chair next to the one Liebman was assigned as litigator. LeBoeuf was present in the courtroom, within the bar but not "at table," as the saying goes, the distinction accorded Healy and Trenticosta.

The irony of being there at all was not lost on Healy. Here he was, a proponent of the death penalty and one of the leading lights in the world of admiralty law, sitting in the U.S. Supreme Court as part of a criminal case to be argued by colleagues with a clear agenda to overturn capital punishment. He looked over at Justice Scalia, the Court's Attila on death penalty issues, among other conservative causes, and wondered if the justice recognized him. It was Healy's great pleasure as president of the maritime bar to have invited Scalia to speak at the group's annual convention one year in Bermuda. He and Mrs. Healy had been the ones to pick up Scalia at the airport and escort him through the convention, but as Healy glanced up at the justice, who was chatting idly with his colleagues on the bench, it seemed clear that he did not recognize the lawyer from New Orleans.

Now the justices were signaling for the oral presentations to begin. Liebman rose, all five feet five of him, and, in his quiet, thoughtful way, plunged right into the thick of things. "Curtis Kyles is on death row for a robbery-murder he steadfastly claims he did not commit, and that his initial accuser, Beanie Wallace, did commit. The issue here is whether the jury had a reliable opportunity to assess the evidence on that identity question, notwithstanding the quantity of evidence that the prosecution suppressed . . . Although legally narrow, the case is factually complicated, and I'd like to take a couple of minutes, if I could, to give the background. When Delores Dye resisted a thief in the parking lot of a Schwegmann's supermarket . . ."

If it were possible to speak and hold one's breath at the same time, that would be a fair description of Liebman's performance in these earliest moments of his allotted half hour—his every word delivered in dreadful expectation that Scalia or another of the conservatives opposed to the Court even hearing the Kyles case would cut short his recitation of fact. The Supreme Court was not about fact; it was about theory. The Court already knew the facts of the case. That would be the argument: have done with your narrative, Mr. Liebman, and get to the point.

But the interruptions did not come. At least not until Liebman was far enough along to sense that he had hooked the justices on his storytelling.

What it all came down to, said Liebman—a man slight enough himself to acknowledge a lifelong sensitivity to the issue—was height, stature, physical bulk. Kyles was bone thin and six feet tall, "a maypole," Liebman told the justices with a turn of phrase that made the observation memorable. In fact, Kyles was an inch or more shy of six feet, but six feet was the figure included in the police record, a rare instance in which the sloven-liness of that record—or was it an overstatement inspired again by the need to portray Kyles as larger and more menacing than life itself—worked to the advantage of the defense. Beanie, on the other hand, was "a fire-plug," as Liebman put it: short and stocky.

How, then, to explain that witnesses mistook them for each other? Here Liebman was well served by a snippet of trial testimony that Judge King also had seized on, acknowledging that Kyles and Beanie, while completely different in stature, resembled one another in profile. Their facial features were comparable; they were similarly dark complected, and like many short and stocky men, what height Beanie had was in his torso, meaning that he would look about the same height as Kyles once seated in a passing car.

With those differences and similarities sorted out, Liebman's next maneuver, logically, was to separate the four eyewitnesses into two cate-gories: those who had seen Mrs. Dye's killer standing beside her, and those whose exposure had been limited to the sight of the man leaving the parking lot in her car. Darlene Kersh, of course, was self-eliminating. She was a confessed perjurer and, in any case, had identified Beanie Wal-lace as the killer in the informal photo lineup arranged by Bunky Healy. Liebman made almost as quick work of Bobby Territo, the young man who had alarmed no one more than himself by shouting excitedly that the "nigger just shot that lady." Territo had acknowledged from the stand that his closest encounter with the killer, the one that shaped his visual impression of him, had occurred in profile as the red Ford pulled right and swept past Territo's truck on a beeline for the exit lane. And further limiting the reliability of Territo's glimpse of the passing driver had been his otherwise commendable instinct to grab a pencil, scrounge for a piece of paper, and try to jot down the Ford's license plate number—which he succeeded in doing, Liebman reminded the justices—as the car swept past.

That left the two laborers, Isaac Smallwood and Henry Williams, and now Liebman stood to prove how valuable the witness statements to the police would have been had Regan's routine demand to see them been honored a decade earlier. Because on examination, Smallwood's actual experience of the killing, though elaborated from the witness stand to include details about the gun and Mrs. Dye's final struggle, could only have begun after the killer had taken his seat in her car and begun to drive off. Liebman read aloud a passage from Smallwood's statement to police: "'I heard a loud pop. When I looked around, I saw a lady lying on the ground, and there was a red car coming toward me.'"

Justice Scalia zeroed in on Liebman just then with a question apparently meant to suggest that Kyles's attorney was hanging this part of his argument on a technicality, a mere turn of phrase at odds with common sense. Surely Smallwood had looked up the moment he heard the shot, which would have given him time to see the killer before he settled into the driver's seat.

But the police had quizzed Smallwood on exactly that point, Liebman answered, and returning to the transcript of Smallwood's interview with detectives, he read aloud their follow-up question and Smallwood's answer to it. "Detective: 'When you heard the shot and looked, was the black man standing near her?' Smallwood: 'No. He was already in the car coming toward me.'"

That left Henry Williams, the grandfatherly gent prosecutors had labeled their best witness. Liebman was willing to concede the point. Indeed, Liebman was about to claim Williams for the defense. "Williams did get the best look at the robbery and the shooting," Liebman told the justices, "and a few hours later he described the man he saw commit it, and this is the description he gave: . . . a black male, about nineteen or twenty years old, about five foot four or five foot five inches, 140 to 150 pounds, medium build, dark complexion, and plaited hair, short. Williams thus gave an identical description of Beanie Wallace." Now Liebman was closing in for the kill: "On that very same day that Williams gave this statement, the police got information and reflected it in a police report that said that Beanie Wallace had committed another murder,"—the Leidenheimer murder—"and in it they gave Beanie Wallace's height and weight, and it was 5 foot 5 inches, 140 pounds—same day—and also twenty-one years old, which is much closer than Kyles, who was a twenty-five-year-old man at the time, six-foot tall, 125 pounds." Liebman hardly needed to belabor the implications of what he was saying, but he did not deny himself the opportunity to spell them out for the benefit of any of the nine justices whose thoughts might have been drifting. The critical importance to the defense of Henry Williams's statement to police was in no way more evident, he said, than in "the length the state went to conceal it." And then, as abruptly as Liebman's moment before the justices had begun, it was over, and he sat back down.

The floor now belonged to Jack Peebles, the envoy from the Orleans district attorney's office who handled appellate work for Harry Connick. Connick himself had not seen fit to dignify the proceedings with his presence, but then he rarely appeared in court, preferring instead to exercise his vision of justice through selected staff. That vision, as Peebles explained it to his questioners on the bench, saw no contradiction between the suppression of so much of the evidence and the legal obligation, set forth in the Supreme Court's *Brady* ruling, to fork over anything that might possibly be exculpatory to a defendant. Connick's reasoning, as Peebles explained it, pivoted—or foundered—on a paradox. Individual pieces of evidence—the list of license plate numbers harvested in the Schwegmann's parking lot, for example—might appear favorable to Kyles, but prosecutors had been within their rights to weigh them against the larger body of evidence from many sources—the photo identifications by witnesses, for example—in deciding that any one item was insufficiently weighty to require disclosure. If, in the aggregate, these individual items of suppressed evidence put the verdict in reasonable doubt, well, that was the wisdom of hindsight. It did not mean that prosecutors Strider and Williams had been bound to turn over everything they had, least of all material the police had not yet forwarded to them.

Maybe so, the justices seemed to say as they questioned Peebles, but how would it be possible for the defense—or anyone else—to appreciate the aggregate power of the state's evidence if each separate piece could, in good conscience, be held back. "I think that's what *Bagley* says," Peebles replied to a question by Scalia, citing a case that had elaborated on the governing *Brady* ruling. "That's crazy, isn't it?" Scalia commented, a remark that made it perfectly unclear whether he was sympathizing with Peebles or making mock of his interpretation of the law.

As the session broke up, Liebman accepted the congratulations of the New Orleanians. Whether channeled from beyond Clarence Darrow's grave or incarnate in the diminutive professor from Columbia, a masterful litigator had been present in the courtroom that morning. But had he mesmerized the justices with his narrative or, in neglecting theoretical considerations, offended a court increasingly impatient with liberal jurists and their obsessive dissatisfaction with laws that empower the state to take the life of convicted killers.

Once back home, the New Orleanians checked in with Kyles to brief him on how things had gone. There was nothing to do, they told him, but wait. He did not need to be told that it would be months before he knew his fate, and he knew the wait would be an agony. But there was a trade-off: every hour of it, every day and week and month, would be time that had to pass before the state of Louisiana could try again to end his life.

It would be more widely known as the day a lunatic blew up the federal office building in Oklahoma City, but for Kyles and those close to his case, April 19, 1995, was a thunderclap of another sort. Kyles would long remember hearing the desk phone ring, and then, a minute or two later, the guard who picked it up telling Sergeant Mayeaux to let him out of his cell. That meant it was a legal call, the kind guards had no choice but to accommodate, day or night. The desk phone was just outside the cellblock, but close enough so that the summoned inmate could reach through the bars and take the receiver. Trenticosta had conferenced in LeBoeuf.

He beat around the bush a bit, playing with Kyles. "Well, you know we've had your petition before the United States Supreme Court, Curtis. We've got some news for you," Trenticosta began. He said it just like that, and suddenly Kyles was not at all sure he could bear the possibility of a disappointment. "Come on, man, don't tell me," he heard himself say. To which Trenticosta started to reply, "Well all right, I won't tell you, then." But LeBoeuf had had enough of the cat-and-mouse routine: "Tell him, Nick. Let him know he got a reversal." Kyles assumed it was just another twist in their idle game. "Don't play with me like this," he said. "I know you all play some serious jokes, but don't play with me like this." And so they stopped and gave it to him straight. The reversal was for real. In the eyes of the law, it was as if the first two trials and the conviction and the death sentence had never taken place. What got said after that, Kyles had no idea. He would remember the sensation this way: "My ears shut down.

Everything went numb." In that condition, he was led back to his cell. To allies on the tier, he whispered his news as he passed, knowing not to be exultant. An inmate's good fortune would engender less hope than resentment in some quarters. And anyway, as Kyles didn't care to be reminded, the reversal might be seized on by the Orleans prosecutor as just another invitation to try him again, especially if Connick was insulted by the ruling, as he surely would be.

In excoriating tones that belied the narrowness of the five-four split among the nine justices, David Souter, writing for the majority, had bluntly declared the district attorney of Orleans Parish guilty of prosecutorial misconduct for failing to cough up material evidence favorable to the defendant. Prosecutors have an "inescapable" duty to disclose all exculpatory evidence, Souter wrote. No longer would prosecutors be able to hide behind the inefficiencies or manipulations of a police department in failing to disclose possibly exculpatory evidence, nor would it be legitimate to look at each morsel of evidence in isolation from all the rest and decide that it alone was not sufficient to undermine confidence in a conviction. Fail to do so, Souter wrote, and the adversary system of justice descends "to a gladiatorial level unmitigated by any prosecutorial obligation for the sake of truth."

In a dissent orchestrated by Scalia and echoing Peebles's line of reasoning, the minority grumbled that the Court had no business reopening the Kyles case, but having done so, it should have concluded that the massive core of evidence presented by the state was sufficient to overwhelm the significance of anything and everything that had been disclosed since then. Souter rebutted the contention this way: "Contrary to the incorrect standard for materiality that the Court of Appeals may have used, the state's disclosure obligation turns on the cumulative effect of all such suppressed evidence." Further, "a prosecutor remains responsible for gauging that effect regardless of any failure by the police to bring favorable evidence to the prosecutor's attention."

Harry Connick greeted the news not with humility, let alone humiliation, but with scorn. "Just because a guy puts on a black robe doesn't mean he's right," the district attorney muttered at reporters who pounced on him for a reaction to the reversal. Over at the Death Penalty Resource Center, LeBoeuf and Trenticosta were prepared to dismiss the comment as a parting shot by a deeply embarrassed public official. Surely now Connick would get about the business of following the dictates of the nation's highest court. In more contrite and measured tones, Connick's first assistant, Camille Buras, assured them that hereafter the district attorney's office would, of course, apply the law as instructed.

But did Connick fully grasp the law he was being ordered to apply? In general comments about evidence suppression, he seemed to have missed the point of the Supreme Court's ruling in the Kyles case. It wasn't just that the prosecution had an obligation to give up exculpatory material once defendants located and demanded it. That had been true at least since the *Brady* ruling three decades earlier. What the *Kyles* ruling said was that the prosecution had an obligation not just to procedure but to justice, and that it extended all the way to rooting out possibly exculpatory evidence and passing it over to the defense, even if that material initially was known only to the state. Connick wanted to leave the burden on defense attorneys. They needed to scour the evidence file themselves, he said, as though oblivious to the fact that the pivotal evidence in the Kyles case had been left out of the evidence file based on trumped-up excuses about a lack of police department typists.

Perhaps Connick was preoccupied. The day the ruling came down, he was looking ahead to a nightclub gig scheduled for the following evening. Since the late 1980s Connick had been actualizing his long-frustrated dream of a career as a crooner at a French Quarter cabaret, but this was an out-of-town opportunity. Connick and his backup band, the Jimmy Maxwell Orchestra, were booked to play a club in Baton Rouge, Louie's on the Levee, owned by a riverboat casino. It was a curious footnote, some thought, to a lengthy and largely unsuccessful battle by the DA to force the riverboat casinos in New Orleans to actually leave their wharves on a daily cruising schedule as required by law. Connick dismissed accusations of impropriety. "I don't see any reason to justify anything," he told the press. "I don't have any jurisdiction in Baton Rouge."

Where Connick did have jurisdiction was New Orleans, and in short order he had declared that Curtis Kyles would be retried there in the following year. The announcement ended Kyles's long sojourn at Angola, at least temporarily, and he was returned to parish prison.

In Houston, Judge King savored the sense of vindication that comes to those who have climbed way out on a limb that nonetheless proves sturdy. The Supreme Court majority might not have bought her every argument, but no one close to the case had any doubt that the passion and meticulousness of her dissent had inspired a closer look at a deeply flawed prosecution. That said, she was not one to overplay the significance of the ruling she had precipitated. King saw it as more clarifying than groundbreaking. It fell into a narrow but crucial category of Supreme Court work, she said, in which the justices take time out from their consideration of unresolved issues of law to demonstrate through close reading of a particular case exactly how the law should be applied.

But after *Kyles*, it would never again be enough for prosecutors to blame police if exculpatory evidence was withheld. *Kyles* would become a watchword against the narrow category of prosecutorial misconduct that might be called prosecutorial lethargy, whether authentic or feigned.

Back in New Orleans, it was particularly offensive to Robert Dye to learn of the reversal not from someone in authority at the district attorney's office, preferably Harry Connick himself, but from a radio reporter calling to ask for a comment. A comment on what? Dye asked. Once he read it, he would dismiss the ruling as another example of a liberal Court fulfilling its own agenda, a solid case thrown out on a trumped-up technicality. Lowell Dye would nurse a deeper grievance. His mother's murder had seemed to trigger a chain of misfortunes in his own life—the divorce from Jan, his father's career-ending bout with bladder cancer, the challenges he had encountered as a single parent rearing a son. And through it all, another disappointment was unfolding in slow motion in civil court as Dye took on the giant Schwegmann supermarket chain in a battle to secure some kind of compensation for his mother's death. The plaintiff's attorney in Dye had been alert to the possibility of negligence on Schwegmann's part ever since that first grief stricken visit to the parking lot after the murder. How could they not acknowledge their liability? he asked himself. The place had been essentially unguarded when the security officer named Miriam stepped inside ahead of her lunch break and her replacement failed to arrive on time. Or so Dye reasoned, in developing a scenario of his mother's last minutes that would be sharply disputed by Schwegmann's. As he dug deeper into the case, Dye was appalled by what he found. The parking lot was a virtual combat zone, from what he could tell. His research turned up dozens of armed robberies, an epidemic of armed robberies, a situation so far gone that employees had to be escorted from the building to their cars in the back lot. Dye quizzed police officers and found some, he said, who had been begging Schwegmann's to do something about the problem.

For the better part of a decade Dye had chased the case up and down the civil court system—hearings and rehearings; appeals and appeals of appeals. He found fault with the judge's jury instruction at the end of the first trial and eventually convinced the Louisiana Supreme Court to throw it out. The day before the case was to be retried, Judge Bobby Katz summoned the parties to the dispute to see if he could broker a settlement. First the lawyers huddled—the posse of them representing Schwegmann's and the buddy Dye had tapped to stand up for him in court. (Dye himself was doing much of the paperwork.) Then Katz called in Lowell and his father, preliminary to a separate meeting with John Schwegmann. Judge Katz began the conversation on a promising note. "If the facts turn out at trial the way the lawyers described it, I want you to understand, Lowell, there's no way you can lose. No way." That was the opener, as Dye recalled it, and of course it was music to his ears. But Katz went on. "Now the regrettable part is, based on your ex-wife's testimony that's coming in a deposition, I just don't think you have very much in damages."

What was this? By Dye's calculation, the case was worth at minimum half a million dollars: $300,000 for depriving Robert Dye of his wife of four decades; $100,000 each for the two sons who had lost their mother. But Jan, now remarried and living in California, offered testimony that Schwegmann's lawyers did indeed use to undercut Dye's claim.

Lowell Dye had a wonderful relationship with his mother, Jan testified. The problem was Robert. In essence, Jan's contention was that there was little affection between Delores Dye and her husband. They bickered; they slept apart.

It got worse. One of Schwegmann's contentions was that Mrs. Dye sealed her own fate—that she was "contributorily negligent" in resisting the gunman's demand for her car or her purse or whatever it was that he was after. Asked about her former mother-in-law, Jan described her as the kind of person who would have resisted an assailant. She was a lovely woman, Jan opined, but tough, argumentative. Jan harked back to an incident of road rage. She was in the front seat, her mother-in-law driving, when someone cut them off in traffic. Mrs. Dye got so angry, Jan said, that she caught up with the other driver at a red light and positively unloaded on him.

Dye would insist that Jan's testimony was a straight-up act of retaliation for losing the custody fight. Whatever Jan's intention, her testimony, combined with other evidence elicited by Schwegmann, effectively undermined the plaintiffs' case. As Lowell Dye succinctly put it, they had been screwed. In the end, the Dyes got nothing at all from Schwegmann, unless you count the donation in Mrs. Dye's name that John Schwegmann bestowed on a local school for children with mental disabilities.

Nothing for the Dyes, yet on top of all that, Kyles was getting a second chance? Might even go free? Flabbergasted by the Supreme Court reversal, Lowell Dye reeled back over the decade since he thought his mother's killer had been meted his just deserts, back to a moment when, in hindsight, he wished he himself had imposed the only appropriate punishment.

It had come during a break in one of the motions hearings that had preceded the first trial back in 1984. The squabbling among Regan and Strider and Williams had crested and subsided and crested again, and Judge Waldron finally saw fit to suspend testimony and see if he couldn't broker an accord on whatever point of law was then in dispute. And so he beckoned the attorneys and the stenographer and led them into his chamber behind the bench. A jury had yet to be impaneled. The courthouse regulars had slipped outside for cigarettes. Even the sheriff's deputies were AWOL as the paneled door swung shut behind Waldron. With a sudden shiver of recognition, a slight elevation of the hairs along the nape of his neck, Lowell Dye realized that there was only one other person in the courtroom just then, a person conveniently shackled and therefore entirely helpless against the surging rage that Dye urgently wanted to direct against him.

"This was my chance," Dye would recall all those years later. He was aware of the absurdity of his fantasy, yet entirely captivated by it. "If I had known then what I know today? If I had known the bullshit that was in store? If I had known how this would turn out? No question I'd have killed him. Right there. Why not? A few years for manslaughter? Oh sure, they'd have caught me. I'd have sat right there until they came back in. A small price to pay for getting rid of that son of a bitch."

PART THREE

SIXTEEN

You had to hand it to Harry Connick. It was no small thing for a white man—for any man—to have kept his grip on citywide public office for as long as he had, least of all during the tumultuous quarter century in which the rest of the New Orleans political establishment, notably excluding the criminal sheriff's department, "went black." It had meant cutting shrewd alliances: in the late '70s with Dutch Morial, the city's first African American mayor; then with his son Marc. Marc Morial took over city hall in 1994, just as the Kyles case was making its way to the U.S. Supreme Court.

The city's black bar was less than dazzled, however. Connick could swing with the jazzmen and chin with the bosses of the black political clubs, but he was regularly accused of not being enough of a friend to the young black attorneys fighting their way into the profession. By the 1990s there was still only a handful of African Americans among the scores of assistant district attorneys who spent their days arguing cases in court and, for better or for worse, were the public face of justice in Orleans Parish.

In fairness to Connick, integrating the DA's office was never going to be easy. What black law student would want what Harry had to offer—a schoolteacher's salary and all the coffee you could drink, maybe a judgeship one day for those with the stomach for politics. The hotshots coming out of LSU Law or even Southern University, a largely African American holdover from the days of segregated higher education in Louisiana, could make twice as much in their first year with the big corporate firms, enterprises no less aware than Connick of the need to get at least a few blacks on board.

With the third trial of Curtis Kyles scheduled for the autumn of 1996, Connick and his first assistant, a young white woman named Camille Buras (she would soon win a judgeship), reviewed their ranks in search of someone to lead the prosecution. A black prosecutor—ideally a black male prosecutor—would help to defuse the racial tension that coursed below the surface of any trial in New Orleans, especially when the defendant was black, as would be the preponderance of jurors, a tension only more pronounced when his victim was white. New Orleans, well before the mid-1990s, had passed a tipping point. In one of modern history's more astonishing capitulations, the white middle class had turned tail and fled the Southern downtowns and schools and hotels and workplaces they had struggled so angrily to immunize against black opportunity, in the process assuring not only the black gains that many whites dreaded, but a black political hegemony more sweeping than the fathers of the civil rights movement had dared to dream.

It was hard to remember the symbolic importance that had attached to the Canal Street lunch counters targeted in the late '50s for an opening wedge of sit-ins. In the two decades since Kyles had haunted Canal, the old department stores had been shuttered or turned into hotels. The mayor's office was long since the exclusive province of the city's African American political clubs, and the chambers of the city council, the municipal legislative wing, were likewise dominated by black representatives, as was appropriate in a city whose African American minority had quickly become a two-thirds majority as the whites bailed out. In the public schools, the citadel the whites had defended most viciously, the rout was only more striking. Integration had been followed by de facto resegregation and the creation of a system that was better than 95 percent black.

Somehow, despite increasingly vociferous challenges from aspiring black politicians, Connick had been able to hang on, his practices and policies more or less intact. And so, in the absence of a readily available black prosecutor for the Kyles case, Connick and Buras turned to a young white woman named Sharon Andrews, bright, balanced, a rising star on Connick's staff, if her marriage to a young defense attorney and plans for a baby didn't sideline her. As her co-prosecutor, they appointed an amiable assistant district attorney named Mike Daniels, another white. Gender would be less potent than race in the chemistry of the courtroom, but gender had its uses. Andrews in her quiet but relentless way would be a living stand-in for the white woman who haunted these proceedings: Delores Dye.

Andrews's counterweight at the defense table would be Denny LeBoeuf, as it happened a classmate during their years at Tulane law. And Nick Trenticosta was still on board as part of the Kyles team. Bunky Healy would remain a loyal consultant to the Kyles defense and a court-room presence to the end of Kyles's legal ordeal, but he had served his time, and now that the case was reversed and about to return to the criminal courts, his services were no longer as urgently needed. To lead them through the retrial, LeBoeuf and Trenticosta were angling for one of the defense bar's more notorious pit bulls. A white Bronx-bred lawyer with the accent to prove it, Mike Fawer had come South some years earlier and, evidently undisturbed by the extreme cultural dissonance between his in-your-face pugnacity and the treacly, soft-spoken Southern approach to life, had fallen in love with the place.

Denny LeBoeuf had worked for Fawer, as had her sister, Marie Campbell, a paralegal and an investigator. An office party late in 1995 provided LeBoeuf with the chance to catch up with Mike socially and, while she was at it, to sound him out about doing the Kyles case. She knew he would be interested, but almost certainly too busy—and too expensive. Fawer was big-time. In the late '80s he had successfully defended Edwin Edwards, the governor of Louisiana, against racketeering charges. And a few years before that, in the months just prior to the Dye murder, he was the wizard who secured an acquittal for millionaire Aaron Mintz by convincing a jury that his wife's death in bed with Mintz was, improbably, a suicide. But there was another side to Fawer, a liberal Northerner's delight in defending the underdog. In the South, most underdogs were black men, the purest of the breed being poor black men charged with capital crimes. But what clinched LeBoeuf's recruitment bid was a coincidence: that John Dillman was the lead detective against Kyles. Dillman was also the lead detective on the Mintz case, and Fawer had taken particular pleasure in dismantling his police work and professional self-esteem. "For another chance to go up against Dillman, I'd do the case for free," Fawer crowed. LeBoeuf called his bluff. There was no money to pay him anywhere near the $250 an hour he could get from the likes of a Mintz or an Edwards.

Fawer settled in to try the Kyles case pro bono. The defendant was grateful. A change at the helm no longer provoked the anxiety that had beset him when Bunky Healy was bumped aside in favor of Jim Liebman. Liebman had worked out rather well, after all. Now LeBoeuf and Trenticosta were telling Kyles that the lawyer before him in the Orleans Parish Prison visitor booth was just the man to tear apart the prosecution's case.

After Kyles's eight years on death row, OPP was a different place. Partly, the prison had changed. The more outrageous barbarisms of the old order—the gang-run free-for-all, with its violence and extortion—had yielded to slightly better regulation. But Kyles, too, had been changed by the passing years. In the eyes of inmates the age he was in 1984, Kyles at thirty-six was an old-timer, a vic, a man who had been swallowed into Angola and survived regurgitation. No longer was it necessary, as it had been during his pre-Angola days, to settle every dispute with flying fists, to follow every misdirected glance with a thumb gouged into the offending eye socket. The hellion of yore now thought of himself as "a laid-back type of person." Everybody knew that, as Kyles put it, "Curtis didn't mess with nobody"—but only because his stature and reputation meant he didn't have to. He had a seat in the dayroom that younger inmates knew to relinquish when he walked in the door. And once ensconced, Kyles would lean back against the wall, to watch TV or, if a combatant worth the trouble presented himself, to play chess, his passion and forte. But even these adjustments to the social order did not guarantee Kyles the perfected immunity he craved. To younger inmates he was a source of fascination as well as power, someone to cultivate—or be seen cultivating—in the hope that some of his authority would rub off on them. It was protection of a sort, enough to make a rapist—a "booty bandit," in the lexicon of prison life—think twice. Of course, some of the knuckleheads among the young men seeking his favor knew no better than to bid for his attention with overly familiar remarks or even jostling. But you didn't call Kyles "nigger" anymore, even in idle conversation, no matter that the word was ubiquitous, almost a term of comradely affection among prison blacks. And if a would-be acolyte encroached even a little on Kyles's space, he would eyeball the upstart or, if necessary, stand up from his chair until the boy saw the error of his ways and backed off.

Finding someone to preside over Kyles's retrial was no simple matter. One after another, Orleans Parish criminal court judges begged off, recusing themselves rather than tangle with a case that had so humiliated Harry Connick, a man they still had to work with, after all. Finally an out-of-parish jurist named Charles Ward, the crusty veteran of many a legal skirmish, agreed to preside ad hoc.

As the trial loomed larger, Sharon Andrews pushed aside other desktop distractions to concentrate on Kyles with a doggedness that was belied by her usual demeanor—soft-spoken, understated, more that of a librarian than a hard-charging and ambitious prosecutor. There were eyewitnesses and police to track down, and Andrews had to figure that some of them might have retired or moved away in the intervening decade. And then there was all that physical evidence to reassemble—the holster, the autopsy, the purse and its contents.

Even in the flush of his victory as Kyles's co-prosecutor in 1984, and notwithstanding the two-day blowout to which Jim Williams had treated himself as a reward for securing his first death sentence, he had known better than to chuck the Schwegmann's bags and old cat food cans into the first available Dumpster, however cathartic that might have been. But there was a carefree informality in the way courtroom exhibits were handled after a conviction, and the Orleans Parish evidence room was famously anarchic. Blood-crusted clothing might be tossed into those same shopping bags and the whole bundle consigned to the roaches and silverfish of long-term storage. Notoriously, as Brent Newton had lamented, the all-important Schwegmann's sales receipt, the only piece of evidence bearing Kyles's fingerprint, had been destroyed by police even before the case came to trial. The ink had been leached out of it by the chemicals used to raise the print. Now it was a blank stub of paper, pure white, and no photocopy had ever been made. There was the purse, Mrs. Dye's purse, dusty, cracked. Andrews turned it in her hands. There was something eerie about a dead person's effects, no denying it. Ten years after the fact, the purse was as out of fashion as Mrs. Dye's hulking Ford sedan, and for that reason only more valuable to the prosecution for its power to evoke a real woman in a particular time and place, a decent woman, an ordinary life snuffed out in a predator's rampage.

The gun. Andrews knew she needed to find the gun. All the ballistics tests known to science would not substitute for the impact on jurors of actually seeing the murder weapon—dark, snub-nosed—handling it, setting it down alongside the purse and the other items that would be dumped on the big table in the jury room as the twelve of them settled in for their deliberations at the end of the trial. Damn. Andrews picked through the heap of evidence a second time to see if the revolver might roll out of a furl in the shopping bags or a compartment inside the purse. No such luck.

Finally, leafing through the folders of paperwork shelved alongside the evidence, Andrews caught a break. She turned up a receipt showing that in early 1985, just after Kyles's murder conviction, the gun had been checked out on the signature of defense attorney Yvonne Hughes, then attempting unsuccessfully to slough a client's imminent conviction for armed robbery onto an available surrogate named Curtis Kyles. Andrews, excited by the responsibility that came with a high-profile case, was not one to leave a stone unturned. It hadn't worked for Yvonne Hughes, but perhaps Andrews could do better. Perhaps she could develop Hughes's former client as another witness against Kyles. She was not unaware of the downside risk: the substance of his testimony might not outweigh the negatives he would bring to the witness stand by appearing in a prison jumpsuit and handcuffs. She decided to go for it anyway and submitted a motion asking the court to let her add him to her witness list. Judge Ward may have been doing her a favor. The motion was denied. Ten years after the fact, there was no more reason to credit Hughes's failed effort to implicate Kyles than there had been in 1985. Worse yet, Hughes couldn't direct Andrews to the gun, except to say that she had returned it to the custody of the Orleans Parish court. Just where was anybody's guess.

Sharon Andrews would recall letting out a shriek when she turned it up some days later in one of several shopping carts full of evidence that had been wheeled into the attic of the courthouse and all but forgotten. There they were, dozens of guns, scores of them, most tagged, some not—hunks of squeezed metal that had spit lead into bodies that fell all over Orleans Parish, years' worth of homicides. A judge presiding on the floor below also found the shriek memorable, and he dispatched a deputy to order Andrews out of the attic until court was recessed. Andrews agreed to pipe down, but there was no getting her out of the attic. She had caught the scent of the Kyles case, and there would be no stopping her. "They'd have had to drag me out of there," she remembered thinking. The shopping cart yielded something equally important—an envelope containing the bullet that the boys in ballistics had linked to the gun found behind Pinkey's stove, the bullet the coroner had picked out of Mrs. Dye's brain.

As Darlene Kersh made clear in the affidavit on file in Bunky Healy's office, she had feared that Kyles or his family would come after her for lying on the stand about what she had seen—or hadn't seen—in the Schwegmann's parking lot ten years earlier. Those fears were not fulfilled. The assault would come quickly, but it would come from the district attorney's office. This they didn't need: some druggy white tramp who discovers love in the arms of black men and decides all of a sudden to recant her testimony. But how to neutralize her? The answer Sharon Andrews hit on was a bounced check, and she wielded the offending slip of paper aggressively. A rubber check—a check for $500 presented at a JCPenney branch across the river on the west bank of Jefferson Parish—was a legal problem usually settled in small-claims court. Not this time. The occasion was a motion hearing, to review the pertinence of evidence and prospective witnesses. The use of Yvonne Hughes's old client as a prosecution witness had been torpedoed at a motion hearing. Now it was payback time. Darlene Kersh had arrived at the hearing expecting to take the stand and rehash some of what she tearfully told Bunky Healy about her perjury in 1984 and John Dillman's role in coaxing the lie from her. Instead, she was confronted with a warrant for her arrest, and just to add drama to the moment, two armed deputies from the Jefferson Parish Sheriff's Department were posted at the courtroom door under orders to haul her into custody as soon as she finished testifying.

With Kersh on the stand, Andrews went on the attack. Kersh remembered it this way: "You are a liar," Andrews began. "You admit that, a perjurer. You are also a thief." Then, turning to the bench, Andrews made her demand: "Judge, I want this witness thrown out for being a liar and a thief." To Denny LeBoeuf, who was preparing to walk Kersh through her testimony, few moments in Kyles's long ordeal laid bare more starkly the ethos of Harry Connick's office, its commitment to conviction at any cost, even if the price paid was injustice. Inconvenient evidence? Suppress it. A witness has backfired on the prosecution? Disqualify her, or at least scare her into submission. But not all of LeBoeuf's dismay was directed at the prosecution. This was not a happy time to be discovering that a star defense witness might be damaged goods.

Kersh would long remember the look on the defense lawyers' faces and her own reaction to their dismay—that "oh shit," empty-in-the-gut feeling, like being jilted in love. She had betrayed the hopes of yet another team that had been counting on her help. But the problem with JCPenney was bogus, a big misunderstanding, she insisted. A druggy relative had swiped her checkbook. Kersh begged them to trust her: "I promise you, it's not me." LeBoeuf and Trenticosta had no reason to believe her. But she was too valuable to abandon at this point. They could only hope she was telling the truth.

The immediate problem was tactical: how to keep Darlene out of the hands of the Jefferson Parish deputies. By law, they couldn't arrest her in the courtroom, but as soon as she stepped outside, she was going to be handcuffed and hauled away. Until the matter could be sorted out, LeBoeuf convinced Judge Ward to grant Kersh asylum in his chambers.

On the phone with the Jefferson Parish judge who had issued the arrest warrant over the kited check, LeBoeuf brokered a deal in which she agreed to take responsibility for Kersh if the warrant could be at least temporarily suspended. The Jefferson Parish constabulary retreated to home turf, and Kersh was ushered out of Ward's chambers and then out of the courtroom without incident or arrest. LeBoeuf called in a favor from an attorney friend who agreed to escort Kersh into the Jefferson Parish courthouse, across the river in Gretna, to attend to the check. It did not instill joy in LeBoeuf's heart to realize that the presiding judge in this matter was Chuck Cusimano, a law-and-order hard-liner not inclined to be amiable with defense attorneys. But even Cusimano soon saw the evidence of overkill. For one thing, the nature of the warrant didn't require anyone's arrest. One look at the photo ID, made routinely as the worthless check was presented at JCPenney, and it was clear that Kersh wasn't the offender. The check kiter was her relative, as Kersh had maintained all along, a hopeless heroin addict who in due course would be sent upriver for a long spell. In Kersh's view: "I swear to God, she was better off there."

Sharon Andrews would always insist that there was nothing improper in her use of the warrant to strike back against Darlene Kersh. "Anybody who comes in this office or that's across the street in the courthouse with an outstanding warrant gets arrested. That's policy. That's the law," she would contend. If so, it was a law that LeBoeuf found more often observed in the breach, and it bitterly amused her to reflect on how differently it had been applied to Beanie Wallace, not a check kiter, but a check forger and also a wanted murder suspect, as he was cosseted by Harry Connick's prosecutors in 1984.

In further preparation for the trial, Andrews tried to get in touch with each of the officers who had a hand in the original case. John Dillman had quit the department by then to set himself up as a private investigator, with a sideline writing pulp fiction accounts of old cases he had handled as a detective. But he was in the area and easy to find. Johnny Miller, Beanie's contact and handler, was still with the department, but barely. A history of disciplinary problems within the NOPD had culminated in his conviction in 1990 on a federal firearms rap unrelated to the Kyles case. He had lied to a licensed gun dealer in the course of purchasing a weapon. In fact, as he would later testify, he had bought seven guns and shipped them to a cousin in South America. Just who he pretended to be in making the purchase and why the subterfuge seemed necessary to him were the more tantalizing questions, but the government settled for nailing him on the technical charge of falsifying a federal record. Miller was fined, put on probation for two years, and forced to do community service. The NOPD settled for a fifteen-day suspension and took him back.

Almost by accident, Andrews ran down another officer with a hand in the Kyles case. She had called the crime lab to order up some photographs of the murder scene and the corpse. The officer handling such requests was a sergeant named Mike Rice, the same Mike Rice who had participated in Kyles's arrest. Andrews had left messages for him here and there, messages that had gone unreturned. Now she had him on the phone. Rice had bounced around the department in the course of his twenty-four years with the NOPD. The Kyles case? Sure, he remembered the Kyles case, he told Andrews. He had been there on Desire Street the day they picked him up. In fact, he had been the cop in the backseat with Kyles when they drove him downtown. Andrews put up with a few minutes of this. She had better things to do than listen to a police department seatwarmer relive his salad days.

"He's guilty, Miss Andrews."

Andrews agreed, of course, and was getting ready to hang up, but Rice continued, and now Andrews found herself listening quite closely.

"He copped to it there in the backseat on the way downtown."

"Oh?"

"He told me he did it, but that he didn't mean to."

Andrews was stunned. A confession? No one had ever told her about a confession. "You could have knocked me over with a feather," she would say, recalling the moment.

SEVENTEEN

On October 11, 1996, Judge Ward gaveled to order the third trial of Curtis
Kyles for the killing of Delores Dye, an act of murder in the first degree.
The charge itself represented a setback for the defense. Mike Fawer had
no problem with high-stakes legal work—and the stakes got no higher than
a death penalty case—but his first instinct had been to seek a reduction
of the charge against Kyles to second-degree murder or even manslaughter, taking into account the prison time already served. A reduced charge
was the fairer charge, Fawer argued. It was also the more obtainable conviction, given the ambiguousness of the evidence, now that all of it had
been disclosed. But Connick's people would have none of it, and Fawer,
LeBoeuf, and Trenticosta were certain they knew why. Connick's team
cloaked its reasoning in the trappings of justice. Kyles had killed; he deserved to die. But the unstated reason for charging Kyles with first-
degree murder was, the defense team assumed, the tactical utility of the
Witherspoon rule.

The variables taken into account in selecting a jury for a murder trial
are several, not all of them particularly subtle, but Witherspoon eliminated
some of the guesswork altogether. Before a first-degree jury could be impaneled, the judge had to ask each prospective juror his or her views on
capital punishment, and those who told the judge they simply didn't have
the stomach for killing a convict would be excluded. In other words, a

Witherspooned jury was going to be a hang-tough jury, a law-and-order jury, a jury less likely to be burdened by bleeding hearts—though they now and then sneaked in. A Witherspooned jury might not always impose the death penalty, but it was more likely to convict than acquit. It tended to see the world in black and white, not the shades of gray that were the domain of reasonable doubt. And in due course, the jury for Kyles's third trial had been well and truly Witherspooned.

Much of the evidence inevitably would be a rehash of the first two trials, and for that reason was familiar to Kyles, now equipped by the years studying law on death row to take a more active role in his defense. Many of the same detectives and police technicians, a decade older but still graven in Kyles's mind from his first exposure to them, would take the stand to tell how the evidence had been collected and analyzed. The laboring men and passersby would once again repeat their oft-told tale of the parking lot shooting. But what had taken two days to tell in 1984 was now a compendium requiring two weeks to review through the lens of documentation and evidence subsequently unearthed and arguments honed before the highest court in the land.

No longer was the pipe-smoking Detective Pascal Saladino merely the instrument of a curbside garbage pickup, a factotum called to the stand to explain how pieces of evidence were secured and transported from Kyles's home to police headquarters. With the Beanie tape to draw on, cross-examining Saladino became an opportunity to establish that the informant had in fact suggested the garbage-bag pickup. There was nothing routine about it, Saladino had to concede. Indeed, in his many years as a detective, never once had police seized curbside garbage, Fawer got him to admit. If that tended to support the defense theory that Beanie orchestrated other aspects of the probe and perhaps planted the evidence as well, so too did the many steps not taken by police—for example, never dusting the garbage bags for Beanie's fingerprints, or the bullets in the murder weapon, or any other evidence that police seemed not to want to examine too closely lest it weaken their circumstantial case against Kyles.

But actions not performed are a weaker basis for argument than evidence actually in hand, and when it came to structuring the defense against this evidence, the U.S. Supreme Court opinion in the Kyles case amounted to a handbook, a set of instructions. Above all, it encouraged Fawer to devote himself to the impeachment of the eyewitnesses, just as Jim Liebman had done with such aplomb in his oral argument before the Supreme Court.

Darlene Kersh had taken herself out of contention. And Fawer made quick work of Bobby Territo after forcing him to acknowledge that his longest exposure to "the nigger" at the wheel of Mrs. Dye's car had been furtive glimpses of him snatched from the rearview mirror of Territo's truck. Yes, Territo might have gotten a better look at the driver as the Ford rolled past on the right, but had he not, by his own admission, sunk down into the seat below the sills of the windows to avoid being shot? That still left the gas-line laborers, Henry Williams and Isaac Smallwood, as troublesome for being of Kyles's race as for the steadfastness of their conviction that he was the killer. Williams would bedevil the defense to the final hours of Kyles's prosecution. But as Liebman had demonstrated, Smallwood was eminently susceptible to being caught in his own half-truths and contradictions.

Sharon Andrews had no more than introduced her witness when she backed away from close questioning and gave him his head. Untethered, Smallwood bolted instantly for the thicket of contradictions in which Mike Fawer in due course would catch him.

ANDREWS: Did there come a time when you saw or heard something unusual?

SMALLWOOD: Yes. They had this lady who was going to her car. They had another guy come walking down—let's see. She was walking like the way her car was parked, she was walking to the back of her car. But the guy, he was walking to the front. But she looked like she thought something was going to happen, so she just opened her trunk and put everything in her trunk and kept her keys.

ANDREWS: What did she put in her trunk?

SMALLWOOD: Her groceries and her pocketbook, and she had her car keys in her hand.

ANDREWS: What happened after that?

SMALLWOOD: And the guy, he just come from the front of the car
              and come to the back of the car where she was and
              grabbed her hand. And it looked like he might have
              told her to give up the keys.

ANDREWS: Did you hear what she said?

SMALLWOOD: No, I couldn't hear what he said, but she was getting
              ready, she was going to scream, so he went in his
              pocket and popped her in the head.

ANDREWS: And when he went in his pocket, did you see what he
              got?

SMALLWOOD: Yes, it was a small gun.

ANDREWS: Did you see the gun?

SMALLWOOD: It was like a small .32, something like that.

None of this was implausible. Mrs. Dye was killed with a slug from
a .32. And others in the group of eyewitnesses saw a tussle over the
car keys after she locked her groceries and her purse in the trunk. The
problem was that in the statement Smallwood gave police immediately
after the murder—one of the several statements prosecutors failed to
turn over to the defense at the time—he explicitly ruled himself out of
that group of witnesses. He had noticed nothing at all, he told police,
until after the gun was fired, indeed until after a man slid into the red
Ford—Smallwood called it a Thunderbird—and began driving out of the
parking lot.

   Mike Fawer was merciless, and he was going to take his time about
it. A desultory quarter hour of questioning rehashed where Smallwood
was standing on the afternoon of September 20, 1984, and precisely the
circumstances under which a detective named Donald Saucier took his
statement down at headquarters an hour or two after the killing. Smallwood readily agreed with Fawer's commonsense suggestion that the accuracy of his memory of the murder was never sharper than in its immediate
aftermath. Saucier had asked him if his statement was wholly truthful,
and then Smallwood signed the document and initialed each page. Fawer
now produced the signed statement and invited Smallwood to read it.

FAWER: Okay. You have not looked at that statement in twelve
              years, have you?

SMALLWOOD: No . . .

FAWER: You told us yesterday, you described the shooting. In
              fact you described seeing the woman before it, right?

SMALLWOOD: Right.

FAWER: You saw grocery bags, you told us about a struggle
              that took place, you told us about the kind of gun it
              even was, right?

SMALLWOOD: Right.

FAWER: You told us about those things, and about seeing the
              shooting, right?

SMALLWOOD: Right.

FAWER: The truth is, you didn't see it, correct?

Smallwood began to hem and haw. He really had seen the killing, he
said, but "I was kind of like on the shook-up side and nervous and all
when I made the statement."

Fawer wasn't buying. "You just told us a minute ago that the most you
knew and the most accurate you ever were was during that afternoon,
right?"

SMALLWOOD: Yes, that's what I said.

FAWER: You understand that at that time, when you were specif-
              ically asked—this is in your words—to describe what
              occurred, you said, "I heard a loud pop. When I looked
              around, I saw a lady laying on the ground." Is that
              what you told them . . . ?

SMALLWOOD: That's what I said.

FAWER: You were asked an even more specific question at the
              top of the second page—do you want to see it, or will
              you take my word when I read it?

The judge admonished Fawer for the contemptuous tone of that last
remark, but Fawer plunged ahead. "'When you first heard the shot and

looked toward the lady on the ground, was the black male standing near her?' Your answer: 'No. He was already in the car coming toward me.' Correct?"

Fawer then moved on from the police statement to remind Small-wood of his testimony before a grand jury some weeks later. Smallwood had reiterated not only that he was unaware of anything untoward occur-ring in the parking lot until after the shot was fired, but that when he heard the shot, so oblivious was he to the act of violence unfolding in the dis-tance, he first assumed the sound was a tire blowout.

The intended effect, one of them anyway, was to cast doubt on Small-wood's reliability as a witness, to establish that he had freely appropriated other people's observations—in particular those of Henry Williams—as his own, perhaps without fully realizing what he had or had not seen him-self. But that didn't necessarily disprove the sequence of events described. The more important effect, even if still subliminal in jurors' minds, was Fawer's insinuation that police and prosecutors were all too willing to overlook Smallwood's inconsistencies. Their commitment was not to the truth, but to the manipulation of it in ways that favored the conviction of a man fingered by an equally unreliable informant. Darlene Kersh was only the most obvious example. In due course, she took the stand herself at this third trial to acknowledge her lies and to contend they had been coaxed from her. As they pushed further into their defense, Kyles's lawyers took a subtler swipe at Detective Dillman, but it stood to undermine con-fidence in the whole process of eyewitness identifications based on the photo lineup he had known better than to use with the reluctant Kersh. What gave John Dillman away was a passage from one of his own books.

Credit for this discovery fell to Denny LeBoeuf's sister, Marie Camp-bell, whose specialty as a paralegal was penalty mitigation, the process of compiling the biographical insights that might entitle a defendant to the compassion of jurors when it came to imposing a sentence after convic-tion. But Campbell was an all-purpose investigator, and so she had ac-cepted the task—a "deeply repugnant" task, she would call it, arching an eyebrow ironically as though she were a mortified literary snob—of reading every word Dillman had published. His oeuvre comprised several books, each of them write-ups of actual NOPD cases, each told from the perspective of a feisty young detective who demonstrates pluck and guile in combating unspeakable criminality. Campbell plowed through *Blood Warning*. She read *The French Quarter Killers*. She was not so many pages into *Unholy Matrimony* when she hit pay dirt. What she had stumbled on was a passage—Campbell highlighted it with a yellow marker—that cut to the heart of any case that hinged on eyewitnesses and the use of a photo lineup to nail a suspect.

Armed with Campbell's discovery, Fawer crept up on his prey: "Is it fair to say, Detective Dillman, that as an experienced homicide detective, there are ways detectives have in conducting photo identifications, of suggesting who the—who they want the individual to pick out, without letting that individual know that?"

Dillman, of course, denied it.

FAWER: You wrote a book called *Unholy Matrimony*, did you not?
DILLMAN: I did.
FAWER: You stand by what you said in that book?
DILLMAN: Yes, sir.

Fawer began to read from the book, page 19: "'Every detective, even relatively inexperienced ones like me,'—namely you, John Dillman, at the time—'knew ways to,' quote, 'coax,' closed quote, 'a witness, to guide her without her knowing towards the "right" identification.'"

Andrews was instantly on her feet, demanding to see the book and any others Fawer might be planning to use against her witness. The passage from *Unholy Matrimony* was the only such exhibit Fawer had in mind, but he was happy to show it to Andrews while Dillman writhed uncomfortably on the stand. Calm was restored to the courtroom, and the defense attorney continued his interrogation. Glancing back down at the printed page, Fawer conceded a point before Dillman could make it: "You go on to say, '. . . such methods are to be avoided.'" That said, Fawer wanted Dillman to tell him just what those methods were, those methods best avoided. "What I am asking you to tell us, to tell this jury, is how homicide detectives would engage in this. You said you know how it's done, 'even relatively inexperienced ones.'"

DILLMAN: What I meant . . .

FAWER: Explain to the jury how it's done.

DILLMAN: What I meant by that particular quote was, during an identification, if you in some way touched a picture, maybe moved a picture up, try to make any type of suggestion. But also in the book, it clearly states before and after that there are ways that you can suggest an identification, but that that's never done. I wouldn't do it in this case. I didn't do it in the particular book. It's strictly . . .

FAWER: Why then, let me ask you this. I understand you're saying it's never done. Then why is it something that's common. You said "every detective," that's your words, right?

DILLMAN: Yes, sir. That's my words.

FAWER: So I take it that it's something that's not intuitive, right? It's not something that people know just by virtue of being anointed homicide detectives, right?

DILLMAN: No. I think it comes from years of working with people.

FAWER: You said "relatively inexperienced ones," like you, so it had to be early in your career as a homicide detective.

DILLMAN: Fawer, you can pick those words apart. That's what's written.

FAWER: It's what you said?

DILLMAN: That's what I wrote.

FAWER: And you wrote what was true, right?

DILLMAN: Yes . . .

Finally it was time to call Sergeant Rice, the man claiming to have been a killer's confessor. Each of the trials had served to remind Kyles of the theatrics that lie at the heart of a well-played courtroom drama, right down to the costume his lawyers had picked out for him: flannel slacks, loafers, and a cardigan, as though he were a young stockbroker freshly showered and ready to head home after a spirited round of tennis at the club. A trial, he had come to see, was a kind of con game, which was to say something not altogether unfamiliar to him. But Mike Rice's testimony pushed beyond theatrics and, for Kyles, into the realm of the surreal. His story, reiterated from the witness-box, was that Kyles sat beside him in silence for the first several blocks of the ride downtown. Finally Kyles had asked what this was all about, and Rice had told him: "The Schwegmann matter." Another long silence. And then this, by Rice's account: Kyles said he "hadn't meant to kill the woman. The gun went off by accident, he had only meant to rob her."

Rice's rendition of the trip downtown differed from Kyles's version not only at its heart—Kyles denied ever confessing to anyone, least of all Mike Rice—but also in its particulars. In Kyles's version of the ride into custody, he was not seated beside Rice; he had been shoved onto the rear floor of the car, and he lay there writhing, trying to fit himself to the hump of the driveshaft while praying that the next time the escorting officer kicked him—and the kicks were frequent—the bullet in his spine would not budge the fraction of an inch that he had been told separated lifelong pain from permanent paralysis.

The defense team was divided on only one issue. Which was the greater affront to justice—the fact that Mike Rice had come forward a dozen years later to testify about a confession not mentioned at the time of the original trials, or the decision by Harry Connick's people to play along, to actually dignify this witness with a place in their case against Kyles?

Fawer's cross-examination of Rice seethed with that sense of scorn: "For twelve years nobody knew of this information that you have been holding to your breast, correct?" Admonished by the judge for his sarcasm, Fawer went on. "And it just happened that after there was a reversal, in the twelfth year, a chance meeting between you and Ms. Andrews led to your sitting on the stand and telling us about this, right?"

Rice, so softly he was ordered to speak up: "Yes."

And why had nobody—not Rice, not Dillman, not anybody working the case—seen fit to at least jot down the gist of Kyles's confession?

Rice's story was that when Kyles started to sing on the way downtown, he told him to save it for the case detective, tell it to Dillman. And once up on the third floor at headquarters, in the cluster of desks and the adjacent interrogation room that was the domain of the homicide division, Rice claimed he passed the word along to his superior: "I told him that Kyles wanted to tell him that the gun went off by accident," Rice testified. "His response was he didn't think we needed it. We had enough."

To the defense team, Rice's testimony was an act of sheer invention. But reference to a confession had set off a bell in the memory of another man who was following the trial as closely as anyone in the room, the dead woman's younger son, Lowell Dye. Once again, by instinct and by training, he was the family's envoy to the courtroom, sometimes accompanied by his father, now a cancer survivor, while Robert junior followed the case from Florida. Lowell Dye thought he could remember hearing Cliff Strider mention a confession way back in 1984. Come to think of it, Dye could remember bugging the prosecutor a bit, wanting to know how he was going to use the confession he was rumored to have.

Strider's reaction had not been a patient one, by Dye's account. The lead prosecutor had been getting a bit tired of Lowell Dye and made no secret of it. Grief was one thing, but meddling in police work was another, even for an attorney—perhaps especially for an attorney, however aggrieved. We don't need the confession. We've got this one nailed, Strider had snapped at Dye, a recollection that mirrored Rice's testimony. But Dye also remembered Strider making a confession of his own: they had screwed up Kyles's confession, which Dye interpreted to mean that they had failed to have an attorney present for Kyles when he said whatever it was that he said. Or was it that Rice had done the screwing up, by recalling—or inventing—a confession that stupidly was phrased in such a way as to frustrate the prosecution's hankering for a death penalty case? Because a gun going off "by accident"—the verbiage Rice attributed to Kyles—was almost by definition an act of second-degree murder or mere manslaughter, not capital murder, only more so if the defendant was to be credited with the cooperativeness implicit in a "confession."

Whatever the reasoning for or against its use by the prosecution, the confession was most vulnerable to attack for one simple reason: the written record from the time—the police logs, the detectives' notes—contained not a single reference to it. Fawer struck a tone of mock incredulity as he tore into Rice on the stand. No one had included it in the police department "daily"—the brief, sometimes telegraphic account of an ongoing investigation? Not one trace of it in the "supplemental"—the expanded report that detectives come back and create at their leisure?

Now Fawer bore down hard. "Have you ever known a homicide detective to blow off a confession?"

RICE: Not . . .
FAWER: In your life . . . ?

Mike Rice cut both ways. Even after Fawer was done with him—perhaps only more so after Fawer was done bullying him—there might have been jurors who would sympathize with a bureaucratic underling possessed of valuable knowledge but brushed aside and cowed into silence by know-it-all superiors. On the other hand, if it was all a lie, it was a big lie, a lie so extravagantly brazen that it was hard to refute. For Denny LeBoeuf, the purest proof that the confession was a fabrication a decade after the fact lay in its absence from the prosecution's case as presented in the second trial. Alarmed by their failure to secure a conviction in the first trial and beginning to panic, there was no way Strider and Williams wouldn't have trotted it out, she reasoned. "If they had it—are you kidding? You think Cliff Strider wouldn't have used that?"

Sharon Andrews saw trouble in Dillman's performance, but she hadn't abandoned hope. After all, it was just a book, a cheesy police chronicle verging on pulp fiction. Jurors would know better than to stake their whole decision on a paragraph in a paperback. Wouldn't they? Rice had been more problematic—a disaster, in Lowell Dye's view, though the prosecutor looked upon him more pityingly. But before the state rested, in fact just moments before, Andrews would indeed abandon hope of anything more than a hung jury, a mistrial. This time the prosecution's comeuppance was of its own creating, a gaffe by Andrews's colleague, the gruffly pleasant and unusually tall Mike Daniels.

Andrews had entrusted the state's summation to him, and Kyles looked on in some dismay as Daniels uncoiled himself from the table beside her and rose to his full height, six five. Kyles was by now enough of an aficionado of these things to be able to read the chemistry in murder-trial casting. Sure, Harry Connick would have been ideally served by a black face on one or another of the prosecutors, but in Andrews and Daniels he had a good mix, Kyles had to concede: the murder victim herself incarnate in the soft-spoken lady leading the team; her partner, Daniels, a gentle giant standing guard against the enemies of order. But Daniels's greatest strengths were other than oratorical, and as he wound up the state's closing argument, he made a misstep that Kyles would relish as long as he had the brains left to recall it.

Mike Daniels, snorting now and then to show his contempt, had been picking at the testimony of a relatively minor defense witness named Peter Frank, one of the young men present at the Sunday night get-together before Kyles disappeared into the catch basin of Desire Street's collective memory, seemingly forever.

Frank's main use to the defense was to establish that Kyles was rarely armed, while Beanie, another partygoer that night, was never without a gun. Frank recalled the sight of the weapon, a blue steel .32, or maybe a .38, that Beanie tucked in his crotch and rearranged showily whenever he sat down or stood up.

Over the years, Frank had learned to give Beanie a wide berth—"just knowing the kind of person he was."

Frank's bona fides as someone who knew guns were six years in the army that had only just ended at the time of the Dye murder. Military service had given him what he called "higher instincts" about guns, by which he meant a sixth sense that told him when things were getting dicey and bullets might soon start to fly.

These credentials were not seriously undermined by the prosecution's revelation that Frank had a prior—a burglary rap several years back. A more effective impeachment of his claim that Kyles was gun-free was the receipt Daniels waved in his face, a document that memorialized Kyles's purchase earlier in 1984 of a .25-caliber pistol, properly registered in his name, though at his mother's address on North Dorgenois Street. The defense had no problem with the receipt; indeed, they had introduced it as evidence that Kyles was forthright in his gun purchases and therefore not likely to associate himself with an unregistered weapon like the one used in the murder of Delores Dye. But harking back to Frank's ignorance of Kyles's pistol provided Daniels with an opportunity for sarcasm: "And the only one to say he ever saw Mr. Wallace with a gun on Sunday, well, that was Mr. Kyles's good friend Peter Frank, who knew him so well that he didn't even know he owned a .25-caliber pistol. And he knew him so well that he lived with Pinkey Burnes on Desire Street, but two months before he bought that pistol, he said he lived with his mom over on Dorgenois Street. And of course Mr. Frank testified . . ."

Just then Daniels interrupted himself to point out a young black man working his way down a row of protruding kneecaps and crossed legs in the visitors gallery to take his place beside Kyles's eldest daughter, Tyteannia. "There he is, right there," Daniels interjected, pointing to the man and then moving on to other themes in his summation. It was a minor moment that would have come to nothing, except for Lela's vigilance. The late arrival wasn't Frank at all. It was another man, black like Frank, but easily twenty years his junior: Tyteannia's boyfriend, a young man named Eric. Lela got word to Marie Campbell, seated at the defense table, and she in turn caught Fawer's attention as he rose to begin his rebuttal. "That's not him," Campbell rasped loudly enough for Fawer, who was partially deaf, to hear. Fawer turned toward her—turned *on* her was more what it felt like to Campbell—signaling by the glare in his eye that she had better be damn well sure of what she was saying, because he was going to go with it.

Fawer was not long into his closing when he played the card, first ordering Tyteannia's friend to rise, then barking imperiously in another direction, "Stand up, Peter Frank. Stand up." Elsewhere in the courtroom, the real Peter Frank, not only much older but also considerably more slender than Eric, stood up. Daniels, in Fawer's retelling, melted into a puddle on the floor, all six feet five inches of him. For a case that hinged on witness identifications, for a case that hinged in particular on the identification of a black man at a distance considerably greater than the distance betwen Daniels and the visitors gallery, for a race-tinged case in which jurors needed no reminding of the inveterate difficulty—a basis of ridicule as well as remorse—that white folks seemed to have telling one black from another, it was a subtle but lethal slipup.

Now Fawer prepared to slide his blade between Daniels's ribs. "Do we have a stipulation, Mr. Daniels, that you spent the afternoon with Peter Frank, with nothing obstructing him, nothing; stood as close as I am, came as close, and one day later failed to identify him?

"And they have the audacity to talk about identification!" Fawer howled, turning away from Daniels to address the jury directly. "I could cry that they have the audacity . . ."

Fawer wasn't crying, of course. He was exultant, certain as the jurors filed out of the courtoom to begin their deliberations that they would re- turn promptly and acquit Kyles of the murder charge that had ruined a dozen years of his life.

Kyles did not dare to be as hopeful. All through the prison years, the emotional equilibrium he needed to avoid despair had also required that he deny himself flights of optimism. But this was definitely looking good, and as he waited to learn his fate from the jury, between chattering with his lawyers or with the bailiff who maneuvered him watchfully into a room off a back corridor and kept him plied with food and even the occasional cigarette, Kyles entertained thoughts of the world that might await him on the outside. It was easy to vow that it would be a different world than he had known. He would play it straight from now on and forever. Amen. But the vow was easier to make than to imagine implementing. What would it be like to live within the confines of a wage earner's income? Rather like limiting himself to one woman, he feared, and with the shrunken financial resources that came with working a legitimate job, fealty to just one woman might be part of the package. He wondered if he'd be that strong. Or if being strong in that way wouldn't come to seem like being weak—a sap's cop-out, a coward's choice. Because there really hadn't been much of an alternative to hustling for a man of Kyles's instincts and ambitions. And if the truth be told, for all the tension and the danger when things were going bad, when they went well, you couldn't imagine much better.

Alone in the courthouse holding cell, Kyles held his umpteenth cup of coffee in both hands and blew gently on the rising steam to cool it, lost in his thoughts as the jury deliberated. It was easy to forget the bad times— the feuds and the menace, the jackers, Beanie—because the good times were so good, and so was the money. Kyles flashed for a moment on a bar he and Johnny used to favor, and he wondered why it had come to mind. Then he remembered. The scene of many an idle and wasted afternoon, it had also played into one of the bigger breaks he caught before his luck ran out completely.

The saloon was walking distance down Desire Street from the apartment and over a couple of blocks. He and Johnny had been nursing beers and smoking cigarettes that afternoon, and it did not quicken their steps in more productive and profitable directions that there happened to be some very fine looking women in there that day, three of them, women with a hard edge on them, an attribute of greater appeal to Kyles than to Burnes, but very foxy by either man's standard. Kyles had no idea, and just then no particular reason to care, that the women were lesbian—bull daggers, to use his term. And from all appearances, the assholes who were hitting on them were equally oblivious to their sexual preference. And so the men persisted, especially the group's alpha asshole. Shortly he had reached that stage in a barroom courtship where he was talking loud, ostensibly to his buddies but loud enough so that everyone in the bar could hear, about the things the best of the women would want him to do to her once she laid eyes on the hank of flesh he carried between his legs. That sort of thing. Finally Johnny had had enough, and he stood up to say something. There were rules for this type of situation, Johnny advised, such as: if she's giving you no play, you move on and give another brother a chance. Of course alpha said something right back, and faster than you could grab a bottle by the neck and smash the butt end of it against the bar to make a jagged eye gouge, chairs were being shoved back and a table got flipped over and everyone was on red alert. That's when Kyles lifted his shirt and showed the revolver in his waistband. Just showed the gun. Didn't touch it, didn't brandish it, because the situation didn't yet require that level of escalation. He captioned the display with a few well-chosen words: "Now you know, man, you really don't want this kind of trouble."

Which appeared to be true. The men filed out of the bar, and Johnny and Curtis followed them to the door to make sure they got into their cars and drove off. That might have been a prudent idea for all concerned, given the probability that the offended party would double back at posse strength to avenge wounded pride. But Johnny and Curtis were not going to deny themselves at least a quick victory strut back inside the barroom, a chance to show themselves in triumph to the ladies whose honor they had upheld, light a cigarette, swill the last of the beer. That's what was happening when one of the girls, the really fine looking one, said, "Hold on, hold on." Johnny did the talking, trying not to sound rushed.

"Look, honey, we got to roll." And she said, "Y'all have any idea who I am?" Which sounded enough like a come-on to bring out the cockiness in Johnny. "Okay, darling, who are you supposed to be?"

She gave her name. Johnny glanced over at Curtis. It didn't mean anything to either one of them. Then she gave her mother's name, and Curtis and Johnny kind of fell back a step. Because the woman she claimed as her mother was a major player, indeed a legend, in the realm of Ninth Ward cocaine dealing. The next thing they knew, Johnny and Curtis were being ushered into the coke queen's place for a round of introductions. She was from the islands—Cuban, as best Kyles could figure out, though Pinkey would come to believe she was Bahamian—and, like her daughter, a lesbian. Indeed, the whole household and the dope-trafficking ring based there were run by women who loved women. This did not rule out a role for men; it just wasn't going to be one Kyles was used to.

As it happened, a shipment had just reached Miami: sixteen kilos of cocaine worth easily one hundred grand wholesale and, of course, many times that on the street. Maybe the gentlemen would care to make a little themselves? It was the movies, only more so: a rented car (all paid for), an armed guard to keep them out of trouble—also to keep them in line in case they got any ideas about diverting to their own use or profit sixteen kilos of pure Colombian blow. Except instead of being a three-hundred-pound goombah with his head shaved and tattoos riding up above his collar line, this particular escort was the hardest, iciest bitch Kyles had ever come up against, "a straight-up gangster," as he would recall her.

They took the interstate along the coast to Florida, past the burned-out Mississippi resort towns not yet revived by casino gambling's magic wand, past the pillared seaside enclave at Pass Christian where the New Orleans gentry summered, past Mobile and Pensacola and the snowy white beaches where the college kids came on Easter break to drink, fuck, crash cars, run naked, and, in other ways not imagined the previous year, celebrate the Resurrection. At Tallahassee they turned south, and eight hours later they were in Miami. They dropped the car where they'd been told to drop it, caught a cab to the designated hotel, and sat around watching television, smoking, napping. The next morning they waited on a phone call, took a cab to where they'd left the rented car, got in, and headed back to New Orleans, $100,000 worth of cocaine packed in the spare

tire. For their trouble Kyles and Burnes split $3,800. For what? For driv-
ing to Miami and back. Twenty-four hours. Thirty-eight hundred dollars.
It didn't get better than that.

The trips started to be a regular thing, though not every week and
not always Miami, the coke capital. More like once a month: Lake Charles,
Galveston. One time they charged extra and drove all the way to New York
for the pickup. Sometimes the Texas trips meant taking a roundabout
route home, maybe all the way north to Little Rock or even Memphis,
after the straight shot—Interstate 10—gained a reputation as the Deep
South's drug corridor and started to heat up. Part of the I-10 problem
was federal agents. But there was also a homegrown menace: small-town
sheriffs who would profile young blacks out on the highway and bust
them on technicalities—changing lanes without a turn signal; driving five
miles an hour over the speed limit. If any drugs turned up in the car, even
residue on a roach clip, the car could be impounded as an ill-gotten gain.
It took a very clean nose indeed, not to mention a lawyer and a lot of
money, for a city black to go back out onto the prairie and contest such
a seizure.

To keep Kyles around between trips, the island women would lay drugs
on him basically at cost: $75 for a quarter pound of weed, at a time when
a pound was going for $400. Two hundred for four ounces of powder that
wholesaled for four times as much and brought another multiple of that in
profits per gram. Just how much or how little Kyles cared to handle was up
to him, especially when it came to the distance driving. He could get superstitious about the trips. "It all depended on what kind of money I already
got in my pocket and how I felt about that trip they was asking me to do. Because one thing I learned: don't do nothing on the spur of the moment."

Eventually it came to an end, as good runs always do. The women
got raided. Cops tore the place apart; the daughter Kyles met in the bar,
the one who introduced him to the big time, split for Texas, from what he
heard; and Kyles fell back into the more marginal hustles that, truth be
told, made it easier for him to sleep at night.

Kyles's reverie was interrupted: a knock on the door and word that the
jurors were descending. Now wholly abandoned to his surging optimism,

he was led back into the courtoom. In the time it took to say two words—not guilty—these twelve men and women filing into the jury box could undo twelve years of incarceration. But it was not to be. Like the first, Kyles's third jury was deadlocked. Two jurors out of twelve—an Uptown socialite and a career military officer, both women—held out against the majority view that the state had failed to prove its case. Judge Ward declared a mistrial.

For Kyles and for his family, the mistrial fell like a hammerblow. His kin had been steadfast in their collective attention to the proceedings in court. If Pinkey or one of the sisters was not present for every day of the two-week trial, another sister showed up, perhaps with one of the older children—Tyteannia was a young woman of nineteen now, Chester and Elmeco well into their teens—all of them fully cognizant of the unfolding events on which their father's fate hinged. The visitors gallery was good at least for a glimpse of the man whose love had been denied them for so long, and a basis for rekindling the hope that he would soon reenter their daily lives. And when the jury had retired to its deliberations, the bailiff had allowed Kyles a brief few minutes in a side room with his family, a moment of almost unendurable intensity as they hugged each other and looked at each other, twining their fingers together or touching each other's faces, scarcely daring to speak of the outcome they wanted so desperately, for fear they would jinx it. Now the very brilliance of Fawer's performance—the successful evisceration of Rice and Smallwood, the artful insinuation that Dillman had manipulated Kersh's testimony and perhaps also that of the men he had exposed to his photo lineup—made the failure to win an acquittal that much more daunting. Here was the best defense imaginable, and still it had not been enough.

The lawyers could console the Kyles family, and each other, with this: the Supreme Court's ruling in the Kyles case pointed not just toward an interpretation of law but to a testable hypothesis. If all the evidence were available to the defense and presented to a jury, the justices said, there was reason to think those jurors would have reasonable doubt about Kyles's guilt; they might fail to convict. Well, the evidence was presented—all of it, at last—and indeed the jurors had failed to convict.

Of course, they had also failed to acquit. But here was the defense team's rekindled hope: that Connick's people might now be willing to drop the case. It wasn't the first attempt at a negotiated end to Kyles's long imprisonment. Even before the third trial, as both sides plowed through endless rounds of pretrial motions and took writs on every conceivable angle of the case, Fawer had broached what he thought might be a face-saving compromise. Rather than go to trial, he suggested, why not present the evidence—all of it this time—to a grand jury. Let that jury see how deeply compromised the detectives were in their every dealing with Beanie Wallace, a key witness no longer on hand to testify. Let the grand jury provide political cover for the district attorney's office by declining to indict. With apologies to Lowell Dye, Connick could explain that his hands were tied. The people had spoken. He had no case to prosecute.

Fawer hadn't really expected that to work. He well knew how stung Connick was by the Supreme Court decision, too stung to settle for time served and move on. But with the third trial behind them, there was reason to hope that Connick had seen the light. His embarrassment would only be compounded by yet another high-profile failure to secure a conviction. The time had come to drop the case—in the shorthand version of courtroom terminology, to "nol-pross" it. As she sat in Connick's conference room in the third trial's immediate aftermath, Denny LeBoeuf found herself sketching out the face-saving press release that would ease Connick's political pain: The people had tried Curtis Kyles once again, pursuant to the Supreme Court's order vacating the original conviction. (In other words, Connick had done his duty.) But as became clear in court, notwithstanding the hard work of the district attorney's office (throw him a rose), the lengthy passage of time since the crime occurred and key witnesses (Beanie) being unavailable made a just trial impossible. In consultation with the defense attorneys, a decision had been reached to drop the charge and release Kyles for time served.

Connick and his first assistant, Camille Buras, listened politely and agreed to take the defense team's view into consideration. Indeed, they were willing to convey it to the Dyes, but as LeBoeuf and Fawer and Trenticosta did not need to be told, Lowell Dye would be calling the shot, and he was not about to be placated.

Robert Dye saw doom in the ten jury votes to acquit. They were never going to get a conviction, he told himself. But for Lowell, the magnitude of the jury split was only another measure of the injustice being visited upon the memory of his mother. There would be no turning back, he told Connick and Buras. Not a chance. It was probably what they wanted to hear, LeBoeuf would conclude in hindsight. But had Lowell's intransigence emboldened prosecutors to act on their own instincts or scared them into acquiescing to a constituent sure to make an unholy fuss if they didn't? That would remain a matter of conjecture. After the huddle with the Dyes, Connick and Buras announced that they had every intention of trying Curtis Kyles a fourth time for murder. And they would shuffle the deck before proceeding: new judge, new jury, and, with Sharon Andrews lost to a maternity leave, a new prosecutor, at long last a black one.

EIGHTEEN

Cockfighting is legal in Louisiana, as in few other states. That is not to say that Louisianans are inhumane in their attitudes toward animals. Stringent animal cruelty laws are on the books, footnoted with a codicil establishing, conveniently, that fighting cocks are not animals. And so a not inconsiderable number of the state's residents have seen the squawking blur of feathers and blood that ensues more or less instantly when two male "chickens," as sportsmen call them, are placed in the ring. It was with some authority then that courthouse regulars dropping in on the fourth trial of Curtis Kyles for the murder of Delores Dye likened the interaction of Mike Fawer and Glen Woods to a cockfight.

If arrogance is the measure of a litigator's prowess—and to some extent it's a good one—Fawer had met his match in Woods. Mike Fawer was the bantam: fiftyish and bearded, his graying hair combed harshly back from an increasingly sketchy widow's peak, his Bronx accent like a buzz saw among the gentler drawls of Southern justice. Glen Woods, fifteen years younger and a good few inches taller, was the cock of the walk, a man with the breezy confidence that comes from knowing that the ladies are impressed even if the courtroom oratory could use a little work. Woods had paid his dues in more than a decade as one of Harry Connick's assistant district attorneys. It was Woods, early in his career, who had bounced Johnny Burnes into the slammer after Beanie Wallace was murdered in

1986, and dozens of murder prosecutions had followed. Out of gratitude for services rendered, Connick had accorded Woods a privilege that was officially denied other prosecutors as a matter of strict policy: permission to take private cases on the side. Other DAs saw the use of part-timers as a way to keep talent in the stable after they had outgrown the poor salaries the taxpayers allowed them, but Connick had held out against it, at least officially. Part-timers would be distracted by their paying clients, he feared. But Woods had leverage. If Connick wanted a talented black prosecutor, he was going to have to give ground.

Most cockfights last for a few minutes, and one of the birds winds up dead. In the fourth trial of Curtis Kyles, Fawer and Woods were at it for close to two weeks, taunting, condemning, carping—Fawer jumping into Woods's face, now Woods into Fawer's—so angrily that it seemed a matter of time until one of the men lost control of himself altogether and they came to blows right there in the well of an Orleans Parish courtroom. Somewhere close to the heart of the matter was Fawer's loathing of Woods, or any other black prosecutor, for participating in a process that to the defense was patently racist. Bad enough that whites like Connick and his boiler room of wannabe young toughs had suppressed evidence and otherwise curtailed the rights of an impoverished black man like Curtis Kyles. Now came Woods, as though to put the imprimatur of his people on the degradation and disenfranchisement of one of their own. And just to make clear the enmity was mutual, Woods did not miss many opportunities to get under Fawer's skin as well, implying that he was hopelessly the dupe of white liberal pieties about the sociology of black crime.

It would take a psychologist to fully fathom the depths of contempt these two men felt for each other as they faced off in the late summer of 1997. And it would have taken a judge a lot tougher and more alert than Alfred Mansour to keep them from each other's throats. A genteel jurist from Alexandria, Mansour was the latest solution to the widespread reluctance of Orleans Parish judges to take on Harry Connick and the Kyles case. But Mansour was disinclined by instinct and breeding to clamp down hard on either attorney, and all but unstrung when his inattention to misconduct only seemed to inspire more of it. In the absence of a judge strong enough to sustain his constant objections to Woods's courtroom strategies, Fawer began making the points of law himself, and he did so with angrier and angrier eruptions from his seat at the defense table alongside the more courtly Nick Trenticosta and Denny LeBoeuf. The problem, LeBoeuf began to fear, was that jurors, whatever they made of his argument, would find Fawer obnoxious, and their disenchantment would extend to his client. Mansour seemed to share LeBoeuf's suspicion that none of this was playing very well with the people who counted. "Stop that," Mansour snapped impotently at Fawer and Woods after one particularly ugly exchange. "The jury is getting very disturbed by your conduct."

After so narrow a brush with acquittal in the third trial, the prosecution had reason to do the most tinkering with its case the fourth time around. Sergeant Rice, for example, was jettisoned, along with his improbable claim to have heard Kyles confess. And Detective Johnny Miller was suddenly unavailable, requiring that stand-ins read his testimony from earlier trial appearances. Stand-ins, of course, could not be cross-examined by defense attorneys seeking to prove that there had been something altogether unwholesome in the way police protected Miller's snitch, Beanie Wallace.

For Kyles, increasingly familiar twists and turns in the state's case did not make them less offensive. The affronts came in all sizes, big and small, witness by witness, starting, he would insist, with the overarching and appalling irreality of the murder charge itself. But Kyles could be galled by seemingly trivial inaccuracies as well: the repeated insinuation, for example, that the Sunday night get-together with his buddies required stolen groceries—Mrs. Dye's groceries—because he could not possibly have provided food for so many people himself. "Like, no black man could be laying out like that for his friends; a black, he ain't got the means. White people believe that, but it would anger me, hearing them say it."

The truth was, Curtis and Pinkey were doing just fine in the days leading up to his arrest. Even without the pin money Kyles picked up hustling pot and fencing stereos, his disability check combined with her food stamps and what she got from welfare covered their needs, if barely, and there was a chunk of savings to fall back on from Kyles's days as a coke runner. No one would call him rich, but it was not a bad existence. Not at all.

Among their friends, Pinkey and Curtis's place had always been a hangout where folks gathered for music and a good time or for no particular reason at all. Put a little something on the stove, a little Isley Brothers on the stereo, the speakers on the porch booming out over the street as a come-on, and you had a party. Marvin Gaye was another of Pinkey's favorites, something to shake and shimmy to.

And when domesticity itself wore thin, they had some built-in escape hatches. The Bassfield farm was just a couple of hours away. The place was rough-hewn and the house eternally unfinished, but a visit from Pinkey and Curtis and the kids rarely ended without Pinkey's brother shoving a bushel of greens into the trunk of their car, or a cut of pork, or some iced chicken. And then there was the older couple upstairs. Pinkey and Curtis had asked them to be Elmeco's godparents. "They just took us for theirs," is how Pinkey put it. "So days when I didn't want to cook or was sick, I had a cook right over my head. And when me and Curtis needed to go anywhere or go out or whatever, we had a babysitter right up there."

You could almost say that in the year or two before the murder charge blew their little world apart, Curtis and Pinkey had begun to grow up. Kyles had started cutting back on the street hustles. With days as well as evenings at his disposal while he recuperated from his bullet wounds, he made a couple of bucks driving elderly or dependent neighbors to clinics or the store or to visit relatives. And if they didn't have the cash, he'd settle for a bottle of beer. He could afford to be a little generous. The years of hustling had paid off. He had been able to put something aside, a small but sufficient fortune, just as his uncle had in bolting from Cleveland following the peculiar death of his first wife. Late at night, after everybody was asleep, Curtis would light up a joint and count out the wad of bills he kept hidden even from Pinkey: the $6,500 he now knew he'd never see again.

Maybe he'd catch a break, Kyles thought to himself as he tried fretfully to imagine what jurors made of the unfolding case. Maybe he'd drawn a jury this time who knew better than the stereotypes prosecutors played on. Maybe it would not seem impossible to them that a black man could lay out a spread for his friends, now and then, maybe even keep a shelf stocked with cat food. Mike Fawer was not one to undo his client's fragile optimism, but he did not share it. Jurors favoring conviction were more likely to increase than to evaporate this time. The reason was simple: an overly rehearsed case doesn't get stronger; it gets stale. The state's witnesses would be that much harder to catch off guard, let alone impeach. Counting appellate and pretrial appearances, some of them had been guided through their paces a half dozen times as they took the stand yet again in September 1997 for Kyles's fourth trial. And if witnesses lacked spontaneity, so, frankly, did Fawer. The first trial had taken it out of him, emotionally and financially. He had no choice but to start charging for his services for the fourth trial, though it would be at the rates paid public defenders: little more than $50 an hour. That his marriage was cracking up—Fawer's wife would leave him shortly after the fourth trial, only to return for a last try several months later—did not improve his mood or morale.

But if the overall momentum of the case was starting to stall, there would be one new witness whose appearance was intriguing enough to set the courthouse grapevine's farther tendrils to quivering. Functionaries and trial aficionados alike traipsed into Mansour's section and swelled the gallery as, on the first day of the fourth trial's second week, the state called Martina "Pinkey" Burnes to the stand. If she was a Jezebel she was an improbable one, this woman at the center of an intrigue that, by one version of events, had cost the father of her children his freedom and his rival for her affections his life. And yet somehow, with her gold dental work, icy self-control, and leggy figure, this impoverished mother of six was entirely adequate to the role.

The years had not got the better of Pinkey Burnes. The baby with Tyrone Joseph—Jean—had been her last, and this child was now in grade school. To get by on her welfare check, Pinkey had taken in boarders at the Desire project apartment the city assigned her—other women, usually with small children. It was a violation, of course, but the rule of laws far more important than that had long since been suspended within the project, an anarchy as intimidating to police as to the city bureaucrats who might have kicked her out of her sprawling warren of rooms if they had caught her subletting them. Up two flights of stairs, the place was as tidy under her management as it was drafty in winter and steamy in summer. But she was keeping food on the table, she had her health, and her kids were still with her. In short, she had survived.

The steeliness of her demeanor that day in court was, of course, alloyed with sheer terror, though some in the gallery mistook it for scorn. Speaking barely above a whisper, and sometimes not speaking at all—Mansour would repeatedly remind her that a shake of the head was not an adequate response to a prosecutor's question—she silenced the background buzz of the courtroom and drew spectators as well as the judge and jury forward in their seats, Kyles among them.

Pinkey had resumed her visits with Kyles since his return to the parish jail, and it was easier for him to keep up contact by telephone, the principal conduit of moral counsel and fatherly advice to his children. Pinkey would not try to hurt him. He was confident of that much, but he was also fully aware that she could do so by accident if not by design, knowing as much as she did about the life he once led.

Whether or not to call Kyles's woman to the stand had vexed legal tacticians from the inception of the case a dozen years earlier. Without quite overcoming his qualms about where her loyalties really lay, Martin Regan had put her on the stand at the first trial, to no particular effect. And he would have again at the second but for the process server's failure to find her on short notice. Perhaps that was just as well, because among the evidence that prosecutors had failed to turn over was one document that might have served their purposes quite well—the statement Pinkey Burnes gave to the police on the afternoon of Kyles's arrest.

The problems with the statement were manifold. For one thing, she had mentioned the time when Kyles's protestations of eternal passion had led to a display of his gun and a threat to use it on the woman he loved if she were ever to leave him. For another, she had described his relationship to the household as intermittent, saying that he stayed there only "off and on." For a third, she had allowed as how it was quite unusual for Kyles to show up with a load of groceries, as he did on the evening of the Dye murder—a statement that nourished the stereotype of the thieving, hand-to-mouth existence Kyles wanted to explode. And yes, she said she had deplored his wasting so much money on something as unnecessary to their daily needs as pet food. Strider and Williams could have wielded the statement like a machete to slash the portrait of a docile family man and provider that Regan was trying to create, but that might have opened the door to the whole slew of witness statements in all their contradictory confusion. Instead, as frustrated as Regan by the failure to track down Pinkey Burnes to testify at the second trial, the prosecutors had tossed a tape of Pinkey's session with police onto the defense table as the jurors went into their deliberations. The implicit message: be grateful that we didn't use this.

Thirteen years later, Pinkey's statement—like all the others that witnesses gave police—was a well-reviewed part of the case, and no small reason why Fawer had decided against calling her in the third trial. No matter what she said, no matter how favorable to Kyles, it would give Connick's people the chance they craved to bring up the 1984 statement as they cross-examined her. This time, Woods decided not to wait passively for that opportunity. He called Burnes himself and was prepared to declare her a hostile witness and lead her aggressively through her testimony if she tried to clam up on him. But he had met more than his match.

For Woods, the trick was to make Burnes repeat—or contradict—what she told police and then to rub her nose in it. He proceeded carefully, methodically, drawing forth from his witness a set of assertions that he knew were at odds with her statement: that Kyles lived with her full-time, that he was a competent and reliable provider, that he was a gentle man. Now, from the animation in Woods's face and the tense, bouncy spring in his step as he whirled around and about in the well of the courtroom, addressing the witness, addressing the jury, firing a snide remark over his shoulder in the direction of the defense table, it was clear that he was ready to spring his trap.

He began with the relatively banal issue of Kyles's domestic arrangements on Desire Street.

WOODS: Now, did he stay there off and on, ma'am, or did he live there permanently?

BURNES: He lived in there permanently.

WOODS: So can you explain to the jury why back in 1984 you said that he lived there off and on?

Burnes was unruffled. "Because when they brought me down for questioning, that is something they wanted me to say." This was stunning, a witness not writhing in the face of contradicted testimony but somehow turning perjury to her advantage as an opportunity to savage the police. She went on: "They were telling me, you know, what to say, and I said, well, he lived there off and on."

Then Woods mentioned the tape. "They put what you said on tape, did they not?"

> BURNES: I'm quite sure they did.
>
> WOODS: . . . Are you telling the jury that before they took your statement down on tape, they sat down with you and told you exactly what they wanted you to say?
>
> BURNES: Yes.

The cat-and-mouse game continued, but now it was the witness who seemed to be playing with the prosecutor.

> WOODS: And did the police make you say that the only time Curtis stayed with you was when you let him spend the night? Did they make you say that?
>
> BURNES: No, they didn't make me say that, but I said it. I told them what they wanted to hear.

Burnes had no trouble explaining why she had portrayed Kyles as a part-time lover. It was the only way she could maintain her status as a single parent in the eyes of the welfare office.

Perhaps Woods had been thinking of the polygraph test as his ace in the hole, but now Pinkey Burnes played it for him.

> WOODS: You gave them the statement they wanted to hear?
>
> BURNES: Yes.
>
> WOODS: You rehearsed it first with them?
>
> BURNES: Yes.
>
> WOODS: And then you went on tape?
>
> BURNES: Yes.
>
> WOODS: Okay. So they didn't write anything down for you, right?
>
> BURNES: Except for the polygraph.

WOODS: I'm sorry, what now?

BURNES: I took a polygraph test.

LeBoeuf handled the cross-examination for Fawer, using it as an opportunity to flesh out the full sequence of events Woods had tried to pick apart: a preliminary interview with police followed by a polygraph in which Burnes answered unchallenging questions truthfully. The next round of interrogation had been essentially a rehearsal for the statement that police meant to tape. And here, according to the account LeBoeuf drew from her witness, the questions got tougher, as did the cops. Where two had been interviewing Burnes, now several men packed the small interrogation room, and when they heard an answer they didn't like, they let it be known.

LeBoeuf: All right. And what sort of things were they saying to you then?

BURNES: They were saying things like they were going to take the children, they were going to place them in a foster home.

LeBoeuf: Okay. And did they appear to be upset with some of your answers?

BURNES: Oh yes . . . Because when they asked me certain things and it wasn't what they wanted to hear, they got to yelling. They were hollering. I knew it wasn't the right answer.

LeBoeuf: And did you then change your answers?

BURNES: Yes, I did.

LeBoeuf: . . . And is that when they turned the tape on?

BURNES: Yes.

Pinkey left the stand wrung out, almost dazed by what she had been through. She did not look at Kyles as she found her way out into the corridor, but she knew she had done well by him, and if she had met his gaze, she would have known that he knew it too.

The pugnacity of Woods and Fawer aside, the fourth trial's only remaining excitement came with the physical collapse of one of the jurors, an enormously fat woman with blood-pressure problems. Earlier in the day, the jurors had been herded onto a bus and driven to the Schwegmann's parking lot to see the murder scene firsthand. Back in the courtroom, the prosecution handed them the photographs of Mrs. Dye's corpse to examine, and the overweight woman began hyperventilating. Soon she was prone on the floor, and other jurors were fanning her with whatever sheets of paper came readily to hand. Her collapse was seized on by the defense in support of their view that the only reason prosecutors insisted on admitting these lurid blowups was to agitate men and women whose deliberations required serenity and reason. When the collapsed juror was overheard the next morning holding forth on the trial from her bed at a local hospital, Fawer moved routinely for a mistrial and, just as routinely, was denied.

NINETEEN

Lowell Dye's failure to win damages or even a judgment of civil liability from John Schwegmann and his grocery chain seemed only to intensify his obsession with bringing his mother's murderer to justice. At whatever price to his law practice, Dye had not been able to keep away from the courtroom as judges gaveled to order the third and then, a year later, the fourth Kyles trial. Lunch breaks were a chance for Dye to scoot back down Canal Street to his office for a few minutes, grab a sandwich, tear open some pieces of mail, and flip through the documents stacked and waiting for his signature. It was on one such occasion, as the fourth trial drew irresolutely to its close, that he had gotten a call from another Kyles trial junkie.

A secretary put her through. It was Victory Wallace, Beanie's mother. Dye's feet thumped back onto the floor from the desktop where, hands cupped behind his head, he had been engaged in contemplative study of the office wall. It was not the first time Mrs. Wallace had called Dye, though they had never met. Early on, she phoned to offer condolences, as Dye recalled, and on another occasion—the time frame was no longer fixed in Dye's mind—she was at pains to let Dye know that her son had not killed his mother, wasn't that kind of boy, no matter what lies the defense attorney told. A mother's zeal to clear her son's name had not ended with Beanie's death. Indeed, the maternal burden seemed only heavier on her shoulders now that her son was no longer around to speak for himself. Worse yet, she had picked up on rumors that members of her own family—her daughter, and a brother she had up at Angola—might be thinking about making themselves available to the Kyles defense. Mr. Dye needed to know that. Maybe he could ward it off.

On the occasion of this third contact with Lowell Dye, Mrs. Wallace began by reiterating her certainty that Joseph, as she called Beanie, was innocent of the murder, but she went beyond a blind-faith testimonial by offering something concrete: leads on two young women who she claimed had been present in the parking lot at the time of the murder. They didn't know Kyles, but they had known Beanie well and could testify that he wasn't the man at the wheel of the red Ford LTD as it exited Schwegmann's and blended into the passing traffic. Lowell Dye recalled the conversation: "I said, 'Well, what are their names?' And she goes, 'I don't really know their names, but my daughter Joanne knows. Joanne was the closest to Beanie, and she can tell you.' I said, 'Well that's fine, but you know what you ought to do? You ought to get Joanne to notify the DA's office.'" Which, by the account of both mother and daughter, is exactly what they proceeded to do, though in Joanne Dotson's case, with a secret agenda her mother would never have shared. Perhaps sensing such a possibility, Dye had decided he'd better hear out this Dotson woman himself. And so it transpired, around ten o'clock one September morning a few days after the call from Victory Wallace, that Dye found himself cruising Elysian Fields Avenue, a central artery in the heart of the city's old Creole redoubt, the Seventh Ward, in search of the address he had been given.

"I want to say she was living somewhere off Elysian Fields," Dye would recall. "You walked down a long driveway, an alleyway, and my memory is you had to walk upstairs, and she's all warm, and it's like, 'Sit down, here in the living room.'"

That feeling of easy conviviality was not mutual, even before Dye whipped out a tape recorder and asked if there would be any objection to his turning it on. Joanne Dotson—forty-one years old and trying to rear two adolescent children on her own—was appalled by the presence of this man in her home, this white man, this lawyerly son of a woman the Kyles family accused her brother of killing. She would tiptoe around and about Dye's questions, and when it was all over and she had closed the door behind him, she would sink against it in relief that he was gone.

They began with small talk, and for Dye, even that was a continuing education in the twined lives and ever-astonishing folkways of the underclass: not only was Johnny Burnes her late brother's closest buddy, but for a time in the early 1980s, while still in his teens, Burnes had lived under Joanne Dotson's roof and fathered children with a young cousin she was raising. Dotson also was under the impression that some months before the Dye murder, Beanie had been dumped by his longtime companion—Valerie Brown, or Noonie, as they called her. This insight moved the conversation beyond idle gossip and into the realm of detail more pertinent to his mother's murder, though not necessarily in ways Lowell Dye found useful in a campaign to return Kyles to death row. Because a rupture in Beanie's relationship with Noonie would explain a couple of things. One was the suddenly reckless urgency of Beanie's long-simmering infatuation with Pinkey in the days leading up to the parking lot murder. Another was Noonie's willingness to contact police in connection with the Leidenheimer murder, that parallel universe in which another woman had died but prosecution was never even attempted, let alone time and time again. The Leidenheimer case had haunted the third and fourth trials like a ghost. The defense tried with limited success to flush it into the open as a way to discredit Beanie as a police informant. Prosecutors, more successfully, fought to restrict references to it as irrelevant to the murder at hand.

Joanne Dotson revered her brother's memory. She had come to think of Beanie as a god—her word—and even before his death she was every bit the doting stepsister. He needed wheels? She gave him her old El Dorado on a more or less permanent basis and did without a car herself. Indeed, Dotson's first inkling of the Dye murder and the transactions involving the bartered Ford LTD was a call from Beanie saying that he wouldn't be needing the El Dorado anymore. Just why he needed the Ford urgently enough to support his claim that he paid $400 for it—money that an addict would be much more interested in putting into his arm—was a meditation for another time. A separate insight that Dye did not pursue was Dotson's offhand observation that her brother had been so tight with police that checks were cut to him on a regular basis, thousands of dollars' worth of checks, a stream of revenue so steady that Victory Wallace, their mother, routinely made the trip down to police headquarters to pick them up on her son's behalf. If unwelcome glimpses into Beanie's life as a snitch were abundant, the information Dye came for— leads on the two young women who had seen someone other than Beanie leaving the Schwegmann's parking lot in Mrs. Dye's car—proved elusive. Dotson had first names for them, Yolanda and Carey, friends of her little sister, she said. But when Dye asked for last names or addresses, Dotson referred him to her mother, just as her mother had referred Dye to Dotson in the first place.

Played back at Dye's leisure, much about the tape was frustrating or even counterproductive. Dotson's answers sounded tentative, even confused. But then, late in the conversation, there it was: a statement that seemed to neutralize her utility to the defense if, as Dotson's mother feared, they ever tried to put her on the stand. Dye was reminding Dotson of the defense team's thirteen-year effort to implicate her brother in the murder as a way of deflecting blame from Kyles. "Did you ever talk to Beanie about . . . did your mother ever talk to Beanie about all of this?" Lowell Dye asked.

Dotson's initial rejoinder was alarmingly ambiguous: "Only thing I know, he told me that he did kill the lady and that it was her car."

DYE: That he . . . that who killed . . . that Curtis killed?
DOTSON: That Curtis killed your mom, and [Beanie] was riding
            around in the car and when he learned that the car was in-
            volved in a murder, he tried to give the car back.

Some defense witness, Dye thought to himself. Let them make what they would of Joanne Dotson. In her statement that Kyles was the killer, he had an all-purpose rebuttal, and he had it on tape. Indeed, he had a witness who just might sway a jury.

Within a day or two of Dye's visit with Dotson, jurors had deadlocked over the matter of Kyles's guilt or innocence. A fourth run at Curtis

Kyles for the murder of Delores Dye had been declared a mistrial. A majority still favored acquittal, but they were barely a majority, and Mike Fawer's gut told him that margin would only continue to shrink. He knew it, and he had every confidence that Connick knew it too.

Again the mood of the Kyles family soared. Once again Curtis had dodged the bullet. Huddled in the courtroom with Kyles's attorneys as the bailiff led the defendant away, they dared to hope that this time prosecutors would drop the case. But again their sense of elation would sputter and die as days passed with no signal from the district attorney's office that Harry Connick was calling it a day. Back in the sweaty confines of the parish prison, Kyles found himself moving beyond the eerie, paranoid sense that had overtaken him at other turns in his long ordeal. This was different from the disorienting discovery that one of his intimates was a police informant, less bizarre than the armed-robbery trial, in which there seemed to be no connection whatsoever between his criminal profile or even his physical abilities and the felonies police were laying off on him. In place of paranoia he contacted a simpler emotion, no less enraging but somehow easier to live with: a feeling of outright persecution. It was a word frequently on the lips of the death penalty and human rights activists now drawn to New Orleans by the legal limbo that had engulfed the case. To Kyles, Connick seemed less sly and dangerous than merely desperate in his zeal to convict the black man who had embarrassed his office at the highest levels of American jurisprudence. But as Kyles sensed in the fretful asides among Nick and Denny and Mike, there was more reason than ever to fear that Connick might finally succeed.

Would Harry Connick have the gall to try Kyles a fifth time? Within days of the most recent mistrial, Nick Trenticosta and Denny LeBoeuf filed a petition with the criminal court seeking to head off that possibility. "Enough is enough," they began. The endless prosecution of Curtis Kyles had become a kind of punishment in and of itself, they argued, a punishment inflicted on a man who, after the Supreme Court reversal, remained legally innocent of Mrs. Dye's murder, no matter how badly prosecutors wanted to believe he had committed it.

So much for legal philosophy. Now the negotiator in Mike Fawer took over. He craved the vindication that would have come to Kyles—and to his attorneys—with an acquittal. But if it took cutting a deal to secure Kyles's freedom, well, Fawer was not going to let his professional vanity stand in the way. He was not above taking his place at the bargaining table; indeed, he rather liked the game. And this time the defense was prepared to offer the district attorney more than a face-saving press release. The state demanded a conviction, even in the face of ambiguous evidence and fractured juries? Well then, let Kyles plead to manslaughter and set him free for time served.

LeBoeuf would remember the air of distraction that Connick brought with him to their meeting on the plea bargain. He was dressed down, as if for a fishing trip, with a jaunty cap on his head that did nothing to counter LeBoeuf's overriding impression: Connick looked old, tired. In a nightclub setting with a drink at the ready, he could still shoot his cuffs and hi de ho with the best of the hepcats, but suddenly the silver-haired swinger was white-haired, and to LeBoeuf's ear, he sometimes sounded a little vague. They'd study the defense proposal, Connick said.

LeBoeuf did not give up hope. She sensed that Connick, whatever convictions he might harbor about Kyles's guilt, was beginning to feel at least a little queasy at the prospect of going yet another round in court. And by now pressure was being brought to bear in ways calculated to make sure he stayed queasy. One source of it was the NAACP's Legal Defense Fund, which had dispatched two young women to New Orleans to drum up media support for Kyles and organize community opposition. Their message was as blunt as it was familiar: the death penalty was inherently racist. Just look at the statistics on the people it was used against. It was also frightfully expensive, not just in human lives but in dollars, the cost of prosecuting the Kyles case already having reached above $2 million, by Mike Fawer's estimate.

The young women from LDF took to sitting in the back of the courtroom as the fourth trial ground to its inconclusive end, and LeBoeuf relished the effect. "Glen Woods hated having them there." The LDF presence instantly transformed him into an enemy of progressive black politics and ceded the moral high ground to the white attorneys Woods was fighting.

Another antagonist arriving on the scene was Amnesty International, the human rights organization that had been honored with the Nobel

Peace Prize. Though Kyles was almost entirely apolitical himself, Amnesty's recognition of his plight had the effect of projecting it into the context of human rights abuses around the world. Meanwhile, the press had gone to work itemizing a pattern of abuses very much closer to home. In a front-page recap of Connick's recent record, a reporter for the local daily, *The Times-Picayune*, put the Kyles case in the context of others that had been overturned because of evidence suppression and prosecutorial misconduct by Connick's crew. In response to the newspaper's inquiries, Connick's first assistant, Camille Buras, estimated at ten the number of cases reversed since 1974 because Connick's people had withheld exculpatory evidence. But the newspaper exposé dredged up several more.

In his own defense, Connick insisted that his staff were duly respectful of the rules of disclosure and the need to play fair with evidence useful to the defense. "We are not frivolous about it, and even if we know the son of a bitch did it, if it is exculpatory, he is entitled to it, and we turn it over," he told the newspaper. But LeBoeuf weighed in with the observation that Connick was not adequately chastened by the Supreme Court's reversal of the Kyles verdict. "If anything, it has gotten worse," LeBoeuf told the paper. "It is worse than anywhere else in the state." And indeed, other lawyers quoted in the article cited examples of evidence suppression by Connick's people in the two years since the 1995 ruling. Judy Clarke, a past president of the National Association of Criminal Defense Lawyers, spoke generally about the issue of evidence suppression, but with the particulars of the Kyles case clearly in mind. "You are supposed to let the jury decide this stuff, not the DA, not the police officers," Clarke told the paper. "Eventually, some gutsy judge down there is going to stop it."

But not, it seemed, in time to ring down the curtain on the continuing prosecution of Curtis Kyles. On September 22, the day after the front-page exposé and one week after the fourth trial jury deadlocked, the district attorney emerged from a huddle with Lowell Dye and Glen Woods and announced his intention to try Kyles again—a fifth time—for the murder of Delores Dye.

Now the activists threw their operations into overdrive. Within a week, Amnesty and the NAACP had been joined on the steps of the courthouse by the American Civil Liberties Union and a busload of supporters for a rally that culminated in a march around the corner to the prison. Chants and picket signs raised the same message in the autumn air: FREE CURTIS KYLES, NO FIFTH TRIAL. The chants gave way to hurrahs and whistles as Kyles appeared in a narrow third-floor window—his arm, anyway—waving a white cloth. For Lela, the moment of jubilation was shot through with a more poignant emotion. What had it been, a dozen years since the Christmas Eve when she and a couple of her brother's kids stood on the windy overpass below the jailhouse and watched Curtis wave a bit of fabric from an upper story? Now at least they were not alone. A throng of people were convinced that Kyles was an innocent man framed by a racist system of justice. Yet there he was, still locked away, still waving his white cloth, with no reason to be confident he'd ever get out.

TWENTY

It was well past lunch one day in late November 1997 when Nick Trenticosta pulled his black hair into his signature ponytail, put on a fresh shirt and slacks, and headed downtown to the offices of the Death Penalty Resource Center. Trenticosta's professional life as director of the center was a balancing act. With Kyles actively on trial, Trenticosta had planted himself at the defense table for the duration, even if Fawer as lead dog and LeBoeuf as staff attorney handled most of the witnesses. Trenticosta was a key tactician, but he was also the case manager, the man who set and met the deadlines, created briefs or supervised their creation by the young law students and staff attorneys who gained exposure to death penalty work under his tutelage.

Now the fourth trial was behind them, and a new judge, an import from Jefferson Parish named Robert Burns, had rejected Trenticosta and LeBoeuf's petition and scheduled the fifth for February 1998, three months hence. That left Trenticosta with time to catch up on other death row cases working their way through the appellate process, perhaps even to catch up on his sleep and come to work late. From a cubicle on the Loyola campus farther uptown, the Resource Center had grown to occupy two floors leased from a small law firm a couple of blocks off Poydras Street and its mile-long spine of pricier office space in the oil-boom towers that ran from the Superdome to the river.

Beyond glass doors framed in aluminum and operated by a squawk box and a buzzer, the center's ground-floor lobby, if that was the right word for it, was unattended—a dusty room with a rump-sprung sofa, the requisite unwatered rubber plant, and a table for the mess of mail that got dumped there once a day. Before heading upstairs to see what his staff was up to, Trenticosta lingered for a moment by the table, leafing through the pile of law journals and letters, bills and advertising circulars. From its return address, one piece of correspondence was readily identifiable as prison mail. It could have been from any of the several Angola inmates the Resource Center represented. Could have been, except that the name and inmate number code above the return address were not those of a current client. Trenticosta settled down for a moment on the sofa, felt the warmth of the autumn sun through the smudged glass behind him, and slit the envelope.

Prison letters to unfamiliar attorneys, to the press, or to public officials are an epistolary subgenre characterized by a tendentious, sometimes delusional tone conveyed in misspelled legalese. The letter in Trenticosta's hands bore none of these hallmarks. The inmate had information, he said, about the Kyles case, and he would be interested to share it with Kyles's attorneys. Simple, to the point. Trenticosta put the letter back in its envelope, took the boxy little elevator up to the Resource Center office, and called Angola. The next morning, he got into his car and three hours later was ushered into a visiting room. A rustling of chains and shackles in an adjacent corridor announced the arrival, moments later, of Herman "Hooks" Wallace.

Trenticosta had had no dealings with Wallace to that time but well knew his legend. Convicted of armed robbery and bank robbery in the 1960s, he was sent upriver for life, but not without first bringing off daring and briefly successful escapes from Orleans Parish Prison, at least two. At Angola he emerged as a political leader, an organizer of the first Black Panther prison chapter to win official recognition from the national organization. And then, early in 1972, he had been placed on "permanent lockdown," Angola's version of solitary: twenty-three hours isolated in his cell, with one hour off for showering and exercise each day. It was the same regimen as for death row, except in Wallace's case without much prospect of release, either through execution or clemency. He and

two other inmates had been on lockdown a quarter century and counting, which, as far as anyone knew, was some kind of record.

Wallace's problem was this: an offed guard. As the general prison
population settled down to breakfast one spring morning in 1972, someone in an otherwise empty dormitory had taken a blade in hand and ten-
derized a twenty-three-year-old named Brent Miller. Miller had grown
up within the grounds of Angola, the son of a guard, the grandson of a
guard, and, at least by reputation, as big a prick as could be found among
the cadre of white turnkeys whose self-esteem depended on the system-
atic degradation of Angola blacks. The coroner counted thirty-two stab
wounds in Miller's flesh, a stabbing frenzy with a handmade shank. The
next day, Wallace was one of thirty "black militants" rounded up on suspicion that they had something to do with the murder. Two years later he
and the other two inmates were convicted of it. The death penalty had been
briefly suspended at this juncture in the history of U.S. jurisprudence.
The lockdown began, the worst punishment Angola could mete out, at
least officially, and in due course Wallace and his alleged accomplices
would come to be known among prisoner rights activists as the Angola
Three. More pertinent to Trenticosta's purposes, the inmate had another, homelier handle, at least among family and friends back in New
Orleans. To a slew of nieces and nephews, including Joanne Dotson and
her late brother, Beanie, Hooks Wallace was Uncle Herman.

Herman Wallace was a figure of towering moral indignation, a black
Muslim with a shaved head and an unshakable conviction that the devil
was a white man and Angola was the ninth circle of his hell. But at their
first meeting Trenticosta realized he was also dealing with a self-trained
jailhouse lawyer of considerable acumen, a black man deeply concerned
to do the right thing by a brother, even one he didn't know—especially if
it tended to point up the deceitfulness of his white overlords.

Wallace had become convinced that Kyles was the victim of an enormous miscarriage of justice, and he was prepared to testify on his behalf.
Trenticosta, with more than a decade under his belt orchestrating testimony by inmates, had no illusions about Herman Wallace's drawbacks as
a witness. He was a convict; the prison jumpsuit they'd make him wear in
court would leave no doubt about that. And there was always the danger
that his politics would get in the way. The last thing Trenticosta needed

was some militant from solitary using his brief moment in the sun to turn the witness stand into a soapbox and begin ranting. But then there was this: if you thought about it, Hooks's credibility was hard to assail. He would pay a huge personal price in testifying for Kyles—a stranger to him and an enemy of his own family. For one thing, it would poison relations with Wallace's sister Victory—Beanie's mother and Hooks's lifeline from Angola to the free world. For another, it would infuriate state authorities who were his only hope, short of another escape, of ever getting released from lockdown. It had to mean something to jurors that he would incur these personal liabilities in the name of the truth. How could it not enhance his credibility?

None of this assessment was lost on Herman Wallace. He understood his shortcomings as a witness as well as Trenticosta, and he had a suggestion for him: get in touch with Joanne Dotson, Beanie's stepsister. She too had come to believe that Kyles was innocent of the Dye murder, and her account would jibe with his, Wallace said. Not only might she corroborate his story, she would be doing so as a woman with no record and in the teeth of her mother's angry disapproval. Joanne had been the closest to Beanie. She idolized him. Make that clear, and she would be a powerful witness.

Trenticosta had no time to waste. As he would soon discover, Victory Wallace and her daughter had already acted on Lowell Dye's suggestion that they make themselves available to Connick's people. For Mrs. Wallace, as for Dye, the important thing was to tell prosecutors about the girls, Yolanda and Carey, who were supposed to have seen someone other than Beanie at the wheel of Mrs. Dye's red Ford leaving the Schwegmann's parking lot. But Dotson, as her Uncle Herman had begun to realize, was trying to find a way to disburden herself of a much weightier insight, one that she knew her mother would find treacherous—if Joanne could ever find a way to speak of it at all.

During lunch break one day, the two of them trekked downtown to the district attorney's office. One of Connick's assistant prosecutors intercepted mother and daughter and, when they told him their business, said they'd better talk to Glen Woods—he was handling the Kyles case. An associate was dispatched to the courthouse, and Woods sent back word that he was in a trial but would meet the women at 1:30. That would have been too late for Joanne if she was going to get back to work on time, so she asked for a piece of scratch paper and left a note with the guard at the DA's front desk: her home number, her work number, a brief message saying who she was and that she needed to talk to someone about the Kyles case.

Woods never called back.

TWENTY-ONE

Mike Fawer had a hunch. He knew the man from somewhere, if he could only place him: a slight, trim-whiskered fellow with graying hair cut short, one in the pool of prospective jurors sent up from the bowels of the courthouse that morning in early February 1998. They came in batches, scores of them initially, traipsing up the courthouse stairs or riding by elevator to this courtroom or that, most of them destined to sit in mounting boredom as others in their cohort were mentally poked and prodded, first by a prosecuting attorney, then by the defense, each seeking the rib of secret bias that might dispose them for or against a defendant. In due time—days on end in the case of a high-profile murder trial—threescore jurors would become a dozen plus two alternates, and the rest would be sent home or, depending on the time of day and the possibility of additional trials, back down into the basement to chat with fellow sufferers, stare vacantly at the TV screens jutting out from the corners of the room, or bang on the vending machines that spat bilious coffee into foam cups, or ate quarters and spat nothing at all.

Fawer was beginning to share their sense of ennui. He would have to be on guard against it. He had not taken this case simply for love of the game. He believed deeply and angrily that Curtis Kyles had been treated to the worst that a racist and class-bound system of justice could deliver. Put to the smell test, the Kyles case stank to high heaven: Would these same abuses of due process—the undisclosed evidence, the cosseted snitch—have been inflicted on a white defendant? On a white man who had killed a black woman? On a middle-class man who had killed a black woman—or any woman—from society's lower depths? Would Harry Connick have tried a banker's son five times for the same murder, or would he have heaved a sigh of relief after the first or second hung jury and settled for a lesser charge or no charge at all? To frame the questions was, it seemed to Mike Fawer, to answer them.

Injustice aside, there had been less noble impulses in Fawer's decision to come aboard and defend Kyles for free: the publicity sparked by a high-profile case; the chance to go another round with Detective John Dillman. An evil man? Fawer really didn't think so. There was nothing about Dillman as dramatic as evil. In Fawer's view, he was more lazy than evil. A strutting, full-of-himself cop, but not in his day a particularly good one, Fawer had decided. Kyles had been a convenience to any detective trying to crack a case, a slam dunk handed off by a snitch. Why question the snitch, even one as suspicious as Beanie Wallace, when you had an easy case already going? One black was as good as another when it came to keeping the solve rate high. And when all was said and done, you had taken "another nigger off the street."

But three trials on, this was starting to wear thin. Fawer had argued the first for free, just as promised. Now he was scraping by on a fraction of his usual fee and, as if that wasn't humbling enough, returning at night to an empty bed.

Damn it. Fawer flashed again on the trim-whiskered man in the jury pool. Something gnawed at the edge of his mind, some long-ago association, then faded before he could coax it into clearer light. A postal employee—Fawer knew that much from the paperwork. His name meant nothing, so Fawer gave it up, preoccupying himself now with other candidates for inclusion on the panel—a sous-chef from one of the hotels; a carpenter so gaunt he brought to mind a Confederate infantryman in the final days of the war; a young and sassy black woman; two older women, one white, one black; and so on.

They had been Witherspooned, this jury of Kyles's peers. They had each agreed that they would be willing to consider killing him if they determined that he had killed Mrs. Dye. But with that advantage ceded to the prosecution, as was unavoidable in a first-degree murder case, Fawer was left to ponder other variables that might tilt the panel just slightly in Kyles's direction. Should it be blacker than white, in the hope that a sense of racial solidarity would engender sympathy for Kyles? Or would the jury pool's inevitable middle-class bent yield a crop of African Americans that much more eager to disown the generation of young black troublemakers who were proving so poisonous to race relations in the era since integration? Would women jurors be seduced by Kyles's boyish good looks, or would their sympathies remain with the grandmotherly housewife so senselessly cut down?

Fawer had represented clients—Aaron Mintz, the accused wife murderer, for one—willing and able to spend tens of thousands of dollars on jury-selection experts, on pollsters good for insights into community mores, on demographers prepared to say just what kinds of people a jury of peers should comprise. The jury selection experts had billed the Mintz defense $20,000. For all the jargon, as far as Fawer was concerned, it still was less a matter of science than of intuition. The high-priced Mintz experts had tossed their yarrow sticks and stuck their collective finger in the wind and proclaimed, among other things, that black men would make good jurors because they would be more sympathetic to a man, like Mintz, caught up in an adulterous affair. Fawer, a white man with an eye for the ladies, had been amused by that reasoning, but he had played along—and sure enough the experts had delivered him a winning jury.

Suddenly it hit him. Of course he knew where he had seen the trim-whiskered man in the Kyles jury pool. Damned if he hadn't been on the Mintz jury as well. Damned if he hadn't been the foreman, foreman of a jury that acquitted a man in the face of evidence many called overwhelming, a man susceptible to reasonable doubt. Fawer riffled back through the stack of forms, one for each member of the pool. Jurors listed their names, addresses, schooling, criminal record (if any), prior jury experience (if any). And sure enough, the post office employee, a man named Glenn Boquet, listed service on an unspecified second-degree murder case in 1984. Mintz was a second-degree case. It had to be the same guy.

Now Fawer had a dilemma. He could reveal the prior connection—increasing to near certainty that the state would use a peremptory challenge and zap Boquet. Or he could keep his mouth shut, hang on to this doubt-prone juror, and see what happened. He decided to keep his mouth shut. Glenn Boquet did not. He had placed Fawer the minute he walked into the courtroom, and if Fawer had not reciprocated in the moment of mutual recognition, Boquet thought he might know why: the Mintz trial had unfolded in the heat of the New Orleans summer, a time of year when Boquet, an avid fisherman lacking even a trace of African blood, generally took on a deep and even tan. It amused him—well, maybe there were other emotions in play as well—to look through the press clips in the trial's aftermath and see himself described as "jury foreman Glenn Boquet, a black." "It was my fifteen minutes of fame," he would remark drily to his wife, "and I had to be black to get it."

Fawer, in fact, had not been confused about Boquet's race, but while the defense attorney kept his own counsel, Boquet saw fit to report to Judge Burns. In essence, perhaps in slightly less salty language, he would remember putting it to the judge this way: "I don't want to have this thing go on for two weeks and then you find this out and the whole damn trial is fucked up because I didn't tell you." Burns appreciated the advisory but was untroubled by it. In coming to him with his concern, Boquet was demonstrating the kind of probity that would make for a good, unbiased juror. He could stay on the panel.

There were other coincidences between the Mintz and Kyles trials, enough of them to make New Orleans seem a smaller town than it is: John Dillman, for one, as Fawer had remembered with relish in agreeing to take the Kyles case. Jack Peebles, for another. Peebles had prosecuted Mintz, the selfsame Jack Peebles who, after graduating to Harry Connick's appellate division, had fought Kyles all the way to the U.S. Supreme Court.

But juries were the wild card. You just never knew. A capital conviction required a unanimous verdict. A single skeptic, one holdout, one juror with the suppleness of mind to see reasonable doubt, and Kyles would walk. A freethinker. That's what Fawer needed, someone like the bright and cocky Glenn Boquet, someone who could stand up to the herd instinct and make fellow jurors think and think some more. Fawer glowed inwardly with the secret knowledge that he had landed a Mintz veteran on Kyles's fifth jury—a $20,000 juror at no cost whatsoever. But in fact, in putting Curtis Kyles's fate in the hands of Glenn Boquet, he had made one of the bigger blunders of his career.

It was easy to be deceived by Glenn Boquet. Bright, with-it, the son of a jazzman, Boquet was a paradox. He had an admiring eye for the ladies, yet he had been faithfully and happily married for some twenty years. Swore a blue streak, yet agonized over moral nuances. A career Postal Service employee, he had put himself through Tulane as a summertime route carrier and had risen through the ranks of his only employer to become the Postal Service's chief financial officer for Louisiana.

Up North, where he came from, Fawer might have made confident assumptions about a man of Boquet's general cut and demeanor, might have enjoyed a beer with him at a college reunion—Cornell, in Fawer's case—might have assumed the jazzman's son would also share Fawer's easy way with blacks and his disgust at the injustices history had visited on them. But this was the South, and Fawer would have been only partly right. Boquet, by his own account, was a right-winger. While many from his generation joined SDS and registered the African American vote in Mississippi and Alabama, Boquet would wryly recall spending the 1960s as a partisan of Young Americans for Freedom. Abbie Hoffman was not his hero, nor were any of the Kennedy brothers. Bill Buckley and Barry Goldwater were the sun and the moon of the YAF cosmos. And as the first college man in Boquet family history, young Glenn was easily able to fend off intellectual assaults on his view of liberal America as a study in terminal decay.

It is true that he had voted to acquit Aaron Mintz, but what Fawer had no way of knowing was that Boquet also believed Mintz was a wife killer. Boquet had acquiesced to the majority only when it became clear that even as foreman, he could not turn them around. That trial had appalled Boquet, not least because of what he perceived as the stupidity of many fellow jurors, but especially because of the trauma endured by Mintz's son and daughter in watching their father's humiliating fight for acquittal. "I will never put these fucking people through this shit again," Boquet told the dwindling cadre of jurors still in his corner as the Mintz deliberations stretched on and on. "We will win or we will lose, but we are not going to have a hung jury." And so, shortly after suppertime on a sweltering July evening thirteen years earlier, the jury filed into the courtroom, and Boquet, as foreman, announced the verdict: not guilty. As gasps and shrieks erupted in the gallery, Fawer had rushed to the jury box and hugged and kissed each man and woman in turn, then rushed, in equal haste, into Judge Frank Shea's chamber, where he vomited his supper all over Shea's fine clean carpet. In the Kyles case, even more quickly than in the Mintz case, Boquet would come to an unshakable view that the defendant was guilty. And he was keenly aware of the obstacles that lay in the path to such a verdict.

With a black defendant, the prosecution wasn't going to probe too deeply into the defense team's unexpected acquiescence to a white male juror with deep local roots. Boquet was just fine with Glen Woods, only more so when his admission to the jury was followed by another bearded white, the carpenter who reminded Fawer of a lantern-jawed Johnny Reb. Jury selection dragged on for the better part of a week, ample time for Boquet and the carpenter, a Tennessean by birth, to discover an easy rapport.

It was a strangely disorienting experience to begin one's day dozing in a jury lounge, waiting to be released to workplace and family, and instead suddenly to find oneself part of a murder jury, sequestered and under guard perhaps for weeks. The goal was to avoid jury tampering, of course, and also contamination of the jury's knowledge of the case by any information not presented in court. Once the panel was complete, sheriff's deputies would escort them to their homes to pick up toiletries and changes of clothing, then bring them back to the hotel that would be their home for the duration.

Kyles's fifth jury was, as justice hopes of all juries, a notably ordinary mix: seven women, five men; about an equal number of whites and blacks. The sous-chef had survived the selection process. The older black woman was a staunch Baptist, but this being Louisiana, there were Catholics from both sides of the color line.

Sequestered juries in Orleans Parish had the run of the hotel's menu, but bedrooms were meted out more thriftily, and most jurors were assigned a roommate—in Boquet's case, the carpenter, a man named Mayo. Jurors are not meant to discuss the case among themselves until all the evidence and testimony have been presented and they have been charged by the judge to begin their deliberations. That doesn't mean they can't discuss one another, particularly on that first night, before any testimony has been heard, and inevitably Boquet had some opinions.

A young black woman juror settled down at the table with Mayo and Boquet at supper that night. Boquet took her measure as they talked. Later, in the bedroom assigned to him and Mayo, he made a prediction: "I don't want to sound like *The Old Man and the Sea*, or like I'm smarter than you," he would remember saying to Mayo, "but I've been through this before. And I work for the post office, don't forget, so I'm familiar with the young black culture. And the concept is, no matter what a white guy does, there's something wrong; there's a motive. Can't trust whitey. She, in the end, will cause us deep trouble, because reason and logic will make no difference with this woman. In the end, it's going to be a black-white thing. Now, I don't know how the trial's going to go, but she's gonna be trouble."

The defense also sensed trouble. It lay in the trend lines of diminishing jury support. Fawer sensed that the momentum of the case was no longer with the defense. To have any chance of an acquittal, he needed to blow the case wide open. Failing that, he'd have to settle for another hung jury and an upsurge of public disgust sufficient to embarrass Harry Connick.

Kyles could read the concern gathering in the faces of his counselors, and perhaps his own anxiety was equally apparent to the inmates he fell in with back at parish prison after each day's court proceedings. It did not win him their sympathy. On the contrary, there were some among them who clearly savored his pain, no matter how he tried to conceal it. Because there was a flip side to the enhanced stature Kyles brought back with him to OPP after his years in Angola. It spawned jealousy, Kyles found, especially among the older prisoners, only more so as his case came to trial—a trial mentioned now and again on the evening news, to comments and sometimes whistles from the inmates gathered around the tier TV. And who did he think he was, with that briefcase he packed with documents and carried off to court each morning? A lawyer? A white man? Something special? It was the aspect of prison psychology that most sickened and perplexed Kyles, the lack of solidarity among inmates, the envy. "If they see the possibility of you going home, they're going to do what they can to blow your chances. That's what I don't understand about prisoners."

What prisoners could do to blow Kyles's chances was to taunt him, goad him, try to shatter the composure that had lifted him above the daily prison fray, draw him into a set-to that might leave marks on his face that a judge and jury would be sure to notice.

"Why would you wish all that torment on somebody?" Kyles remembered asking himself. "If they're innocent, let them go home. If they've paid their dues, let them go home."

He yearned for it, of course, the little world he had made with Pinkey and the respite from it that he found at his mother's place or with his mistress. But to that yearning had been added an urgent sense that he was needed there more than ever. Meco's legal troubles had worsened acutely, as Kyles was the last to learn. He had received intimations all along that Meco was on a slippery slope, the very same landscape of petty crime and escalating violence that had eased Kyles into the criminal underworld twenty years earlier. Pinkey had tried to keep her son's problems from his father for a while, not wanting to worry Kyles needlessly or break his concentration on his own legal predicament. And anyway, what could he do from OPP besides exhort and importune, as he had been doing in intermittent phone calls all of Meco's life? Now Meco wasn't there in the cluster of his children who gathered in Pinkey's kitchen to pass the phone back and forth among themselves in a roundtable conversation with the dimly remembered man on the other end of the line. Meco was behind bars himself, a seventeen-year-old held on an attempted-murder rap in St. John the Baptist Parish, some thirty miles upriver. Kyles's grasp on the details behind the charge remained sketchy at best and was going to stay that way as long as he was in prison, mindful that his every call and conversation might be monitored. From what he could tell, the charge stemmed from a bit of business between Meco's buddies and a rival posse involved in the only line of business that held much promise for them: drugs. A door had been pushed in, bullets had flown more or less randomly, more a matter of intimidation than a calculated hit. Meco could say in all honesty that he had no idea whether the slug that dropped one boy was from his gun or someone else's. He hadn't waited around long enough to find out.

Like father, like son. They had always said that Meco was the image of his old man, from his gait to his temperament, and in a secret chamber of his mind Kyles registered a smidgen of fatherly pride in a boy as ballsy as Meco was turning out to be. He knew it for a sentiment that he would never be able to share with the high-minded white people who clung to their belief in his own gentle innocence, and it was more than eclipsed by the deep fear he felt for his son now that he was behind bars. But there was good news as well—joyous news, really—from Tyteannia. His oldest daughter, now twenty and married, was going to make Kyles a grandfather. Indeed, she was due any day now, as Kyles realized from her appearance one day in court, the first time he had seen her in months. An image of her as a little girl, a third-grader in her school uniform, bubbled up from the mists of Kyles's memory, at first random and without context. Then suddenly Kyles could place it: the snapshot he had taped onto the dashboard of the Monterey, the car he was working on when the takedown squad swooped in on him that Monday in 1984, a lifetime ago. His little girl had grown up without him, and in that same interval, he had grown old.

TWENTY-TWO

By Thursday, four days into the voir dire process, the jury was complete. Judge Burns could schedule opening arguments for the following morning. At the state's table with Glen Woods was a new face, Margaret Lagattuta, a tall, hefty white woman, from the ranks of Harry Connick's assistant DAs. The defense was again in the hands of Mike Fawer, with Nick Trenticosta and Denny LeBoeuf beside him and LeBoeuf's sister, Marie Campbell, ever present to keep orderly their swollen accordion folders of briefs and notes, prior testimony, affidavits, witness statements—the accumulated record of a murder case litigated for fourteen years.

Glen Woods had only just begun a long-winded and desultory opening statement when it became clear that something was up. For those fourteen years the state of Louisiana had portrayed the defendant, Curtis Kyles, as a lone wolf, a fearsome predator who had stalked and killed a loving wife and mother as she shopped for groceries. But now Woods was recasting the whole scenario. He would, he claimed, prove that Kyles committed the crime with an accomplice or accomplices, a whole pack of running buddies, among them the police informant known as Beanie Wallace. Kyles was still the killer, Woods contended, still subject to the state's ultimate penalty. But he needed to be seen in context, as part of an ensemble of predators—Beanie, Johnny Burnes, Don Powell, Kevin Black, the whole lot of them. They preyed on the Schwegmann's parking lot and divvied up their spoils. Whatever the merit of Woods's new theory of the case, the state would never see fit to charge Black and Powell with any of the imputed crimes.

In her seat in the visitors gallery, Kyles's sister Lela Johnson felt her blood pressure begin to rise with her rage. Once again the DA seemed to be rewriting the case to suit his convenience. She had seen it happen between the first and second trials, with the suddenly more prominent role assigned to Kevin Black, and then again in the third, with a police sergeant claiming to have overheard a confession. To Lela, the malleability of the truth in the prosecutor's hands "was like he don't care what kind of lie he have to tell." In hindsight, as she looked back on the sudden transformation of her brother from lone predator to team player, it would seem "like they was trying a different man." The tactical shift was equally stunning to Lowell Dye, though for different reasons. He too was present in the visitors gallery, and as Woods launched into his enunciation of the "running buddy" theory, as it came to be called, Dye began to shake his head in astonishment and dismay. Here Dye was with new evidence—Joanne's taped statement; the eyewitness account by Yolanda and Carey, if only they could be tracked down—that seemed finally to remove Beanie once and for all from the murder scene, and now Woods was trying to put him right back in the Schwegmann's parking lot.

Dye could be caustic. And when he caught up with Woods, dragging nervously on a cigarette in the courthouse corridor during a break in the first day's proceedings, he would remember not mincing his words. "That's a joke, right, Glen?" And then, less coyly, "What planet are you coming from, man? That's the stupidest goddamn thing I ever heard in my life." To which, as Dye recalled it, Woods answered, "Well, that's the way these guys were; they ran together."

"But Glen," Dye remonstrated, "you're forgetting something, man. One little thing: there's no evidence putting Beanie in the parking lot—none. You've got nothing to go on." As though morbidly fascinated by the onrushing fiasco, Dye said he then asked the origins of so cockamamy a strategy. "I said, 'Glen, where did you come up with that?' and he goes, 'Well, we were thinking about it, about theories of the case, and Camille and I came up with that. We thought it would be a good thing.'"

In truth, it might have been a masterstroke. Having failed to disentangle Beanie from the possibility that eyewitnesses mistook him for Kyles, Woods and Buras decided simply to finesse the issue, inviting jurors to bind the two men inextricably in their minds. After all, only one of them was still around to convict, whether as accessory or triggerman, it didn't matter which; and only one of them was still eligible for execution, the only one who mattered for present purposes—Curtis Kyles.

For all Dye's skepticism, Woods did have at least a little bit of evidence putting Beanie in the parking lot. A new witness—someone whose name Woods had found jotted down on a 1984 police report but who, evidently lost in the shuffle, had never been interviewed by prosecutors. From the witness stand Bernard Cloud described himself as a guard at Halter Marine, one of the big shipyards along the Industrial Canal adjacent to Schwegmann's. His story was that he had heard the shot, perhaps two, and then he saw a man run down the roadway—a running buddy truly running. A second man in a "dark-colored car" had overtaken him and paused long enough for a heated exchange of words. The men, Woods suggested, were Kyles and Beanie Wallace, but Cloud was able to offer no proof nor any insight into what they yelled at each other. Woods had not played his whole hand, however. The running-buddy theory laid the groundwork for another courtoom surprise, a second fresh witness against Kyles.

Hooks Wallace's letter to Trenticosta, it seemed, was not the only correspondence from Angola in the interval between the fourth and fifth trials. Connick's people also were in receipt of a letter from an inmate who, like Sergeant Mike Rice, claimed to have heard Kyles confess to the Dye murder years earlier. After Rice's disastrous performance in the third trial, the prosecution scratched him from their witness list, but Glen Woods still needed a clincher for so wobbly a case, ideally someone who had heard Kyles sing or was at least willing to say so. How very ardently Woods yearned for this kind of testimony was evident in just how dubious a witness he was willing to call. The letter writer was an armed robber named Chris Alphonso. Better known throughout Angola as a jailhouse informant who had been of service to Connick's office even before he went to prison, Alphonso, by then thirty-five, was also a minister, thanks to a correspondence course he had taken. But it was not in the line of pastoral duty that he claimed to have served Kyles as confessor. The occasion was impromptu, a chance encounter in a prison yard back in 1987, he said. There, according to Alphonso, Kyles had disburdened himself of his guilty secret by sharing it, inexplicably, with a white man he didn't know.

At any rate, that was the story Alphonso laid out in his letter to the district attorney's office. Ironically—or was it a kind of false naïveté meant to buttress his otherwise shaky credibility—Alphonso initially postured as a supplicant on Kyles's behalf. The defendant did not deserve the death penalty, Alphonso wrote, because in confessing Mrs. Dye's murder, Kyles said he was sorry about it—a bit of filigree not unlike Mike Rice's discredited account in which Kyles admitted the killing but called it accidental. Blond and doughy looking in his orange prison jumpsuit, on the stand Alphonso elaborated on the alleged confession by saying that Kyles identified Beanie as his accomplice in the killing. "He said that [it] was him and . . . Beanie that did it," Alphonso testified.

In the four preceding trials, that detail would have been most unwelcome. Beanie, after all, had been portrayed all along by prosecutors as the hapless victim of Kyles's effort to fob off a hot car. But Alphonso's account required that he be an accomplice, a running buddy. Whatever Alphonso's role in the invention of this theory, defense lawyers suggested that his letter was transparently unreliable, an attempt to curry favor with authorities in the hope of cutting short a prison term that might otherwise run until 2018. Failing that, Alphonso was angling for transfer to a comfier prison. To the embarrassment of his handlers, under questioning by Fawer, the witness made no bones about it. It was his understanding, Alphonso testified, that Glen Woods agreed to tell the judge who presided over his conviction that he had helped out with the Kyles case. But Alphonso also threw up another motive for his testimony. He said he agreed to come forward in exchange for "protection" from inmates on his "enemies list," a roster that had grown to seventy-five names, only some of them people he had ratted out as an informant. That revelation, with its undertone of grandiosity and rampant paranoia, jibed with a 1997 psychiatric evaluation the defense team dug up. The diagnosis: Alphonso was a schizophrenic.

Is there anything you wouldn't say to please the district attorney? Fawer asked as his cross-examination reached a peak of sarcasm and scorn. Any lie you wouldn't tell?

Alphonso's answer was cheerful and succinct: No, he said, with a fawning glance toward the prosecution table.

As informants go, Alphonso served the Kyles prosecution less brilliantly than Beanie Wallace. But his contribution was not unrequited. Three years later he popped up on a list of a half dozen inmates eligible for a state Pardon Board hearing. Five were denied. Alphonso was the one set free. Police had written a letter to the Pardon Board hailing his work as a snitch.

By the fifth trial's second week, the exhaustion and frustration in the courtroom were palpable. On Tuesday, the Woods/Fawer forensic cockfight got physical as the defense attorney actually shoved his counterpart during a bench conference with Judge Burns. Woods came back like a barroom pugilist with an offer "to take it outside," inspiring Burns to threaten them both with contempt citations and jail time. Fortunately, the jury was out of the room.

Woods's relationship with Lowell Dye was also worsening. The prosecutor was growing increasingly irked by Dye's kibitzing. It got on his nerves the way Dye haunted the courtroom, sometimes with his father in tow, second-guessing every tack the prosecution took, strutting around as the seasoned professional, when as far as Glen Woods knew, he had never tried a criminal case in his life. And then inspiration struck. To get Dye out of his hair, Woods needed to make him a witness, if only to corroborate from the stand that he had had contact with Joanne Dotson some months earlier. It meant that Dye would have to sit outside the courtroom, out of earshot of testimony that might warp his own. "As if I hadn't already heard every witness four times before," Dye snorted. But there was no reasoning with the procedural rules. Dye was relegated to the company of police detectives and black laborers, the appalling Darlene Kersh, and others smoking and fidgeting out in the majestic vaulted hallway that ran the length of the courthouse behind its Tulane Avenue façade. And there he would be confined when, on Valentine's Day 1998, the defense called two witnesses with the potential to blow the case wide open, Uncle Herman "Hooks" Wallace and his niece Joanne Dotson.

Wallace went first, and his appearance would have been striking even if he hadn't reached the stand breathing heavily, a lifetime of prison smokes having told on him during the climb up the back staircase to the second-floor courtroom. He was also shackled and in a borrowed prison overall with the initials OPP emblazoned on the bright orange fabric. LeBoeuf dealt with the unavoidable by way of introducing him to the jury. "Mr. Wallace, you're obviously incarcerated presently in Orleans Parish Prison. Where are you normally incarcerated?"

"I'm normally incarcerated at the Louisiana State Penitentiary at Angola." Still panting, he asked for time to compose himself. "I'm a little out of breath right now . . ."

And lest anyone accuse her of candy-coating her witness's record, LeBoeuf drew it from Wallace himself: convictions for armed robbery and a federal bank robbery, both in 1967, and five years after that the murder of the Angola guard. Then they got down to business. What had been on Wallace's mind in contacting Trenticosta, and what he—and then in turn his niece—reiterated under questioning by LeBoeuf, was this: Thirteen years earlier, during a collect call to the New Orleans home front, Herman Wallace found himself chatting for a few minutes with his sister's boy, the one they called Beanie. Beanie had been a mere sprite of three or four when his uncle went upriver, but Victory had brought him along on visits to Angola over the years. It was the seed of a relationship that was then sustained by phone. On the occasion of his call in the autumn of 1984, Uncle Herman had been concerned to find his nephew a little agitated. In only partially coded language, Beanie had unburdened himself of his worries, which centered on a purse snatching gone wrong. "It went down bad; it broke bad," he said, leaving his uncle to imagine the worst. "But I think I got it fixed up. I'm going to be okay."

Herman Wallace's deep and embittered estrangement from the process of jurisprudence in which he was participating told in the almost mechanical precision of his answers. Asked his relationship to Beanie Wallace, he corrected LeBoeuf: Beanie was "an alias"; his nephew was named Joseph. Eased toward a recap of that first conversation with Beanie after the Schwegmann murder, Wallace had no patience with euphemism or indirection: "Basically, Joseph explained to me that he had recently killed someone."

Joanne's demeanor on the stand was very different. Where Wallace was curt and imperious, she was whispery and petrified, her dread expressing itself in a frozen half smile that some in the gallery took as a sign of deceitfulness. But her testimony fitted seamlessly into the narrative begun by her uncle. She picked it up with an account of another phone call from Hooks several months later. This time he was looking for her, but again Beanie had answered. He was living upstairs from Joanne at the time, in an apartment with no phone. And so, at the sound of hers ringing, he had come bounding downstairs to see who it was. That was just as well with Joanne; she was packing up her kids' things, trying to get away for the weekend, and she really didn't have time to chat.

From the kids' room, she overheard bits and snatches of the conversation—a reference to Schwegmann's, to the parking lot murder that had gone down over there, and to somebody named Curtis. Beanie knew somebody named Curtis, the Curtis who was married to the sister of his friend Johnny Burnes. Maybe it was that Curtis, except then she thought she heard him say something about setting somebody up. As a rule, Joanne knew better than to mess in Beanie's business, but this was upsetting to her, and so she quizzed him a little bit after he got off the phone. Who was he talking to, and what was this about setting up somebody? It was Uncle Herman on the phone, Beanie said, but he wasn't ready to say much more. "Well, you need to tell me when you're ready," Joanne scolded.

A year would pass before Beanie was ready. It was easy for Joanne to be precise about the date. June 20, 1986, was the day she turned thirty. Maybe it was the birthday grog, or maybe it was a sixth sense that told Beanie he was coming to the end of his own days and needed to make a clean breast of something that was eating at him. In any case, Joanne would contend, on that day he told her everything. He had killed Delores Dye "because the bitch didn't want to give up her money." And he had put his contacts in the police department onto Kyles, basically because he hated Curtis, and he knew that Curtis hated him right back. Joanne didn't need any reminding about the woman at the center of all that hatefulness. She didn't know Pinkey, but she knew of her.

Before the conversation ended, Beanie pulled out his wallet and showed Joanne a card on which he had listed the various cops he'd fed information to during his years as a snitch. Johnny Miller's name was on that card, and so were other detectives, along with their phone numbers. Joanne jotted some of them down, people to get in touch with if Beanie got into more trouble. Beanie swore his sister to secrecy about everything he told her. Eight days later he lay on the train tracks alongside Johnny Burnes's house on Law Street, and this time there was nothing the police could do to help their boy out of a jam.

Woods would make much of the fact that it had taken Hooks Wallace and Joanne Dotson so long to come forward with their secret—just as Fawer had lacerated Mike Rice for so conveniently providing prosecutors with Kyles's "confession" twelve years after it had gone unnoted on police records. But Joanne could claim that she had not waited long at all. In fact, as soon as she was liberated from *omertà* by her brother's death, she had tried, she claimed, to tell authorities what she knew. Her recourse was to Melvin Mackie, an ex-cop she had been seeing. Mackie had a sense of priority. First we're going to bury Joseph, he told Joanne. Then he'd take her downtown to talk to someone he still knew in the department.

It would not enhance the credibility of Joanne's account that she could no longer remember the name of the detective Mackie connected her with, and Mackie was no longer around to jog her memory. But her account of the visit rang true in its description of the police station, of her mother waiting with Melvin while the detective led her into the headquarters elevator and across a room crowded with desks. The detective took her statement, the whole story of Beanie's confession—the Dye murder, framing Kyles—and she signed it, she said. Somehow that statement never turned up in the prosecution's records of the case, at least not the part of it disclosed to the defense team.

As far as Joanne could figure, she had done her part. The wheels of justice would begin to turn, and the man Beanie set up would go free. Or so she assumed. In any event, she had been unable to think of what else she could do until years later—just a couple of months ago, to be precise—when she left her note for Glen Woods with the guard at the district attorney's office. "He gave me the pad, and I wrote my name on there," Dotson recalled under questioning by LeBoeuf. "I wrote the time that I was there, and I put my name down there. I put my home number, my work number, and I left a brief . . . a brief message letting him know who

I was and the reason why I needed to speak with him. 'Cause I put on there it was pertaining about the Kyles case."

LeBoeuf: And did you say whose sister you were?
Dotson: Yes.
LeBoeuf: And did Mr. Woods ever return the call?
Dotson: No, he did not.

In his cell at Angola, Hooks Wallace also had lost track of the Kyles case when, in the course of his ceaseless prowling through legal developments that might provide an avenue of escape from his own predicament, he came across the 1995 U.S. Supreme Court ruling *Kyles v. Whitley.* It was a jarring moment for him. There in every particular was the murder Beanie had mentioned to him. It had to be. But for Hooks, it was also his first awareness that the man his nephew framed had actually been convicted of the crime—indeed, sentenced to die for it. Wallace's consolation was this: that Kyles would now surely be set free, even if it took a pro forma third trial to tidy things up. And then, to Wallace's astonishment and disgust, there had been a fourth trial and then, in the offing, a fifth. And so he had written his letter to Trenticosta at the Death Penalty Resource Center.

For Joanne Dotson, the wake-up call had been the man on the TV news one night saying that Curtis Kyles was facing trial again—his fourth—for the murder of Delores Dye. Somehow the third trial had not caught her attention, and she had drifted on with her life as she had for a decade, reasonably sure that Beanie's confession and her statement to the police had restored Kyles to freedom. In romantic moods she sometimes wondered idly if he knew the role she played in his release and might even drop by one day to thank her. Instead, it was Lowell Dye who dropped by, eliciting from her the taped statement that seemed to contradict everything she had been saying.

LeBoeuf knew she had to deal with it preemptively. The tape would be devastating on cross-examination, just as Dye had hoped in giving it to the prosecution. LeBoeuf needed to do what she could to defuse its impact. She wrapped up her questioning by asking Dotson about Dye's visit.

"He came to my house one morning," Dotson began. "He identified himself, and I let him in my house. We sat down. He had a . . . He say, 'I hope you don't mind if I put a tape recorder on.' I say, 'No problem.' So I sit in the chair and he got one of those little fold-up chairs and sit in front of me. Set the tape recorder on my coffee table and he was . . . Before we started, he was like telling me, 'I'm trying to clear your brother's name because I know your brother didn't do it.'"

The recollection seemed momentarily to overwhelm Dotson, and LeBoeuf eased up on her, turning away from the content of the conversation to ask her witness banal questions: how many children she had (three), which of them were home that day (Ralph and Hilton, and also Beanie's fatherless son, Joseph, a twelve-year-old). Finally Dotson seemed to have composed herself, and LeBoeuf got back to business: "When you had this conversation with Mr. Dye, did you tell him what you testified to this morning, that Joseph Wallace confessed to the murder of his mother?"

DOTSON: No, I didn't.
LEBOEUF: Why not?
DOTSON: Because I couldn't tell him that my brother had killed his mother.
LEBOEUF: Did you lie to him?
DOTSON: Yes, I did.

The witness seemed unable to go on. But then, rallying, she muttered the words, "And I'm sorry." They seemed directed as much at her mother as at the absent Lowell Dye.

Banishing Lowell Dye from the courtroom had not, of course, ended his meddling with the case. If anything, the way the prosecutors had bungled his leads—letting Joanne morph from a potential star witness for the prosecution into a key witness for the defense; never tracking down Yolanda and Carey, the two young women who watched the Ford leave the parking lot with someone other than Beanie at the wheel—left him only that much more zealous to see Woods make the most of the witness who he now was convinced could clinch the case: Pinkey Burnes.

"She's the key," Lowell told Connick and Buras. "You absolutely have to do an excellent job cross-examining Pinkey." And of course Connick and Buras assured him that Woods and his assistant in the courtroom, Margaret Lagattuta, would not disappoint. Dye was not convinced. With Pinkey scheduled as the closing witness, he went to work, drawing up a list of questions seventeen pages long that he believed would tease out inconsistencies between her previous testimony and the statement taken from her by the police at the time of the arrest. They were subtle discrepancies—about household pets, or the lack of them; about Kyles's unreliable habits as breadwinner (so why the sudden bounty of food that Pinkey was able to ladle up for friends and neighbors that Sunday night?); and about his lack of sexual fidelity to the mother of his children—questions that Dye had come to believe could be fatal to the defense. His list completed, and with Pinkey scheduled to testify on Monday, Dye called Glen Woods over the weekend. "He tells me to meet him at, like, four o'clock in the afternoon down at the DA's office, right?" Dye said, recalling the moment. "And I've got the questions all worked out, everything annotated as to what she said in the different trials: This is what you need to ask. This is what you focus on. This is where you go on cross . . ."

A front was coming in as Dye banged on the locked doors of the district attorney's office that Sunday afternoon, waiting for someone to let him in. A thirty-mile-an-hour wind blew icy drizzle that slicked his hair and soaked his clothes. Dye had been there maybe five minutes, banging on the glass door and shivering mightily, when Lagattuta emerged from the catacombs of the DA's domain, padding across the industrial felt carpet in her stocking feet. Dye asked for Woods. "'I'm here to see Glen.'

"She says, 'You ain't gonna see Glen today.'

"I said, 'No, you don't get it. I made an appointment. He's meeting me here.'

"She goes, 'You ain't gonna see Glen.'"

And then it dawned on Dye. She wasn't playing gatekeeper; she wasn't protecting Woods. She was making a prediction, and she was right. Woods wasn't going to show up. Dye was incredulous. "I'm soaking wet. I've wasted all this time. I have all the questions worked out. I know Pinkey is the key witness. Woods knows I know she's the key witness. She's the final witness. He's already screwed the whole Joanne Dotson thing up . . ."

Dye finally got his crack at Woods in court the next morning, but Woods seized the initiative: As Dye tells it, "He walks up to me, and he says, 'Lowell, I've been thinking about it all weekend. I know you want me to call Pinkey, but I've made a trial decision: we're not going to call Pinkey.'" Dye was seething, but he strove to mask his disgust with sweet reasonableness, at least at first. "I went, 'I understand, Glen, that anytime a case goes to trial and there's multiple lawyers on any one side, that one trial lawyer has to be the captain of the ship.'" And then he began to lose himself to his rage: "'But you know what? Sometimes the captain of the ship can make a very tragic mistake, and this is the worst fucking mistake I've seen in twenty fucking years of practice.'" The outburst was theatrical. It was also heartfelt, and years later, after the case had faded from the press and the recollection of all but those most intimately involved, Dye would remain convinced that he was absolutely right.

TWENTY-THREE

Glenn Boquet's breezy certainty that the young black woman on the jury would jam its deliberations revealed, of course, as much about him as about her. But dismissing Boquet as nothing more than a garden-variety Southern bigot prone to hasty assumptions about both blacks and women would be to miss a more complex psychological reality. With Boquet as the jury's alpha male and, ultimately, as its foreman, that psychology would play a shaping role in the fate of Curtis Kyles.

For Boquet, the trial had been like the rending of a veil, the one that separated the races in New Orleans (only more so in the mid-'80s), but also one that divided Boquet from his own past. The Boquets were not black, but neither were they Cajun, as the surname might suggest. The French-speaking Cajuns (a corruption of "Acadians") had reached the prairies and bayous of south Louisiana in the eighteenth century, following their expulsion by the British from Canada. The Boquets, just three generations back, had come direct from Bordeaux to cut cane in the fields of Terrebonne Parish, southwest of New Orleans—white workers doing jobs once largely the province of black slaves. Boquet's great-grandfather was born aboard the ship. Boquet's grandfather made the leap from field labor to petit bourgeois respectability as a barber, offering fifteen-cent haircuts in the back room of the family's apartment off Franklin Avenue, not all that far from Desire Street, albeit a very different Desire Street from the one Curtis Kyles would know.

Boquet père had inherited the barbershop business, and by working jazz gigs at night, he was able to put Glenn through a Catholic high school and then Tulane, the first Boquet to go to college. The family had made it, and to certify that success, they followed a generation of New Orleans whites out to the suburbs on the eastern edge of the city, leaving behind the blacks who would, by the 1980s and 1990s, find themselves the sole denizens of the inner-city neighborhoods they had fought to integrate just twenty years earlier.

In the racial cosmology of Glenn Boquet's New Orleans, Mrs. Dye couldn't have picked a more portentous place to die. Schwegmann's—a grocery store so big it was almost glamorous when it opened—had come to seem like a giant floodwall to him. On one side was the world of the white middle class, the world of Glenn Boquet and Lowell Dye and, a few rungs below them, of Darlene Kersh. Behind the store and beyond a tangle of elevated interstate ramps and bypasses were the miles and miles of trim cottages raised on pilings above the eternal threat of floods, the old working-class neighborhoods, once the last hurrah of inner-city white ethnics and now all but entirely black. On the one side, as Boquet saw it, law and order. On the other, a world of unprincipled violence. "People killed and lied and cheated and degraded each other, and every now and then, apparently, somebody would hop through the fence, and bam, she's dead, a Mrs. Dye. It freaked me out so goddamn much, it was like a science fiction movie. There's a curtain. Over here is heaven; over there is hell. All the rules of heaven don't apply in hell. All the rules of hell don't apply in heaven."

But here was the moral conundrum that elevated Boquet's two-tone view of the world from the realm of simple bigotry: "Do you forgive hell for not being heaven?" he asked himself. "Do you hate heaven for not being hell?" Because, reactionary as his politics might seem, Boquet was willing to concede that working-class whites—Boquet's own stock—had made their escape up the economic ladder and out of the inner city by placing their feet squarely on the upturned faces of the black people hoping to be next in line. "I'm not a bleeding heart," Boquet would offer in explaining himself years later, "but I'm an observer. Curtis Kyles killed that lady be-

cause he could not escape the world that had replaced what was there before. The truth is, he killed her. The other truth is, we created the world
that allowed that to happen."

That deviation from right-wing orthodoxy was perhaps as close as
Boquet would ever get to the mind-set he assigned to Mike Fawer. This is
not to say that he had no respect for Fawer. His views of the defense attorney were complicated. Based on the job Fawer did for Aaron Mintz, Boquet
could sincerely describe him as "brilliant," perhaps even "a genius"—but
a fallen genius, Boquet had decided, a man corrupted by his liberal faith
in the innocence of the oppressed. After two trials with him, Boquet also
thought he could see through Fawer's courtroom legerdemain, and once
deliberations began—if this damn testimony ever ended—he intended to
warn his fellow jurors not to be taken in. Boquet would summarize his
insights his way: "Fawer has an incredible ability to say, 'Don't think
about what the police found; think about what they didn't find.' And of
course the minefield of things they didn't find is endless—tests not performed, evidence not dusted for fingerprints, witnesses not summoned."

"Fuck Fawer," Boquet wanted to exhort his peers as Fawer regaled
them with his courtroom theatrics. "Go back to what they *did* do, and
what that means. Go with what you know." The corollary, of course, was
that along with putting the police on trial, Fawer's case hinged on shift-
ing guilt from Kyles to Beanie Wallace, from a flesh-and-blood defendant
tied in a dozen ways to the evidence, to a dead man not present to defend
himself. "He made Beanie Wallace the convict in that trial, and I kept
wanting to tell these sons of bitches"—Boquet here refers to his fellow
jurors—"that's not what's going on here . . . We have more than enough
evidence to convict Kyles."

Brilliant though he might be, Fawer was also capable of tactical errors, Boquet decided. And the biggest error, unless you count not bounc-
ing Glenn Boquet out of the jury pool in the first place, was the way he
handled the rough-cut laborers who testified as eyewitnesses, in particular the elderly, bearded Henry Williams. Boquet had taken to calling him
Uncle Remus. Fawer, borrowing from Jim Liebman's Supreme Court
script, had easily hog-tied Isaac Smallwood and Bobby Territo with the
loose twine left over from their not very well packaged accounts of what
they saw that day in the parking lot at Schwegmann's. But whatever could

be said of its fidelity to actual events, Henry Williams's testimony was too simple, too straightforward to allow for much teasing out of inconsistencies. He had been watching a woman stride across the parking lot, because he had an eye for women, he told the jury. Then suddenly that woman went down, and her killer was at the wheel of her car driving right past Williams's work crew. Just as simple as that.

"Mike could tear apart a genius," Boquet had decided. "He could wipe him out. He could tear apart a specialized expert, just rip him to shreds. But the one thing Mike couldn't do—what he couldn't deal with—was simple."

Rather than assail Henry Williams, Liebman's strategy before the Supreme Court had been to enshrine him as the only reliable eyewitness in the bunch. This he had done by focusing on the statement Williams gave to the police and by declaring the details of height and weight and age ascribed to the killer as a precise description of the short and stocky Beanie Wallace. But what worked well in Washington was rendered more than a little problematic when the same Henry Williams was present in the courtroom to insist that whatever he had said to police, the man he had seen kill Delores Dye was the gentleman at the defense table, the black man right over there, Curtis Kyles. Sometimes slyly, sometimes with the blunt force of redundant questions, Fawer challenged Williams to reconcile the police statement with his persistent identification of Kyles as the killer, and finally Fawer began to sound like a bully.

"What happened was he began to brutalize the witness," Boquet said, "and guess what? It didn't play well with anybody. And by that I mean even the black jurors. The white man with the New York accent and the fine brown suit was kicking ass on this poor black man with the gray beard."

Jury service, particularly if the jury is sequestered, is a little like being trapped in a high-rise elevator with a bunch of strangers during a lengthy power outage. By the time the final arguments ground to a halt on the afternoon of February 14, the Kyles trial was playing to a jury that was starting to come apart at the seams. Mostly it was the tension and the tedium of two weeks of hairsplitting testimony, brutally clashing lawyers, and prolonged periods of introspection among men and women who were under orders not to begin discussing the case, even among themselves, until the last witness had been heard from and the attorneys on both sides had loosed their final harangues.

Boquet found some relief in nighttime scribblings, endless notes—twenty, thirty pages at a pop—on what he had heard in court, along with character sketches and reflections on fellow jurors. These he would slip into the bundle of post-office paperwork that his secretary came by each morning to pick up. It was therapy mostly, but it also amounted to a record he wanted to keep. And on the eve of deliberations, some further relief—a bit too much, perhaps—was found in the six-pack that the sheriff's deputy in charge of the jurors, a gold-toothed, three-hundred-pound sweetheart of a woman named Liz, sneaked in to Boquet and Mayo's room, a room as thick with smoke as any barroom, since Mayo's cigarette habit was almost as intense as Boquet's. In any event, it all began to close in on Boquet that night, so much so that at about three a.m. he found himself sitting cross-legged and stark-naked in the bathroom sink and talking to himself in the mirror. "Who are you? What right do you have to decide someone's life?" Questions like that, amounting if not to a full-blown identity crisis, then to a very rough drunk for the bantam 125-pounder whom jurors were about to elect as their foreman. Suddenly, bringing the soul-searching to a ludicrous conclusion, the sink broke away from the wall, and Boquet found himself lying on the floor amid shards of porcelain. Mayo, jolted awake by the crash, was standing over him. It was time to get some fucking shut-eye, Glenn. There was a long day ahead, man, and some important decisions to be made: like whether Curtis Kyles would fry or go free.

As that fifth jury went into its deliberations, Mike Fawer would remember a very bad feeling—an ominous, deep-in-the-gut feeling that told him he had blown it. No one was more aware than he that his cross-examination of Henry Williams had become overbearing. It was the risk you took. To break a witness, you had to get rough. If it worked, you were a hero. If it failed, if the witness hung tough, you looked like an ogre. Thank God for Denny. She had handled more of the crosses after that—Denny, with her big brown eyes and quiet, steady way with a witness. But even Denny had not been able to settle Joanne Dotson down. That was another disappointment. Joanne was a witness who really had heard a confession—an honest-to-God confession—and with no reason to lie about it. Or put it this way: Joanne had every reason to lie—namely her mother—yet she had come forward anyway. But with that nervous little grin on her face, had she been any more credible than Mike Rice? Or the ridiculous Angola inmate Chris Alphonso? Fawer could only hope so. The irony was that Joanne was supposed to have been Uncle Herman in civilian clothes. She was supposed to bring credibility to the story of a confession as told by a convict in a prison jumpsuit, yet somehow she had managed to undermine the power of the confession itself.

In the tense and cluttered jury room, with its countless coffee cups and soft-drink cans and take-out trays of half-eaten fried catfish, Boquet did what he could to further erode the impact of the Wallace family's secret. As the deliberations began, the jury elected him foreman, just as the Mintz jurors had, and he took the role seriously enough to want to be more than the member who merely announced their verdict. He wanted to forge that verdict, which meant achieving the unanimity that a murder conviction requires.

Inmate or not, in some ways Uncle Herman had been the better witness, and God knows Chris Alphonso had been a disaster for the prosecution. But Boquet had a strategy for nullifying both of them, the strong witness and the sniveler, and that was to play them off against each other. Use one to destroy the other. Okay, Alphonso was a lying son of a bitch, a psycho, Boquet conceded to those in the room who thought so. That's what you could expect when you hauled convicts into court to testify. They'd say anything. By all means reject Alphonso, but then you also had to reject Herman Wallace, and his strange niece Joanne, with her weird little liar's smile.

It was like herding cats, Boquet thought, trying to bring these eleven jurors along with him. Forget Fawer, he told them. Remember Henry

Williams, the witness Fawer badgered. Forget all these accusations against the police. Remember Henry Williams. It became his mantra. Remember Henry Williams. Forget Beanie. Beanie's dead. Forget about the Leidenheimer murder. This is the Dye murder we're deliberating. Curtis is on trial, and to say that he's not guilty, to say that he wasn't the man at the wheel of Mrs. Dye's Ford is to call Henry Williams, that simple, decent man, a liar. Sometimes it seemed to be working. The jurors would verge on consensus and then break apart again into separate camps. One would see the light, and another would stray. Now it was the sous-chef who needed hand-holding. He was having an attack of the heebie-jeebies. It was all about the death penalty, of course. He had passed the Witherspoon test, or he wouldn't be on the jury. He had told the judge that he'd be able to consider the death penalty, if it came to that. But now he was having second thoughts. If they convicted Kyles of the crime, were they sentencing him to death? Forget the death penalty, Boquet fairly shouted. This was about guilt and innocence. The sentence—that could wait. First they needed to decide whether Kyles was guilty. But the sous-chef still needed reassurance, and so Boquet sent a message to the judge asking for confirmation that it was possible to convict Kyles without condemning him to death. The jurors clambered down the back staircase and into the courtroom, where Judge Burns verified Boquet's understanding of the law.

In the end, it came down to the young black woman, just as Boquet had predicted. She wouldn't budge from her view that the state's case was inconclusive, and another couple of jurors were standing with her. The foreman whined and he wheedled, he argued and he cajoled, and finally, as he had done with Aaron Mintz, he gave in. Except giving in this time meant a mistrial, a hung jury, not the acquittal that Boquet and his cadre of holdouts finally bestowed on the millionaire furniture store heir. The jury deliberations had gone on all day, and it was late in the evening of February 17, a Tuesday, when Boquet sent a note to Judge Burns saying that unanimity eluded them and he saw little chance of that changing. Burns pulled the plug.

It was a painful moment for Boquet, made only worse in the trial's aftermath as friends and neighbors assailed him for caving in. How could he do it? they wanted to know. How could he let a scumbag like Kyles off the hook? Boquet did not shrug his responsibility for what happened. "A foreman can do a lot," he would say in a reflective moment—and there was no denying Boquet had been an active and aggressive foreman— "but I am eminently guilty of having failed in two great trials. It hurts." The second time hurt worse. "I believe Aaron Mintz killed his wife," Boquet said, "but I *know* Curtis Kyles killed Delores Dye."

TWENTY-FOUR

There were times when Kyles wondered if a conviction wouldn't be better than this endless limbo. Be done with it. Get it over with. And the announcement by Judge Burns that the fifth jury to have heard his case was, like all but the second, unable to reach a verdict was such a time. A darkness settled over Kyles even before he could huddle quickly with his family, touch and kiss them, then look to his keepers and his defenders and tell them to get him the hell out of the courthouse—a darkness as deadly as he knew, a sense of defeat from which the only imaginable relief was to hurt somebody, kill somebody. It would be a kind of suicide by proxy.

In all his long years in prison Kyles had seen the struggle this way: prisons were about turning men—and not just wrongly convicted men—into the monsters their jailers needed to think of them as being, all in order to justify the barbarities the system meted out to them. It was an old and hoary saw, but in his disgust Kyles knew it for the truth. Don't be the animal they want you to be. The words came back now to Kyles—Marty Regan's words of warning as the judge ordered Kyles to rise and stand in silence beside Beanie Wallace during the second trial back in 1984. Kyles had struggled with himself to keep from savaging Wallace right there in the courtroom in front of judge and jury, in front of Cliff Strider and Jim Williams, not to mention Lowell Dye and his father, who would have been only too happy to see him lose control.

The message had echoed down the years. Burl Carter, the quiet, brooding vic who, the very night of Kyles's arrival at OPP, had begun tutoring him on ways to rise above the gangsterism that ruled the prison, had been one variation on the theme. The suspect decency of the Angola guard who clapped Kyles on the back when the Supreme Court reversal came through was another. And what did these enticements to civility and restraint earn him? Another year in prison, another decade, another opportunity for a man like Harry Connick to condemn him to a further stretch in prison simply by declaring his intent to try him again. It was a world turned upside down, punishment preceding the verdict it was supposed to follow, and from a prosecutor, Connick, who had broken the rules of evidence and still failed to make that verdict stick. If Kyles had the name, well then by God he'd have the game. Let there be no possibility of respite, no more equivocation. Let his incarceration—if it was to be a permanent condition—finally be squared with the spirit of the laws that were being used against him. If the state needed him to be a monster, maybe it was time to oblige. And as surely as the feeling gripped him, that by hurting someone—killing someone—he would feel alive again, however briefly, he knew exactly who that someone should be.

Kyles's fantasy life had always been specific, and often it was self-actualizing. Now the focus of his thoughts was an inmate over in the parish prison, the one they called Duke. There would be no particular advantage in killing Duke, but there would be great pleasure in it, in letting Duke feel the self-restoring fury of his shiv as Kyles thrust it again and again and again into the immensely muscled chest of this supreme son of a bitch. There would be no glory in this execution, nothing heroic about it. Duke, despite his handle, was not part of the prison peerage. Duke was a rapist and a snitch. More to the point, Duke was a troublemaker, a taunter, a dayroom drag who could be counted on to mock Kyles when he returned from court with no acquittal, just as he had mocked Kyles for keeping to himself, for trying to keep out of trouble in the months before the trial. As Kyles would put it, Duke was one of those men who had decided "his shit don't smell." It would be testament only to Kyles's utter degradation that the ritual by which he would take himself out of the game he had played for the past fourteen years, the game of trying to prove his innocence, would entail spilling the blood of someone so ordinary and vile. Yes, it would be Duke. The only question was where.

Kyles had two shivs. One was sheathed inside a tiny slit in the mattress of his cell bunk. Lying there in the night, Kyles was vaguely aware of it, less a lump in the mattress than a kind of valence, as though the metal in his own bullet-riddled, pinned-together body was tugged magnetically by the thin hand-honed blade. The other shank was beneath the freestanding water jug in the dayroom. As the inmate assigned to clean up when the lights went off at midnight, Kyles owned the room for a few minutes in each twenty-four-hour cycle, time enough to have found the hiding space and put it to use as his own.

With the force of clairvoyance, Kyles could see the look that would wrench Duke's face as the metal slid beneath the plates of his sternum and found the bloody bulb inside his chest. The thought of it focused Kyles's mind as he sat in the holding cell on his way back from court after the mistrial was declared, waiting once again to be processed back onto the tier. And it was at that precise moment that a bailiff caught up with him, the tolerant one who had kept Kyles in coffee and let him smoke in the back corridors of the courthouse when no one was around. He had something for Kyles more urgent than coffee, more urgent even than a cigarette. "Curtis, man. They're dropping the case, man. They're going to let you go." That was the message as Kyles remembers it, and of course it infuriated him to be teased like this, and by a man he had come to think of as decent.

"No, Curtis. I'm not playing with you."

There was a phone handy, and the bailiff managed to get through to Lela. Kyles could hear little more than shrieking, his sister shrieking and the people with her, everybody shrieking. But the shrieking was confirmation of a kind. Connick had given up, thrown in the towel, cut his losses, eaten his plate of shit, topped it off with a slice of humble pie. Kyles put the phone down in a daze. It was over. Fourteen years had been carved out of his life like a cancer. Now the question was this: Had the patient survived the surgery? What was left of his life? Kyles wondered. What was life like among free people after fourteen years, many of them years of brooding silence on the row?

In hindsight, LeBoeuf's hunch was that Connick had been less keen than Woods on a fifth trial and that the district attorney had set conditions before agreeing to it: if Woods couldn't win a conviction this time, it was over. Done with. Time to move on. Time to do what LeBoeuf thought should have happened after the third trial, if not after the Supreme Court reversed the second. And in conversation with the press the following day, Connick confirmed at least that the decision not to go for a sixth trial had been made at some point prior to the jury deadlocking. That said, Connick took a swipe at Judge Burns, suggesting that he had cut off deliberations prematurely in declaring a mistrial. The judge, aware that jurors were at an impasse, should have suspended deliberations until the following morning and let them get some sleep. "We had spoken to the judge and encouraged him to let the jury deliberate longer," Connick said. The note from the jury room, as Connick read it, hadn't said a verdict was impossible. "They didn't say they were hopelessly deadlocked. I think the judge took the note to mean they were."

After the mistrial declaration, Connick phoned the Dyes with his apologies. "It's going to be difficult to go forward," he said. "I hope you understand that."

Robert Dye had been prepared for defeat, however painful. The hung jury in the third trial had been an augury to him. "After the first, you were going to have more of them," he said. The pattern bespoke cowardice, he suggested. "These people know if they hang a jury, nobody needs to be responsible. It's my feeling all along that that was what was going to happen."

Lowell was bitter with the outcome and frank about it: "It's a miserable gaping wound," he told a reporter. "Not only is a murderer on the street, but the legal system, in my mind, has failed."

Connick could only agree. Kyles, he would tell the press, was "a free but guilty man."

Kyles did not go to bed that last night in Orleans Parish Prison. He knew better than to bother trying to sleep. First he hauled his earthly effects into the dayroom—T-shirts, books, knickknacks—and parceled out that paltry estate to some of the men he would be leaving behind. And then midnight came, and the men with whom he was on decent terms embraced him, wished him the best, and padded back to their cells ahead of the lights-out. He stayed on in the dayroom past midnight. The guard didn't give a damn. Past one, past two, until finally Kyles was watching the predawn test pattern on the television, and the sky outside the prison turned from black to pearl gray.

After the languorous pace of the appellate process, when rulings would follow arguments by months and as long an interval would pass again before parties next met in court, the events of Kyles's last morning in custody unfolded at breakneck speed. Suddenly every turn of the wheel seemed intolerably creaky. Here was Connick's consent to Kyles's release, but where was Judge Burns? He presided over the mistrial. His signature was needed. Now Burns turned up, but to invest the occasion with proper gravity, he needed to find a robe. One was purloined from the chambers of Judge Frank Marullo, a man only slightly taller than he was wide, a robe that fit the more conventionally proportioned Burns like a bib. The ritual, if not the dignity, of the court restored, the release was signed and then rushed several hundred yards to the parish prison.

Blinking in the acid clarity of the south Louisiana winter sun, shying bashfully from the equally radiant glow of family and friends who had gathered hours earlier to wait for him, Kyles was scarcely capable of speech, let alone oratory, as he stepped from behind the squat, razor-wired walls of Orleans Parish Prison and onto a street called Perdido. It was a Wednesday, February 18, 1998. A week earlier, Kyles had become a grandfather. A week later he would mark his thirty-ninth birthday. More than a third of his life—thirteen years and 146 days—had passed in prison. Dressed in slacks and a starched white shirt that Lela sent in to the prison, he had this for the bouquet of microphones that a handful of reporters thrust into his face: "All I can say, man, is I'm happy to get out. I just wish I could have been vindicated." The reporters pressed for more. "I just feel like I'm going to pass out." And with that, Kyles succumbed to the multiarmed Siva of his laughing and weeping friends, lovers, lawyers, family. The knot of them staggered down Perdido, clinging to Kyles, twining their arms around him, around his shoulders, his waist, his neck, passing him from one to the next and back again. Finally Marie Campbell was able to ease Kyles into Mike Fawer's van, and they headed downtown along tree-lined avenues draped with strings of beads: it was the Carnival season in New Orleans, and some of the beads hurled out into the crowd from passing parades had inevitably snagged in the overhanging branches. Such festivities as had been planned in Kyles's honor were up ahead at the Resource Center office on Baronne Street. But first, was Kyles hungry? They stopped to get him a shrimp po'boy to go. He couldn't eat it.

They were within blocks of the Resource Center, passing the federal court establishment on Lafayette Square, when Kyles had to get out. There was grass in Lafayette Square and trees and people to walk among, people who would not challenge Kyles or beat him or order him back into his cell. His knees buckled with his first step out of the van, and it was all he could do to walk. There were small wildflowers in among the wintry blades of grass, violets and the occasional dandelion. Thinking of his mother, who had loved flowers and cultivated them, Kyles bent to pick one up, then froze in place as though caught in the act. He looked up at Marie. She nodded. And he picked a bluet and rotated it slowly in his fingers, staring at it as if in disbelief.

At the Resource Center, a predictable pandemonium broke out as Kyles stepped out of the elevator and into an open workspace decorated for the occasion with crepe paper and balloons. It was almost more than he could bear: dozens of well-wishers, many of them youngsters, but also old hands who had disentangled themselves from their own sentences at Angola and affiliated themselves with the Resource Center to work for others. There were law students and the people from Amnesty International and the NAACP. More than once Kyles fled to the bathroom on a wave of nerves and stood over the toilet, trying to empty his stomach.

At last Tyteannia arrived, Kyles's eldest, holding the newest addition to his tribe, and he seized on the baby, his first grandchild, like a life ring. He clung to her as he made his rounds, losing himself to the smell and feel of her whenever things started to get weird for him and self-consciousness froze his tongue. And here was Pinkey, staging a late entrance, and Chester and Cutina and little Tyra, the baby born after his incarceration, now a young lady going on thirteen. Everyone but Meco, who was struggling in the jailhouse in LaPlace against the serpentine coils of his own legal dilemma.

When it was possible to stage a decorous retreat, Kyles begged off and slipped away. Lela offered him a ride and said yes when he asked if he could drive, figuring this was one of those things Kyles needed to remember how to do. One of his sisters had agreed to take him in the first night, not because they were particularly close, but because she had the room, a place where he could decompress, or try to. More than a couple of her young girlfriends came by to check out what a decade without would do to a man known for his way with women. But Kyles declined the come-ons and retired early—to sleep, to collect himself. After so long alone, "I didn't want to be no two-minute man," Kyles remembered thinking.

The sense of estrangement was not a condition that went away simply by packing people into a room. Release was like a time machine, and the next morning it landed Kyles all the way back where the giant hole in his life had been torn open, in Desire—not the apartment, that was long gone, but the public housing project, his first home in New Orleans and now Pinkey's. His kids were there, all except Meco. Tyrone Joseph, the man who had loved Pinkey enough to see her through her long ordeal, now loved her enough to clear out and let her find out if there was anything left of her relationship with the Lazarus from death row. "Basically, we sat up for two days," Kyles would recall of this family reunion. "We sat up and we talked and we ate and we cried."

Denny LeBoeuf had not noticed Kyles slipping away from the party on Baronne Street. "Where did he go?" she asked, a note of apprehension in her voice as she looked around for him. "I don't know," someone piped up, an answer that drew a footnote from LeBoeuf's sister, Marie Campbell: "And for the first time in fourteen years, it doesn't fucking matter." It did matter, of course, maybe not that day, but soon enough. Kyles was off the hook for the Dye murder, but as part of the deal, he was still on probation until the fifteen-year sentences for armed robbery had run their course, and that would not be for another year and then some. Kyles was going to have to watch his step, and parole officers were only part of his problem. The world to which he had returned was at once welcoming and strange. The welcome, family aside, was extended most heartily by every dope-dealing, burglarizing, carjacking hustler who recognized this figure from out of the past—and that was all of them, because as grand-fathers go, Kyles looked remarkably like the twenty-five-year-old he had been when he last cast a shadow in the city's Ninth Ward.

Kyles hadn't been out of prison but a couple of months when he was subjected to a temptation worthy of Gethsemane. The coke dealer's daughter, the woman who had led him into his one brush with real money, was back from her own exile in Texas and well on her way to rebuilding her mother's scuttled empire. "You need work, Curtis? Plenty work? Anytime, Curtis. You just say the word."

The strangeness was everywhere, and nowhere more so than in Kyles's own head. If the streets were haunted by the ghosts of a past life, so was the decision to move in with Pinkey. Fourteen years earlier, he had freed her to do what she had to do to keep the children together, and now he could not help resenting that she had somehow succeeded. Within weeks, there were other women in Kyles's life, women who didn't raise a moment's suspicion in his mind that they might once have had an eye for Beanie Wallace. And shortly Pinkey tired of his unexplained absences and belated returns to her bed, and she threw him out.

Lela, remarried following a divorce and making payments on a small house with a tidy lawn across the river in Algiers, took him in for a while. She would remember the little things about his adjustment. There was the simple matter of time's passage and the changes wrought—call-waiting on the telephone, for one. Kyles would master that after only a few minutes of bafflement. The much greater challenge lay in trying to re-trace the lines that divide one person from another and connect him to everyone else.

Depending on how you looked at it, Kyles had spent fourteen years with nothing at all, or with his every need—well, many of them anyway—attended to. That was the paradox of prison. Returned to civilian life, he had both less and much more that he could call his own, and a much harder time determining where the difference was supposed to lie. Lela would remember the call she got at work one morning: Curtis, his voice edged with anxiety. He woke up hungry, Kyles said, and took something from her cupboard and ate it, only to be consumed by uncertainty. Had he stolen from his own sister? She told him he was welcome to what he could find. A practical sort, she also put him to work. The lawn needed cutting, and Kyles was wailing away at it one day when the mower's blade caught a masonry drainage duct hidden in the grass and broke apart. "You'd have thought he had totaled my car," Lela would recall. Was it a reportable offense? She assured him it was just between the two of them, though she wouldn't mind a little help replacing the mower, a few bucks a week.

Kyles also checked in with Project Return, a nonprofit organization that helped ex-cons find jobs and adjust to civilian life. Project Return put a premium on punctiliousness and other signs that the former inmate was taking full responsibility for himself after a period of time in which he had had no responsibility whatsoever. The drill sergeants in this regimen were themselves ex-cons and usually black, but the style of their assault on bad habits, whether born of arrogance or sloth, grated on Kyles, as it was surely meant to. It was "nigger this and nigger that," Kyles found, and his time with Project Return was short-lived. Besides, he had work laying brick, at least when the weather was decent. Kyles's arrest for the Dye murder had been excised from his record, but most employers would toss the application of any man whose résumé showed three priors for armed robbery, not to mention that fourteen-year interval with no work at all. Brickwork contractors didn't need to give a damn, though, and one of the men Kyles had worked for in the old days took him back on.

The counselors at Project Return offered a lightning rod for Kyles's disenchantment with the program, but the worst of his anxiety was free-floating. The overwhelming pressure he had felt at the big homecoming party at the Resource Center office had not dissipated in smaller gatherings. Kyles had spent fourteen years largely talking to himself. It was hugely difficult remembering how to bring someone else in on the conversation. One exception was Pat Blackburn, the woman he had seen secretly all through the years when he and Pinkey were raising a family. She had continued to keep up with him in prison. With Pat he could be his old self. More important, with Pat he could be his new self, and after a few weeks at Lela's he moved back across the river to live with her. She would not quickly forget the moment of terrible and beautiful communion when all of Kyles's hardness and pride had not been enough to keep him together. They had been talking that night about his mother and the terrible loss he felt at the time of Gracie's death, and Kyles just let go. It seemed like forever before the last of the sobs stopped racking this boy-ish grandfather curled up in Blackburn's lap and she was able to move his head onto a pillow and think about getting some sleep herself.

Another respite from the deep sense of alienation that hung over Kyles was a nephew of his, one of Brenda's boys whose companionship he found easy to take. Aggravating Kyles's people problem, in some cir-cles he had achieved the status of a minor celebrity. Strangers would rec-ognize him in public, unaware that he wanted anonymity above all else. They would come up to him on the street, in stores, at lunch counters. The worst of them would start off by saying that they knew all along he was innocent—and then proceed to ask him if he had done it. His nephew sometimes had to intervene, pull Kyles aside, hose him down. These people might be ignorant, Kyles needed to remind himself, but they meant no harm. Just curious, that's all they were. Ignorant and curious.

The terms of Kyles's probation left him subject to random drug tests, and that stood to cost him his most reliable social lubricant, mari-juana. He was also obliged to observe a nighttime curfew and stay within the confines of Orleans Parish. He was in violation of two of the stipula-tions and on his way to testing the third when he paused along the inter-state somewhere in Alabama and took a hit off the joint proffered by his traveling companion. They were en route to Atlanta for freaknik, the an-nual spring break ritual popular with the African American college crowd. Parole officers did not immediately descend on Kyles there along the roadside; nor, upon his return, did Orleans Parish seem to have heard about his excursion to Atlanta. Probation might be a more flexible con-dition than he had imagined.

And then suddenly Kyles found out that it wasn't, at least not in his case. He and Pat had returned to her place just ahead of curfew one evening in late June, when there came a knock at the door. A spot check, a random drug test, and unfortunately, Kyles had shared a joint with other bricklayers on his crew earlier in the day. He did not deny the in-fraction. Maybe his candor would inspire forgiveness, or at least a will-ingness to cut him a break. The officers were chummy, sympathetic even, but they were not disposed to bend the rules. He was a felon in violation of his probation. On September 16, seven months almost to the day since his release, a three-member panel of the state parole board remanded him to prison.

They had got him at last. The sense of satisfaction that spread among interested parties in the Orleans Parish district attorney's office was matched by the dismay among Kyles's family and allies. Some, like Fawer, were frankly disappointed in Kyles. Others sympathized. What could you expect? they asked. Look what he's been through. Over the next year and a half, Kyles would be posted to a variety of prisons throughout the Louisiana system, an experience that cost him, along with much chagrin for letting down his family and defenders, an exposure to tuberculosis and the arduous course of treatment it required. The greater loss was this: Kyles's release from his fourteen years of confinement had been marred by Meco's being in jail. Now it was Kyles who would be away when Meco's release date arrived in September, the same month in which his father was returned to the pen.

By the time Kyles got out of prison for the parole violation, late in 1999, Elmeco was again behind bars, on a second-degree murder rap, a charge that was dropped for lack of adequate evidence and witnesses early the following year. The presiding judge was Dennis Waldron, the same Judge Waldron who had sent Kyles to death row.

Elmeco's release from custody coincided with his mother's birthday, as wonderful a gift as Pinkey could imagine. And for Kyles, it was the beginning of four good years together with his second son, a bookend to their four years, dimly remembered, before Kyles had disappeared into the rabbit hole of the Louisiana prison system. Now a grown man with street cred certified by his own time in jail, Elmeco proceeded to sire a bunch of kids by as many different women and, like his father before him, set about the business of living as large as hustling availed. And then, on a Tuesday evening in July 2004, it all went to hell. In a warren of low-rent tract housing some twenty miles downriver from New Orleans, three gun-toting wiseguys in a feud with Elmeco went down in a hail of bullets sprayed through the open window of their van. One of them, a twenty-two-year-old, died of multiple gunshots, including one to the neck. Two others were treated for less severe wounds and that same evening provided the sheriff of St. Bernard Parish with what he needed to issue a warrant for the arrest of Elmeco Burnes, twenty-four, on two charges of attempted murder and a separate charge of murder in the first degree.

For twenty-four hours, Elmeco agonized over his options: flight or surrender. For Kyles, who joined him in his hideout, the choice was not less tormenting. To convince the young man to turn himself in was, Kyles feared, to guarantee "that he will hate me for the rest of his life," a life that might well be played out in prison, perhaps on death row. And yet Kyles, horrified as he was by the prospect of prison, knew that surrender was his son's only real hope. The alternative—a delirious and furtive few months of freedom—would almost certainly end in Elmeco's early death, either at the hands of officers in pursuit or the ever more desperate associates he would knock up against in a losing struggle to sustain an outlaw life.

Finally, on the afternoon of the second day of cigarettes and talk and more talk and more smoking, a hoarse and bleary-eyed Kyles prevailed. With Denny LeBoeuf brokering the surrender, Elmeco turned himself in. Perhaps he could convince prosecutors he had been acting in self-defense, an argument buttressed by the arsenal of guns and ammo cops found in the van. If not, Elmeco would face a legal peril eerily similar to what Kyles himself had confronted at almost exactly the same age twenty years earlier. A father's worst fear had come true. Elmeco had become the man a son most admires.

TWENTY-FIVE

Robert Dye was not one to gloat over the misfortunes of others. He had known enough trouble in his own life. Nearly twenty years after Dee's death, now in his eighties, Dye lived on alone in the house where they had raised the boys. Lowell, married and divorced a second time, was across town and alone himself. Robert junior's marriage had worked out better than either of Lowell's, and he was still living in Florida and working with the National Park Service. A quizzical, keen-witted man, the senior Robert Dye found pleasure in reunions with his war buddies, those of them who could still make it. He dreamed of writing up a history of their service flying over the hump in Italy, the time they took flak, the plane fighting for altitude and finally easing over the Apennines to a crash landing on the other side.

A fundamentally benevolent temperament probably contributed to his longevity. It surely made him less bitter than Lowell about the legal fiasco—in both the civil and criminal courts—that followed Dee's death. But if he was not inclined to gloat, neither was he unaware that fate had dished up more than the usual serving of ironies and comeuppances to the ensemble of players touched by his wife's murder and the prosecution of Curtis Kyles. His estimation of John Schwegmann's intelligence was nicely affirmed in the collapse of his supermarket empire not long after the courts exempted the grocer from liability in Mrs. Dye's death. Suckered into the mergers-and-acquisitions frenzy by the big boys from Wall Street, Schwegmann had bet his chain on a buyout that would have given him overwhelming dominance of the local market. Instead, he lost his shirt. Before the ax fell, Schwegmann's wife, Melinda, had parlayed a seat in the state legislature into a turn as lieutenant governor. A thoroughly unsuccessful run for governor landed her back in the legislature, whereupon her district was gerrymandered into oblivion by political sharks who smelled only blood where once there had been oceans of Schwegmann greenbacks. The Schwegmanns had shown up at Mrs. Dye's funeral. That was decent of them. That Mrs. Schwegmann also showed up in civil court as Lowell's case against her husband went down in flames was an unfriendly way of reminding the judges of her political clout, the widower decided. To the end of his days he would chuckle over the memory of their third encounter, the time she rapped on his door while campaigning in the neighborhood.

"Hi, I'm Melinda Schwegmann," she began—a big, good-looking blonde.

"Sure, I know you are, and I'm Robert Dye," he said with a smile no less radiantly insincere than the politician's. Whereupon, as Dye told it, Mrs. Schwegmann beat so hasty a retreat down the walkway to her waiting car and driver that her disembodied grin hung in the air like the Cheshire cat's in *Alice in Wonderland.*

Then there was the TV reporter, so smugly confident of Kyles's innocence. He had not missed an opportunity during breaks in the trials to pester the Dye family with questions that seemed snide if not downright hostile. Within a couple of years he had been caught with underage boys, cocaine, and a batch of pornography and was bundled off to the federal pen. Johnny Miller, Beanie's main contact on the police force, had been a better friend to the prosecution and the aggrieved Dye family, but he too had run afoul of the law. With the federal firearms rap on his record, he had eventually thought better of staying on in the police department. He landed on his feet, however, fetching up as a bodyguard and all-purpose flunky for Hollywood actor John Goodman and his entourage after Goodman married a local woman and set up a household in New Orleans. And neither Jim Williams nor Cliff Strider, the assistant prosecutors whose misconduct was excoriated so scathingly by the U.S. Supreme Court, was punished or even disciplined by his employer, Harry Connick, before drifting out of Orleans Parish, Williams to a middling career as an attorney in Jefferson Parish, Strider as a prosecutor in the more rustic parishes of north Louisiana.

The definitive end of the era came in 2002, with Connick's withdrawal from the New Orleans political fray after three decades as prosecutor. There was the adulatory send-off at a hotel ballroom, the nabobs and political power brokers, the judges, the tycoons. The glamorous Harry Connick Jr. had bounded onto the stage for the obligatory father-son rendition of the Sinatra signature piece, "My Way." But Connick's chosen successor as district attorney was soundly defeated, notwithstanding the automatic, if not ardent, support of the political establishment in which Connick had managed to remain entrenched for so long. Spurning Connick's candidate, voters turned to Eddie Jordan, a Clinton-era federal prosecutor, an African American who had just brought down another emblem of the "Louisiana way"—the silver-haired, silver-tongued, and thoroughly corrupt ex-governor, Edwin Edwards.

In the early rounds of the Eddie vs. Edwin brawl, Jordan had accepted a plea bargain negotiated by Edwards's attorney that would have cost the ex-governor at most a short stint in prison for taking kickbacks from operators vying for Louisiana casino licenses. His son and coconspirator, Stephen, would have been spared prison altogether. Instead, Edwards fired the attorney, gambled on hanging tough, and by trial's end could look ahead to spending, in all likelihood, the rest of his life in federal prison. The fired attorney with a penchant for negotiation? Mike Fawer.

The final irony of the Kyles case was not lost on Robert Dye, but neither was it one to savor: if the prosecution of Curtis Kyles had been better calibrated with the ambiguities of the case against him—if, for example, he had been tried for second-degree murder or, once convicted of first-degree murder, given a life sentence—he would almost certainly have been in prison to the end of his days, lost to view, uninteresting to death penalty foes, unqualified for the legal services they could bring to bear on his behalf, a forgotten man.

A half decade after Harry Connick gave up on Curtis Kyles and the prosecution's dream of taking a life in atonement for the murder of Delores Dye, tufts of grass and weeds had sprouted in the rectangular seams of the vast fenced-off parking lot where she died. With the supermarket chain in bankruptcy, the empty lot had the look of a giant picture puzzle in shades of black. The shuttered store, once so awesome in the public imagination, now seemed dwarfed, shedlike, alongside surrounding office buildings and the elevated highway behind them. The case, of course, was itself a puzzle that had never been truly solved. The perfidy of the district attorney's office had been laid bare for all to see, and the wisdom of the nation's highest court had been tested and affirmed. There was reason to believe, the Court had declared, that if all the evidence were presented, jurors might reasonably doubt Kyles's guilt. And indeed, with all the evidence in front of them, three juries in a row had been unable to convict him. But supposing defense attorneys had a complete file when the case was fresh? Even with key witness statements and documents hidden away or ignored by prosecutors, the first jury had been unable to convict. With the complete record in front of them, might the second have agreed to acquit Kyles altogether? Might a subsequent grand jury have bound Joseph Beanie Banks Brown Wallace over for trial, not just in the Dye murder but perhaps as well for the death of Patricia Leidenheimer?

Within a few years of Kyles's release from prison for the parole violation, it was possible to call him a rehabilitated man. He had been penalized for crimes he insisted he did not commit and, by his own lights, had paid a debt to society for crimes that had eluded prosecution. But for all that, he recovered in himself the ability to be a loving man, still indiscriminate in his enthusiasm for women, but devoted to his children and grandchildren. No longer eligible for disability payments, he laid brick for a living when the weather permitted, and he scraped by on an unsteady income. A blown motor on his fifteen-year-old Chrysler could set him back a month. When one of his women discovered that she had a rival, Kyles came back to the boardinghouse where he was staying to find that his room had been trashed and the landlord was throwing him out. At times like those, it would take everything in Kyles's power to resist the lure of the streets, the hustles he had learned there, and the sustaining dream that the next score would be the big one. One definition of a civilized man is knowing the difference between dreaming and living, but that does not mean the dreams are always civilized.

One of Kyles's dreams was a waking vision, a vision of the hereafter to which he might have consigned Beanie Wallace had Beanie lived long enough to see Kyles released from prison.

It is a sweet hereafter, a land of honey and rolling hills and wildlife. The hills are up around Bassfield, and the wildlife includes a small army of ants, the big red ants that work the red and clayey Mississippi soils— red ants swarming like soil come to life—and they are everywhere. From a distance, Beanie would seem to be hugging the trunk of a tree, as though he too is relishing this communion with the natural realm. At closer range, he is hugging it backward, his back against the trunk, his arms wrenched around to the rear of the trunk and bound there, as are his ankles. He is naked. Bound and naked. With the tethers satisfactorily in place, Kyles drops to his haunches, settles back for a cigarette to ponder his handiwork. Beanie is not gagged, nor is he screaming. Not yet. His terror registers in his eyes, which have widened like a child's. There is nothing much to say, no call even for cursing. Beanie knows why he is here. Asking for mercy would be futile, as futile as it would be for Kyles to ask for an apology, or even an explanation of what went down between them.

Kyles stubs out his cigarette and rises back up off his haunches. As he does so, he slips his thumb and forefinger into his shirt pocket and retrieves a single-edged razor. Seeing the razor, Beanie works his bindings a bit, writhes uselessly against the tree trunk. But the razor is sharper than pain, and Beanie settles for wincing as Kyles nicks him with it here and there, everywhere, carelessly but methodically, like an abstract artist, each stroke of the blade releasing a thin beaded line of brilliant red that widens smoothly against the man's black flesh. Kyles lances an eyeball, more out of curiosity than cruelty—now there is screaming—and decides to leave the other intact. The penis he stretches out, so as to slit it with some precision, stem to tip, like a sausage link ready for grilling. But for the most part, his brushwork is random, detached, neither favoring nor avoiding any portion of Beanie's anatomy.

The ants would have found Beanie anyway. The blood was bait

enough. But in his fantasy, Kyles has brought along a jar of honey, a jar from the shed where Pinkey's father stores the harvest from his hives. Kyles perfects his composition with a last few strokes of spreading red, then upends the jar over Beanie's head and walks away, flicking the razor into the brush. In the night, he hears the screaming. But from the house, way beyond the hedgerow and across the twenty acres in corn, it could be the sound of bobcats mating. Kyles reaches for Pinkey and pulls her toward him. Of course, it is not Pinkey anymore, but it should have been, to make the dream complete.

EPILOGUE

Did Curtis Kyles kill Mrs. Dye? In the eyes of the law, it's an open question. I began working on this book with an assumption in mind, which was that the answer most likely was yes. My faith in that assumption strengthened in direct proportion to the clamor from those among his champions and defenders who insisted it could not possibly be so. I nursed a secret hunch: that maybe Kyles was sick of the subterfuge and the ministrations of all the earnest young people hovering about the case, requiring, in furtherance of their own agendas, that he be portrayed as the innocent martyr of a corrupt and brutal system. I wondered if a man like Kyles, embittered as he had become and cynical as he had been all along about the processes of justice, might not utter a final fuck-you as he looked over his shoulder at the system whose snares he had taken so long to escape. I wondered if, once acquitted of the murder charge, he might not be ready to confess. It was a fantasy, perhaps, but an interesting one in which Kyles, protected against further prosecution by the rules against double jeopardy, would admit what had seemed so obvious to so many people: that of course he killed Delores Dye. By accident, perhaps, but without a doubt—killed her dead. It would be a clearing of his conscience. It would also be a mocking commentary on a system of justice so sloppy and corrupted it could not get out of its own way and bring off a binding conviction. But then the fourth trial came and went, and then the fifth, and for lack of a conclusive verdict the double-jeopardy provision never kicked in.

In the course of five years, getting to know Curtis Kyles and his family, I learned many things about him and his life before he was convicted, some of them too delicate for publication. But Kyles never wavered from his contention that he had nothing to do with the Dye murder. I no longer give a pat answer when asked whether I think that's true. I have my strong assumptions, but it's a complicated and ambiguous case. The best evidence I can provide is this book.

What seems certain is that Kyles was framed, first by Beanie Wallace in cahoots with the police, perhaps as well by prosecutors in their failure to disclose exculpatory evidence. I leave it to readers to decide whether, by illegal means and for dishonorable reasons, they framed the right man.

To some of Kyles's champions, the treatment accorded him was nothing more than a latter-day lynching by a Deep South courthouse mob so incompetent that the rope snapped before they could haul him aloft. The metaphor has its uses. New Orleans in 1984, and perhaps two decades later, was not completely purged of the Jim Crow mind-set of the segregation years, much as we liked to think all that was over. But the sense of purpose implicit in a lynch mob obscures something about the Kyles frame-up that needs to be acknowledged: however deeply racist, in many respects what happened to Kyles was as much the result of sloth and indifference by police and prosecutors as it was the outcome of a devilish manipulation. Prosecutors were correct to assail the idea advanced by the defense that a thug like Beanie Wallace could have orchestrated an elaborate cover-up so artfully. But the truth is that he didn't have to. Kyles was a convenience, too handy for police to want to pick apart the contradictory stories told by the convicted felon who brought him to their attention. Wallace had some value to police as an informant. Kyles had none, least of all to the district attorney in the final weeks of a high-profile reelection campaign. And so Kyles went down, and Wallace got a payoff. The same mix of corner-cutting and debased ethical standards also might seem to explain the behavior of Harry Connick's prosecutors: the failure to study contradictory witness statements, if their suppression was not deliberate; the coarse intimidation of Kyles's witnesses; the failure to explore Beanie Wallace's implication in the Leidenheimer murder. To the Kyles camp, it was behavior they never could have got away with—never would have dared try—if the defendant was a white man, a rich white man, an Aaron Mintz, for example.

In botching the Kyles case through prosecutorial misconduct, the district attorney's office cost the survivors of Delores Dye any chance of judicial—let alone emotional—relief. Kyles's ordeal also provided evidence, if evidence was needed, of the folly in retaining capital punishment as the capstone of the nation's legal edifice. The Kyles case would become a watchword in the continuing American dialogue on these themes—only more important at a time when the precision of DNA testing has caused a diversion of energies into cases that hold the tantalizing prospect of proving "innocence."

Innocence is a concept without relevance in a judicial system that presumes it of everyone. Under the common-law tradition that is the bedrock of American jurisprudence, the prosecution's obligation is to prove guilt, and it must be proved beyond a reasonable doubt. The defense is not required to prove innocence. The Kyles case had its idiosyncrasies, some of them fascinating, but it stemmed from a garden-variety crime. And as with most crimes of violence, there was no DNA evidence to tie a perpetrator to his victim, no basis of irrefutable proof. The rash of faulty convictions overturned by testing old DNA samples will be worked through, leaving people of conscience once again to contemplate the central flaw in any system that presumes to play God and take lives: doubt, and the ineradicable possibility of human error.

Those were philosophical concerns. But there was another way I found myself thinking about the Kyles case, one not grounded in law and politics.

New Orleans, the least American of America's big cities, was a town in which the official version of reality—the reality of courts and government and the taxable economy—had only a casual congruence with what was actually going on. This was, after all, the city whose culminating civic ritual was Mardi Gras, an anarchic mayhem that masked at its heart a conservative tradition—the annual presentation of marriageable young women—a tradition as hidebound and intricate as the rigmarole of monarchy. New Orleans was a city that grieved to the blare of a ragtime street band, the largest city in a state where careers in public service not infrequently made millionaires and land barons of sheriffs, judges, and other officials on salaries roughly equal to a schoolteacher's.

That criminal law was only partially comprehensive of the lives and even the crimes of Louisianans had been tacitly acknowledged in the rules of jurisprudence itself, most notably in the vestige, well into the twentieth century, of the concept of the *crime passionel*. This is a crime of the heart—the murder of an unfaithful spouse, for example. Such a crime, under Louisiana's Napoleonic Code, fell beyond legal redress and exempted the perpetrator from punishment.

The murder of Delores Dye emphatically was not a crime of passion. On the contrary, it was a crime reptilian in its cold-bloodedness—the exchange of a woman's life, a woman apparently unknown to her killer, for her car, her groceries, and the meager contents of her purse. But the extraordinary thing about the ordeal by trial of Curtis Kyles was the way in which, over time, the tragic fate of Mrs. Dye became incidental and then almost irrelevant to the intrigue that it laid bare.

Prosecutors sensed this and, in court, railed impotently against the ambition of the defense team to transform the trial from an evaluation of Kyles's putative guilt into a prosecution of the police and the district attorney's office for abuses of their respective powers. And even this plaintive analysis, however true, didn't get to the heart of the drama. Because underlying all of it—underlying the murder of the housewife and the overweening, deeply corrupting zeal to nail someone for it—was a lover's triangle that inspired scheming perhaps desperate enough to have made a dupe of the state.

The fourteen-year prosecution of Curtis Kyles was like a slowly fading print. As Kyles's lawyers protested every time Connick resolved to try him again, details of the Dye murder got no clearer with repetition. They blurred. Memories clouded. Testimony was recanted or embellished improbably. Witnesses were no longer available, and their prior testimony had to be read by stand-ins. But—and this was the fascinating part—as the details of the Dye murder paled and faded, the outlines of an altogether different tableau became visible beneath it.

If the Dye murder was, in essence, the portrait of a young man with his gun to the head of a kindly grandmother, the underlying pentimento depicted three people: two men and a woman. One of the men is Kyles. The woman is his common-law wife and the mother of his children. The other man is the friend of theirs named Joseph Beanie Wallace. Maybe acquaintance is a better word for the relationship, because no friend, however tangled their lives had become, would do what Kyles contended this man had done to him. That the agents of law and order let him get away with it—that they were, in effect, complicit in a cover-up—only added to his sense of outrage.

The Kyles case is a study in persistence: the persistence of a determined prosecutor; the persistence of racism in the post-segregation South; the persistence of memory, both true and false; the persistence of grief (Lowell Dye's) and punishment (Kyles's) when a district attorney substitutes a zeal to convict for a commitment to justice and, as a consequence, botches his case. Kyles will persist in Glenn Boquet's nightmares for as long as Boquet can dream. His case also will persist as a touchstone in criminal defense work as long as there are police and prosecutors inclined to cut corners in the name of getting "another nigger off the street."

Preconceptions about race and class made it easy to assume that a street-toughened black man like Curtis Kyles could have killed a grandmotherly white shopper. These preconceptions were trite even in 1984, well understood and yet deep-rooted enough to be still capable of working their mischief. The psychologically more interesting phenomenon was the persistent inability of the prosecution to make the course correction that would have led them to another low-income black, Beanie Wallace, as his involvement in the case became clearer and deeper. Lowell Dye couldn't make the shift. His obsession with Kyles—sparing Wallace, a man he would have found equally loathsome—was bound up in the emotionalism of his grief. Harry Connick and the team he assembled to root out the enemies of public order and safety in New Orleans had no such excuse.

ACKNOWLEDGMENTS

It can be said, and often was by his defenders, that Curtis Kyles was a victim of summary justice. That he was tried twice and sentenced to death within three months of Delores Dye's murder bespoke an appalling rush to judgment by the Orleans Parish district attorney. Only a man marginalized by race and poverty would have been accorded the same treatment. But this much can also be said for the process of jurisprudence that cost Kyles fourteen years of his life: by 1998, the Kyles case was one of the most thoroughly adjudicated in history. The record of that case—including witness statements, affidavits, tape transcripts, and investigators' reports, as well as the transcripts of five criminal trials, the evidentiary hearings of 1989, and the briefs and arguments accompanying appellate maneuverings in state and federal court—provided a lode of material invaluable to this project. As I saw fit to remind people who declined to talk with me about the case, I really didn't need their cooperation, much as I wanted it. The record could speak for itself, I pointed out, perhaps a bit testily. My incentive in approaching them was fairness and the likelihood that they would speak more passionately and eloquently than they had on paper.

In truth, this book was made much richer and more readable by the many people who did choose to tolerate my meddling in memories that sometimes ranged well beyond what got said in court. Some had a little time for me, others a lot, and all were deeply appreciated. It was Denny LeBoeuf who first introduced me to the case and to the family of a man then still in prison and awaiting his fourth trial. Nick Trenticosta, Mike Fawer, and Marie Campbell took time from their busy schedules for this project, and so did Bunky Healy, Sheryl Bey, and their consultant, Gerard Rault. Jack Peebles and Sharon Andrews helped me to grasp something of the prosecution's perspective and also to understand how it is possible for honorable people to be caught up in a process that leaves a bad odor. Martin Regan was generously forthcoming about his role in the early phases of a case that pains him to this day. Kyle Schonekas and Joe Roberts took questions about the unsuccessful civil suit the Dyes brought against Schwegmann's. Cliff Strider spoke with me briefly and then apparently thought better of it, as did John Dillman. Glen Woods engaged an entertainment lawyer and asked for a contract before he would talk, and so we did not. Harry Connick referred me to statements he made at the time, which I found odd, because they reflected so poorly on a man whom I had encountered on numerous occasions in my capacity as a New Orleans newspaper editor and thought of as well able to explain and defend himself. All efforts to reach Sgt. Mike Rice were unavailing.

My goal, whether or not it was realized, was more than the record of a case in court. I wanted to tell the story of a murder through the lives of the people impacted by it, above all Kyles, but also Lowell Dye and his father, Joanne Dotson, Darlene Kersh, Glenn Boquet, Pinkey Burnes, Kyles's sisters Lela Johnson and Brenda Jenkins, and Kyles's children, in particular Elmeco, the one who seemed most like his father. All of these people gave generously of their time, none more than Kyles himself. Their insights were crucial to my understanding of this case. Errors made weaving those insights into a coherent whole are my own.

From the outset I was concerned that Kyles participate financially in this project. I told him that his story was worth something and that I did not mean to be the only person to profit from it. Generosity was not my only motive, however. I told Kyles that along with his cooperation, I expected autonomy over the final product and was prepared to pay for it. He needed the money more than I did; I needed his story, but also the freedom to tell it as I saw it. And after only a few conversations, it no longer seemed likely to be a story of an altogether innocent victim of a corrupt and racist system, the paradigm that some of his defenders, and perhaps Kyles himself, had hoped to impose.

Kyles accepted these terms, and a contract was drawn up. For reasons of his own, Kyles could never bring himself to sign it. We continued talking anyway, a properly ambiguous arrangement, I told myself, for a book about a thoroughly ambiguous case.

Claudia Menza, the New York book agent, had faith from the start that there might be general interest in this material. Ross Martin, originally with Spike Lee's company, Forty Acres and a Mule, more recently the director of programming at MTV-U, saw the movie possibilities and, over bacon and eggs in a Union Square eatery, caught the attention of Ayesha Pande, the editor at Farrar, Straus and Giroux who turned the light green and presided over the transformation of an idea into a book. She was ably assisted by Stacey Barney and Kabir Dandona, and our collective effort was scanned by the implacable Ellis Levine. To all, deep thanks for your faith and your patience.

—PINKY BURNES

" last modamn "
CHRIS, WILTZ ?,

- DUDLEY GARRETT - PSEYNO